CHARLES KINGSLEY

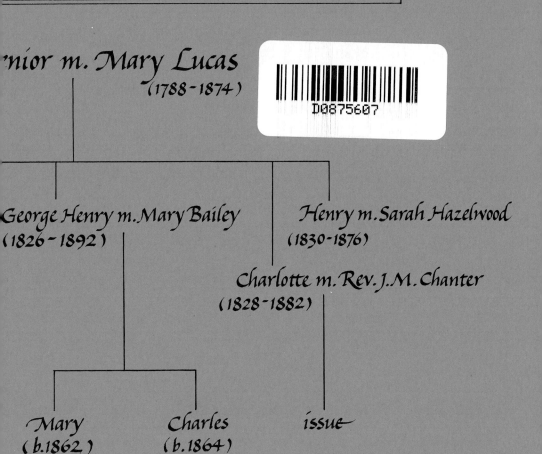

...nior m. Mary Lucas
(1788 - 1874)

George Henry m. Mary Bailey
(1826 - 1892)

Henry m. Sarah Hazelwood
(1830 - 1876)

Charlotte m. Rev. J. M. Chanter
(1828 - 1882)

Mary
(b. 1862)

Charles
(b. 1864)

issue

THE BEAST AND THE MONK

THE BEAST AND THE MONK

A Life of Charles Kingsley

Susan Chitty

MASON / CHARTER

NEW YORK 1975

First published in the United States by Mason/Charter Publishers, Inc.,
384 Fifth Ave., N.Y.C. in 1975.

Library of Congress Cataloging in Publication Data

Chitty, Susan, Lady.
   The beast and the monk.

   "Supposititious works of Charles Kingsley": p.
   Bibliography: p.
   Includes index.
   1. Kingsley, Charles, 1819-1875--Biography.
I. Title.
PR4843.C5   823'.8 [B]   75-15680
ISBN 0-88405-121-8

Only connect, and the beast and the monk, robbed of the isolation that is life to either, will die.

E. M. Forster, *Howard's End*

For my mother
Antonia White

Acknowledgments

Any writer of a new biography of Kingsley must feel gratitude for the painstaking research contained in the two books on him that have appeared since the Second World War, Una Pope-Hennessy's *Canon Charles Kingsley* (Chatto and Windus, 1948) and R. B. Martin's *Dust of Combat* (Faber, 1959). I would also like to extend my thanks to the following who have given many hours of their time in assisting me with this book: E. M. Cunnack (President of the Helston Old Cornwall Society), Mary Stella Edwards, Stanton Mellick (University of Queensland) and David E. Muspratt (Curator of Muniments, Working Men's College).

Help has also been forthcoming from many others, including the following: Dorothy Allen, Mary Boast (Newington District Library), M. A. Bowdler, F. J. Braybrooks, Colonel Rixon Bucknall, Christine Case, The Chester Society of Natural Science, Literature and Art, Donald Cummings, C. H. Dale, Anne R. Dawkings, Edgar Todd, The Rev R. O. H. Eppingstone, The Rev D. A. Farquarson-Roberts, Florida State University of Tallahassee, The Flyfishers' Club, Geoffrey Gilbert, The Rev M. B. S. Godfrey, Kenneth Goodridge, Rudolph Glossop, F.G.S., G. N. Gurney, The Rev R. H. Gurney, Nigel Haigh (Secretary of the Bermondsey and Rotherhithe Society), W. Kingsley Hartley, Peter Hickson, Winifred Jenkins, P. I. King (Northampton-shire and Huntingdonshire Archives), The Rev E. H. Loasby, Lilah Locke, The Rev P. M. Lloyd, R. J. McGarel-Groves, W. S. G. MacMillan, John S. Mayfield, C. H. B. Morris, R. A. Nanayakkara, Emily V. Scott, Ian Sutherland, Leonard Taylor (The University of Iowa), Dorothea Wakelyn-King, Major F. G. B. Wetherall, Elizabeth White, Judith Williams, Edith Winn, Elspeth Yeo (National Library of Scotland) and Rose Yeomans.

I would also like to thank Phyllis Jones, who typed the manuscript, and my husband, Thomas Hinde, who corrected it.

Contents

Acknowledgments   9
Introduction   15

PART I: THE RECTOR'S SON

Chapter 1   The Haunted Rectory 1819–1830   23
Chapter 2   A Devonshire Lad 1830–1838   34
Chapter 3   The Cambridge Undergraduate 1838–1842   51

PART II: PARSON LOT

Chapter 1   The Lonely Curate 1842   65
Chapter 2   The Lover for all Eternity 1843   79
Chapter 3   The Parish Priest 1844   87
Chapter 4   The Father of a Family 1844–1848   98
Chapter 5   The Year of Ferment 1848   105
Chapter 6   The Year of Collapse 1849   118
Chapter 7   *Alton Locke* 1849–1851   130
Chapter 8   Across the Water 1851–1853   147
Chapter 9   *Westward Ho!* 1853–1855   164
Chapter 10 The Years of Drought 1856–1858   179

PART III: CANON KINGSLEY

Chapter 1   Royal Favour 1859–1860   201
Chapter 2   *The Water-Babies* 1860–1863   211
Chapter 3   'And all the wheels run down' 1863   224
Chapter 4   The Newman Controversy 1864   229
Chapter 5   *Hereward the Wake* 1865–1866   238
Chapter 6   Exit the Professor 1867–1869   248
Chapter 7   The Tropics at Last 1869–1870   259
Chapter 8   A Canon at Chester 1870–1873   268
Chapter 9   The American Lecture Tour 1874–1875   283
Appendix 1 Letter-pamphlet on the Crimean War,
         February 25th, 1855   298
Appendix 2 Supposititious Works of Charles Kingsley   302

Bibliography   303
Index   307

List of Illustrations

following page 160

The Murder of Queen Gertrude of Hungary[1]
St Elizabeth and her Burden[2]
Crucifixion of StElizabeth[1]
Charles doing penance
Absolution of Fanny
The Thorn.
The hallowed lovemaking of Charles and Fanny
The reapers
Ascension of Charles and Fanny
Charles Kingsley[2]
Fanny Kingsley[3]
Helston Grammar School[4]
Henry Kingsley[2]
Mary Kingsley[2]
Eversley Rectory[2]
Rose Kingsley[2]
Maurice Kingsley[2]
Mary Kingsley[3]
Grenville Kingsley with his mother[3]
F. D. Maurice[5]
Thomas Hughes[5]
J. M. Ludlow[5]
Charles Mansfield[5]
Bramshill Park [6]
Jacob's Island, Bermondsey
Danae and her baby[7]
Tom, the water baby, and Mrs. Doasyouwouldbedoneby[7]
Charles and Fanny Kingsley at Eversley[8]
Charles Kingsley dressed to go fishing[2]
Charles Kingsley the year before his death[3]

Acknowledgements
1 Trustees of the British Museum
2 Rev Maurice Godfrey
3 Angela Covey-Crump
4 *Radio Times* Hulton Picture Library
5 The Working Men's College
6 Leslie North
7 Messrs Macmillan & Co., Ltd.
8 *Country Life*

Introduction

When the clock on the study mantelpiece at Eversley strikes noon on January 23rd, 1975, Charles Kingsley will have been dead a hundred years. After such a lapse of time a fresh assessment of what he is remembered for today is surely not out of place.

Kingsley was undoubtedly one of the most prominent men in England in his century, and deeply involved in the religious, scientific and social conflicts that exercised the minds of his contemporaries. He achieved distinction, or, in some cases, notoriety, in many fields. As a churchman he rose to become chaplain to Queen Victoria and he died holding the post of Canon at Westminster Abbey. As a theologian he entered the lists with John Henry Newman who wrote his *Apologia* to confound him. As a Christian Socialist he founded three periodicals and headed many distinguished committees. As a scientist he rose to become a Fellow of the Geological Society and a friend of Darwin and Lyell. As a historian he held the post of Regius Professor at Cambridge for nine years. Yet it is for his books rather than any of these achievements that he was best known. Thirty years after his death Macmillan was still doing a brisk trade in a nineteen-volume *de luxe* edition of his works, and an even brisker one in sixpenny pocket editions of the novels and poems.

And it is as an author that Kingsley is remembered today, but not as author of such books as *Alton Locke* and *Hypatia*, serious novels with social and theological themes, that Max Müller, Taylorian Professor of Modern European Languages at Oxford, predicted would earn him a 'niche ... in the Temple of Fame', but of a handful of children's books, or perhaps one children's book, *The Water-Babies*. *The Water-Babies* can claim the rare distinction of being among the dozen or so juvenile classics of the last century still available today in half a dozen editions (nine, to be exact). *The Heroes* does not share this distinction, although it is still bought, and *Westward Ho!* and *Hereward the Wake* are familiar titles but today rarely read even in the schoolroom. A local bookseller tells me he has not sold a copy of either for several years. Both have however been serialised by the BBC: in 1965 a thirteen-episode version of *Westward Ho!* on radio was running concurrently with a ten-episode adaptation of *Hereward* on television.

As a poet, too, Charles Kingsley is almost completely forgotten. Few of us could probably name a single poem by him, and yet a surprising number of the lines he wrote have passed into the language. They are so familiar that we take them for traditional sayings, and forget that they originated from his pen: 'Do the work that's nearest'; 'Be good, sweet maid'; 'O that we two were Maying'; 'When all the world is young, lad'; 'For men must work and women must weep', are but a few examples.

My own interest in Kingsley was aroused quite accidentally by a reference to his love of horses quoted as an introductory paragraph to early editions of *Black Beauty*. Tracing the paragraph to its source I came upon that treasure house of Kingsley material, from which every biographer brings home fresh jewels, *Charles Kingsley: His Letters and Memories of his Life. Edited by his Wife*. Any quotation in the present volume, that is not ascribed to another source, comes from this, the original biography.

Fanny, Kingsley's adored wife, wrote her massive life of her husband immediately after his death. It was published in December 1876[1] and, considering that she was so prostrated for months after the tragedy that she could not even travel to the Abbey to see his bust, it is hard to imagine how she found the strength for the task. It is generally supposed that John Martineau, Kingsley's faithful pupil and neighbour, gave her some help in soliciting testimonials and amassing letters (for it is of these that the book mainly consists). Fanny's (or John Martineau's) work as a biographer was limited to contributing paragraphs that linked one letter to the next and, alas, excising indiscretions. Apart from these small alterations in the cause of respectability the letters were printed very much as they were written, and it is for this reason the book is such an excellent source of biographical material. From it emerges a picture of a strange, but extraordinarily likable, person.

Kingsley was above all a man of immense enthusiasms, many of them inconsistent or even flatly contradictory. Indeed the inconsistencies in his personality are one of its chief charms. To the world he appeared the muscular Christian he so much admired. Only to his wife did he admit to moments of black despair from which death seemed the only release. To the world he was a preacher with mesmeric qualities, in private conversation he suffered from a stutter, the result of an unhappy childhood. To the world he was a passionate champion of the working man, in private he condemned Irish labourers as 'white

---

[1] The book was originally published by Henry S. King & Co., but the copyright passed within a few months to C. Kegan Paul & Co., and eventually to Macmillan & Co. It has passed through over thirty editions.

chimpanzees' and blacks as 'ant-eating apes'. He was a keen hunter of foxes, yet had a long friendship with a wasp he saved from drowning. He toured the snowy Rockies, throwing open windows and complaining of the central heating, and came home to die of pneumonia at the age of fifty-six. He was convinced his wife would die before him, yet it was he who was to fill the grave he had prepared for her at the bottom of the rectory garden.

The picture that Fanny gave of her husband was a detailed one, but there was one aspect of him over which she drew an impenetrable veil; his private life. She published few of his love letters to her and those she did publish were heavily edited. Now, at last, around three hundred of these closely guarded documents, never before seen by anyone outside the family, have been generously made available by Kingsley's literary executrix, Angela Covey-Crump, who recently inherited them from her aunt, Gabrielle Vallings, Kingsley's grandniece. These letters make fascinating, and at times bizarre, reading. A whole new side to Kingsley's character, the side that he used to refer to as 'the forbidden depths', is revealed. Mrs Covey-Crump has also released a locked diary kept by Fanny in Nice during her year of separation from Charles in 1843. This diary not only sheds sidelights on the couple's four-year courtship, but contains certain of Kingsley's drawings, drawings that, in the opinion of Nathaniel Hawthorne 'no pure man could have made or allowed himself to look at'? It is because of these that the present biography can claim to give a fuller and more intimate picture of Kingsley than any that has till now appeared.

The love letters revealed that Kingsley combined an extremely sensuous nature with strict inhibitions instilled by a formidable upbringing. He could only accept the idea of carnal relations with his wife once he had convinced himself that the body was holy and the act of sex a kind of sacrament in which he was the priest and his partner the victim. Before the marriage could be consummated the bodies of the lovers must be purified by mortification, but their rewards would be great, for heaven, he declared, would consist of one perpetual copulation in a literal, physical sense. 'Those thrilling writhings are but dim shadows of a union which shall be perfect', he wrote to Fanny when she was his fiancée. Some of the drawings he made of naked women, often saints, undergoing atrocious tortures have now been found and are printed in this book for the first time.

It is as well that the love letters *have* become available, for other sources of original material are few. No direct living descendants of Charles Kingsley can now be traced. Although he was the father of four, only his oldest son, Maurice, had children, two boys named

Ralph and Frank. They, however, were born in the United States, whither their father had emigrated in 1873, and when they failed to come home and volunteer for the First World War, the English branch of the family ceased to recognise their existence. Maurice, who died at New Rochelle, New York, in 1910, had, in any case, made it clear that he was no longer interested in his mother country, for he refused the offer of his father's papers and possessions when his mother died, on the grounds that he could not afford the cost of transporting them across the Atlantic.

If help has not been forthcoming from direct descendants, it has come in abundance from more distant relatives, and from members of the general public. A letter to the *Daily Telegraph* produced well over a hundred replies, from people of widely different interests: there was the elderly canon who has been writing a life of 'the most lovable character in the Nineteenth Century' for the last twenty years, and the Eversley dressmaker whose father was baptised by him; there was the man who shared a flymaker with him on Dartmoor and the lady who has started every day for the last fifty years with a reading from his *Daily Thoughts*; there was the man who has devoted his retirement to an exclusive study of Kingsley's views on the survival of marriage after death, the lady who met Tom the chimney sweep when she was a girl and the Ceylonese student who thought *The Water-Babies* was 'all true' when he was a boy.

It is not only people, but places that remember Kingsley today. In Bideford, his statue, in professorial robes, stands beside the River Torridge in Kingsley Road, flanked by the Kingsley Café and the Kingsley Service Station. In Eversley church a brass memorial tablet commemorates the restoration of the church in his memory in spite of the fact that, during his lifetime, he opposed it. Eversley also celebrated the centenary of his ordination (with a 'Water-Babies' window) in 1942, and the one hundred and fiftieth anniversary of his birth (with a Flower Festival) in 1969.

Perhaps the only place associated with him that has not done him quite the honour that is his due is Westminster Abbey. As soon as Kingsley died Dean Stanley sent word to Fanny that the Abbey was open to 'the Canon and the Poet'. Fanny explained that it had always been Kingsley's wish to be buried at Eversley and it was therefore decided that a marble bust should be placed in the Abbey to commemorate him. The bust was duly executed by the sculptor, Woolner, sent to Fanny to contemplate for a couple of hours, and then conveyed to the Abbey. It is its fate after its arrival there that has been a cause for some dissatisfaction among Kingsley's admirers. The visitor to the Abbey today will find it, not in Poets' Corner, but on an obscure windowsill in St George's Chapel. This, Fanny had been assured, was to be the New Poets' Corner, but no other poets overflowed into it. Kingsley remained alone in what, three years after his death, was described by an Australian admirer as 'an obscure corner of the Abbey' and there he remains to this day. Perhaps the centenary of his death may be considered an appropriate occasion for his removal to the company of Thackeray, Dickens and Tennyson, who were his friends during life.

PART I

The Rector's Son

CHAPTER 1

The Haunted Rectory
1819–1830

Charles Kingsley was born on June 12th, 1819. He shared the year of his birth with Queen Victoria, appropriate enough for one who combined in his person so many of the conflicts that racked the Victorian era. He came of an old but landless family and was taught to be proud to be a Kingsley. 'We are an ancient house laid low, with mammon and fashion riding roughshod over our heads',[1] he told the woman who later became his wife. 'Our Kingsley is a ruined grange in Cheshire in the depths of Delamere Forest and we lost it in fighting the battles of our Country and our God against Charles, the Miscalled Martyr.'

As a historical statement this is no more accurate than many others from the same pen. The original Kingsley estates were indeed probably in Cheshire, inherited from Ranulph de Kingsley who was granted the 'office of Bailiwick and Keeping of the Forest of Delamere' in the twelfth century. But the Kingsley relative who is supposed to have lost them was Colonel George Fleetwood, the regicide, and the estates that he forfeited were in Buckinghamshire not Cheshire. The Kingsleys continued to be far from destitute for a hundred and fifty years after the Restoration and produced some distinguished soldiers, including General William Kingsley, whose horse was shot under him at the Battle of Minden and whose portrait by Reynolds hung in the rectory at Barnack beside that of another ancestor, Archbishop Abbot by Van Dyke.

For the immediate cause of Kingsley's landless state we have to look no further than his father. Charles Kingsley Senior was born in 1781, near Lymington in Hampshire, the only son of a wealthy man who probably made his money by dealing in East and West Indian produce. He died when his son was five years old but left him well provided for. The boy grew up to be gifted both as an artist[2] and a naturalist and

---

[1] Letter 52, 1843, from a collection of unpublished letters to Fanny. The collection will hereafter be referred to as ULF, i.e. Unpublished Letters to Fanny.

[2] A bound volume of his landscape sketches still remains. They are in ink and wash and are both delicate and imaginative, if somewhat formal.

became widely read in the literature of several languages. They said of him, 'He had every talent except that of using his talents.' After two months as an undergraduate at Brasenose College, Oxford, he retired to Battramsley House near Lymington in the New Forest, a large, yellow brick hunting lodge which still preserves its privacy from the Brockenhurst road with a thick belt of laurel. It had stabling for four horses, spacious grounds, a walled kitchen garden, a home farm and some land. In this pleasant place Mr Kingsley Senior devoted himself to the pursuits of a country gentleman, chiefly shooting and fox-hunting. At the age of twenty-six he discovered that all his money was gone.

It was at this juncture that his young wife, Mary, came to the rescue. Mary Kingsley[3] was a remarkable woman who to a late age combined 'a quite extraordinary practical and administrative ability with the sensitivity and fancy of a young girl.'[4] Her father was Nathan Lucas, a judge whose family had owned estates at Farley Hall in Barbados for five generations. He was a man of a scientific turn of mind and a close friend of two of the leading scientists of his day, Sir Joseph Banks, President of the Royal Society, and John Hunt, the surgeon. His grandson Charles used to tell the story of how, when the volcano at St Vincent erupted in 1812, he lighted a candle and, ignoring the negroes shrieking in the darkened streets, retired smiling to seek its cause among his books.[5] When Mary was old enough to go into society he acquired Rushford Lodge in Norfolk and brought her over to complete her education. She was gay as well as studious and enjoyed the round of parties that was arranged for her. On one occasion she danced with Byron at a ball in Norwich and thought 'he looked like a butcher boy, his face was so red'.

The story of her courtship by the handsome New Forest squire is not known but she must have married Charles Kingsley Senior around 1804, fifteen years before the birth of her first child. Reading between the lines of Victorian discretion one suspects that the marriage was not an entirely happy one. Perhaps the contrast between her husband's ineffectual personality and her own bustling and organising one was too great. In a letter to Fanny written when he was twenty-five

[3] Kingsley's mother, Mary, must not be confused with the famous African traveller of the same name, who was his niece, the daughter of his brother George. Kingsley himself had a daughter called Mary who became an author but she wrote under the name of Lucas Mallet and was known in private life as Mrs St Leger Harrison.

[4] Letter of Charles Kingsley to Francis Galton, 1865. All the letters quoted in this book are from Mrs Kingsley's *Charles Kingsley: His Letters and Memories of his Life*, unless otherwise stated.

[5] Charles Kingsley, *At Last*, 1871.

Kingsley said of his mother, 'if she has learnt to love her children more than her husband . . . is it not because she has not been able to rest upon a husband's love? She has always been her own helper — her only helper.'

Yet her husband was to find that her organising ability stood him in good stead when his money gave out a few years after their marriage. She it almost certainly was who surveyed the careers open to a penniless gentleman and picked upon the Church. Certainly it was she who handled the administrative work and did most of the visiting in his future parishes. In 1807 Charles Kingsley Senior entered Trinity Hall Cambridge to study Divinity and, a leisurely nine years later, came down with a degree of LL.B. at Sidney Sussex College. He was by then thirty-five years old.

And now began the nomadic period of moving from curacy to meagre living that was the lot of most newly fledged clerics. It was at his second curacy, at Holne on the edge of Dartmoor, that Charles, his first son, was born. The young Kingsley in fact spent only the first six weeks of his life at Holne but Dartmoor and Devonshire were to mean so much to him in later life that it is worth dwelling a little upon the place.

The rectory at Holne (now in private hands) must be one of the most beautiful places in the west of England. It is tucked into a secret fold of the moor, its lawn flanked by fine trees, its views descending over the glebe fields to Holne Wood and the glittering Dart. The house itself is old, with cream-washed walls three feet thick, a thatched roof and leaded windows. When the Kingsleys moved in, it was in a dilapidated condition, which explains why the curate was allowed to live there, but the view from the corner bedroom where Kingsley was born more than compensated his mother for its damp walls and peeling wallpaper.

Indeed so great was Mrs Kingsley's passion for the Devonshire landscape, that she walked about it constantly during her pregnancy, hoping to communicate her love to her unborn child. As she wandered among the gnarled moss-laden trees of Holne Chase or over the magnificent gauntness of the moor she willed her child to see what she saw, and in a way she succeeded. Kingsley always called himself a Devon man and claimed that to think of the West Country made him weep.[6]

---

[6] A German psychiatrist, who wrote a pamphlet to prove that *The Water-Babies* was proof of Kingsley's desire to return to the womb, based his case on its author's oft-expressed wish to go back to the West Country. Unfortunately the author of the pamphlet, not being familiar with the English language, read it as 'The Wet Country'.

The family's next move was to Burton-on-Trent where Charles
Kingsley Senior had been offered a position as curate in charge. Here
we have our first glimpse of the 'little delicate Charles' wrapped in his
mother's shawl during a dangerous crossing of the River Trent in
flood.[7] In 1820 Kingsley's brother Herbert was born, only eighteen
months his junior. A year later came Gerald[8] but by then the family
had moved yet again, this time to a living at North Clifton, near
Newark in Nottinghamshire.

The wanderings of Charles Kingsley Senior ended, for the time being,
on January 23rd, 1824, when he was collated by the Lord Bishop of
Peterborough to the rectory of Barnack, near the charming old town
of Stamford in Lincolnshire. The bishop was Herbert Marsh, who, as
Lady Margaret Professor of Divinity, had been a close friend at
Cambridge. The two men shared an interest in the scientific approach
to biblical criticism which Marsh had studied in Germany. There was,
however, one condition attached to the gift of the living: it must be
surrendered to Bishop Marsh's son when he was old enough to be
ordained. Such arrangements were common in the lax state of the
Church of England at that time and six years later the young Marsh
duly took over from Mr Kingsley — to remain rector incidentally
until he was declared insane in 1850.

Barnack was, and still is, a handsome village built of the golden
limestone quarried on its outskirts. Barnack stone was famous. It was
used not only to build Barnack church, with its fine Saxon tower, and
all the fine churches whose spires punctuate the surrounding country,
but also the cathedrals at Ely and Peterborough. Barnack Rectory
was built from it too. It was a rambling fourteenth-century house
known locally as the Palace of Barnack, out of all proportion to a
parish of six hundred and twenty souls, but a suitable headquarters for
the administration of one of the richest livings in England. Several
stone walled gardens stood round it as well as an orchard, a stable-
yard, and a farmyard. The land that went with it was extensive enough
to be described as a park. It must have been an ideal playground for the
three little boys so close in age. Yet Kingsley's memory of those years
was strangely clouded, perhaps because neither of his brothers survived
to full manhood.

Kingsley himself was five years old when he first went to live in

[7] Letter from Miss Martineau to Charles Kingsley about 1855.

[8] I am indebted to R. B. Martin for discovering the date of Gerald's birth. Mary
Kingsley erroneously ascribed it to the year 1816 in the preface of her *Notes on Sport
and Travel*. His name appears in the baptismal register at South Clifton beside the
date October 20, 1821.

the ancient house with its walls supported by massive buttresses, its endless passages and its cavernous rooms. It was midwinter and 'dark and sad were those short days, when all the distances were shut off, and the air choked with foul brown fog and drenching rains from off the eastern sea.'[9] For the first year there he suffered from frequent and dangerous attacks of croup and it took all the skill of Betsy Knowles (an old servant of his father's family) and of the nursemaid Annie Simpson (a Devonshire girl who had been a member of Mrs Kingsley's scripture class at Holne) to keep him alive. Not only did these devoted women have to nurse him through various childish afflictions but through the effects of the medicines that were prescribed for them. In later years Kingsley claimed that the heavy doses of calomel (mercurous chloride) that he was given for 'biliousness' as a child inhibited the development of his jaw and increased his tendency to stammer. So strongly did he feel about doctors who treated 'a baby's inside . . . much like a Scottish grenadier's' that, in *The Water-Babies*, he had them stood in a row and given a dose of their own medicine by the formidable Mrs Bedonebyasyoudid:

First she pulled all their teeth out; and then she bled them all round; and then she dosed them with calomel, and jalap, and salts and senna, and brimstone and treacle; and horrible faces they made; and then she gave them a great emetic of mustard and water, and no basins.

Because Kingsley was so delicate as a child he slept in his mother's room. This explains why, when ill with 'brain fever', he found himself in the Great North Room, commonly known as Button Cap's Room. His mother used to move into this room when she was near her time, and in it were born Kingsley's youngest brothers and sister, George (1826), Charlotte (1828) and Henry (1830). It was a handsome book-lined room with an oriel window overlooking the flower garden at the front of the house. As a bedroom it had one drawback. It was said to be haunted by the ghost of Button Cap.

Charles was an imaginative child. As he admitted in a letter written many years later, 'I could never distinguish dreams from imagination, imagination from waking impressions, and was often thought to be romancing when I was relating a real impression.' Needless to say he had no difficulty in seeing Button Cap.

I knew him well [he told his niece, Alice Pelham]. He used to walk across the room in flopping slippers, and turn over the leaves

9 Charles Kingsley, *Hereward the Wake*, 1866.

of books to find the missing deed, whereof he had defrauded the orphan and the widow. He was an old Rector of Barnack. Everybody heard him who chose. Nobody ever saw him; but in spite of that, he wore a flowered dressing gown, and a cap with a button on it. I never heard of any skeleton being found; and Button Cap's history had nothing to do with murder, only with avarice and cheating.

Sometimes he turned cross and played Polter-geist, as the Germans say, rolling barrels in the cellar about with surprising noise, which was undignified. So he was always ashamed of himself, and put them all back in their place before morning.

I suppose he is gone now. Ghosts hate mortally a Certificated National Schoolmaster and, being a vain and peevish generation, as soon as people give up believing in them go away or perhaps someone had been laying phosphoric paste about, and he ate thereof and ran down to the pond and drank till he burst. He was rats.[10]

A sad event occurred at this time which must also have worked upon the child's morbid imagination. A baby sister, Louisa Mary, who had been three months old when the family came to Barnack, died at seven months.[11] This tragedy reinforced the child's already firm belief in the shortness of this life and the importance of the one to come. Before the family even moved to Barnack he was fully aware of the eternal rewards or punishment that await us in the next world and used to preach sermons on the subject. According to his mother 'His delight was to make a little pulpit in his nursery, arranging the chairs for an imaginary congregation, and putting on his pinafore as a surplice, give little sermons.' Mary Kingsley, unknown to him, took them down at the time and showed them to the Bishop of Peterborough, who thought them so remarkable for such a young child, that he

[10] Barnack Rectory still stands although shorn of its lands which now accommodate an estate of a hundred newly built houses. The present rector no longer lives there. Limited, like his fellows, to 'the diocesan minimum' he prefers a small house up the road. It is not entirely the same house as it was in Kingsley's day. After a fire in the middle of the last century (perhaps the work of Button Cap?) half of it was replaced by an imposing Victorian Gothic structure. The old part of the house survived until recent years when it was largely demolished but for one outer wall. Button Cap's room at the end still survives, however, without its floor. It forms the upper part of a garage. The arrangement evidently does not suit the ghost. He has not been seen at his oriel window for many a year. But the present occupants have, on several occasions, been aware of a wholly inexplicable smell of burning at one particular point in the sitting room of the new wing and in the bedroom immediately above it.

[11] I am indebted to David Newton, of the East Midland Allied Press for tracing the death notice in the Stamford Mercury.

begged they might be preserved predicting that the boy would grow up no common man. At the same time he wrote a short hymn which his mother also preserved.

SONG UPON LIFE

Life is, and soon will pass
As life is gone, death will come
We rise again
In Heaven we must abide
Time passes quickly
He flies on wings as light as silk
We must die
It is not false that we must rise again
Death has its fatal sting
It brings us to the grave
Time and Death is and must be

By the time he reached Barnack the sensitivity of his conscience had, if anything, increased. Old Betsy Knowles recalled an example of it:

I have never forgotten one day when he and his little brothers were playing together, and had a difference, which seldom happened. His mother, coming into the room took the brothers' part, which he resented and he said he wished she was not his mother. His grief afterwards was great, and he came crying bitterly to the kitchen door to ask me to take him up to his room. The housemaid enquired what was the matter, and said his mamma would be sure to forgive him. 'She has forgiven me, but don't cant, Elizabeth (I saw you blush). It isn't mamma's forgiveness I want, but God's.' Poor little fellow he was soon upon his knees when he got into his mother's room where he slept.

Two letters of Kingsley at this time, however, prove that his young life was not entirely overshadowed with disease and death. One was written to Betsy Knowles at the age of eight from the East Coast resort where the children spent their holidays. The original can still be seen in the National Library of Scotland. It is written in an exquisite copperplate hand which, alas for his biographers, was to deteriorate into an almost illegible scrawl in later years.

Dear Mrs Knowles,
    I got both letter and cake quite safe and liked the latter very

much. The night before last Georgy was very ill, indeed we have all been unwell. Mama wants you to send our spades directly; together with half a dozen very small geraniums. We all join in love to you and Knowles. We long to see you, and promise you that when you come we will be good boys and learn our lessons well. Pray how do the little lamb and the little pigs and the old sow do?

Adieu! my dear Mrs Knowles!

Believe me ever your affectionate friend

Charles Kingsley

The other letter was written a year or two earlier to a young woman (a friend of his parents) whose beauty had captured his already susceptible heart.

My Dear Miss Dade,

I hope you are well is fanny well? The house is completely changed since you went. I think it is nearly 3 months since you went. Mamma sends her love to you and sally browne Herbert and geraled but I must stop here, because I have more letters of consequence to write and here I must pause.

Believe me always,

Yours sincere friend,

Charles Kingsley.

Besides 'letters of consequence' the young Kingsley no doubt had lessons to prepare, for the alarming business of his formal education at the hands of his father and a tutor had begun. Kingsley never felt close to his father. In an early letter to Fanny he described how, as a child, his 'love and devotion were only enticed out to be played with for a moment, and when it became *de trop* in any way was rudely struck aside and made to recoil weeping into itself.'[12] In another letter, written about the same time, he confessed 'I have nothing to care for in reality but my mother and you'[13] and it was only in the last year of his father's life that he found him at all 'affectionate and reasonable'.[14] The Reverend Charles Kingsley, like his contemporary the Reverend Patrick Brontë, was a remote figure to his children, and spent much time behind the doors of his study. Charles's only excursions through these doors were for the purpose of reciting lessons, for this was the method of education in vogue in his day. Children were given long

12 ULF No. 182, September 1843.
13 ULF March 31, 1841.
14 ULF No. 352, 1859,

passages in Latin and Greek to get by heart and then called into the presence of a parent or tutor to recite them. How much Kingsley detested the method is shown by the picture he drew of one of its victims in *The Water-Babies*. In the underwater world Tom meets a boy whose head, overstuffed with facts, has turned into a turnip, filled with water. It called to Tom as he passed:

'Can you tell me anything at all about anything you like?'
'About what?' says Tom.
'About anything you like, for as fast as I learn things I forget them again.'
And the more he listened the more he forgot, and the more the water ran out of him. Tom thought he was crying but it was only his poor brains running away from being worked so hard.

Little heads were stuffed with facts by liberal applications of the birch, and Kingsley's horror of corporal punishment stemmed from his own childhood. He would never beat his own children and after Mrs Bedonebyasyoudid had dealt with the doctors, he saw to it that the schoolmasters also had a taste of their own medicine.

She boxed their ears, and thumped them over the head with rulers, and pandied their hands with canes . . . and at last birched them all round soundly with her great birch-rod, and set them each an imposition of three hundred thousand lines of Hebrew to learn by heart.

It must surely have been while standing in his father's presence, searching for forgotten words, that Kingsley developed the stutter that was to plague him for the rest of his life. Half a century later his widow wrote to a friend:

He suffered so bitterly as a child from the want of delicate tact on the part of his own Parents (fond as they were of him) with regard to his own stammering. They observed upon it before him, instead of appearing perfectly unconscious as they ought to have done . . . so that he lived in a most painful state of self-consciousness, feeling that he vexed his parents, till the defect became confirmed, and almost irremediable. But then he was a very sensitive child, leading a solitary spiritual life, and they were very quick excitable people.

There is, however, one cheerful recollection of these sessions in the study that proves that the boy's fear of his father was not as great as his curiosity about natural history. A friend happened to be in the room when Kingsley was repeating a Latin lesson to his father. Charles's eyes were fixed all the time on the fire in the grate and at last he could stand it no longer. There was a pause in the Latin, and he cried out, 'I do declare, papa, there is pyrites in the coal.'

It was in the field of natural science that father and son came closest. Like many sportsmen, Charles Kingsley Senior was keenly interested in the habits of the creatures he hunted, and at Barnack he was able to pursue his interests both as a sportsman and a naturalist to the full. He was now the recipient of an income of £1,200 a year (to which was added the living of North Clifton where he had installed a friend, Mr Penrose, as curate) and the Fens, that paradise of the wildfowler, lay only a few miles to the east. As soon as he was old enough Kingsley was set before the keeper on his horse to accompany his father on shooting expeditions. On autumn mornings 'waked by many a gun' they must have passed through Helpston where John Clare, the Northamptonshire peasant poet still lived, and entered Peterborough Great Fen at Peakirk. Eight years before his death Kingsley recalled that still undrained waste in one of the finest prose passages he ever wrote.

The fancy may linger without blame, over the shining meres, the golden reed beds, the countless water-fowl, the strange and gaudy insects, the wild nature, the mystery, the majesty — for mystery and majesty there were — which haunted the deep fens for many hundred years. Little thinks the Scotsman, whirled down by the Great Northern Railway from Peterborough to Huntingdon, what a grand place, even twenty years ago, was that Holme and Whittlesea, which is now but a black unsightly steaming flat, from which the meres and reed beds of the old world are gone, while the corn and roots of the new world have not yet taken their place, when . . . dark green alders and pale green reeds stretched for miles round the broad lagoon, where the coot clanked, and the bittern boomed, and the sedge-bird, not content with his own sweet song, mocked the notes of all the birds around, while high overhead hung motionless, hawk beyond hawk, buzzard beyond buzzard, kite beyond kite, as far as eye could see. Then down the wind came the boom of the great stanchion gun, and after that sound, another, louder as it neared; a cry of all the bells of Cambridge and all the hounds of Cottesmore; and overhead rushed and whirled the skein of terrified wild fowl, screaming, piping, clacking, croaking — filling the air with the hoarse rattle of their wings, while clear above all sounded the wild whistle of the curlew and the trumpet note of the great wild swan. They are all gone now . . . Gone are ruffs and reeves, spoonbills, bitterns, avosets; the very snipe, one hears, disdain to breed. Gone too, not only from the Fens but from the whole world, is that most exquisite of butterflies — Lycaena dispar — the great copper; and many a curious insect more.[15]

[15] Charles Kingsley, 'The Fens', *Prose Idylls*.

CHAPTER 2

A Devonshire Lad
1830–1838

Nursery days ended when the Kingsleys left Barnack. Convinced that she would have no more babies, Mrs Kingsley ordered that the cradle in which they had all been rocked should be taken to Annie Simpson's cottage at Easton-on-the-Hill. (Annie was by now married to a labourer, Mark Cox, and about to become a mother herself.) The rest of the Kingsley possessions were loaded on to a boat and conveyed to Ilfracombe, on the coast of North Devon.

It is not clear why Charles Kingsley Senior chose to remove to Ilfracombe. Certainly he had no living to go to there. Perhaps he had happy memories of his stay at Holne, although that had been in South Devon, and not on the coast either. He was in poor health, having contracted the ague (malaria), then still prevalent in the Fens, and perhaps hoped the mild climate of the town 'with its rock walled harbour, its little wood of masts within, its white terraces rambling up the hills'[1] would cure him. For a year the family of eight and their servants lived in lodgings. Then a well-born friend came to the rescue. James Hamlyn-Williams of Clovelly Court, an open-hearted man in spite of his ferociously expressed prejudices, succeeded his father to the baronetcy and appointed Mr Kingsley curate at Clovelly. A year later the rector died and the living, worth £350 a year, was his.

Clovelly was, and out of season still is, enchanting. Arthur Mee called it 'the place incredible, one of the loveliest corners of England'. It is some forty miles west of Ilfracombe, if you take the land route. The Kingsleys went by sea across Bideford Bay, not only because it was quicker but because this was the most practical method of approach to that 'steep stair of houses clinging to the cliffs.'[2] In one of his first articles for *Fraser's Magazine*[3] Kingsley described his arrival

[1] Charles Kingsley, *Prose Idylls*.
[2] Charles Kingsley, *Westward Ho!*
[3] Charles Kingsley, 'North Devon', July 1849. Reprinted in *Prose Idylls*, 1873.

crawling up the paved stairs inaccessible to cart or carriage, which are flatteringly denominated Clovelly Street, behind me a sheer descent, to the pier and bay, 200 feet below, and in front, another 100 feet above, a green amphitheatre of oak and ash, shutting out all but a narrow slip of sky, across which a mist was crawling. Suddenly a hot gleam of sunshine fell upon the white cottages, with their grey steaming roofs, and bright green railings, and on the tall tree-fuchsias and gaudy dahlias in the little scraps of garden courtyard, calling out the rich faint odour of the verbenas and jessamines, and, alas! out of the herring-heads and tails also as they lay in the rivulet; and lighting up the wings of the gorgeous butterflies, almost un-known in our colder eastern clime, which fluttered from woodland down to garden.

The rectory stood above Clovelly. It was a tallish eighteenth-century house very similar in design to one of those elaborate doll's houses one sees in museums, having four rooms on each of its three floors. It was comfortably set among tall trees with a lawn and a circular drive in front and a coach house and stables near the entrance gates. A bank rising at one side was, and still is, a mass of wild daffodils in the spring and at the top of this bank stood an oak tree where the Kingsley boys (and all subsequent rectory children) had a tree house. From this retreat Charles could see the furrowed red soil of his father's glebe land on one side and on the other, the bay 'with its restless net of snowy foam'.[4]

As the boy looked westward across the level blue of the ocean, he longed to see over the horizon to the West Indies and the Spanish Main. His mother had often told him of her home, Farley Hall, with its pillared portico, in Barbados. There was a cabinet in her sitting room full of shells that she had picked up on the beaches of that sunlit island, and in the library was the collection of books she had inherited:

lordly folios on whose maps many a sturdy coastline dwindled into dots — full many a line of dots went stumbling on to perish at the foot of pregnant nothingness. Volume on volume of famous voyagers — Dampier, Rogers, Shelrocke, Byron, Cook and grand old Esquemeling — the Froissart of the Buccaneers — and respect-able Captain Charles Johnson, deeply interested and very properly shocked by 'the Robberies and Murders of the most Notorious Pyrates'.[5]

[4] Charles Kingsley, 'North Devon', *Prose Idylls*.
[5] Mary Kingsley, Introduction to George Kingsley's *Notes on Sport and Travel*.

Books like these filled the boy's head with stories of the 'old sea heroes', Sir Walter Raleigh and Sir Richard Grenville, Drake and Hawkins, Carleill and Cavendish, Cumberland, Preston and Frobisher. He longed to see for himself such wonders as the Sargasso Sea, that 'sunken Atlantic Continent' and relive 'the memorable day when Columbus' ship plunged her bows into the tangled ocean meadow, and the sailors were ready to mutiny, fearing hidden shoals, ignorant that they had four miles of blue water beneath their keel'.[6]

His father's church, just across the road from the rectory, up a lordly avenue, was also full of reminders of the old heroes, for its walls were, and still are, studded with ornate tablets commemorating members of the sea-going Cary family. (Beside these there is now a brass one to Kingsley himself, put there by his daughter, Mary, who married a later rector of Clovelly.) The church crouches under the shadow of Clovelly Court, home of the Carys for generations, and then of James Hamlyn-Williams, Mr Kingsley's benefactor. This fine eighteenth-century house commanded a view of the sea from its parapeted terrace. Parts that had survived a fire went back to Tudor times and had known the tread of the feet of Will Cary himself, one of *Westward Ho!*'s Companions of the Rose.[7]

Charles Kingsley Senior encouraged his son's interest in courageous exploits at sea. When the boy was only eight years old he took him to Plymouth to see Sir Edward Codrington's fleet return after sending the Turkish and Egyptian fleets to the bottom at the Battle of Navarino. The experience, which has been overlooked by previous biographers, made a deep impression on Charles. He was fascinated not only by the ships, but by the 'moral beauty' of Plymouth Sound itself:

> Even then, as a mere boy, I was struck by the grand symmetry of that ample basin: the breakwater — then unfinished — lying across the centre; the heights of Bovisand and Cawsand, and those again of Mount Batten and Mount Edgecumb left and right; the citadel and the Hoe across the bottom of the Sound.[8]

Not only naval fortifications, but military ones also, were a subject of interest to him at this age. He spent hours drawing plans of imaginary fortresses and, for the rest of his life automatically picked out points suitable for defence in any landscape.

[6] Charles Kingsley, *At Last*, 1871.
[7] Clovelly Court suffered another serious fire in 1945, and is now smaller than it was. It is still inhabited by a descendant of the Hamlyn-Williams family.
[8] Charles Kingsley, *At Last*, 1871.

The country round Clovelly was peculiarly suited to such games. The three Kingsley boys had their own ponies, bred on Exmoor, and were free to explore the moors of Bursden and Welsford that lay to the west, 'a rolling range unbroken by tor or tree, or anything save, few and far between, a world-old furze bank which marked the common rights of some distant cattle farm'. Only native ponies could be trusted on those moors for there were bogs twenty feet deep in the low-lying parts. It was over them that Amyas Leigh and the Companions of the Rose were to pursue the Jesuitical Eustace and into one of those bogs that they feared, or rather hoped, he had vanished.

There were also fine rides, westward again, along the tops of the cliffs to the howling bleakness of Hartland Point, where the lighthouse now stands, and to what Kingsley took to be a ruined Roman villa 'tumbling into the sea, tesselated pavements, baths and all'. It was perhaps that ruined villa that first gave Kingsley his feeling for the past. He imagined, rather surprisingly, 'the strange work' that went on 'in that lonely nook, among a seraglio of dark Celtic beauties.'[9]

But the strongest call to his imagination came from the sea and

those delightful glens, which cut the high table land of the confines of Devon and Cornwall, and open towards the boundless Western Ocean. Each is like the other, and each is like no other English scenery. Each has its upright walls inland of rich oakwood, nearer the sea of dark green furze, then of smooth turf, then of weird black cliffs which range out right and left far into the deep sea, in castles, spires and wings of jagged iron-stone. Such are the 'Mouths', as these coves are called; and such the teeth which they display, one rasp of which would grind abroad the timbers of the stoutest ship.[10]

Just how terrible those teeth could be he was to learn on a night of autumn gales soon after his arrival at Clovelly. In the morning he and his father had sighted a great barque in distress off Hartland Point and had followed it along the cliff tops all day with a company of 'parsons and sportsmen, farmers and Preventive men, with the Manby's mortar lumbering behind us in a cart'. At nightfall the ship finally ran

[9] Charles Kingsley, 'North Devon'. What Kingsley took to be a Roman villa was in fact probably the second century B.C. Iron Age fort at Embury Beacon, the ramparts of which are now three-quarters fallen into the sea. The Romans barely penetrated North Devon.
[10] Ibid.

upon the rocks and the whole company of followers descended to the beach and waited for her to break up.

Under a wall was a long tent of sails and spars filled with Preventive men, fishermen, Lloyd's underwriters, laying about in every variety of strange attitude and costume; while candles, stuck in bayonet handles in the walls, poured out a wild glare over shaggy faces and glittering weapons. I recollect our literally warping ourselves down to the beach, holding on by rocks and posts. A sudden turn of the clouds let in a wild gleam of moonshine and against a slab of rock on the right, for years after discoloured by her paint, we saw the ship, rising slowly on every surge, to drop again with a piteous crash.[11]

The little trawlers of the Clovelly fishermen as well as big ships came to grief in Bideford Bay. It was not too uncommon to see

the old bay darkened with grey water spouts and the tiny herring boats fleeing from their nets right for the breakers, hoping for more mercy from those iron walls of rock than from the pitiless howling waste of spray behind them; and that merry beach beside the town covered with shrieking women and old men, casting themselves on the pebbles in fruitless agonies of prayers, as corpse after corpse swept up at the feet of wife and child, till in one case alone, a single dawn saw upwards of sixty widows and orphans weeping over those who had gone out the night before in the fulness of strength and courage.[12]

The night that Kingsley described was that of October 4th, 1831 when a sudden gale drowned thirty-one fishermen and pilots. His father was deeply concerned for the families they left behind and was a member of a committee set up at Bridge Hall, Bideford, for the dis-tribution of funds to them. Mr Kingsley became more involved with his parishioners at Clovelly than with those of any of his other parishes. To him these folk of Devonshire with their courage, their physical beauty and their vivid modes of expression, were a race apart from the 'South Saxon clods',[13] and he spent much time down on the quay with the fishermen in their 'red caps, blue jackets, striped jerseys and bright brown trousers'.[14]

[11] Ibid.   [12] Ibid.   [13] Ibid.
[14] Charles Kingsley, *Two Years Ago.*

He could steer a boat, hoist and lower a sail, 'shoot' a herring net and haul a seine with the best of them and when the fishing fleet put to sea, whatever the weather, he would start off 'down street' to give a short service and join in the singing of the old Prayer Book version of the 121st Psalm:

> Though storms be sudden, and waters deep
> Thy Guardian will not sleep.

The Kingsley boys soon caught their father's enthusiasm and learnt the 'maddening excitement' of managing their own little trawler under sail. Nor were they blind to the wonders of the shore. Both parents were keen amateur conchologists and, while Mrs Kingsley, helped by the new nurse-maid from Parracombe, Susannah Blackmore (now buried in Clovelly churchyard) explored Clovelly beach with George, Charlotte and Henry,[15] the three older boys went farther afield with their father. Nets full of shells were lugged to the door of 'poor dear old opium-eating Doctor Turton', a physician living at Bideford who was an expert on shells.

But Kingsley did not always 'naturalise' with his father. He began to know a few of the local boys and acquired a knowledge of the Devonshire dialect which was to serve him well at dinner tables in future life. It was one of these fishermen's sons that became his first close friend, 'my especial pet and bird's nesting companion, a little, delicate, precocious child who might have written books some day if he had been a gentleman's son'. But that was not to be his fate. He died at sea, like so many of Kingsley's companions, and was afterwards found lashed to the rigging of his father's wrecked boat. Perhaps it was his friendship with this boy that made the memory of Clovelly especially dear. In a letter written to Fanny in 1854 he said, 'Now that you have seen Clovelly you know what was the inspiration of my life before I met you.'

School put an end to the idyllic seaside life. Kingsley had been lucky to escape it so long, for he was now twelve. In the autumn he was sent, with his brother Herbert, to a preparatory school at Clifton, on the downs above Bristol, owned by the Rev William Knight.[16] Number 34 Richmond Terrace is one of a row of eighteenth-century terrace houses raised above the quiet little street in which they stand, with a public garden in front of them. The school can only have been a

[15] Clovelly featured in the novels that Charlotte and Henry were eventually to write.

[16] Previous authorities have wrongly given his name as John Knight.

modest establishment but the rough-house of even so small a school-room proved a rude shock to the sensitive solitary boy and in after years he compared 'the treatment that we poor brutes of the old world received' somewhat enviously with 'the care and attention' given to his own sons at school.[17] He took refuge from his fellows with Mr Knight's daughters and their governess or in long walks on the downs. According to Mr Knight, his only academic distinction lay in making remarkable translations from Latin verse into English, when he chose, and in his knowledge of natural history. He lost his temper on one occasion when the housemaid swept away as rubbish the specimens he had collected on his walks.

Although he was only there for one year, an event occurred soon after his arrival at the school that made a deep impression on him. He was walking on the downs on a Sunday afternoon of sullen autumn rain.

The fog hung thick over the docks and lowlands. Glaring through that fog I saw a bright mass of flame — almost like a half-risen sun — the gate of the new gaol on fire. By ten o'clock that night, one seemed to be looking down upon Dante's Inferno and to hear the multitudinous moan and wail of the lost spirits surging to and fro amid the sea of fire.

Without asking permission he ran down to the docks and saw sights not normally considered suitable for a small boy. The mob was completely out of control and the mayor, uncertain of his authority, had refused to give the soldiers orders to disperse them. Shops were being broken into and casks of brandy hacked open in the streets by the drink-crazed mob, and all the while the soldiers sat motionless on their horses, blood streaming from wounds in their heads. The young Kingsley was in fact witnessing the Bristol riots of October 1831, occasioned by the refusal of the Lords to pass the second Reform Bill, riots which culminated in the burning down of the Mansion House. In one alley he saw a sight he never forgot. Brandy from some broken casks was running down the gutter and rioters were on their hands and knees lapping it up. Suddenly there was a sinister hissing sound. The brandy had caught fire and the drinkers were, according to Kingsley, instantaneously transformed into blackened corpses.

The riot did not end until the Tuesday afternoon. When the young Kingsley played truant once more he witnessesd a sight hardly less edifying. Along the ruined north side of Queen Square was layed a row

[17] ULF No. 352, 1859.

of mutilated corpses. There was one fragment of charred flesh with a scrap of old red petticoat adhering to it, 'which I never forgot. What I had seen made me for years the veriest aristocrat, full of hatred and contempt for those dangerous classes, whose existence I had for the first time discovered.'[18]

When the time came for Charles to leave the school at Clifton there was much discussion between his parents as to whether or not their oldest son should be sent to a public school. Dr Hawtrey, the famous master of Eton, had heard of him and was anxious to have him. Rugby, under Dr Arnold, also had attractions, but these were not strong enough to counterbalance the strong Tory principles and evangelical views of Mr Kingsley. In the end, and to Kingsley's lasting regret, the Grammar School at Helston in Cornwall, was chosen.[19] In later life he was convinced, almost certainly wrongly, that only the rough and tumble of a public school could have cured him of his shyness and his stammer. It is worth noting, however, that he was most reluctant to send his own sons to those very public schools which he so regretted not attending himself and which, incidentally, continued to present his books as prizes until far into the present century.

His parents in fact probably made a good choice in Helston. Under the headmastership of the Rev Derwent Coleridge, son of the poet, this small local school became known as the Eton of the West. There were day boys from good local families such as the Bolithos and the Borlases,[20] and boarders from farther afield. Among these were Archer Thompson Gurney, author of the satirical poem *The Transcendentalists*, and the young Coleridge, who was to become Lord Chief Justice. When Kingsley first went to the school it was housed in an early-seventeenth-century terrace house at the bottom of the famous curving main street of Helston. The house still stands[21] and it is hard to imagine how even a small number of boys could have been accommodated in its rabbit warren of tiny rooms, no two of which

[18] Charles Kingsley. Lecture delivered at Bristol in 1858 entitled 'Great Cities and their Influence for Good and Evil'. Collected in *Miscellanies*, 1859.

[19] According to an advertisement in a local paper to which Mr E. M. Cunnack has drawn my attention, the fees at Helston were 32 guineas a year with 8 guineas extra for tuition. This fact, and the proximity of Helston to Clovelly, may have influenced Mr Kingsley's choice. Nevertheless even so short a journey seems to have put a strain on his resources, for on at least one occasion the boy spent his Christmas vacation at school.

[20] Unpublished memoir of Archer Gurney by A. W. Gurney, in the possession of the Rev. R. H. Gurney.

[21] It is now a solicitor's office.

appear to be on the same level. During Kingsley's third year at the
school it moved to more suitable premises, built from vast blocks of
granite, at the top of the hill. Of this building the impressive gothic
porch is still visible.[22] According to the *Royal Cornwall Gazette* the
move to the new premises coincided with Flora-day 1835, and on that
memorable occasion two of the young gentlemen stood under an
archway of green branches and spring flowers and recited odes of their
own composition. Their names were Messrs Kingsley and Powles.

Certainly the school was primitive in some respects. Coleridge employed only two assistant masters. One was a young clergyman called
Charles Alexander Johns, later to become famous as the author of
Flowers of the Field, the other a teacher of mathematics, an 'inferior'
person, but of a gentle nature. French and music were taught badly
by a visiting Frenchman. It was the duty of C. A. Johns to supervise
the boys all day in the large schoolroom but he gave only one ear to
their Virgil. The greater part of his attention was given to setting up
the botanical specimens that were to make him famous.[23] The headmaster did not teach, but would occasionally sally forth from his comfortable library to administer a lecture. He had an odd trick of saying
'here' at the end of each sentence. 'I am given to understand that you
go into the town on market days — here — which you know is against
the rules of the school — here!'[24] He disliked administering corporal
punishment and would leave his cane on the schoolroom chimney
piece. The boys used to cut lengths off it and smoke them.

Although the pupils were the sons of gentlemen, they had the sing-
song West Country manner of speaking. Coleridge and his wife
(who was a clever handsome woman), were known as 'The Maister'
and 'The Misses'. The boys never said 'I know' but 'I do knaw', never
'I can't' but ' I ceant'. To the end of his days Kingsley spoke with a
slight accent, and his spelling was never perfect. He invariably spelt
the name of *Frasers' Magazine* as Frazer's although he was a regular
contributor.

But the school had advantages, the chief of which was the freedom
it gave the boys to explore both the headmaster's private library and
the surrounding countryside. Coleridge was a noted theologian of

[22] The rest of the building has been incorporated into the premises of a club.
Coleridge's Latin dedication to the unknown founder, carved on stone, is preserved
in the cocktail bar.

[23] Before C. A. John's attention became completely absorbed by botany he showed
some interest in teaching history and even published a book called *Chronological
Historical Rhymes*, 1883.

[24] This rule was regularly disobeyed. The boys used to go into market on Saturday
mornings and buy eggs which the cook boiled for them.

wide interests, fluent in Arabic, Coptic, Zulu and Hawaiian, and these interests were reflected in his books. Among them Kingsley could satisfy undisturbed his taste for the exotic. His headmaster was gratified to come upon him one day 'busily engaged with an old copy of *Porphyry and Iamblichus*' — two Neoplatonist philosophers who lived in Alexandria in the fourth century.

The school took a liberal attitude to boys going off on expeditions into the country, provided they went with a companion (a rule which Kingsley frequently broke). Wednesdays and Saturdays were half-holidays and there were whole holidays on saints' days. They could go where they liked provided they wrote their destination on a slate and did not miss a meal. The young Kingsley spent long hours on the Lizard and botanising along the oak-fringed banks of the Helston estuary. His letters to his mother were at times little more than lists of specimens.

Give my love to Emily Wellesley, and ask her to dry me some *Adoxa*. The plant in the moors is in flower now. *Menyanthes trifoliata* is its name and we have found it here long ago. I question whether that is *Arabis stricta*; *Hirsuta* it is very likely to be. If it is *stricta* it is a most noble prize; but Mr C. wrong-names his plants dreadfully, between you and I. If you go to Bragels you will find a very large red-stalked spurge, *Euphorbia amygdaloides*, growing by the path, before you enter the wood, as you come up from the beach — pray dry me some of this. I have found *Spergula subulata*, *Vicea angustifolia*, *Asalenium lanceolatum*! ! ! *Scilla verna*, *Arenaria verna*, *Teesdalia nudicaulis*, *Ornithopus perpusillus*, *Carex strigoa*, *Carex auden*, and several others, all of which I can give Emily specimens.

But Kingsley's interest in nature was not merely physical. It bordered on the metaphysical. In one of his earliest letters to Fanny he told her of the strange excitement, often culminating in tears, that was aroused in him by 'the beautiful inanimate . . . sun and stars, wood and wave'. In a more intimate letter he planned the revelations he would make to her on their wedding night:

not about people but about the nature-lore I have been studying from a child. I saw some dead moles hanging in a hedge today and my first thought was 'I wonder if Fanny ever saw a mole! If she were here I would take one down and show her its wonderful form and preach her a whole sermon about moles and their use and try to find some mystic meaning in them.'[25]

25 ULF No. 49, 1843.

As a schoolboy Kingsley did not always commune alone with nature, however. C. A. Johns was in the habit of allowing certain favoured pupils to accompany him on his collecting expeditions. (Those who were left behind affected to prefer the manly fishing basket to the 'soppy' collecting tin.') Kingsley and Johns became close friends in spite of the eight years difference in their ages. They even spent a summer holiday exploring the flora of the Plymouth area together.

Derwent Coleridge has left us a portrait of his former pupil at this time:

> Charles was a tall slight boy of keen visage and great bodily activity, earnest and energetic, original to the point of eccentricity, a genuine out-of-doors English boy. He was popular alike with tutor, school fellows and servants. His account of a walk or a run would often display considerable eloquence, the impediment in his speech rather adding to the effect. We well remember his description of a hunt after some pigs, from which he returned (not an uncommon occurrence) his head torn with brambles and his face beaming with fun and frolic.

In fact 'the dear old master', as Kingsley used to call him, was not entirely accurate in his account. Charles could never qualify as a 'genuine out-of-doors English boy', for he was no good at cricket, and indeed was described by one of his contemporaries as 'a milksop who was afraid of a cricket ball'.[26] He did, however, excel in feats of daring and had only two rivals in jumping the lane at the bottom of the school garden from wall to wall. The lane was a deep one and a fall would certainly have meant broken bones. But this was not enough to make him popular. His researches in the library gave him an air of superiority which others found hard to stomach. Also he was absurdly easily upset; as a grown man he was never able to read *Uncle Tom's Cabin* because it was 'so terribly sad'. For this tender-heartedness he was teased unmercifully. His nickname, according to his great-niece Gabriella Vallings, was Cave, on account, she told me, of his large mouth, which seemed all the larger as it gaped in search of an elusive word. By the time Kingsley reached the top of the school he had earned some respect. His name, written in large letters in boot blacking on the wall of the playground, was piously preserved after he left.

Kingsley's brother Herbert was quite the opposite, distinguished for nothing but his jolly extrovertness. He was liked by the boys and a

[26] Collier, *The Cornish Magazine.*

favourite with Aunt Betsy the housekeeper. Yet the end of his short
life was strangely clouded. Two months before he died he stole a silver
spoon, sold it and ran away from school, spending a night in the open.
He was arrested in Helston the next day 'by a bailiff named Hawk,
who found him in the street in such a wretched plight and looking so
ill that he knew at once who he was, put handcuffs on him, and marched
him back to the school.'[27] He was locked in his room and fed on
bread and water and, although kind Aunt Betsy, into whose apron
he cried, brought him illicit meals,[28] he soon became very ill with
rheumatic fever. He was on the way to recovery when he died suddenly, presumably of the heart condition that so often accompanies the
disease. Yet rumour persists in Helston to this day that he drowned
himself in Looe Pool, a land-locked arm of the sea that lies in the grounds
of Penrose estate and is visible from the main street of Helston. The
fact that Herbert's grave in Helston churchyard is marked only by a
stone bearing the letters H.K. lends some substance to this rumour.[29]

Whatever the circumstances of Herbert's death, its effect on Charles
at the age of fifteen can well be imagined. Cowley Powles, a school
friend, was present when he received the news.

Charles was summoned from the room where we were all sitting in
ignorance of what had just taken place. All at once a cry of anguish
burst upon us, such as, after more than forty years, I remember as if
it were yesterday. There was no need to tell the awe-struck listeners
what had happened.

After the tragedy Kingsley's friendship with Cowley deepened.
Like the Devon fisherman's son at Clovelly, Cowley was small and
frail. Kingsley described him as having a 'manly heart in the most
delicate womanly body',[30] and his pet name for him was Corculus, a
term of endearment used by Plautus meaning 'little heart'. But friendship with him was not destined to be cut off in its prime. It lasted a lifetime and it was a source of great happiness to Kingsley when, towards
the end of his life, Cowley became one of his parishioners at Eversley.
Powles never forgot their first meeting.

[27] Journal of C. A. Johns, 1811–1863.

[28] Unpublished reminiscences of W. J. Winn, a nephew of Aunt Betsy (whose
real name was Elizabeth Williams.)

[29] The grave is marked by a large slab of stone lying on the ground. Anyone
interested can find it by standing due north of the church tower and walking towards
it over other graves.

[30] ULF No. 23, October 3, 1843.

It was at Helston, in January 1833, when we were each in our four-teenth year. He and his brother Herbert had been spending the Christmas holidays at school, and I was introduced to them on my arrival from London, before any of our schoolfellows had returned. I remember the long, low room dimly lit by a candle at the further end, where the brothers were sitting, engaged at the moment of my entrance in a series of (not uncharacteristic) experiments with gunpowder.

Charles and Cowley confided their most intimate thoughts to each other and, when at the age of sixteen Cowley fell in love with the girl who was to become his wife, Kingsley wrote him long letters of advice which read very like the ones that, later, he was to write to his own fiancée. 'Teach her a love of nature. Stir her imagination, and excite her awe and delight by your example.'

He himself was occupied by personal thoughts of the love of women at this time. He had conceived a mild admiration for a young lady with a pleasant singing voice at the school, probably Coleridge's only daughter. But the poems he began to write were to a lady of an alto-gether less fleshly kind, who sat alone by a holy well all day:

> And as I gazed with love and awe
> Upon that sylph-like thing,
> Methought that airy form must be
> The fairy of the spring.[31]

Another poem was about a lady actually dead:

> Her grave should be
> Upon the bare top of a sunny hill.
> There should be no tall stone, no marble tomb
> Upon her gentle corse; the ponderous pile
> Would press too rudely on those fairy limbs.[32]

There was also a long prose fable called *Psyche* about a woodland maiden in search of love. She sought it in nature, but the sight of the hawk striking the dove told her it was not there. She sought it in the

[31] Charles Kingsley, *Trehill Well*, 1835. No doubt based on Trelill Well, a holy well which can still be seen on a farm 1¼ miles from Helston. The only lady associated with it however, was the farmer's wife who, according to a local historian, exhorted visitors to drop a pin in to fend off bad luck.

[32] Charles Kingsley, *Hypotheses Hypochondriacae*, 1835.

palaces of the rich and the hovels of the poor but found that death walked in both. She thought for a moment she had run it to earth when she

> gazed upon two fond ones, as they lay with their fair limbs wreathed round each other, and their lips mingled in sleep, while their white breasts heaved together in mutual throbs. But she looked, and she perceived, in their dreams, that there was one chill thought — that such bliss might not last for ever.

In the end the maiden found love, suitably enough, 'with Him above . . . and she was seen by her blue well no more'. Kingsley sent all three of these productions to his mother, but it was Cowley's copies that were treasured and preserved for posterity.

In the January of his sixteenth year Kingsley received a letter which he was instructed to burn. It informed him that he was to leave Helston and come home to complete his education under a tutor. The reasons for this decision can only be guessed at. It is possible that he was not learning enough. He disliked school subjects and was inclined not to work until the eve of an examination. His mathematics were poor and even his Greek and Latin, so essential for entry into a university, were below standard. Nor was Helston the kind of school where he was likely to be pushed. He and Cowley were considered privileged students in their senior years. They were allowed to work in their own room and in their own time. On occasions they were called upon to teach the younger boys. There may have been another reason, however, for the decision to withdraw him. Mr and Mrs Kingsley were about to leave the West Country for London, and Charles, usually so healthy and active, was not well. He had only recently recovered from an attack of cholera and although it was of the mild variety (English and not Asiatic) it had left a permanent mark. For the rest of his life he was to suffer from periodic trouble with his liver, which he designated his 'insides'. Under the circumstances his parents may have wished to have him living nearer to them.

When Charles Kingsley Senior accepted the living of St Luke's, Chelsea, he probably made the biggest blunder of his lifetime. His reasons for taking it were understandable enough. He had four boys to educate and St Luke's was a large and wealthy church (you pass it on the left in Sydney Street when you go from South Kensington to Chelsea Town Hall). It had just been built in the neo-Gothic style (which Kingsley detested)[33] to serve the newly built Cadogan estates.

[33] 'I intend one day to get up a club for the total abolition of Gothic art.' Charles Kingsley, 'My Winter Garden', *Prose Idylls*.

Indeed it was probably only because he was a relative of Lord Cadogan that Mr Kingsley was appointed to so rich a living.[34] Mrs Kingsley was a close friend of Lady Louisa Cadogan, who admired young Charles's verses.

Privilege, however, brought responsibilities. Mr Kingsley now numbered his parishioners not in hundreds but in thousands. Gone were the easy days of chatting with the fishermen down at the quay at Clovelly or sketching the neighbouring coves. After he moved to Chelsea he never painted another picture and Mrs Kingsley finally established an ascendancy that she was never to relinquish. With parochial schools and Bible classes and district visitors and committees to manage she had at last found scope for her organising abilities and she took over the running of the parish without hesitation.[35] As far as Charles was concerned, the house became uninhabitable. In a letter to his beloved Cowley at Helston he wrote, 'We have nothing but clergymen (very good and sensible men, but), talking of nothing but parochial schools and duties, and vestries and curates, etc., etc, etc. I begin to hate these dapper young-ladies-preachers like the devil.' Kingsley was not alone in hating them. 'As you may suppose,' he continued, 'this hatred is hereditary, and the governor is never more rich than when he unbends on these points.' But the youth was not only missing Cowley; his thoughts often strayed to the charming young lady he had left in Cornwall.

Here are nothing but ugly splay-footed beings, three-fourths of whom can't sing, and the other quarter sing miles out of tune, with voices like love-sick parrots. Confound!!! They have got their heads crammed full of Schools, and district visiting, and baby linen and penny clubs. Confound!!! And go about among the most abominable scenes of filth, wretchedness and indecency, to visit and read the Bible.

Strange words from a future clergyman and philanthropist, but Kingsley never got over his aversion to 'talking shop' and made it a rule in his own home that parish affairs should never be discussed at table.

In London it was no longer possible to escape into the green embrace of nature. The garden behind the Georgian rectory[36] was very large;

[34] His predecessor at the rectory was a brother of the Duke of Wellington.

[35] Kingsley once described his mother as 'A second Mrs Fry in spirit and action'.

[36] The rectory, at 56 Old Church Street, within a stone's throw of the King's Road, is still inhabited by a rector, and its vast garden is miraculously preserved. It serves as a playground for handicapped children.

it contained gravel walks and pools and a mulberry tree which Queen Elizabeth is supposed to have planted — but it was not large enough. The Thames embankment was lined with bird-filled trees and Carlyle, who had just moved to Chelsea, claimed that the air was 'hardly inferior to Craigenputtock', but to the young Kingsley, the marshes of Battersea were a poor substitute for the moors of Helston and Clovelly. Charlotte and Henry (now nine and six respectively) found interest in the life of the great river. Indeed Henry was to use the old tomb-crammed church on the embankment (which St Luke's had supplanted) as the setting for his best novel, *The Hillyars and the Burtons*. But Charles could find consolation only in work.

The plan to engage a tutor for him seems to have been dropped and instead he was entered at King's College, London, an Anglican foundation which had recently been given the power to grant degrees. But Kingsley, like Ruskin, preferred to use it as a cramming establishment to prepare him for one of the older universities. For two years he worked unremittingly at Greek and Latin literature and mathematics, walking up to the West End every day, reading all the way, and walking home late to study all evening. He became interested in the works of Plato and did well in the examinations but made little impression otherwise upon his teachers. One tutor later admitted surprise that anyone so abnormally shy should have made a mark in the world, and another confessed that he could not remember him whatsoever.

During those two years Kingsley appears to have had no recreations at all apart from reading any book he could lay his hands on, (fortunately his father's library was well stocked with works on history and travel). He had no one of his own age at home to talk to, since Gerald had joined the navy, and he got little companionship from his parents. He had never found it easy to talk to 'the governor' but now he found himself inhibited in his conversation with his mother as well. He wrote 'the only persons before whom I am dull are my father and mother. I know not why, but I cannot try to make them smile. They *set me down* so.'[37] He had occasional talks with 'two or three good male acquaintances', one of whom was sub-secretary to the Geological Society but, because of his father's Low Church views, all worldly amusements, such as the theatre, music and parties, were forbidden. It was hardly surprising that he became ill. He lost weight, grew spotty, and started to suffer from 'spectral illusions (one as clear as any of Nicolai's) often accompanied with frightful nervous excitability, and inability to settle to any work, though always working at something

[37] ULF No. 23, October 3, 1843.

in a fierce, desultory way'.[38] Eventually it was discovered that he had a seriously congested left lung. In the opinion of the family medical adviser, 'old Dr Chambers', there was a danger of permanent disease[39] and some 'tartarised blistering stuff' was applied which left lifelong scars, but had little other effect. In the end a cure was found in the form of a holiday at Clovelly with his father. It was as if the two years of absence had never been. Sir James lent him a boat and a black pony and he swam every day in the sea without ill effects. His joy in returning to the old home still rings through the letter he wrote home all those years ago. 'I seem like some spirit in metempsychosis which has suddenly passed back, out of a new life, into one which it bore long ago, and has recovered, in one moment, all its old ties, its old feelings, its old friends, and pleasures!' Nevertheless he was left with a large adhesion of the pleura and a lung which troubled him in heavy fog for the rest of his life.

[38] Letter to John Bullar, March 19, 1857.
[39] Unpublished letter to Dr Ackland, quoted with the permission of Mary Stella Edwards.

CHAPTER 3

The Cambridge Undergraduate
1838–1842

Cambridge in the 1830s was still a place where the majority of under-graduates enjoyed a spell of high spirits and hard drinking before settling down on their family acres. And, among many lax colleges, one of the most permissive was Magdalene, where Kingsley was entered. For his first term the shy young man continued his studious habits and spent much time in his attic-like rooms at the top of C staircase in the front quadrangle. But his mathematics tutor, Samual Waud, soon put an end to that. He was a sociable man whose habitual greeting to those studying under him was 'Come to my rooms, and we will have a problem or two and an oyster and cigar.' He realised that Kingsley was too shy to fraternise with the fast public school men who dominated the college, and encouraged some of them to call on him. They soon discovered his sporting tastes. He was already an excellent horseman and, although he could not afford his own hunters, he began to have adventurous days with the hounds on hirelings. And he took up rowing. By the spring he had worked so hard at his oar that he had earned himself a place in the college second boat and done himself some small internal injury which was not discovered until after he went down.[1] With sport went some degree of dissipation. Magdalene Boat Club dinners were renowned for their conviviality and at one of them fifty-four bottles of champagne were drunk, along with a dozen each of sherry and hock and twenty bowls of punch. A vice that took a far stronger hold of Kingsley than drink, however, was tobacco. At Cambridge he took to smoking not a gentlemanly cigar but a clay pipe of the sort used by working men. So great became his passion for the weed that he was eventually to devote a page of *Westward Ho!* to eulogising 'the lone man's companion, the bachelor's friend, the hungry man's food, the sad man's cordial, the wakeful man's sleep, and the chilly man's fire'. To Amyas Leigh, and not Walter

[1] ULF, October, 1843. 'My complaint is due to rowing, not to lifting my darling over a fence!'

Raleigh, he allotted the honour of having first imported the 'lotus leaf of Torridge' and only with its fragrant mist inside his head was he capable of prolonged thought. 'At twenty I found out tobacco,' he told a friend. 'The spectres vanished, the power of dull application arose: and for the first time in my life I began to be master of my own brain.' At first his mother, and later his wife, attempted to break him of the habit. Neither succeeded for long, and his indulgence cannot have helped the lung complaint that killed him in his fifties.

With a pipe between his teeth, and in congenial company, the shy young man became an eager, if stammering, talker, though according to one of his contemporaries, a Mr Stewart, what he talked was the 'most awful rot'.[2] In spite of his reputation for being 'odd' and 'cracky' he did make several close friends, one of whom was to supplant, for a time, the beloved Cowley Powles in his affections. Charles Blachford Mansfield came from a rectory background like Kingsley, but unlike him he was handsome, socially poised and able to charm. To compensate for an invalid childhood he had trained himself as a gymnast and used to perform 'strange feats' on a gymnastic pole in his room. To his friends 'he seemed more antelope than man'. Add to this the fact that he was a brilliant scientist with a mind of 'Baconian breadth' and it will be easy to see why Kingsley succumbed to him. According to Dr Stubbs, later Bishop of Ely, 'while Kingsley was at university Mansfield was to him what Hallam had been to Alfred Tennyson'. Kingsley himself confessed, in a letter written at the time of Mansfield's early death, 'He was my first love. The first human being, save my mother, I ever met who knew what I meant.'[3]

The friendship with Mansfield was Kingsley's third close association with a member of his own sex, and the one that involved him most deeply. In a letter to Fanny a year later he defended the brotherly love of men, and told her she must not depreciate it. 'Remember, the man is the stronger vessel. There is something awful, spiritual, in man's love for each other.' He considered he was paying her a high compliment when he said, 'Had you been a man we should have been like David and Jonathan.'[4] He was always much moved by the beauty of the male body. In an essay in which he denigrated mountains he remarked how much more beautiful was the body of the mountaineer, 'if you but strip him of his jacket and breeches', than the mountain he climbed. In the same essay he described a young keeper on a trout

[2] Letter to the author written by Stanley Harold, one time curate to Mr Stewart, now living in Australia.
[3] Letter to Ludlow.
[4] ULF No. 30, October 28, 1843.

stream as 'a river god in velveteen'.[5] After he had been married eight years he claimed he would walk ten miles to see a certain butcher's nephew playing cricket, 'in spite of the hideous English dress. One looks forward with delight to what he would be "in the resurrection".' His younger brother Henry came to share these views, but whereas with Charles any element of homosexuality remained latent, with Henry it became more overt. No doubt Kingsley's fear of such tendencies in himself accounts for his constant emphasis on 'manliness' and athletic prowess. In fact several of his acquaintances remarked on a certain *womanliness* in him. Justin McCarthy wrote that 'despite his rough voice and vigorous manner, he was as feminine in his likes and dislikes, his impulses and prejudices as Harriet Martineau was masculine in her intellect and George Sand in her emotions'. Certainly Fanny recognised how serious a rival Mansfield had been. In her biography of her husband she firmly omitted all mention of the Cambridge friendship.

The two young men were constantly together. They rowed on the Cam, they smoked, they experimented with magic and Mesmerism, they observed birds. Most of all, they discussed religion. In the late 'thirties religious doubts were fashionable. Dr Pusey and Mr Newman had blown the first trumpet blast of High Anglicanism at Oxford six years before and no earnest young man could be without views on the position of the Church of England. Kingsley, sickened by the theological quibbling of both High and Low, rejected Christianity outright, although he never admitted to being an atheist. In adolescence his faith had not been strong. The only mention of religion in his letters to his mother was a dutiful promise, too often repeated, to read his Bible. It was in Nature, not in God, that he found inspiration. Now, under the influence of Mansfield, a materialist, he surrendered himself to Pantheism and even addressed a poem, *Palinodia*, to the Great Mother.

With so many distractions it is hardly surprising that Kingsley's studies suffered. He often persuaded the man who shared tutorials with him to finish his essays for him. The rigid curriculum of classical and mathematical studies enforced at Cambridge in his time never appealed to him and if its intention was to train the mind in logical thinking, it failed notably with him. 'As for my studies interesting me,' he wrote, 'if you knew the system and the subjects of study here you would feel that to be impossible. Vanity and Avarice are the great incitements to hard reading here, for the practical and applicable knowledge gained here is almost nothing.'[6] Nevertheless he summoned up sufficient

[5] Charles Kingsley, 'Chalk Stream Studies', *Prose Idylls*.
[6] ULF No. 7, 1841.

vanity and avarice to put in a period of hard cramming before the college examinations at the end of his first year. He came out first both in Classics and in Mathematics and broke the news to his father in a mood of high elation, for, as he pointed out, 'you know I am not accustomed to be successful'. The way was clear for a rewarding long vacation, although just how rewarding he was not yet to know.

In the summer of 1839 the Rev Charles Kingsley, tired of London, exchanged duties with the Rev Twopeny, and removed to his rectory in the village of Checkenden near Ipsden, in Oxfordshire. In this way he could afford two months' holiday in the country for all his children including Gerald, on leave from the navy, and George and Henry, who were at King's College School. But it was for his oldest son that the move was to have the most momentous consequences, because at Braziers Park, a large house in the neighbourhood, resided the wealthy Misses Grenfell: Georgiana, Charlotte, Henrietta and Frances Eliza. Frances Eliza was known to her friends as Fanny.

The Misses Grenfell, all in their late twenties or early thirties, were the orphans of the recently deceased Pascoe Grenfell, a Cornish tin magnate who had been the member for Truro and later for Great Marlow. Their mother had been the daughter of Lord Doneraile of County Cork and one of their great-aunts, a Miss St Leger, was the only woman who had ever been admitted to the Order of Free-masons. Seven other brothers and sisters had all married well, and they had been installed at Braziers Park with comfortable portions but little expectation of marriage. The four had wisely made a virtue of necessity and espoused the cause of Dr Pusey and voluntary virginity. They had formed themselves into a kind of sisterhood,[7] spent long hours dis-cussing the Tracts and even fasted, although only in moderation. For these ladies did not allow their 'hot-bed' religion to interfere with worldly pleasures. They dressed magnificently, were received at the best houses during the London season and were altogether typical products of the 'Bond-Streetism'[8] Kingsley so much detested.

Yet Fanny was not quite like her sisters. She was considerably younger than they and because her mother had died when she was four years old had been largely brought up by them. She was less of a 'proud, fine lady' than they.[9] She was also prettier. Her portraits show a well upholstered young woman with a creamy skin, glossy brown

---

[7] ULF No. 46, 1843. 'You are a woman brought up from childhood in a nunnery, brought up not as a young woman should be in the hope of marriage but on the present enjoyment of sisterhood, among women who have no intention or hope of marrying.'

[8] ULF No. 24, October 4, 1843.

[9] ULF No. 31, October, 1843.

hair and fine eyes. Kingsley first saw her on his return from a ride on the 4th of July[10] a date that became sacred to both of them. She and her sisters had come to call at the rectory and were seated in chairs on the lawn being entertained by Mrs Kingsley.

There was something peculiar in her profile that reminded him of his beloved Cornishmen. And there was a roundness in her figure that he admired for he did not care for 'grace in woman which is obtained at the expense of honest flesh and blood'.[11] He felt he had known the girl in some former life; this was not a first meeting but a reunion with a twin sister. 'That was our true wedding day,' he said to her twenty years later in a letter written admittedly to excuse himself for having forgotten the anniversary of their actual wedding. Fanny, looking back, felt the same. 'How I remember your wild troubled look that first day, as if you lived such a *lone* life, and I felt, from our first conversation, that I alone could understand you, that I alone had the key to your spiritual being and could raise you to your proper height.'[12]

At last Kingsley had found someone to whom he would be able to open his heart unreservedly. He would feel it possible to say things to Fanny that he could not even say to Mansfield. 'Everything I say seems to sink into your mind as if you had a receptacle fitted for each thought of mine,' he told her. She was the calm being, secure in her Christian faith, at whose feet his battered soul unburdened itself. But the couple did not at once embark upon intimate confessions. In the 1840s there were formalities to be gone through before a shy young man and a well-brought-up young woman could feel quite free to confide in each other. And at this time there was certainly no thought of marriage, at any rate on Fanny's part, for she was already half committed to joining Pusey's community at Park Place, Regent's Park. Even if she had considered marriage as an alternative she well knew the awkward undergraduate, with no money and a 'twang' in his accent[13] would never be accepted by her family.

At the end of the summer Kingsley went back to Cambridge in a state of confusion, and devoted his second year, as have many young men before and since, to running up debts. He found that in violent physical exertion he could best escape the thoughts that tormented him. 'You cannot understand,' he told Fanny, 'the excitement of

---

[10] Fanny's Nice Diary, July 3, 1843. Hereafter FND.

[11] Charles Kingsley, 'My Winter Garden', *Prose Idylls*.

[12] Unpublished letter from Fanny to Charles, March 14, 1854.

[13] ULF No. 39, November 11, 1843. Kingsley always hotly denied the twang of which Fanny accused him. It was probably a left-over from his West Country upbringing.

animal exercise to a young man.' He plunged into an exhausting programme of boating, hunting, driving, fencing, boxing, fishing and
duck-shooting. He was later to look back with disgust upon what he
described as that 'year of dissipation' but at the time there were moments
that must have seemed pleasant enough. A sporting companion,
Pitcairn Campbell, described a meeting with him.

We happened to be sitting together one night on the top of one of
those coaches which, in our time, were subscribed for by a number
of men paying 10s or £1 each, for various expeditions into the Fens,
driving men taking the management wearing wonderful coats and
hats, and providing the horses. I remember the drive very well. The
moon was high, and the air was frosty, and we talked about sport
and natural history whilst the cornopean professor astonished the
natives with what he called Mr Straw's waltzes. At last we got upon
fishing, and I invited your husband to come to my rooms to view
some very superior tackle which had been left me by a relative. He
came at once, inviting me to join him in some of his haunts up the
Granta and the Cam, where he had friends dwelling, and hospitable
houses open to him.

I shall never forget our first expedition. I was to call him, and for
this purpose I had to climb over the wall of Magdalene College.
This I did at 2 a.m. and at about three we were both climbing back
into the stonemasons yard, and off through Trumpington, in pouring
rain all the way, nine miles to Duxford. We reached it about 6.30.
The water was clouded by rain and I espied, under the alders, some
glorious trout rising to caterpillars dropping from the bushes. In
ten minutes I had three of these fine fellows on the bank, one of them
weighed three pounds, the others two pounds each. We caught
nothing after the rain had ceased.

Besides these expeditions, we made others on horseback following
the great Professor Sedgwick in his adventurous rides, which the
livery stable keepers called jolly-gizing.[14] The old professor was
generally mounted on a bony giant, whose trot kept most of us at
a hand gallop. Gaunt and grim, he seemed to enjoy the fun as much
as we did. When we surrounded him at the trysting place even the
silliest among us acknowledged that his lectures were glorious. It
is too true that our method of reaching those trysting places was not
legitimate, the greater number preferring the field to the road, so
that the unhappy owners of the horses found it necessary to charge
more for a day's jolly-gizing than for a day's hunting.

[14] Geologising.

There was another professor whose lectures we attended together, but he was of a different type and character, one who taught the gentle art of self defence, a negro of pure blood, who appeared to have more joints in his back than are usually allotted to humanity. In carrying out the science which he taught we occasionally discoloured each other's countenances.

But to Kingsley there was a sinister element in these boisterous goings-on, for he knew that they were only attempts to escape from something in himself that frightened him — his own sexuality. The romantic friendship with Mansfield could not satisfy his animal cravings and indeed it was with Mansfield, judging from the letters they later exchanged, that he had his first physical encounter with a member of the opposite sex. The name of the woman is not known but she was probably a prostitute at Barnwell or Castle End, both popular brothels with undergraduates. The experience filled him with shame and self-loathing. He felt so dirtied by it that three years later he offered to release his fiancée from her marriage obligations because of it. 'Darling,' he wrote, 'I must confess all. You, my unspotted, bring a virgin body to my arms. I alas do not to yours. Before our lips met I had sinned and fallen. Oh, how low! If it is your wish, you shall be a wife only in name. No communion but that of mind shall pass between us.'[15]

The second long vacation from Cambridge passed in a mood of black despair. He felt that not only his own soul had been darkened by the 'uncleanness' of his 'wild beast life' but the world about him, even beautiful nature, was coated with a sooty pall of guilt. He considered opting out completely and escaping to lead the life of a 'wild prairie hunter — pursuing bison and grizzly bear, mustang and big horn, Black foot and Pawnee'.[16] It is possible that, like the hero of his novel *Yeast*, he even considered suicide at this time. Perhaps the thoughts that he put into the mind of Lancelot were in fact his own. 'More than once, as he wandered restlessly from one room to another, the barrels of his pistols seemed to glitter with a cold devilish smile, and call to him. "Come to us! and with one touch of your finger send that bursting spirit which throbs against your brow to flit forth free, and never more defile her purity with your presence".' Gradually he came to see that there was only one escape from this torment: Christ. 'Without Him,' he told Fanny, 'everything, even the very flowers and

[15] ULF No. 45, 1843.
[16] Charles Kingsley, 'My Winter Garden', *Prose Idylls*.

insects, yes, even your beautiful face is hell, dark, blank, hopeless.'[17]
But he did not believe in Christ. Who could help him regain his foot-
hold in the Christian faith?

Fanny had waited patiently in the wings for her cue and he poured
out his heart to her that autumn in a long formal letter that commenced 'My dearest Lady' and ended simply with the word 'goodbye'.

> I have a kind of awe that almost amounts to fear in writing to you.
> I feel that in the tumult and grossness by which I am surrounded my
> mind is seldom, very seldom, in a tone capable of approaching the
> subject as it ought to be approached, and of coming pure and calm
> into your pure and calm presence. I feel that I am insulting you
> when I sit down reeking with the fumes of the world's frivolities
> and vices to talk to you. I feel too that my mind is becoming ener-
> vated, that I cannot remember or think or invent with the variety
> and distinctness of which I was formerly capable, in short that I
> have injured not only the moral sense but the mechanical system
> of the mind which I once had. I have however, I assure you, struggled
> to alter lately and this alteration has been remarked with pleasure by
> some and with sneers by others. 'Kingsley,' they say, 'is not half so
> reckless as he used to be.' You are to me a middle point between
> earthly and ethereal morality. I begin to love good for your sake.
> At length I will be able to love it for God's sake.[18]

This letter was a landmark in the relationship of the two young
people, for in it Kingsley suggested for the first time that he was beginning to think of Fanny not only as a mediator between himself
and the Almighty but also as a woman he might marry. 'Oh Fanny,'
he sighed, 'shall we ever be *real friends*?' Meantime the hard path to
conversion had to be trodden. The 'young-ladies-preachers' of Chelsea
had instilled in Kingsley a horror of conventional religious phraseology
and he felt that he must come to Christianity anew. 'I find,' he wrote,
'that if I allow myself to use, even to my own heart, those vague and
trite expressions, which are generally used as the watchwords of
religion, their familiarity makes me careless.' He was repelled by the
tepid Christianity of men like his father. If he was to be a Christian
it must be a Christian of an extreme, even fanatical variety. And what
was the most extreme and fanatical variety of Christian. Could it be a
monk?

The suggestion that Kingsley, who was to go down in history as the

[17] ULF No. 58. January 10, 1844.
[18] ULF No. 3, November 1840.

leading opponent of Cardinal Newman, ever flirted with the Church of Rome, may appear absurd. Yet in later life Kingsley was often to repeat that he knew the attraction of Rome better than any convert, and to Fanny he confided 'There is no middle course. Either deism, or the highest and most monarchical system of Catholicism.' Further proof of his leaning towards not merely Catholicism but monasticism has recently come to light in a letter which Fanny always intended to burn. 'I once formed a strange project, I would have travelled to a monastery in France, gone barefoot into the chapel at matins (midnight) and there confessed every sin of my whole life before the monks and offered my naked body to be scourged by them.'[19]

But there was one very serious obstacle to becoming a monk: Fanny's beautiful white body. Gradually Kingsley was becoming convinced that he was a creature that could not survive without a mate. Eventually he sat down and penned a detailed account of why celibacy was an impossible condition for him. That account was preserved in the small leather deed box in which he kept his most precious possessions such as the gloves that Fanny was married in and letters from Royalty. When that box was opened recently the document was found to be missing. No doubt some discreet relative had burnt it. Its contents can only be guessed at.

Meanwhile throughout the winter Kingsley struggled with his doubts and confided them to Fanny. 'I have no faith,' he wrote. 'You cannot conceive the moments of self-abasement and shame.' At times he was tempted to fall back into his old ways. 'The last week has been a period of violent struggle, of continual temptations to return to old courses.' 'Long, long must I wander through the night,' he said in the New Year of 1841. Yet already 'a gleam, fitful but certain', glimmered across his 'darkling path'. On January 11th Fanny paid him a visit at Chelsea Rectory and he took her in his arms for the first time. Three years later he commemorated that first kiss with a drawing of a young man with a feathered hat and swelling codpiece embracing a young woman. Underneath the drawing he copied out a quotation from Frederika Bremer which ran: 'Long reposed they heart on heart; and life seemed to have no enigma, no question for them.'[20]

On the last Sunday in March the couple met and kissed once more and this time Fanny confessed her love to Charles. Within three days he wrote to her to announce he was at last safely inside the fold.

Day after day there has been an involuntary still small voice directing

[19] ULF No. 53, 1843.
[20] FND, September 1843.

me to the Church as the only rest for my troubled spirit in this world. I did not know then the reason of this strange haunting of the mind, though I felt it was the only 'atonement' which I could make in the eyes of the world for my offences. I feel, Fanny, that I am under a heavy debt to God and how can I pay this better than by devoting myself to the religion I have scorned, making of the debauchee a preacher of purity and holiness, and of the destroyer of systems a weak though determined upholder of the only true system.[21]

Kingsley sealed his return to the Faith with a vow to become a clergyman. This he made in a moment of deep emotion on the night of his twenty-second birthday, three months later. He wrote and told Fanny of it at once. 'I have been for the last hour on the sea shore. Before the sleeping earth and the sleepless sea and stars I devoted myself to God, a vow never to be recalled.'

It was fortunate that Kingsley's conversion occurred during his third year at Cambridge, the year in which it was essential that he should settle down to a sober and industrious life if he was to achieve a degree that would reflect any kind of honour on him. He now began to work in earnest, aware that only thus could he win Fanny's hand. The Misses Grenfell, he was well aware, did not approve of him. They had observed a change in Fanny, an unwillingness to partake in worldly amusements and a tendency to spend long hours in her bedroom. They associated it with the frequent letters from Cambridge and expressed disapproval. Even Mrs Kingsley said the correspondence must stop. Up to this point she had encouraged her son in his affair and had even forwarded occasional letters to Fanny so that they would bear a Chelsea postmark. He confided his most intimate feelings to his mother in a way few modern young men would dream of, and she shared in them, perhaps finding in them compensation for the dryness of her own marriage. But even she now saw that if Charles was to be regarded as anything but a 'penniless adventurer' in pursuit of an heiress he must prove himself worthy of her. 'My only reasons,' he told Fanny, 'for working for a degree are that I may enter the world with a certain prestige which may get me a living sooner. I can yet take high honours in the university and ought to get my fellowship.'

He now adopted a strict regime of study, attending morning chapel at eight, reading from nine till one or two, attending chapel again at five, dining, and reading two or three hours in the evening. He refused hunting and driving and made a solemn vow against cards.

[21] ULF No. 6, March 31, 1841.

He even begged Fanny to forbid him 'wine or spirits or any fermented liquor for the rest of the year'.[22] His only recreation was an occasional ten-mile walk along the Cam in a Fen wind with a fishing rod in his hand, his infallible cure in after life for 'over-mentation'.

Poor Fanny had no such programme of work to distract her. On that fateful Sunday in March she had discovered that she was deeply in love with the intense undergraduate with the wide mouth and uncouth manner. Her sisters held a council of war and decided on the standard cure for love-sickness — a long trip abroad. Fortunately Lady Gainsborough was at that moment planning to do a round of the German watering places. She would be glad of Fanny's companionship. Fanny had no alternative but to go. During those long summer months she wrote endless letters to Charles which she never posted. At first they were written on sheets of notepaper pinned together in pamphlet form. Then at Baden she bought a red notebook and at Marienbad and Carlsbad she poured into it her passionate longing for her lover.

Charles meanwhile was spending his last long vacation studying hard at Sir Charles Wales's house at Shelford, near Cambridge, where he had often spent fishing weekends. Certainly he had not forgotten Fanny. Indeed he went to London to see a portrait of her which had been hung in the Royal Academy exhibition that year. He considered it a poor imitation of the original. 'You cannot think how horribly ugly they have made her,' he told his mother. 'He has given her a pair of little staring glassy eyes stuck close together, a huge heavy red round jaw and an expression of amazed ill-temper. And a Scot plaid dress the ugliest thing possible in make and colour.'[23] Yet he sent a rather cool reply to a letter Fanny wrote him when she returned from Germany, suggesting they should become engaged. 'Are we not eternally engaged now Fanny? Perhaps not formally in the eyes of men but in our own consciences and hearts. I have always been afraid of being too successful at first. I think sorrow at the beginning augurs well for the happiness of a connexion.' He did, however, accept some books from her, which he had refused to do a year earlier, admitting 'we are now perhaps in a different relation to each other from what we were then'. The books were the works of Carlyle, which were to make a profound impression on him. But in the meantime the study of Greek, Latin and mathematics had to be pursued.

The last Michaelmas Term at Cambridge was a weary grind, for Kingsley was trying to cram into six months the work of three years.

[22] ULF No. 7, 1841.
[23] Unpublished letter to his mother in the British Museum.

To his mother he wrote:

> That degree hangs over me like a vast incubus keeping me down. I
> feel deeply what Manfred says of an order
>
> > Of mortals on the earth, who do become
> > Old in their youth, and die ere middle age.·
>
> I shall be an old man before I am forty. If you rejoice that you
> have born a man into the world, remember that he is not like com-
> mon men, neither cleverer nor wiser, nor better than the multitude,
> but utterly *different*.

In this presentiment of early senility he again resembled his brother
Henry who, in his time as an undergraduate often expressed a longing
for 'cheesy death'. Charles himself was only twenty-three when he
wrote the famous verse

> Oh! that we two lay sleeping
> In our nest in the churchyard sod;
> With our limbs at rest on the quiet earth's breast,
> And our souls at home with God.[24]

In January, to his astonishment, and to the greater astonishment of
Dr Samual Waud, he achieved a second class in Mathematics. The
Classical examination was due to begin in the middle of February
but by the thirteenth, as he confided to Cowley Powles, who was
undergoing the same ordeal at Oxford, his brains were in such an
overworked and 'be-Greeked state' that he could study no more.
'I read myself ill this week, and have been ordered to shut up every
book till the examination,' he wrote. 'The last three weeks have been
spent in agonies of pain with leeches on my head.' In fact he gained a
first class. His examiner, Dr Bateson, praised his Latin prose and verse
but was frank enough to admit that 'their excellence was due far more
to native talent than to industry or study'. Kingsley, however, was
well-satisfied, and went down confident that he would soon be recalled
as a fellow.

[24] Charles Kingsley, 'Oh! that we two were Maying', *The Saint's Tragedy*.

PART II

Parson Lot

CHAPTER 1

The Lonely Curate
1842

The strain of the Cambridge examinations brought on a breakdown that was a mild version of many that were to come. Kingsley applied to it what was to be his infallible remedy in such cases, a generous dose of the 'Far West'. While he was still working for his degree he had asked his mother to book rooms at Holne, the village on the southern edge of Dartmoor where he had been born, but which he had never seen. Now, armed with a fishing rod and a small library he went there and invited Cowley Powles to join him.

> I shall be most happy to have you as temporary sharer in the frugalities of my farm house lodgings. Whether you will despise hard beds and dimity curtains, morning bathes and evening trout fishing, mountain mutton and Devonshire cream, I do not know, but you will not despise the chance of a few weeks in which to commune with God's works.

It was not only with God's works that Kingsley was to commune, but with man's works on God. He had precisely three months in which to absorb the theology required for his ordination. It is doubtful whether he was able to make a very profound study of the Fathers in that time but he dipped into the work of some of the modern divines and confirmed views he already held. 'Don't read Palmer,' he told Fanny, 'I began it and in the first ten lines he establishes a fallacy.' 'My chief knowledge of the Jesuits is from the quotations of their great adversary, Goode.' And about the Tractarians, 'I read Tract 90 scientifically and made up my mind at once, as to them and their opinions much more safely than if I had waded through a thousand pages of their verbiage.' His letters to Fanny were full of attacks on the Tracts, for he was anxious to cure her of what he called her Manicheanism, the doctrine that the flesh is evil. This was understandable since from that doctrine Pusey had drawn the unpalatable conclusion that the clergy should not marry.

Fanny was well read in modern theology and she did not give up her allegiance to what her lover called the 'moaning piety' of Pusey without a struggle. 'So you still like their *tone?*' enquired Kingsley after many letters on the subject. 'And so do I. There is a solemn and gentlemanlike earnestness which is most beautiful, and which I wish I may ever attain. But you have just as much reason for following them, or even reading them, as a moth has for fluttering round the candle because it is bright.'

At the beginning of July Fanny was once more a guest at St Luke's Rectory, this time for 'five blissful days',[1] days whose bliss was not clouded by the fact that Charles spent part of the time on the sofa with acute toothache. One evening, as Fanny sat by him, he turned to her, pale with pain, and said 'in such a wild way . . . "God only knows how, but if my eyes are closed I know when you are looking at me" '.[2] She longed to throw herself on her knees beside him 'and kiss away the pain' but modesty forbade it. The following day however there was a tender scene when she surprised him half asleep in the armchair in his mother's drawing room. He started up, folded her in his arms and gave her a long kiss ('my blood boils and bounds as I recall it', she wrote). On July 8th, his 'frame still thrilling' from Fanny's parting kisses (the expression was hers) Charles left for Farnham Castle to be examined by the Bishop of Winchester. He had scruples about his motives. Was he for instance desiring to be a deacon only so that he might marry his beloved? He prayed that the bishop might reject him if he was not worthy in the eyes of God. The bishop accepted him and he took this as a sign that 'I have not sinned too deeply for escape'. On Sunday, July 10th, he was ordained. It was a day of deep solemnity. On it he dedicated not only himself, but also Fanny, to a lifetime in God's service. 'Oh my soul, my body, my intellect, my very love, I dedicate you all to God. And not mine only, to be an example and an instrument of holiness before the Lord forever.'

Now Kingsley was free to take up the curacy in Hampshire that his father's influence had procured for him. When he preached for the first time from the pulpit of the red-brick Georgian church at Eversley he little guessed that he would be preaching from that pulpit for most of the Sundays of his life. The church, with its square tower topped by four weather vanes (one of which persistently disagreed with its neighbours) was to become very dear to him. But there is a certain

[1] FND, January 6, 1843.
[2] Ibid.

irony in the fact that it should have been dedicated to the Blessed Virgin, for there was nothing Kingsley detested more than 'Mari-idolatry'.

Eversley parish was situated a few miles south of Reading, within earshot of the drums of Aldershot when the wind was in the right direction.[3] It lay in the green valley of the River Blackwater, but included stretches of moorland on either side, barren land of little use even today except to soldiers on manoeuvres. It comprised the two hamlets of Eversley Cross and Eversley Street, a mile apart from each other. The church was isolated from both of these, and so was Bramshill Park, the home of Sir John Cope, patron of the living.

Eversley Cross, the larger of the two hamlets, looks a prosperous enough community to the traveller on the A327 from London to Reading, and so it looked in Kingsley's day with its cheerful green, used as a cricket ground at weekends and as a communal poultry yard for the rest of the week. Round it 'were scattered red brick cottages each with its large neat garden and clipt yews and hollies before the door'.[4] But the inhabitants of many of the outlying cottages were a wild crowd, mostly 'heath croppers' and 'broom squires' who worked as farm labourers when they could and cut turf and made heath brooms when they couldn't. They had eked out a meagre living by poaching since the days when deer from Old Windsor Forest could be caught by an apple-baited hook hung from an orchard bough and their mothers could still remember wearing muffs and tippets made of pheasants' feathers 'not bought with silver'. The sporting instinct in these men appealed to Kingsley and he thought none the worse of them when the satisfaction of that instinct resulted in a spell in Winchester gaol. He drew a flattering portrait of a parishioner after twenty years among them:

Far shrewder, owing to his dash of wild forest blood from gipsy and highwayman, than his bull-headed and flaxen-polled South Saxon cousin of the chalk downs. Dark haired he is, ruddy and tall of bone, swaggering in his youth, but when he grows old, a thorough gentleman, reserved, stately, and courteous as a prince.[5]

[3] Oh blessed drums of Aldershot!
Oh blessed south-west train!
Oh blessed, blessed Speaker's clock,
All prophesying rain.
   Charles Kingsley, *The South Wind*, 1856.
[4] Charles Kingsley, 'My Winter Garden', *Prose Idylls*.
[5] Charles Kingsley, 'My Winter Garden', *Prose Idylls*.

No sooner had Kingsley arrived at the new parish than he found himself, at the age of twenty-three, in full charge of it, for the incumbent, Mr Toovey-Hawley, immediately left for one of his frequent six-week tours of the continent. Sunday, July 17th, was his first day of public ministration at Eversley and he was afraid he might stammer during the sermon. His fear, no doubt, was not diminished by the fact that, in those days, the pulpit at Eversley was an elaborate three-tiered affair of carved wood with a sounding board above it. 'I was not nervous,' he wrote to Fanny, 'for I had prayed before going into the desk that I might remember I was not speaking on my own authority, but on God's.' In fact he never stammered when preaching, provided he had the written version of the sermon before him. He sometimes, though not always, got into trouble if he was speaking without notes.[6] During the rector's absence he lived in the rectory, and Henry, now aged twelve, came to keep him company and enjoy a country holiday. As soon as Mr Toovey-Hawley returned, he moved into lodgings at a cottage called 'The Brewery' which still stands on a corner of the village green opposite the pond.[7]

One of the tasks that the rector was only too glad to hand over was that of teaching in the village school. 'I teach as long as I can stand the heat and the smell,' Kingsley told Fanny. 'The few children are in a room ten foot square and seven foot high.' On the other hand he enjoyed visiting the poor and reading to the infirm. The stretches of moorland that lay between the scattered dwellings of his parish gave his long legs the exercise they craved. He was concerned, however, lest the muscles of his chest became slack, now that he was no longer rowing, and he wrote to his mother for a pair of dumb-bells. 'Pray get them. They are about 5d. a pound properly if they are lead, but secondhand you may get them for a song.' Another pleasure of moorland walks was bathing in the little streams that trickled off the moors 'with the hum of bees, and the sleepy song of birds around me, and the feeling of the density of life in myriads of insects and flowers strong upon me. And over all, the delicious sense of childhood and simplicity and purity and peace, which even a temporary return to the state of nature gives.'

In spite of such idyllic intervals the young curate was lonely. The possibility of marriage to Fanny seemed remote and there were times

---

[6] In an unpublished letter to Fanny written in the autumn of 1849 he announced proudly, 'I have today preached an *extempore* sermon to the club without the least hesitation.' He always referred to his stammering as 'hesitation'.

[7] The cottage has been renamed Dial House and can be seen on the right as you pass through Eversley Cross on the A327 going from London to Reading.

when he supposed that he should live the rest of his life 'reading old books', and knocking his head against the ceiling of his room, 'like a caged bird. Not a human being to speak to but Stapleton, who is one and a half miles away and always busy.'[8] Augustus Granville Stapleton, one of the churchwardens, was to become a close friend. He was a man who combined an immensely aristocratic bearing with great kindness. Kingsley once said of him, after watching him warm his coat-tails before the fireplace of somebody else's stately home, 'he ought to have been a peer'.[9] Perhaps he knew that Mr Stapleton was a natural son of the first Lord Morley. More important, he had been Canning's secretary, and the young curate spent some happy evenings 'politicking' at Warbrook, the Stapletons' fine Georgian house that still stands in the belt of woodland between the church and Eversley Street. Stapleton, however, was a considerably older man than Kingsley, and the young curate was somewhat in awe of him. He confided to Fanny that he once spent a sleepless night when he thought he had lost an important document belonging to Stapleton.

Conceive my terror! I got up at 2 a.m. and searched in vain. At last I set out to Stapleton's in pouring rain. As I got to his gate, praying all the way, I remembered one pocket book where I had not looked. I went home and it was there. What a powerful weapon is prayer!

For friends of his own age he had to rely on visitors, and wrote to a wealthy Cambridge friend, Peter Wood, asking him for introductions to people with trout fishing in the area.

Whether in the glaring saloons of Almack's or making love in the luxurious recumbency of the ottoman, whether breakfasting at 1.0 or going to bed at 3.0, thou art still Peter, the beloved of my youth, the regret of my parochial retirement. Peter! I am alone! Around me are the everlasting hills, and the everlasting bores of the country! My parish is peculiar for nothing but want of houses and abundance of peat bogs; my parishioners remarkable only for aversion to education, and a prediliction for fat bacon. I am wasting my sweetness on the desert air. I say my sweetness, for I have given up smoking, and smell no more. Oh Peter, Peter, take pity on me! I am like a kitten in the washhouse copper with the lid on. Come and

[8] ULF No. 42, November 1843.
[9] ULF No. 201, 1860.

eat my mutton, and drink my wine, and admire my sermons, some
Sunday at Eversley.

Your faithful friend Boanerges Roar-at-the-Clods.

Peter responded to his call and was rewarded by having the brace of
pheasant he had brought roasted to a cinder by Kingsley's well-meaning
landlady.[10] He reported, however, that Charles was 'as happy as a
king' in his simple lodgings. Another visitor was a young officer from
Sandhurst who used to ride over to see him and claimed to love him
'as well as man can love man'. It was to this soldier that Kingsley confided one day, when looking down upon the rectory from the hill
opposite, 'how hard it is to go through life without wishing for the
goods of others. Look at the Rectory! If I were there with a wife how
happy I would be!'

Meanwhile he had to content himself with writing letters to the
wife of his dreams. Fanny had recently sent him Frederick Denison
Maurice's *Kingdom of Christ* (a book, incidentally, dedicated to his old
headmaster, Derwent Coleridge) and it proved a turning point in his
life. So great was his admiration for Maurice that, when the two men
became friends, he insisted upon always addressing him as 'Master'.
Maurice's views on Church unity and the holiness of matter echoed
Kingsley's own. Kingsley was so excited by them that he set about
writing a theological work of his own. It was a lengthy essay entitled
The Two Dispensations[11] and he had high hopes that it would win him
the Cambridge fellowship that he was still expecting. No sooner had
he completed it than he commenced another entitled *What is the real
error of the Tracts for the Times?* In it he deplored not only the High
Church party, but also the Low Church party to which his father belonged. He had been shocked at the absurdity of not being allowed to
mention either the Catholic and Apostolic Church or Baptismal Grace
when preaching at St Luke's and he now recommended a middle way,
neither high nor low. 'We must be catholic, we must hold the whole
truth; we must have no partial views like the Dissenters and Tractarians.' He called for a leader for a new latitudinarian party. 'We
want a new Luther,' he told Fanny in a letter at this time, but added
modestly, 'I am not he.' It was clear, however, that, at this stage, he
saw his future as a theologian.

Fanny was as enthusiastic about the essay as he and offered to copy it
out for him, which was perhaps a mistake, for in so doing she com-

---

[10] The willow-pattern-covered dish in which the vegetables were no doubt served
on that memorable occasion is still preserved at Eversley.

[11] This title referred to the Old and the New Testaments.

mitted herself to copying out most of the twenty-eight books he was eventually to produce. A questionnaire she sent him at the time brings us as near as we shall ever be to hearing a conversation between the two. It was enclosed with a letter which carried the request, 'Send this back with "yes" or "no" immediately.'

FANNY   Must I copy out the Essay on foolscap leaving a blank page on each side?
CHARLES Yes.
FANNY   Will you write out the 'rules'?
CHARLES Little by little.
FANNY   Will you promise me not to do the drawing as you cannot have time, what with the essay and my rules?
CHARLES No, I will do it.
FANNY   Will you let me know the name under which you will publish? If it is not simply Ernest (my name for you) let it be some Greek or German word with a deep meaning.
CHARLES Let the name be Ernest Lackland; a fine name will seem senti-mental and ridiculous if discovered, and Lackland has meaning enough for the head of a ruined family.
FANNY   You need not write to your mother yet, for I have written.
CHARLES How my filial duty is thereby excused I do not know except on the supposition that you and I are the same person. Darling! Kiss me![12]

The domestic tone of this interchange shows how close the couple had become. They exchanged letters almost daily and signed them 'Your own husband' and 'Your own wife'. On one occasion Fanny hungered all through a day's sightseeing in London, 'that Babylon', for a letter she expected from Charles. When she returned in the evening to the house of a married sister at Woodford Bridge, no letter. 'Did you not write because you went away with Gerald Wellesley? I could hate G.W. but will not, that is wrong. Only *write*,' and so on for four close-packed pages. This letter, written only a few days after Charles's arrival at Eversley, was typical in its verbose meandering style of many that were to follow. Charles, concerned for her health, some-times pleaded 'Don't *overwrite* yourself', but Fanny persisted. 'When I am sad I plunge into a letter to you and tell you *everything*.' She sometimes apologised for her ignorance but Charles denied it. In a letter which commences with a somewhat schoolmasterly definition of the word anthropomorphic, he insisted, 'You are as delicious in

[12] ULF No. 80.

intellect as in everything else.' Elsewhere he spoke of her 'deep and delicate mind'.

The correspondence was not always maintained on the elevated plane of theology, however. Sometimes it descended to quite mundane matters such as how long Charles should wear his hair. Fanny wrote saying it was too short. Charles replied:

> I am very much obliged to you for your commands, for I hate wearing it so very short, as I am not boating or hunting or following some of the old destructive sports of which it always puts me in mind. But my mother informs me about ten times an hour that if I have my hair more than about two inches long I look a mixture of footman, pick-pocket and Methodist parson, that she is ashamed of me and that you will be ashamed of me (that most unlovely of all arguments and like to be the one which drove me mad) and so on so I could have cut off not only my hair but also my nose.

But more serious matters than the length of Charles's hair were to divide the couple. Fanny's family still remained adamant in their refusal to accept Kingsley as a suitor for their sister. On one occasion he asked one of the Grenfell sisters what was her objection to the marriage and she replied, 'My objection is *you*.' In their opinion his financial position had barely improved on what it had been three years before. His salary only amounted to £100 a year, his chances of securing a fellowship seemed remote and, until he secured a living, he admitted that he must continue to be dependent on his parents. Charles made vain attempts to prove to the three formidable maiden ladies that he was no longer a boy. Georgiana, the oldest sister, he found the hardest to win over, for she was dominating, hysterical and too stupid to be convinced by argument. 'Have I not sat peaceably listening to Miss Grenfell for hours when I disagreed with every word she said?' he enquired of Fanny. Miss Henrietta he claimed he liked the best: 'I would do anything to win her.' Indeed on one occasion when Fanny was accusing him of not trying to love her sisters, he cried, 'If you go on mistaking me I shall go and make love to Miss Henrietta and run away with her.' In more sober moments he felt his best chance of success was with Charlotte, the intellectual one, who was eventually to marry J. A. Froude the historian. 'I had hoped to make a friend of Charlotte,' he said wistfully and begged Fanny to impress her by reading her the weightier passages from his letters.[13] But all these efforts were doomed to failure. The real reason for the Grenfell sisters' dislike

13 ULF No. 46, 1843.

of Charles, as he well knew, was that he was a threat to their 'improper ascendancy'[14] over Fanny, and particularly to the improper ascendancy of Georgiana, the mother superior of the little sisterhood. By the end of August Georgiana's hostility had reached such proportions that Charles suggested he and Fanny should undergo a test to prove their love. They would agree not to write to each other for a year. Previous biographers have assumed that the cessation of the correspondence was imposed by the Grenfells, but entries in Fanny's diary prove that this was not the case.

Fanny was appalled at the prospect of separation and she wrote Charles a letter filled with guilt and foreboding. The ending of their happiness was a punishment for her sin, she was a creature wicked beyond redemption. Charles's reply was in a very different tone. This was to be a period of trial to make them worthy of each other, either in this life, or, if need be, in the next. She must cure herself of her morbidity or she would ruin her marriage, should it ever take place. With prophetic truth he told her, 'You will dread the possibility of dying in childbirth and when the child is born you will always be expecting it to die.' She must stop 'sin hunting' and 'squirrel caging'. She must learn to laugh. 'Shall I ever make you laugh?' he wrote. 'If you are sensitive to the ridiculous uncombined with malice, which is what I delight in, how happy I shall be.'[15] It is amusing to hear Kingsley, who was said never to be seen to laugh himself, accusing Fanny of the same failing. But whereas he undoubtedly had a sense of humour, she almost certainly had none.

Charles's cure for Fanny's melancholy was work. She must study Nature, read Buckland's *Bridgewater Treatise* on geology, learn to draw the human figure, to sing (for that is the duty of every clergyman's wife), to do elementary doctoring. She must keep a commonplace book and 'put into it not only facts and thoughts but observations on nature and little sketches, even the form of beautiful leaves'. Above all she must follow the example of her beloved. 'Look how I have spent my day,' he said in the concluding paragraph of his farewell letter. 'I have, since nine this morning, cut wood for an hour, spent an hour and more in prayer and humiliation, written six or seven pages of my Essay, taught in the School, thought over you and your mind while walking round two-thirds of the parish visiting and doctoring, and written all this. Such days are lives and happy ones.'[16]

Charles also instituted a weekly festival and fast, that he and Fanny

[14] ULF No. 23, 1843.
[15] ULF No. 23, 1843.
[16] ULF, September 15, 1842.

were to keep respectively at eleven o'clock on Thursday nights and
ten o'clock on Friday nights. He wrote Fanny two letters, one to be
read on each occasion, and these she read faithfully once a week, describing one as 'thrilling' and the other as 'agonising.'[17] On festival
nights the two lay, in imagination, in each other's arms, but on Friday
nights they did penance. Charles had forbidden Fanny bodily self-
torture, but she suffered mentally in the knowledge that, at that time
each week, he stripped himself naked in his cottage bedroom and
scourged himself. 'Oh, how I long to kiss away those stripes,' she
confided to her diary.

Once more Fanny's family prescribed the conventional cure for a
broken heart — a trip abroad. This time a winter in Nice was decided
upon, and a companion found in the form of a devout older woman
who also had the name of Fanny. The other Fanny proved a sympathetic friend who occasionally teased her charge for her extreme
innocence about married life but respected her need for privacy and
always allowed her to breakfast alone in her room. The two women
arrived in Paris on October 27th and reached Nice nearly a month
later, having passed through Avignon and Nîmes and admired the
Pont de Gard in weather so fine that neither a bonnet nor shawl were
necessary.

It was in Paris that Fanny bought a locked notebook with a marbled
cover and a green leather back and commenced writing letters to
Charles in it, just as she had on her tour of Germany a year earlier.
The notebook has only recently been discovered and for convenience,
I am calling it the Nice Diary. In it Fanny poured out the
tale of her sufferings and loneliness. She longed passionately for
the man she called her husband and lay in bed imagining 'delicious
nightery' when they would lie in each other's arms 'and I will
ask you to explain to me my strange feelings'. Sometimes these feelings became so strong that she hardly knew what to do with herself.
She longed to wring her hands, groan, roll on the floor, scream, run
until she dropped. At times she even considered taking poison. Often
she was ill and lay in a darkened room, unable to read even a verse from
the Bible Charles had given her. At the end of January she consulted a
homoeopathic doctor because of her heart 'which stops beating every
five minutes in a strange way', and on January 6th an agonising head-
ache threw her 'nearly into convulsions' and caused her weeping companion such concern that she was on the point of sending home for one
of Fanny's sisters. She lost weight, which worried her 'for I know men

[17] FND, December 8, 1842.

like a nice round figure' and declared 'my maid said today, after dressing me, that the only flesh I had was on my face'.

Yet she bravely attempted to persevere with the programme that Charles had set her. She took lessons in French and Italian (but not singing, for which she regretted having no talent) and copied out long passages in French from the works of Rousseau, D'Alembert and Bernardin de St Pierre. 'Tough' reading she found burdensome however, and she was often tempted to fall back on the 'feeling' poetry of Tennyson, and on executing rather wooden flower paintings in water colour, an occupation that she had always despised 'because silly young ladies did it'. Now it had a new significance because Charles was interested in botany. On one occasion she painted, from memory, a rather charming little water colour of the garden at Ipsden where she had met Charles, with a glimpse of a freshly harvested field showing through the dark summer foliage of the trees.

Fanny's companion, the other Fanny, encouraged her to make expeditions into the town, although the sight of the five hundred Catholic priests who inhabited Nice worried her with thoughts of the celibate fate her Charles had so narrowly escaped. Even a trip into the country on a donkey reminded her of such matters, for the object of the journey was a monastery. Evening gatherings were made irksome by the attentions of a newly widowed captain who insisted upon paying court to her. Nor did she share her companion's predilection for religious meetings where 'the gentlemen talk and the ladies listen'.

During the first autumn of the separation Charles kept himself busy, as he had promised, and undertook the added burden of attempting to educate Henry who had once more come to stay with him, this time in his cottage digs. But life was not easy for him. He was by now passionately in love with Fanny and thoughts of her body haunted him not only by day but in his dreams. To punish himself for impure thoughts and to purify himself for their eventual realisation, he tortured his body. In Lent he fasted, ordering nothing but gruel, bread and water from his bewildered landlady and on Wednesdays he neither ate nor drank till evening. He dressed 'as scantily as possible with decency', slept on the floor one night a week and rose at three to pray. On November 1st (All Saints Day) he inflicted pain of a more violent sort on himself. 'I went into the woods at night and lay naked upon thorns and when I came home my body was torn from head to foot. I never suffered so much. I began to understand Popish raptures and visions that night, and their connection with self-torture. I saw such glorious things.'[18] He was evidently somewhat

[18] ULF No. 36, November 1, 1843.

embarrassed about confessing this pious exercise not because of the scandal it would have caused had one of his poaching parishioners been in the woods that night, but because he could see that this behaviour came perilously close to the kind of mortification practised by the hated shavelings of medieval monasteries and the latter-day Manicheans of the Oxford Movement. However, as he pointed out to Fanny when their correspondence was reopened, his sufferings were intended not to destroy the flesh as in the case of St Bernard of Clairvaux, but to make it fit for love and bliss. Indeed, he assured her, he grew fat and calm on his ascetic regime. 'My face is so changed into calm in the last twelve months and I have filled out and become broad chested. You remember what a "wild deer" I was.'[19] And, he added, if they met again she would have stripes but not scars to kiss, 'for I have done nothing that would disfigure me'.[20]

Towards the end of the year of separation Kingsley found another outlet for his frustrated sexuality in the series of illustrations he now began for his biography of St Elizabeth of Hungary. He had no doubt been introduced to the saint by a biography of her written by a French Catholic, Count Montalambert, which had appeared in a richly illuminated English version in 1839. St Elizabeth was a popular thirteenth-century saint, portrayed on the walls of many a German peasant's hut as a lovely young mother with her lap full of roses. Kingsley proposed to show her in a more realistic light, as the victim of the monkish torturer under whose influence she fell after the death of her nobly born husband on a crusade. The story was to be inscribed on vellum and presented to Fanny on her wedding day as a solemn warning against Puseyite practices. In fact Kingsley only completed a lengthy introduction and part of the first chapter. Eight illustrations were, however, roughly sketched 'infinitely superior to anything I have ever done'.[21] Most of them depicted naked women under torture. The most horrific shows the saint's mother being lynched in a peculiarly obscene manner.[22] In others we see the saint suffering self-inflicted penance. In one she carries a cross up the pointed crags of a mountain, in another she is crucified on an anchor and in a third she is whipped before an altar. But in none of these pictures do we see 'the

[19] ULF No. 20, September 26, 1843.
[20] ULF No. 21, September 28, 1843.
[21] ULF No. 19, September 1843.
[22] At least one assistant in the Manuscripts Room of the British Museum regards this drawing as the 'most disgusting exhibit in the whole collection', and considers that it should be kept under lock and key.

shrunk limbs stiff from many a blow'[23] described by the monk Dietrich of Thuringia, from whose chronicle Kingsley took his facts. Instead there is a well-rounded, well-cared-for body with long dark hair becomingly draped about the shoulders, unmistakably the body of Fanny. And Kingsley admitted as much: 'St Elizabeth is my Fanny not as she is but as she will be. I feel I draw worse and worse. If my baby will be model I will be able to draw such lovely pictures for her.'[24] The sexual content of these drawings did not go unobserved by his contemporaries. A tutor at Cambridge confided to Nathaniel Hawthorne (whose delicate protestant nose could scent out sin a mile away) that Kingsley had made drawings such as no pure man could have made or could allow himself to show or look at, and furthermore he believed him to be 'a sensualist' (not that he practically sins in that way) in his disposition.' Kingsley would have disagreed with this verdict. He once said, 'I am the most sensuous (not sensual) of men.'

The young curate had inherited a gift for drawing from his father, but whereas Charles Kingsley Senior specialised in landscape, his son admitted he was 'no drawer of trees' and specialised in the human figure which to him alone expressed 'the broad natural childish emotions'. As an undergraduate he had been keenly interested in art and admired the then unfashionable paintings of Tintoretto and Reubens.[25] Frank Penrose, who later became architect at St Paul's, said he was the only man at the university with whom he could discuss painting. Another undergraduate used to push a pencil and paper in his direction whenever he dropped in for a chat, 'for I knew his wont to go on sketching all sorts of fanciful things while we worried our young heads over other dreams as fanciful'. In fact Kingsley's drawings never got far beyond the state of glorified doodles but they served him well in his final examination. Being at a loss for an answer to the question in a mechanics paper 'Describe a Common pump', he drew a village pump guarded by a stately beadle in front of a church door. Round the pump stood villagers of all shapes and sizes and carrying empty vessels, and from the pump itself hung a notice which said, 'This pump locked during divine service'. The moderator of the year had the drawing framed and hung in his room, and no doubt with good reason. Kingsley's chief talent for drawing lay in caricature and by far the best drawing for *The Life of St Elizabeth* shows a crowd of medieval peasants most amusingly portrayed.

In May Fanny returned home to find her longing for Charles only

[23] Charles Kingsley, *The Saint's Tragedy*.
[24] ULF No. 36, November 1, 1843.
[25] Charles Kingsley, 'My Winter Garden', *Prose Idylls*.

increased by the sight of 'the letter bag now empty of comfort to me' and of the bed 'where I slept in your arms on our festival nights'.[26] When she moved to the London house of her sister, Mrs Warre, her sufferings increased, for her maid one day saw Charles walk past the door. After spending several days watching at the window, 'hoping yet fearing to see that beloved face',[27] she retired to bed complaining of agonising pains in her heart and left side and resorted to large doses of morphine and salvolatile. By now two of her married sisters, Caroline Warre and Emily Osborne, had relented and were ready to do anything to arrest what appeared to be a serious decline. It was agreed that Fanny should be persuaded to reopen her correspondence with that wild young curate in Hampshire.

[26] FND, May 12, 1843.
[27] FND, June 10, 1843.

CHAPTER 2

The Lover for all Eternity
1843

Fanny's letter announcing the good news to Charles arrived at the end of September 1843. It was written in a strangely dead tone which he feared might be due to 'the collapse of a mind overburdened with pain'.[1] He wrote three replies to it on one day, one of them covering eight closely written pages. When he reached the bottom of the eighth page he exclaimed, 'Must I stop? Oh finite paper and ink and infinite mind!' But he did not stop and proceeded to cross-write all eight pages. He was as he put it 'beserk with joy. I cannot spell or talk sense. I could write on for ever for I have no one to speak to but you. The ages have spoken to me since I kissed you last.' It was as if a heavy curtain had suddenly been drawn aside to reveal a dazzling prospect. Not only was Fanny restored to him but his financial affairs had taken a turn for the better. His mother had been able to give him £100 from a legacy with which to pay the Cambridge debts which had been hanging over him for a year and his father had secured for him the sinecure of Clerk in Orders at Chelsea which carried with it a salary of £120 a year. It even looked as if the long-awaited fellowship might be about to materialise.[2] For a moment he was able to see the Grenfell family as 'noble hearts, God bless them all — Riversdale Pascoe — your sister, I begin to understand them and love them better and better'.[3]

The *Life of St Elizabeth* was now abandoned, for Charles had a flesh and blood martyr[4] to whom he could pour out his thoughts. Fanny was still too weak after a twelve-month torture to bear the shock of seeing him but she could read his letters. Now began one of the strangest outpourings in the history of love. For the last three months

[1] ULF No. 18, September 25, 1843.

[2] ULF No. 17, 1843.

[3] ULF No. 16, 1843.

[4] ULF No. 18, September 1843. 'Blessed living martyrdom! You bear in your body the marks of the Lord Christ.'

of the year 1843, Charles unloosed the floodgates of his most private fantasies on to paper. Such was the make-up of his mind that his feelings of guilt about his body and its functions could only be allayed by sanctifying both. 'Matter is holy,' he told Fanny, 'awful glorious matter. Let us never use those words *animal* and *brutal* in a degrading sense. Our animal enjoyments must be religious ceremonies.' He carried the analogy to almost unbelievable lengths. 'When you go to bed to-night, forget that you ever wore a garment, and open your lips for my kisses and spread out each limb that I may lie between your breasts all night (Canticles I, 13).'[5] 'At a quarter past eleven lie down, clasp your arms and every limb around me, and with me repeat the *Te Deum* aloud.'

But prayers alone were not sufficient to cleanse the bodies of the lovers of guilt. Between suggested cures for Fanny's illness, which ranged from mesmerism and cocoa to copying out his sermons, Kingsley imposed penances hardly suitable for an invalid. In several letters he enjoined fasting. Sometimes the fasts he imposed had a medicinal purpose, as when he wrote, 'This periodic illness is an effort by your system to throw off superabundant nourishment. Yours is an over stimulating regime for one of full blood, which your rosy cheeks declare you to be. *Give up wine.*' In other cases he demanded the sacrifice of more vital items of diet. In one letter he enclosed instructions for the manufacture of a pair of hair shirts which were in fact made of canvas, 'the thinnest and at the same time the coarsest and roughest you can get. They should be just a yard and two inches from the shoulder downwards, as tight as you can make them. I am a yard and an inch round the chest and very small in the waist. And make yourself two also, of the same pattern, just long enough not to be seen.'[6] He did, however, draw the line at whipping Fanny. 'And so you would let me scourge you. Dear Woman, No! No! Your own hands or your maid's must give the stripes. I will kneel outside the door and pray.'[7] Though he did agree to hear her confession and give her absolution. 'You shall come to me some morning when we can ensure solitude and secrecy, come as a penitent, barefoot, with dishevelled hair, wearing one coarse garment only and then I will, in God's name solemnly absolve you. Afterwards I will bathe you from head to foot in kisses and fold you in my arms.'[8] A sketch was included in this letter showing

[5] ULF No. 22, October 2, 1843.

[6] ULF No. 26, October 6, 1843.

[7] ULF No. 24, October 4, 1843.

[8] ULF No. 21, September 28, 1843.

Charles, decorously dressed, laying his hand on the head of the kneeling Fanny clad only in a shift.

Seven days after he reopened his correspondence with his future bride Kingsley made a strange request of her. 'Darling, one resolution I made in my sorrow, that I would ask a boon of you and I wish to show you and my God that I have gained purity and self-control, that intense though my love is for your body, I do not love it but as an expression of your soul. And therefore, when we are married, will you consent to remain for the first month in my arms a virgin bride, a sister only?' Kingsley assured his bride that by postponing their bliss in this way they would purify and prolong it, so much so in fact that when they reached heaven they would be able to enjoy uninterrupted sexual intercourse. 'Will not these thoughts give us more perfect delight when we lie naked in each other's arms, clasped together toying with each other's limbs, buried in each other's bodies, struggling, panting, dying for a moment. Shall we not feel then, even then, that there is more in store for us, that those thrilling writhings are but dim shadows of a union which shall be perfect?'[9]

So strong was his belief in the eternity of marriage that he was deeply shocked by a letter from Fanny suggesting he would marry again should she die. 'If you died tomorrow I would never, never marry another, but live a quiet old bachelor, loving other people's little children. The idea that communion with you is a mere temporary self-indulgence is so horrible to me that if you really believe it I could never bring myself to touch your body.'[10]

During that October Charles and Fanny became officially engaged. His officer friend from Sandhurst happened to call on him the morning that he received Fanny's letter accepting his proposal of marriage. He found Kingsley madly stamping his clothes into a portmanteau and shouting, 'I am engaged! I am going to see her now today!' Outside the cottage Stapleton's gig was waiting to take him to the station.

Fanny had wisely chosen the home of her brother-in-law, the Reverend Sydney Godolphin Osborne, as the scene for the reunion, for she knew what a blighting effect the Misses Grenfell would have upon her beloved. The Osbornes lived at Durweston, on the Dorset downs, in a large rectory which now houses forty boys of Bryanston School. It was a romantic place for the lovers to meet, with its large garden and its alley of clipped yews leading down to the little church below. Yet with so much stored-up passion on both sides the meeting might have been an awkward one. In fact it was outstandingly successful.

[9] ULF No. 53, 1843.
[10] ULF No. 30, October 1843.

Fanny rose from her bed of sickness, ran to her lover, hid her face against his lapel and confessed to him the joy she had found in their mutual mortifications, so different from the sensations aroused in her by previous Puseyite ones. For 'the most delicious four days'[11] the young couple rambled, no doubt well-chaperoned, through the copses and up and down the chalk downs of Cranbourne Chase. When a slope was too steep, Fanny would take off her shoes and stockings and astonish Charles with the beauty of her bare feet. He found bare feet peculiarly affecting. He once told Fanny, 'Your letter about bare feet almost convulsed me. I have such *strange* fantasies about bare feet.'[12] When a fence had to be crossed he would lift her over it. Although the lovers were left very little alone they learnt 'how much may be done in a moment',[13] and indeed they contrived to so thoroughly overstep the bounds of propriety that Charles was afterwards to exclaim with some satisfaction, 'we did all we could before we were one!' When he left Durweston he wrote Fanny a letter in a huge euphoric script which contrasted sharply with the neat copperplate of his early letter to her from Cambridge. What he said in the letter implied that they had indeed only just stopped short of the rituals of the wedding night.

What can I do but write to my naughty baby who does not love me at all and who of course has forgotten me by this time? But I have not forgotten her, for my hands are perfumed with her delicious limbs, and I cannot wash off the scent, and every moment the thought comes across me of those mysterious recesses of beauty where my hands have been wandering, and my heart sinks with a sweet faintness and my blood tingles through every limb for a moment and then all is still again in calm joy and thankfulness to our loving God. Tomorrow I fast, not entirely, but as much as I can without tiring myself. Only to acquire self-control and to keep under the happy body, to which God has permitted of late such exceeding liberty and bliss.'[14]

A footnote that Fanny added, at this time, to the passage about 'delicious nightery' in her Nice Diary, also suggests that she had permitted her lover exceptional liberties; 'I did not know,' she wrote, 'what I said *then* about night.'

The Grenfells now decided to make the best of a bad job and accept

11 ULF No. 32, October 1843.
12 ULF No. 39, November 11, 1843.
13 ULF No. 41, 1843.
14 ULF No. 29, October 24, 1843.

Kingsley as a brother-in-law. Riversdale Pascoe Grenfell, the head of the family, invited him down Tresavean, one of his Cornish mines,[15] while he was on a visit to his former schoolmaster C. A. Johns.[16] Charles, anxious to make a good impression, insisted on being let down forty feet deeper than anyone else in the party on the end of a rope and, at the bottom, took a pickaxe and 'astonished the miners by doing a stroke of work'. Cowley Powles was also present and was greatly exhausted by the expedition and Kingsley's own hand shook somewhat as he executed a sketch of the occasion for Fanny afterwards. Not to be outdone in hospitality, one of Fanny's sisters, Mrs Frederick Hill, who also lived in Cornwall, invited him to stay and 'almost ate me up with kindness'. The children, he wrote, were the image of Fanny, especially the boy: 'I did pet and play with him so.'

But among Fanny's relatives it was the Osbornes who had the most to offer. They did not merely supply hospitality. They found Charles a house to live in, and a very beautiful one at that. The rectory at Pimperne was, and still is, a four-square eighteenth-century house built of alternate layers of flint and brick. Above the front door is an elaborate fourteenth-century oriel window, preserved from the original manor house (at one time the property of Henry VII) and the garden is surrounded by a ha-ha and vast trees. In this splendid house Charles would be able to live as curate-in-charge. The living was in the hands of the absentee Dr Wyndham, but Osborne extracted a promise from Lord Portman, the patron of all the livings in the area, that Charles should have the next one to fall vacant.[17]

Plans for the wedding were now hurried on, for Fanny was producing new and alarming symptoms in the form of spasms which the family doctor declared only married love could cure.[18] Charles insisted on waiting until after Christmas, partly because his father was short of money, but more because he wished to avoid any appearance of unseemly haste. 'We ought,' he told Fanny, 'to do everything to prevent this marriage appearing private or *hurried*. I would beg you send cards.'[19] Plans were made for a five-week honeymoon at a farmhouse near the Cheddar Gorge, to be lent to them by yet another of Fanny's sisters, the wealthy Mrs Warre of Lowndes Square.

[15] Tresavean was a productive copper mine.

[16] Johns had just succeeded Coleridge as headmaster at Helston Grammar School.

[17] This was presumably before he fell out of favour with Lord Portman by encouraging many of his tenants and labourers to emigrate to the United States and personally escorting them to the docks.

[18] ULF No. 29, October 24, 1843.

[19] ULF No. 59, January 1844.

The tone of the correspondence continued intimate. At Durweston Charles had discovered that Fanny's passion matched his own, and that there was little of the blushing maiden about her. 'I want to coax some ministering angel to carry you here and put you down in my little room, and lay you on my bed, and undress you with my own hands and cover you all over with burning kisses till you were tired of blushing and struggle if you did struggle which I fancy you would not.'

At Durweston Fanny had given Charles her commonplace book and annotated Bible to read and their thoughts were now so closely in tune that they sometimes dreamed the same dreams on the same nights. Fanny even cured him (temporarily) of his habit of lying in bed till nine or ten in the morning. She willed him to rise early and on two mornings succeeded. They also shared mortifications. 'I woke in the night and thought "perhaps she is wearing that horrible chain", so I threw off night shirt and bed clothes, all but one blanket and lay in the cold and read your journal.'[20] Both lovers felt they were closer to God when naked. 'When I feel very near God I always feel such a need to *undress*, as if everything which was artificial jarred me. What bliss to see that you feel the same.'[21] Charles told Fanny of the nights on which he would sleep naked and they agreed to 'keep the festival' as often as they could. He designed a sleeveless nightshirt for occasions on which they could not and sent Fanny a sketch of it (lost, alas). 'I send you a sketch. Do you like my nightdress in it? My mother does not, because the idea of no sleeves is *so coarse*. She is such a prude though by no means a "refined" person.'

The lovers looked forward eagerly to the shared mortifications of their married life although Charles sometimes wondered whether Fanny would enjoy them so much when they actually came. 'I am afraid when we are married that you will be disappointed at the amount of bliss you expect when you find me asking you to labour cold and hungry, girded in sackcloth, and to sleep at night shivering on the hard floor.' And Charles had other mortifications in store for Fanny. 'In your parish you must walk on foot, in your household you must wash yourself in earthenware and make your own bed, you must mend your husband's and your children's clothes. Nursing your own children will preserve your health ten times as long as sedentary habits, late hours and that infernal tea with all its disquieting effects.' Their home would be simple and unrefined.

[20] ULF No. 35, October 1843.
[21] ULF No. 31, October 1843.

What do you mean when you said Mrs Johns house must have plenty of *refinement* scattered about it. I hope you do not mean all those pretty artificial knick-knacks, with which you, darling, and Charlotte and others make their rooms look so ladylike. We must not require them. I shall be more obliged to the friend who gives us a substantial grid iron, than a Paris envelope-case. We must be above artificial refinements you know. All I want is plenty of *baths and soap and clean linen*. I am afraid you will find me very homely but I am accustomed to care for nothing more than a labouring man has except cleanliness, divine cleanliness, the type of spiritual fruit, without which no corporal of domiciliary comfort is possible.[22]

One concession he did however make to Fanny's desire for decoration. He promised to 'ornament the walls of our bedroom with arabesques and groups. I would we could let no one but ourselves ever enter the bedroom. Your maid must be the only person allowed to do so. It shall be our chapel and our study and our heaven on earth.'[23]

Charles found great satisfaction in the snub implied to Fanny's relatives in this way of life. 'We will show them that money is *nothing*,' he wrote. 'I have prayed for a good living so that it might stop your brothers' mouths. *I* should be glad to see you sacrificing yourself in poverty.' He had reason to be bitter, for the men in the Grenfell family had insisted that he should settle £100 a year on Fanny to which he would not have access. Charles was outraged by the slight to the family honour. 'I have determined to prove that I am more trustworthy than they think by never touching a farthing of your money,'[24] he told her. 'In this way only can I relieve my mind of a feeling of soreness at the extraordinary way in which I have been treated.'

The Grenfell women showed themselves in an equally unappealing light. Now that the wedding was unavoidable they proceeded to indulge in an orgy of what Charles called 'maudlin misery' in which Fanny seemed willing to share. Only a month before the wedding Charles wrote:

I am pained by the manner in which you seem to look forward to and dwell on the parting with your sisters. It is one of the fashions of this carnal age to extol and almost deify emotion. Do not tell me that your family are *above* exciting themselves and your family

[22] ULF No. 27, October 15, 1843.
[23] ULD No. 23, October 3, 1843.
[24] Fanny brought with her a settlement of £300 a year.

never make scenes and so on. You are all a very excitable family and very very much given to make scenes and at the present rate are preparing for a scene, such a one as will make angels weep.[25]

In another letter he faced the situation with more humour. 'I will come Tuesday afternoon and choose the ring. You shall have all Monday to cry in and then you will be too tired to cry Tuesday afternoon, and then you can start again as soon as I go, and cry all night.'[26]

As the last days before the wedding ran out both parties became quite ill with the strain. Fanny's grammar and spelling, never good, deserted her completely. 'It is the warm weather coming on my being so week which has given me soar throat,'[27] she explained. Charles could only express relief at their vow of chastity. He had always feared that the sight of Fanny naked might unman him. Some months before the wedding he had written, 'I have been thinking over your terror at seeing me undressed, and I feel that I should have the same feeling in a minor degree to you, till I had learnt to bear the blaze of your naked beauty. You do not know how often a man is struck powerless in body and mind on his wedding night.'[28] It was not the blaze of Fanny's naked beauty that he now feared, but sheer exhaustion. 'I rejoice more and more in the thought of our month's abstinence,' he wrote. 'I am too worn for my mind to bear such bliss!'[29]

[25] ULF No. 43, December 9, 1843.
[26] ULF No. 59, 1844.
[27] ULF No. 57, January 1844.
[28] ULF No. 49, 1843.
[29] ULF No. 57, January 1844.

CHAPTER 3

The Parish Priest
1844

The wedding of Charles and Fanny took place at Trinity Church, Bath on January 10th, 1844. Fanny was married from the house where her sisters now lived at 24 Queen Square. Sydney Godolphin Osborne officiated (at the suggestion of Charles Kingsley Senior who was first offered the honour) and the formidable Georgiana Grenfell signed the register as a witness. The Kingsley family was not unrepresented. Charles's sister Charlotte (now sixteen years old) was a bridesmaid and there were several of what Kingsley described as 'our West India relatives' who lived in Bath. No doubt Cowley Powles was also there, since he had given the couple 'a handsome horse to ride or drive' as his wedding present.[1]

After the wedding the young couple went by train to the farm-house at Cheddar lent them by Caroline Warre, wife of the Member of Parliament for Ripon. We have no account of their first night to-gether but a few weeks before the wedding Fanny had written, at Charles's request, 'a long, wanton letter about what you will do to me and I will do to you at Cheddar'. We may take that letter as a fairly accurate account of what actually happened. It is worth quoting at length, for surely a stranger wedding night was never passed.

> After dinner I shall perhaps feel worn out [wrote Fanny] so I shall just lie on your bosom and say nothing but feel a great deal, and you will be very loving and call me your poor child. And then you will perhaps show me your *Life of St Elizabeth*, your wedding gift. And then after tea we will go up to rest! We will undress and bathe and then you will come to my room, and we will kiss and love very much and read psalms aloud together, and then we will kneel down and pray in our night dresses. Oh! What solemn bliss! How hallow-ing! And then you will take me up in your arms, will you not? And lay me down in bed. And then you will extinguish our light

[1] ULF No. 50, December 1843.

and *come to me*! How I will open my arms to you and then sink into yours! And you will kiss me and clasp me and we will both praise God alone in the dark night with His eye shining down upon us and His love enclosing us. After a time we shall sleep!

And yet I fear you will yearn so for *fuller* communion that you will not be so happy as me. And I too perhaps shall yearn, frightened as I am! But every yearning will remind me of our self-denial, your sorrow for sin, your strength of repentance. And I shall glory in my yearning, *please God*![2]

Charles and Fanny set out on their five-week honeymoon well supplied with occupations. Fanny had suggested they should learn German and Charles had eagerly agreed. He in turn proposed that they should bring all their love letters with them.

My baby will classify them and keep a box on purpose for them, and often look at them in after years and at last leave them as a heirloom to our children. How much they may learn from our struggles! How it may 'attendrir' the heart of a son or a daughter, just struggling impatiently with opening life, to call him apart and open that sacred box and read him some of those letters and say, 'My son, see how I felt when in thy place and age!'

There was only one fly in the ointment of their happiness: Fanny continued to be ill. Indeed it was Charles who had to write the bread-and-butter letter to Mrs Warre, thanking her for lending them the house, for Fanny was not well enough to write. Perhaps her indisposition was understandable, considering that she was not getting the medicine that had been prescribed for her. On February 8th (presumably) the marriage was consummated and Fanny conceived at once. The couple found themselves perfectly attuned physically almost from the start. A few months later Charles wrote, 'My love to the naughty baby whose begetting was the most delicious moment of my life *up to that time*. Since then, what greater bliss!'[3] When they left Cheddar they moved to the spare room in the rectory at Chelsea and experienced such physical ecstasy that, twelve years later, Kingsley found himself quite unable to work there.

'I am sitting in my mother's old dressing room where we spent those four days of heaven twelve years ago. I have turned it into a

[2] Unpublished Letter from Fanny, December 9, 1843.
[3] ULF No. 64, April 17, 1844.

study though the room is so full of the gleam of your eyes and the scent of your hair I cannot help thinking of you and love all the while.'[4]

All through his life Kingsley remained enormously attracted to Fanny. He had only to be away from her for a few days to become incapable of sleep from longing for her. 'I am all naked and *half* without you,' he said a few months after their marriage. Twenty years later he wrote in similar vein. 'I dreamt of you last night in *all* your beauty and loved you. I wont say more for fear the letter should miscarry.'[5] When he was away from home he constantly entreated her to perform the impossible athletic feat of kissing herself all over from head to foot in the bath on his behalf, and despite his chronic shortness of cash, was never happier than when she spent money on pretty clothes. 'I am delighted to hear of the bonnet,' he wrote on one occasion. 'It will be a great enjoyment to foolish me.'[6] Edmund Gosse remembered eavesdropping as a boy on a party where the grown-ups were answering in turn the question 'What is the most beautiful thing in the world?' He never forgot the solemn reply of the then grey-haired Kingsley, 'My wife's eyes.'

All, however, was not sweetness and light even in those early months of marriage. The living at Eversley suddenly became vacant and the parishioners began a campaign to have Kingsley back. As a result when he set out for Pimperne in Dorset he was in a state of uncertainty. He left Fanny with relatives. While they had been together she had started to take morphine, of which he disapproved, to counteract the discomforts of early pregnancy, and he lost his temper with her several times, a thing he had not done since his Cambridge days when he used to 'get angry and shout at people'.[7] All his life he was a nervous, restless man and, according to G. W. E. Russell[8] who knew him, could seldom bring himself to remain seated at table until the end of a meal. Now, under the strain of his new-found bliss, he said things that he later repented. His letters from Dorset were full of contrition. 'Oh forgive, *God* forgive, my carelessness, my discontent for the last month. *Now* I feel how your presence, under whatever disagreements, is a bliss for which nothing can make up!'[9]

While he was in Dorset Kingsley stayed once more with the Sydney Godolphin Osbornes, for the rectory at Pimperne, although beautiful,

[4] ULF No. 337, 1855.
[5] ULF No. 311, 1861.
[6] ULF No. 85, 1845.
[7] 'I had a dreadful temper once.' ULF No. 23, October 3, 1843.
[8] G. W. E. Russell, *Afterthoughts*, 1912.
[9] ULF No. 62, April 1, 1844.

was in a state of dilapidation as a result of forty years of neglect on the part of Dr Wyndham.[10] He walked daily across the three miles of Cranborne Chase that separated Durweston from Pimperne, three miles that spoke to him of the happy days he had spent there with Fanny before they were married. He was enchanted by the grey-green beauty of the beech copses that are still scattered about the smooth rolling downs of that part of Dorset. 'I never was before in a chalk forest,' he told Fanny. The downs themselves he found even more beautiful, 'with their enormous sheets of spotless turf, those grand curves and swells, as if the great goddess-mother Hertha had laid her-self down among the hills to sleep, her Titan limbs wrapt in a veil of silvery green.'[11] Those downs, he felt, had a message. 'I should like to preach a sermon on chalk downs and another on chalk streams. They are so *purely* beautiful,' he told his beloved.

The Osbornes were the only relatives of Fanny with whom Charles was at ease, probably because they were the only ones who were not rich. He had been disposed to like them even before he met them. 'God bless those Osbornes,' he had written, 'two or three things in your letter showed me they were so homely and simple and so *like other people*.' It is true that he found Mrs Osborne (Fanny's sister Emily) touchy. 'I could never feel safe with her, bright as she is,' but he adored her children, particularly Georgie who was a favourite with both his uncle and his aunt. All through his life, even after he had children of his own, he had affection to spare for other people's children. There were few of his letters from Durweston that did not end with a reference to the Osbornes' 'chicks'. 'The children,' he wrote on one occasion, 'with many screams, and pulling of coat tails, send a shower of incoherent loves.'[12]

It was the father of the family however, the Honourable and Reverend Sydney Godolphin Osborne who was to change the direc-tion of the young curate's life. Osborne, later Lord Sydney Osborne, was a social reformer whose letters to *The Times*, particularly about the housing conditions of the Dorset peasantry, chilled the nation's blood. The series covered forty years and was never signed with more than the initials S.G.O. Its author was a younger son of Lord Godolphin, who had gone into the Church from convenience rather than convic-tion. Once there, his parochial duties had taken him into houses the like of which he never knew existed. He became a passionate collector of abuses and statistics.

[10] Dr Wyndham's incumbency had yet another twenty years to run.
[11] Charles Kingsley, *Yeast*.
[12] ULF No. 51, April 1844.

Kingsley's admiration for Osborne himself was a qualified one. He admitted he had faults, even hoped *he* might do *him* good.[13] He described him as 'conceited and contrary' and soon discovered he could not be relied upon to support any campaign he had not himself initiated, 'because the dirt is not of his own finding'. But for Sydney's causes his enthusiasm was unbounded. During that month of April in 1844 Kingsley turned from 'the veriest aristocrat' he had been in youth into a devoted champion of the right of the people to a decent standard of living. After his stay with Osborne he wrote:

I will never believe that a man has a real love for the good and the beautiful except he attacks the evil and the disgusting the moment he sees it. It is very easy to turn our eyes away from ugly sights, and so consider ourselves refined. The refined man to me is he who cannot rest in peace with a coal mine, or a factory, or a Dorsetshire peasant's house near him in the state they are.

He himself was to live up to his own measure of the refined man. The one cause in which he was absolutely consistent for the rest of his days was that of sanitary reform. 'A dying child,' he once wrote, 'is to me one of the most dreadful sights in the world,' and children were dying because they lived in roofless crowded cottages without sanitation or clean drinking water. It was appropriate that the Public Health Act for which Kingsley campaigned all his life should have been passed in 1875, the year of his death.

While Kingsley was at Durweston he continued to write Fanny long letters about the kind of household they would set up together, although it was still uncertain whether that household would be at Pimperne or Eversley. His parents had agreed to let him have some furniture including a double bed, about which he wrote jubilantly.

Darling! Darling!
The dear bed that we both have slept in! I had hoped that that should become our marriage bed, our altar. That there, where we have moaned and languished for each other alone, you should be the victim and I the priest, in the bliss of full communion! Perhaps our children will be born in it! And perhaps, unless God reserves us for higher honours, we may die in it. They have given us the bedding and all appurtenances and window curtains to match, a sofa (a very good one) and a rosewood drawing-room table and a library table.[14]

13 ULF No. 62, April 1, 1844.
14 ULF No. 50, December 1843.

But most of his letters were not about how much they would have but about how little they would manage on. Charles's income was now £670 a year, compounded of his salary as a curate (£100), Fanny's allowance (£300), the Chelsea clerkship (£120) and an allowance which his father had been able to make him on his marriage (£150).[15] This sum he proposed to hand over to Fanny, retaining only £100 to buy his own clothes and pay the gardener. In this way he would be able to prove to Fanny's family that not a penny of her money had passed through his hands.[16] He assured her that the sum he was handing over to her, even after the deduction of £90 for insurance and £100 for alms, would be double what they needed to live on.

> My parents [he wrote] have been calculating that housekeeping, taxes, servants, and your horse ought not to cost us £250! They say we ought to keep the same number of servants as Emily and Sydney Godolphin Osborne did on our income, a man to groom and garden and wait at table when there is company (£25), a cook (£25) who must do some housemaid's work, and a maid (£25) to look after you, our bedroom, and to wait on us when we are alone. Shall we not be comfortable? We shall be richer than the Osbornes, for I shall keep only one horse, and that only to drive my baby over to see her noble sister, and take her about the Parish when it is very wet. I shall not hunt or shoot, of course, or fish but very very seldom, when we want a dish for a friend.[17]

Charles planned to give away in charity any money that was not required for their immediate needs, although he made one concession in the matter of babies. His mother had told him that the expenses involved in bringing a child into the world amounted to £50, and this money, he assured Fanny, he was prepared to set aside. His conscience was so delicate, at this time, in money matters, that he regarded cumulative insurance policies as immoral, and claimed that he would accept only the value of the premiums when his policy matured. The interest he would give away.

In May a summons came from Arthur's Club in London. There, Sir John Cope, the patron of the living at Eversley, informed Kingsley that he was the new rector, and advised him to proceed thither with all speed. Kingsley dashed off a letter to Fanny which is still preserved

[15] ULF No. 50, December 1843.
[16] ULF No. 44, 1843.
[17] ULF No. 50, 1843.

at Eversley Rectory. It had neither a beginning nor an end and it announced in large scrawling letters, 'I have a living *for my very own*!' By the end of the week he was installed at the rectory with a van-load of furniture from Chelsea and was able to tell Fanny 'by hard work we have made the whole place look very neat indeed'.[18]

Eversley Rectory was, and still is, a rambling seventeenth-century house with large light rooms. Because parts of it go back to the fifteenth century, however, it is full of steps up and steps down and odd corners and cupboards. Perhaps its strangest feature is the divided Y-shaped staircase that leads to the maids' bedrooms in the attics. A rope dangling from the ceiling above it takes the place of a banister. All the principal rooms of the house, Fanny's drawing room on the left of the front door and the main bedroom above it, the dining room on the right of the front door and the guest room over it, had bow windows looking towards a green mound topped with trees. It was from that mound that Kingsley, as a curate, had looked down en-viously upon the rectory. He loved the view of it from the first moment he saw it and attempted to draw it for Fanny. 'The ground,' he wrote, 'slopes upwards from the windows to a sunk road, and then rises in the furze hill in the drawing, which hill is *perfectly beautiful* in light and shade and colour.' That hill still looks much as it did in Kingsley's day, except that, of the summer house he built, and papered with pages from the *Illustrated News*, only the foundations remain. In its place stands a giant Californian Redwood, brought back by Kings-ley's daughter Rose from their tour of the United States in the last months of his life.

The rector's favourite room was his study, entered by a heavy studded door (later converted to a french window) at the opposite side of the house from the church. It was a long low room and the hooks from which he used to sling his South American string hammock are still preserved in its beams. The brick floor was covered with matting, and the walls were lined with book-shelves. In Kingsley's day it was usually in a state of comfortable disorder with fishing rods propped against the walls and the table spread with papers, clay pipes and fishing flies. The fireplace was vast and contained footholds used by the real life Toms who swept the chimneys in those days. Kingsley liked to place his chair (a comfortable reclining one of buttoned leather still in the possession of the present rector) in front of the door leading to the garden. Outside this door he created a strip of lawn known as 'the quarterdeck' which stretched to a group of acacia trees, some of the earliest planted in this country. 'Behind the acacia on the lawn,'

18 ULF No. 70, 1844.

he wrote, 'you get the first glimpse of the fir forests and the moors, of which five-sixths of my parish consists. Those delicious self-sown firs!' Three of the famous firs stood on the front lawn, on the church-yard boundary. On summer evenings Kingsley would sling his ham-mock between them.

One of Kingsley's first duties after he arrived at the rectory was to give a small reception for his patron and other pillars of the parish, which was an ordeal for a shy young man of twenty-five. 'I introduced everybody, gave them wine and sandwiches, and all went off like greased lightening, but I was in a dreadful fright. I have been fearing and fearing this day for weeks. Oh that I could flee away to the wild moors and get a day's fishing!'[19] Fanny was soon able to join him and share the strain of such occasions. At last the young couple could settle down to a proper married life together, only marred by the presence of Henry, who had once more been sent to stay with his big brother. Kingsley comforted Fanny with the observation that 'little Henry's presence will be a good mortification to us' and that anyway he could not follow them to the bedroom. 'From 11.0 at night until 6.0 in the morning we shall be on our own. What bliss!' he told her.

The church services at Eversley had been shockingly neglected by John Toovey-Hawley, who made the slightest indisposition on a Sunday an excuse for sending his clerk to the church door to announce that there would be no service. His interest in his parishioners had been limited to the female section and it was not with their souls that he was concerned. It was the discovery of an indiscretion 'of a most revolting nature' concerning one of these ladies that led him to flee the country and so leave the living vacant. He had completely neglected the upkeep of the little church with its elegant eighteenth-century memorial plaques and its box pews. Church furniture was almost non-existent. At the altar, which was covered by a moth-eaten cloth, stood one broken chair. A cracked kitchen basin inside the font held water for baptism; such alms as there were were collected in an old wooden saucer. The classical rood screen had faded to 'dun-duckety mud colour'[20] and sheep kept the grass down between the graves in the churchyard. Many of the new rector's seven hundred and fifty human flock had gone to the folds of the local Baptist ministers, a breed for whom he had little charity to spare. He described them in terms worthy of his beloved Carlyle, as 'muck enthroned on their respective

[19] ULF No. 70, 1844.

[20] This, according to an unpublished letter written by Rose Kingsley in 1918, was how Kingsley always described it.

dung hills, screeching on their scrannel pipes of ragged straw', and never dared leave his parish without thoroughly tarring his sheep 'to keep off the schismatic flies and mosquitoes who will be at them the moment I am gone'.[21]

Kingsley knew that the only way to win his parishioners back was to visit them in their homes. He always got on well with working men. Indeed, like the hero of his first novel, *Yeast*, 'he suffered from a continual longing to chat with his inferiors', while at the same time being careful to preserve his dignity as a superior. At Cambridge he had drunk with all classes in the public houses, 'to learn Englishmen'. Because of this, he explained to Fanny, 'some people think me un-refined. And what's the truth? That the lower orders worship me, and *never* take liberties.'[22] Fanny tells us he was not above swinging a flail with the threshers in the barn, turning his swathe with the mowers in the meadow or pitching hay with the haymakers in the pasture. He was never at a loss for a subject of conversation with either a hunts-man or a poacher 'for he knew every fox cover on the moor and every pike hover and chub-hole' in the local waters. With farmers he could discuss the rotation of crops and with their labourers the science of hedging and ditching. For these people he organised confirmation classes at the rectory, since many of the younger ones, and even some of the middle-aged, had never been to communion. The classes were so popular that Sir John Cope's stud groom, 'a respectable man of thirty-five' came with a message from his fellow hunt servants to say that 'they had all been confirmed once, but if Mr Kingsley wished it, they would all be very happy to be done again'.

Kingsley's style as a preacher was 'quiet but compellingly earnest'.[23] He took a pride in preaching a simple sermon each week full of homely allusions, too homely in the opinion of the Bishop of Winchester. Remarks like 'there was a great poet once, Dante by name', or 'there was a heathen king once, named Philip of Macedon, and a very wise king he was, though he was a heathen',[24] might insult a modern churchgoer. But it must be remembered that the majority of his hearers had never read a book. And the content of the sermons was often arresting. 'If thou art not in heaven in this life, thou wilt never be in heaven in the life to come,' he said once. 'Get rid of those notions that tempt men to fancy that having misused this place, they are to

[21] ULF No. 31, November 1843.

[22] ULF No. 24, October 4, 1843.

[23] Sir William Cope's funeral sermon for Kingsley.

[24] Man's Working Day, 25 *Village Sermons*, by Charles Kingsley, Jun., Rector of Eversley, Hants and Canon of Middleham, Yorkshire, 1849.

fly away when they die, like swallows in autumn, to another place they know not where, where they will be very happy, they know not why or how.'[25]

Kingsley had yet another method of bringing his parishioners under his influence. Like the missionaries of our own day, he offered them education. Unbelievable though it may appear, there was not a grown man or woman among the labouring people at Eversley who could read. The village schoolmaster was also the shoemaker, and caning and cobbling went on simultaneously in his stifling shop. There was little inducement for children to attend, for they were anyway needed at home to mind younger brothers and sisters while their mothers worked in the fields to bring in a few extra shillings. At the age of ten they themselves were sent out to work for the local farmers. As a result of agitation on Kingsley's part, an intelligent young parishioner was eventually sent to Winchester Training College and was still at his post as village schoolmaster when the rector died. Adult evening classes were held at the rectory three nights a week in winter and a lending library was established. Sunday school was also held at the rectory and there were cottage lectures twice weekly at Bramshill for those who were too old and feeble to get to the rectory. Kingsley often had to ride through foul weather at night to reach them. 'I expect to finish in the ditch,' he told a friend one winter, 'but this rain has made it soft lying.'

Not content with supplying the spiritual and intellectual needs of his parishioners, he also ran a one-man social welfare service. Most of the labourers' families were miserably poor, earning less than ten shillings a week with no prospect but the workhouse at the end of it all. Kingsley was determined that none of his people should go to the workhouse to rot on a straw pallet until they would oblige the parish by vacating it for the graveyard. Various small savings schemes were established to help the people to help themselves, such as a shoe club, a maternal society and a loan fund.

There was always a steady stream of callers at the kitchen door for bread and soup, and to all who he considered deserving he gave. Only to those who obstinately persisted in folly did he refuse, and then with difficulty. A friend recalled him striding up and down in agony between the breakfast room and a miserable crying woman outside, and his look of pain and disgust when he finally sent her away. 'Look there!' he said, as he pointed to his own well-furnished table.

To those who could not come to him he went on foot or on horseback. He would walk miles to comfort a sick cottager or a gypsy

[25] Charles Kingsley, Heaven on Earth, 25 *Village Sermons.*

dying in a ramshackle van on the moors. On one occasion a farmer tried to dissuade him from crossing one of the boggy patches that still persisted on the moor and were occasionally fatal to strangers. But he would not heed the warning. 'There's a man dying in that cottage. Would you have me leave him to go, without trying to be at his side?' he enquired.[26]

For four years Kingsley worked unremittingly at redeeming his parish from a state of barbarism. Yet he was happy, for he was a man incapable of idleness, and wrote what could have been his own epitaph in the lines.

> Be earnest, earnest; mad if thou wilt;
> Do what thou dost as if the stake were heaven.[27]

He saw himself as a parson in the style of George Herbert, 'not quite as holy' as the beloved poet-priest of Bemerton, 'but trying to be as busy'. He had outlined a daily programme for life at the parsonage even before he was married and earnestly attempted to adhere to it.

Let us rise at 6.0 and have family prayers at 7.30. We will breakfast at 8.0. From 8.30 to 10.0 must be given to household matters, and from 10.0 to 1.0 we will study divinity together, having our doors open for *poor* parish visitants. At 1.0 I must go out in all weathers and visit the sick and poor and teach in the school (I speak of our first *childless* ten months). We will dine at 5.0 and then draw and feed our intellect and fancy all evening with your head on my bosom and our lips meeting every now and again to tell each other something that is too deep for words. Then family prayers and bed at 11.0.[28]

---

[26] This story was told to Leonard Taylor by his grandfather who knew Kingsley. He recounted it in *The Sunday Companion*.

[27] Charles Kingsley, *The Saint's Tragedy*.

[28] ULF No. 34, October 1843.

It is interesting to see how Fanny altered this letter to make it suitable for publication in her biography of her husband:

1 She omitted the suggestion that they should rise at 6.0.

2 She added 'or settling parish accounts and business', to the morning study of divinity.

3 She omitted the italics from the phrase '*poor* parish visitants'. Kingsley had elsewhere emphasised that he was not prepared to admit idle morning callers of his own class.

4 She omitted the tenderer part of the evening's entertainment.

CHAPTER 4

The Father of a Family
1844–1848

On November 7th, 1844, exactly ten months after the wedding of her parents, Rose Georgiana was born. The baby, who Charles nicknamed Cocky, brought him great happiness. 'My little baby,' he called her, 'the next link in the golden chain of generations, begotten of our bliss.'[1] He leaned over her cradle for many long minutes, lost in 'reverent yet passionate wonder'. Like Wordsworth he believed that heaven lay about a child in its infancy. For each new baby he felt the same delighted awe.

He was no remote Victorian father, barricading himself in his study. He saw his children many times during the day and the current baby was always carried upstairs to play on its parents' bed in the morning, even if Fanny was away. There is barely a letter from this time on that does not contain a message for Fanny to pass on to one or other of 'the infantry'.

The next year Fanny became pregnant with 'another pledge of our love'. Early in this pregnancy, as in all her subsequent ones, she became unwell and had to be sent to the Isle of Wight in the hope that immersion in 'the Happy Water' would produce 'a strengthening effect'.[2] Charles missed mother and child equally. 'I cannot sleep without you, but lie tossing or else getting up and walking about. I fancy you and Baby romping in bed in the morning, my two beautiful treasures.'[3] As usual, when Fanny was absent, he repented his impatience with her. 'At Whitsun,' he told her, 'I prayed to God to forgive me all my crossness to my darling love and to make us both holier and wiser.'[4] Early in 1847 Kingsley's first son was born and named after the beloved master, Maurice. He was a child of extraordinary beauty, at any rate in

1 ULF No. 37, November 7, 1843.
2 ULF No. 71, June 1846.
3 ULF No. 76, 1846.
4 ULF No. 81, May 31, 1846.

his father's eyes, and Kingsley never ceased to find satisfaction in the impression he made on ladies passing in the street.

With the birth of her children Fanny abandoned the programme of cold water, hard work and simple food that Charles had laid down for her before their marriage, if she had ever adhered to it. For the rest of her life she was a devoted, perhaps too devoted, mother. She had longed for a baby ever since she herself was a child, wishing her dolls were made of flesh and blood[5] and in her year of exile from Charles she had planned a 'Babe's Book', a collection of 'poetry, fairy tales and fables . . . for Ernest's edification'[6] (it was always assumed that the first child would be a boy called Ernest). She was now determined that Rose and the children who might follow her should have only the best. She was never able to abandon the standards of her wealthy background and remains, to this day, 'a very *grand* lady' in the memory of her family. After the first autumn rains she decided that the rectory, which had seemed to her husband so 'neat and comfortable', was damp and unhealthy. 'It was an old house,' she wrote, 'that had not been repaired for more than a hundred years. It was damp and un-wholesome, surrounded by ponds which overflowed with every heavy rain, and flooded, not only the garden and stables, but all the rooms on the ground floor, keeping up master and servants, sometimes all night, baling out the water in buckets.' She omitted to mention that these periodic innundations were a source of delight to Charles, at least in his younger days. 'Up to my knees in water,' he wrote exultantly 'working with a pick axe by candlelight to prevent all being washed away. But it all goes with me under the head of "fun". Something to do.' The next job that Charles was given to do was to help the gardener, George White, fill in the chain of fish ponds which stretched across the garden from the home farm at the far side of the house to the group of Scotch firs in front of it.[7] These were considered responsible for the flooding.

Fanny was temporarily satisfied and added a late entry to her Nice Diary to that effect, dated February 21st, 1846. 'I am a wife and a mother — in such a sweet peaceful home. It is nearly two and a half years since I last wrote in this book. We have been married two years and a month and I shall now begin writing a diary when I can. My dearest Husband is sitting at his writing table in our sweet little drawing room writing his sermon — and I full of influenza — but full of

[5] FND, November 23, 1842.
[6] FND, July 3, 1843.
[7] A hollow which was formerly one of these ponds can still be seen near the last remaining fir.

happiness — am sitting at mine very near him, and our darling child, nearly sixteen months old, after trotting about all day is upstairs fast asleep in her little white bed — and her faithful nurse watching her — and our garden is so improved and full of pretty trees and flowers of our own planting and our walks are fresh gravelled and the whole place is getting gradually into order . . . We are fitting up a new Nursery for our darling Rose and that makes me very happy for it is such a sweet sunny room and such a nice view from the windows.'

Three months after Rose's birth Kingsley's brother Gerald died at sea at the age of twenty-three, under circumstances very similar to those described by the *Ancient Mariner*. We know very little of Gerald, the only remaining brother of Kingsley's own age. So jealously did Fanny guard her husband's reputation that she barely spoke of his sister and brothers and even omitted to mention that Henry Kingsley spent six years in a cottage at Eversley. But there is some evidence to suggest that Gerald was a straightforward young man of slightly frivolous tastes. His ship, the *Royalist*, was becalmed for a year and a half in the Torres Straits and there he died of fever. 'The sailors say that there is but a sheet of paper between Torres Straits and Hell,' Kingsley told Fanny. 'And there he lay, and the wretched crew, in the little brig, roasting and pining day after day, for a year and a half. The commander died, half the crew died and so they died and died on, until in May no officer was left but Gerald, and on the seventeenth of September he died too, and we shall never see him more.' Old Mr Kingsley overheard the news by chance in a public library in Chelsea and fell down in a dead faint. Charles hastened to London to be with him and his mother.

It was on a visit to Chelsea about this time that Kingsley met the author of *The Kingdom of Christ*, a book that he always claimed changed his life. F. D. Maurice had rented St Luke's Rectory for a few months and Kingsley wrote to him asking for advice about the non–conformists in his parish and also for a meeting. He expected to find him sympathetic, for Maurice had also come to the Church of England by a tortuous route. His father had been a Unitarian minister in Suffolk, and it was only after a brilliant career at Cambridge and a spell as editor of a literary magazine in London that he took orders. He was a disciple of Coleridge whom he had originally admired for his Romanticism and whose thoughts on the relationship of Church and State he eventually came to share. His conversion did not pass unnoticed, for the publication of *The Kingdom of Christ*, his first major work, accompanied it. It was a clarion call for peace between warring sections in the Anglican Church. The Church, Maurice declared, is a constitution binding men together and transcending different opinions. A party can only claim partial truth. Such views were not likely to appeal either to Evangelicals or Tractarians, but they appealed enormously to Kingsley. So did the theory that the Church had social responsibilities, a theory that was soon to lead Maurice to Christian Socialism.[8]

We have, alas, no account of the first meeting of the two men at St Luke's Rectory, but certainly there was an instant liking on both sides. Kingsley found himself in the presence not only of one of the greatest theologians of the nineteenth century, but of a man with wide knowledge of literature and philosophy. Some years later, when Maurice was lecturing on ethics at Cambridge, Tennyson went so far as to describe his mind as 'the greatest since Plato'. If you add to this the extraordinary beauty and sensitivity of Maurice's face (which was said to have a mesmeric effect on his congregations) and the complete lack of condescension in a man who was a professor at King's College, and a highly popular chaplain at Lincoln's Inn, the impression made on the younger man is understandable. And Kingsley's liking was reciprocated. 'Mr Maurice's affection for him was unspeakable,' wrote Ludlow, who knew them both. 'I have often doubted whether he really ever loved anyone except Kingsley of all the young men who began to gather round him.'

A Cambridge friend whom Kingsley saw much of on his visits to London was Charles Mansfield, now engaged on the experiments for the extraction of benzol from coal tar which led to the foundation of the aniline industry. Mansfield had always been given to strange beliefs. As an undergraduate he began to be haunted by a seal he had shot on holiday. He had taken to vegetarianism and cloth shoes, convinced that not only eating meat but even the collecting of insects was wrong because it deprived God's creatures of life. Now Kingsley found him undergoing the agonies of a late conversion to Christianity. 'He is discovering,' he told Fanny, 'that God and the Devil are living realities, fighting for his body and soul. This for a man of vast thought and feeling who has been for years a confirmed materialist is hard work.' On one occasion when Kingsley called on him in his rooms, he seemed in danger of losing his sanity. He would not leave Kingsley for the rest of that day. They walked together to Temple Bar where they

---

[8] Since the Second World War there has been a revival of interest in F. D. Maurice, and at least five books about him have appeared. His views on ecumenism and the social responsibility of the Church were couched in language that was sufficiently misty and obscure for them to appear applicable to present-day conditions.

met F. D. Maurice in the street, then to Clapham, where they dined, and finally back to Chelsea.

Kingsley also continued to see Peter Wood, the man whose pheasants his landlady had spoiled in the cooking. In 1845 the two young men spent a pleasant holiday together in Yorkshire. Peter's father, Dean of the Collegiate church of Middleham, had two canonries to dispose of and offered them to his son and his son's friend. The posts carried no duties and no salary and accepting them involved attendance at the church for one Sunday only, no great sacrifice as Yorkshire was a hospitable county that showed excellent sport. Kingsley enormously enjoyed the stay in the little racing town with jockeys and grooms crowding the streets. The magnificent countryside round it was one day to supply him with the background to *The Water-Babies*.

Two years later Kingsley took his first long family holiday, albeit a working one, earned by taking the Sunday services at Pennington, a church near his father's old home in the New Forest. The health of Fanny and the babies demanded the benefit of sea air so Kingsley rode over from Milford, on the coast, to take the services. The ride through the forest, with its historical associations, was a pleasure to Kingsley. It was only either at a great crisis in his life, or at a time when all his surroundings were in perfect harmony, that he was able to write poems. The latter was now the case and he wrote several ballads including one of the most successful of his songs, *Airly Beacon*, a strangely prophetical forerunner of the poems in *A Shropshire Lad*.

> Airly Beacon, Airly Beacon;
> Oh the pleasant sight to see
> Shires and towns from Airly Beacon
> While my love climbed up to me.
>
> Airly Beacon, Airly Beacon;
> Oh the happy hours we lay
> Deep in fern on Airly Beacon,
> Courting through the summer's day.
>
> Airly Beacon, Airly Beacon;
> Oh the weary haunt for me
> All alone on Airly Beacon,
> With his baby on my knee.

A far more serious and considerably less readable production was now about to be given to the public. Ever since his marriage Kingsley had been working on his life of St Elizabeth, now recast as a five-act blank verse drama in the style of Shakespeare, and renamed *The Saint's*

Tragedy. The play took five years to write, for Kingsley was determined to make a masterpiece of it. He told his wife, 'I do not like to be hurried or bound to time in St E'[9] and refused to serialise it, saying that the saint should not be chopped up into sections. When the time came to publish, no publisher could be found. The Romish violence that Elizabeth did to her person was very shocking to the Victorian reader and even to the author who retained in Latin certain passages in his footnotes about the exact nature of the saint's mortifications.[10] The scene most likely to cause offence came at the beginning of Act II. The curtain rose on the naked saint pacing her nuptial chamber, torn between Christ, her heavenly bridegroom, and Lewis, her earthly one. Eventually Lewis wakes and cries out as he touches her,

> Alas! what's this! These shoulders' cushioned ice,
> And thin soft flanks, with purple lashes all,
> And weeping furrows traced!

Elizabeth tries to explain the joy she receives from her penances, but, failing, leads her husband back to bed and more earthly pleasures with the rhyming couplet

> Now I must stop those wise lips with a kiss,
> And lead thee back to scenes of simpler bliss.

Later in the play Conrad of Morpurg, Elizabeth's spiritual adviser, steals most of the limelight, as bad characters so often will. There were certain aspects of *his* character that were destined to raise a blush or two in Victorian drawing rooms. At times it seemed as if the satisfaction he gained from torturing the comely saint was not entirely a spiritual one, as when he stood looking down on her dying body and blurted out:

> O happy Lewis! Had I been a knight —
> A man at all — what's this? I must be brutal,
> Or I shall love her: and yet that's no safeguard:
> I have marked it oft; ay — with what devilish triumph
> Which eyes its victim's writhings, still will mingle
> A sympathetic thrill of lust.

At the request of Fanny and his mother Kingsley 'resolutely scratched

---

[9] ULF No. 81, May 31, 1846.

[10] He also conveyed in Latin the fact that relic hunters removed the nipples from her corpse.

out' some of the 'coarser passages'[11] and F. D. Maurice, who had at first feared the bedroom scene might cause offence,[12] contributed a preface explaining that the author only wrote of these Popish practices in order to condemn them and that he did not necessarily agree with all that his characters said. Even thus supported the play was turned down by two publishers, Moxon and Murray. Derwent Coleridge, whose opinion of the play Kingsley described as 'far higher than I had expected' then sent it to a third publisher, Pickering, with a highly recommendatory note. Even this however, Kingsley explained to Fanny, was 'not sufficient to persuade him to take the thing off my hands'. Eventually the unhappy saint found a home with John Parker of the Strand, who, as Kingsley put it, 'though a burnt child, does not dread the fire'.

John Parker, who was in partnership with his father of the same name, had been at King's College with Kingsley. He was a small fiery man who was to become a close friend of both Charles and Fanny. He was also the owner of *Fraser's Magazine*, in future issues of which much of Kingsley's work was to appear. Under his auspices *The Saint's Tragedy* appeared in 1848 and sank almost without a trace except at Oxford where a small group at Exeter College, who were in revolt against the High Church teaching that was sweeping the university, admired it. The group included Arthur Clough, J. A. Froude and Kingsley's old friend Cowley Powles.

Unbeknown to Kingsley, the play also won the approval of two very distinguished Germans. One was Baron de Bunsen, the German ambassador, who privately expressed the opinion that Kingsley was a second Shakespeare and ought to continue to write the historical plays where the Master had left off. The other was no less a person than the Prince Consort himself. He told his oldest daughter, the Princess Royal, in a letter written many years later,[13] that he was profoundly moved by the fate of St Elizabeth. 'The reader's own nature shudders before the image of what the Church has substituted for God's Work.'

Of more immediate importance to Kingsley at the time, however, was the admiration of his parents. 'St Elizabeth's success with my father and mother is quite glorious,' he told Fanny. 'They are astonished at it.' And for the first time Mrs Kingsley showed Charles 'a quantity of beautiful poetry that she herself had written'. Alone together mother and son enjoyed 'a delightful evening of peace and intellect'[14] at St Luke's Rectory.

[11] ULF No. 83, 1847.   [12] ULF No. 82, April 15, 1847.
[13] January 25, 1860.   [14] ULF No. 84, 1847.

CHAPTER 5

The Year of Ferment
1848

While Kingsley was on holiday in the New Forest, his parents stayed at Eversley and looked after the parish. When he returned they sided with Fanny in insisting that the rectory was not fit for children to live in, although it can hardly have been worse than Holne where Charles spent the first months of his life. To Fanny it always seemed at its dampest and dreariest after a seaside holiday. Builders were called in to level and rebuild a tumbling block of chimneys, put new fireplaces in all the rooms but one and replace certain 'disgusting nuisances' with 'necessary conveniences'. Also, not surprisingly, it was discovered that the filling in of the ponds had not solved the problem of flooding. The rectory stood on blue clay and the graveyard drained into it. New drains had to be dug and Fanny did not believe in half measures. The drains she caused to be dug were long and deep and have survived to this day; the fireplaces she installed, even in the children's bedrooms, were broad affairs of cast iron decorated with moulded foliage (the present owner has recently uncovered several of them). Such standards required money to support them. Kingsley applied to the patron of the living, Sir John Cope, Bart., for help, but received none. Cope lived at Bramshill Park,[1] a magnificent Tudor palace built of red brick and approached over four thousand acres of heathland by a straight avenue a mile long. Bramshill was famous for the vast size of its rooms, the largest being forty yards in length and hung with tapestries. Kingsley always felt he had a certain family association with the place for Archbishop Abbot, an ancestor of his, had accidentally shot a keeper in the park there and was said never to have smiled again.

Amid all this splendour, perpetually worried about money, lived Sir John, a bachelor, master of the Bramshill Hounds[2] and much given to the bottle. As he grew older he became increasingly eccentric and fell under the domination of his overseer, George Clacy, and Clacy's

---

[1] Now a police college.
[2] Now known as the Garth or the South Berkshire.

wife, Sophia. To Kingsley the Clacys seemed the evil geniuses of Bramshill, concealing from their employer the impoverishment of the tenants. 'I am certain that Sir John would be furious at some of the things which go on, the complete serfage of half the inhabitants to Clacy's will and pleasure. And Madame, alas, is a worse thief and tyrant.' It seems, however, that Sir John was not eager to be told the true state of affairs by his rector, for on more than one occasion Kingsley was ordered to leave the house forever, only to be called back during Sir John's next bout of drink-sodden repentance.

Sir John's meanness sometimes drove Kingsley to the point of frenzy. Two undated letters show how far he was pushed by it at times. The first ran as follows: 'This place sickens me. Cope has not done one of the sanitary improvements. He will certainly make the place too hot to hold him and I shall have to send the police inspectors round.' The second, written in the almost illegible hand he adopted when deeply distressed, sounded an even more desperate note. 'This plot has been Sophia's alone, and there are three or four more cases undisposed of I fear. If my mother were not alive I should go to Germany for three years, take a foreign chaplaincy or something. As it is I must stop at the stake and be baited like a bear.'

Sir John's curmudgeonly behaviour had two important effects on Kingsley: it made him acutely conscious of the plight of tenants, particularly agricultural tenants, and it forced him to use his pen for supplementing his income. The living at Eversley was worth £600 a year, but out of it Kingsley had to find £100 a year in salary to Charles Smith, the curate he had inherited from his predecessor, and large sums in poor rates and other dues. It was ten years before the living became remunerative and in the meantime he had been forced to borrow £300 from Glyn's bank.[3] There was nothing for it but to write to John Parker requesting regular employment for his pen 'because bricklayers and carpenters in an old tumble-down house' had overtaxed his resources. He offered 'to furnish poetry of almost any pattern at a very moderate sum per yard' and in fact supplied *Fraser's Magazine* with two articles on the National Gallery and one entitled 'Why should we Fear the Romish Priests?' in which he displayed the ignorant and prejudiced attitude to the Church of Rome that was to land him in such hot water fifteen years later when he crossed swords with Newman. How grossly he underestimated his future opponent was shown in a paragraph on converts. 'Have we lost a single second-rate man even? One indeed we have lost, first-rate in talents, at least, but has he not, by his later writings, given the very strongest proof,

[3] Eventually £1,000 of Fanny's money had to go towards improving the house.

that, to become a Romish priest is to lose, *ipso facto*, whatever moral or intellectual life he might previously have had?' This outpouring did not receive the answer it deserved because of the obscurity of its author and the fact that *Fraser's* mostly circulated in country homes whose inhabitants shared Kingsley's views. It is nevertheless of interest as the first of that fusillade of 'grape and canister'[4] with which Kingsley, embattled at Eversley, was to bombard his contemporaries for the rest of his life, in the form of books and pamphlets on a wide variety of subjects.

In the very month of the publication of the Roman article, Kingsley did in fact, for the only time, become involved physically in a major national event, the Chartist rising. It is hard now to realise what a frightened city London was on the morning of April 10th, 1848. The memory of the February Revolution (in which Kingsley's brother George had received a slight wound) was still fresh in people's minds and blood was expected to flow as freely in the streets of London as it had in those of Paris. The old Duke of Wellington himself had barricaded the Thames bridges, regiments had been brought in from all over the country, the Queen had left the capital, and nearly a quarter million members of the middle class, including Charles Mansfield, had transformed themselves into special constables.

By chance John Parker had been spending the weekend at Eversley and, on the spur of the moment, Kingsley decided to accompany him to London. Parker's parting remark to Mrs Kingsley was that he expected to land up in the fountain in Trafalgar Square. The two men found most of the shops of London closed and the streets deserted. One young barrister had, however, ventured forth to his office. His name was John Malcolm Ludlow and he had seen enough of revolution in Paris to doubt its likelihood in London. His clients were not so hopeful and he sat in an empty office until at eleven his clerk announced Mr Kingsley, a clergyman from Hampshire. This gentleman entered the room and, stuttering something unintelligible about M-m-maurice, handed over a note. The note ran as follows: 'Meantime (as I am confined to the house by a cough myself) will you let me introduce my friend Mr Kingsley. He is deeply in earnest and seems to be possessed with the idea of doing something by handbills.'

Ludlow's first impression of Kingsley was of a man 'thin and gaunt, lanthorn jawed I might say; with a large mouth indicative of great resolution, but at the same time singularly mobile. A single glance at him showed that you had no ordinary man before you.' Kingsley was

---

[4] An expression of Kingsley's, quoted by Thomas Hughes in his preface to the 1876 edition of *Alton Locke*.

equally impressed by the young Ludlow, whom contemporary photos show as a small man with a finely shaped brow and dark eyes of remarkable brilliance. Kingsley explained that he was anxious to prevent bloodshed by addressing the mass meeting of Chartists taking place at that moment on Kennington Common. Ludlow agreed to accompany him, and as they walked Kingsley talked. Ludlow found his

> conversation fascinating by its originality, keen observation, strong sense and imaginative power; deep feeling and broad humour succeeding each other without giving the least sense of incongruity or jar to one's feelings. His stutter, which he felt most painfully himself as a thorn in the flesh, in fact only added to a raciness in his talk as one waited for what quaint saying was going to pour out, as it always did, at full speed, the stutter once conquered.[5]

The gist of Kingsley's remarks that day was that the Church needed to work with Socialism, not against it. Ludlow agreed and Kingsley loved him for it, little guessing how many things they were to disagree about in the future. Indeed within three days of their meeting F. D. Maurice had to write a note to Ludlow smoothing over some misunderstanding caused by Kingsley's 'sense of inferiority'. Describing their friendship long afterwards, Ludlow wrote: 'Kingsley, I must own, was very prompt in flinging himself into intimacy with anyone whom he found congenial to his many-sided nature. He was essentially an artist, and was fascinated for the time by a newly made friend, and I am afraid for a time he over-valued me.' So deep were the young men in conversation that they were surprised, on reaching Waterloo Bridge, to find themselves in the midst of the rain-sodden remnants of the Kennington meeting on its way home. Kingsley asked one of them what had happened and he was informed that Feargus O'Connor had made an impassioned speech recommending, rather surprisingly, that they should disperse and leave him and the committee to convey the three rolls of the charter to the House of Commons strapped to the tops of cabs. The denouément of the story is well known: how the Charter was discovered to weigh not five tons but barely five hundredweight and to contain not six million signatures but fewer than two million, including those of 'Pug Nose', 'No Cheese', 'Duke of Wellington', 'Prince Consort' and 'Victoria Rex'.

Although the Chartist movement ended with the Charter, working-class discontent did not. A series of disastrous harvests, combined with the potato blight that had caused so much havoc in Ireland, had sent

[5] Ludlow, 'Some of the Christian Socialists of 1848', *Economic Review*, 1893.

food prices rocketing and the misery of the poor, both in town and country, was extreme. Kingsley had been greatly heartened by the ability the Chartists had shown to work together and he was convinced that it was in association that the hope of the working man lay. He did not, however, believe in the electoral reform demanded by the Charter. On the night of April 11th he worked until four in the morning writing out a poster which he caused to be printed over the signature 'a working parson'. In it he ridiculed the idea of universal suffrage ('this fifty thousandth share in a Talker in the National Palaver at Westminster')[6] and pointed out that one could not be free while one was 'a slave of one's own stomach, one's own pocket, one's own temper'. He concluded with a promise that 'a nobler day is dawning for England, a day of freedom, science, industry.' These words must have seemed so vague as to be meaningless to a slave with an empty stomach, but to the middle classes they were deeply shocking. Never had a Socialist manifesto been issued by a clergyman of the Church of England.

Kingsley spent the rest of the week in a state of wild euphoria, as a typical letter to Fanny, written in a large scrawl, shows.

> Parker's, Strand, April 12, 6 p.m.
>
> I really cannot go home this afternoon. I have spent it with Archdeacon Hare, and Parker, starting a new periodical, a Penny People's Friend, in which Maurice, Hare, Ludlow, Mansfield, and I are going to set to work to supply the place of the defunct Saturday Magazine. I send you my first placard. Maurice is delighted with it. I cannot tell you the interest which it has excited with everyone who has seen it. It brought the tears into the Old Parker's eyes, who was once a working printers boy. I have got already £2.10.0 towards bringing out more, and Maurice is subscription hunting for me.

The new periodical, *Politics for the People*, enunciated the principles of the new Christian Socialism, with which Kingsley's name has remained indissolubly linked. The creed of the Christian Socialists was not an extreme one. As Kingsley pointed out in the two 'Letters to Chartists' that he contributed, the new movement took nothing more dangerous than the Bible as its reformer's guide. But its name alone was enough to make him suspect among most of his fellow clergy. *Politics for the People* ran to seventeen issues before it died,

[6] Thomas Carlyle.

Chilled early by the bigot's curse
The pedant's frown, the worldling's yawn.[7]

Ludlow was the editor, and Kingsley his assistant, but both deferred
to F. D. Maurice. It appeared weekly, was printed by John Parker, and
consisted of short paragraphs giving the religious angle on political
questions of the day, interspersed with articles on a variety of subjects.
Sydney Godolphin Osborne and Tom Hughes (author of *Tom Brown's
Schooldays*) were among the contributors, and it was from this time
that Kingsley's friendship with the hearty Welsh squire dated. Charles
Mansfield and Kingsley provided essays that were designed to help the
working man escape from 'dull bricks and mortar and the ugly colour-
less things which fill the workshop and the factory'. Mansfield — who
wrote about birds — used the pseudonym Will Willow-wren. Kingsley, under the name of Parson Lot[8] wrote two further articles
on the National Gallery, and instructed the labourer to take
comfort from 'those baby cherubs in the old Italian painting. How
gracefully they flutter and sport among the soft clouds, full of rich
young life and baby joy. Yes, beautiful indeed, but just such a one at
this very moment is that once pining, deformed child of thine over
whose death cradle thou wast weeping a month ago.' In the same
article Kingsley affirmed his belief in the right of free entry to national
art collections. 'In the British Museum and in the National Gallery alone
the Englishman may say, "Whatever my coat or my purse, I am an
Englishman and therefore have a right here. I can glory in these noble
halls as if they were my own house."' Three years earlier, in a letter to
Fanny from Oxford, he had told her how much he resented having to
pay a shilling to visit the bones of beloved Democritus Burton at
Christchurch Cathedral. Now he suggested that 'those useless relicts',
the cathedrals of England, should be converted into winter gardens
for the recreation of the working man, though he made no suggestions
about what would grow in them.

During the summer of 1848 Kingsley was frequently in London.
A railway line had now been built between London and Wokingham
and the journey could be done in an hour and a half. His letter from
London often ended with a request to send the brougham to meet
either the two forty or the four forty from Waterloo. Editorial meetings of *Politics for the People* took place at Maurice's house in Lincoln's
Inn or at Parker's in the Strand, and at these two places Kingsley met
many of the leading socialists of the day including Robert Owen

[7] Charles Kingsley, *On the Death of a Certain Periodical.*
[8] Like Lot, Kingsley was alone amid the Cities of the Plain.

of New Lanark Mills fame, and one genuine member of the working classes, Thomas Cooper, the author of a Chartist poem in ten books entitled *The Purgatory of Suicides*. Kingsley introduced himself to Cooper by letter. 'Ever since I read your brilliant poem,' he wrote, 'I have been possessed by a desire to thrust myself, at all risks, into your acquaintance. I felt myself bound to write to you to see if among the nobler spirits of the working classes I could not find one friend who would understand me.' Kingsley and Cooper did in fact become friends and as a result of Kingsley's influence Cooper became a Christian but lost much of the support of his own class. Kingsley eventually saved him from the workhouse by setting up a subscription for him.

Fanny disapproved of her husband's political activities, fearing, with reason, that they would damage his chances of preferment. 'I cannot bear to think that I cause you a pang', he wrote, 'but you must remember that these battles and abuse, painful as they are, are what every man has to go through who does any good'.[9] In another letter he wrote, even more forcefully, 'I will speak in season and out of season. Every man on earth who ever tried to testify against the world has been laughed at, misunderstood, slandered, and that, bitterest of all, by the very people he loved best.' Kingsley was not a man to whom the flouting of public opinion came easily. In a letter to Thomas Hughes he spoke of 'the weak terror I have of offending people, trained as I am to think first, not whether a thing was right or wrong, but whether it would offend Lady A or Mrs B.' He was to pay the penalty of giving offence sooner than he expected. As a result of F. D. Maurice's influence he had recently been made a professor of English Literature at the newly founded Queen's College and had been led to expect the greater honour of a post at King's College. He was now informed by Dr Jelf, the principal of King's, that the post would not be his. An added insult was that it was not given to anyone else.

Undismayed, Kingsley plunged into the writing of his first full-length book, a novel entitled *Yeast; a problem*, the first instalment of which appeared anonymously in the July issue of *Fraser's Magazine*. *Yeast* is indeed a problem today, although in its own day it moved many hearts including that of Fanny, who wanted to be buried with it. This was because many scenes of the courtship of the heroine Argemone by the hero Lancelot Smith, were taken from her real-life romance. It went into fewer editions than any of Kingsley's subsequent novels and after reading it Ludlow implored him never to write another while Mansfield condemned it as 'decorated lies'. Parker, the editor of *Fraser's*, instructed him to bring it to a speedy conclusion because it

[9] ULF No. 96, 1848.

was upsetting his readers. Kingsley obeyed and thereby upset the balance of the book.

The plot of *Yeast* is so slight as to barely cast a shadow. Lancelot, 'a huge awkward Titan cub of a man', is out hunting when he meets the queenly Argemone beside a chapel in the hills, 'her resort every Wednesday and Friday for an hour's mystic devotion, set off by a little graceful asceticism'. So unsettled is he by the 'eye-wedlock' that occurs between them that his seat on his horse is seriously affected and he comes a cropper at the park palings of her father, Squire Lavington. An enforced stay as an invalid at Whitford Priors, Argemone's home, ensues, during the course of which Lancelot is reconverted to Christianity by Argemone. He recovers only to find that all his money has gone in a bank failure. For a time he lives in penury in London, supporting himself by free-lance journalism. He is then removed somewhat peremptorily from the scene by the mysterious Barnakill who transports him to Utopia.

Weak though the book was it showed flashes of Kingsley's power to describe nature with an affectionate humour that was to be his most attractive trait as a writer. The book opens with a description of a morning at the cover side.

A dim, distanceless, day in March. The last brown leaf which had stood the winter's frost spun and quivered plum down, and then lay like an awkward guest at a great dumb dinner party. A cold suck of wind just proved its existence by toothache on the north side of all faces. The spiders, having been bewitched the night before, had unanimously agreed to cover every brake and briar with gossamer cradles, and never a fly to be caught in them, like Manchester cotton spinners madly glutting the markets in the teeth of 'no demand'.

This charming tone was, alas, quickly abandoned, for the intention of the book was a serious one: to air the problems that were exercising the minds of thinking young men of the day. Religious matters were discussed (with Argemone and with a cousin who was about to enter the Church of Rome) and Art was talked over with the artist Claude Mellot. But the chief question to be considered was the condition of the agricultural labourer. With Tregarva, Squire Lavington's young gamekeeper, as a guide, Lancelot sets out to view the species at a country fair and is disillusioned by what he sees.

The ill looks of the young girls surprised him very much. Here and there smiled a plump rosy face enough; but the majority seemed undersized and underfed. He remarked it to Tregarva. The keeper smiled mournfully. 'You see these little creatures dragging home babies in arms nearly as big as themselves, sir. That and bad food, want of milk especially, accounts for their growing up no bigger than they do.'

Matters are no merrier inside the beer tent booth, in spite of the efforts of a singer of folk songs that would have rejoiced the heart of Cecil Sharp.

As soon as Lancelot's eyes were accustomed to the reeking atmosphere, he saw seated at two long temporary tables of board, fifty or sixty men wrangling, stupid, beery, with sodden eyes and drooping lids, interspersed with girls and brazen faced women, with dirty flowers in their caps, whose whole business seemed to be to cast jealous looks at each other and defend themselves from the coarse overtures of their swains.

Lancelot had been perfectly astonished at the foulness of the language that prevailed; he whispered a remark on the point to Tregarva. Tregarva explained that the chief cause of this degradation was wretched housing conditions. He had even written a ballad on the subject entitled *A Rough Rhyme on a Rough Matter*, inserted into Squire Lavington's game book by an enemy. 'How', says the keeper to the squire, 'can he expect decent behaviour among working men

> When packed in one reeking chamber,
>   Man, maid, mother and little ones lay:
> While the rain pattered in on the rotting bride bed,
>   And the walls let in the day.'

Lancelot never actually gets inside one of these rotting hovels. The stench from the sewer in front of one of them is enough for him.

'No wonder you have typhus here,' said Lancelot, 'with this filthy open drain running right before the door. Why can't you clean it out?'

'Where's the water to come from to keep a place clean,' answered the woman peevishly. 'It costs many a one a shilling a week to pay fetching water up the hill. We've work enough to fill our kettles.'

At this moment two cloaked and veiled figures come to the door.

They are Argemone and her sister Honoria, bringing succour

to a child ill with typhus. Unlike Lancelot, they go inside the stricken cottage and Argemone contracts the dread disease and eventually dies in Lancelot's arms, burbling of clean water. 'The Nun Pool! Take all the water, every drop, and wash Ashy clean again. Make a great fountain of it, beautiful marble to burble and gurgle and trickle and foam, for ever and ever, and wash away the sins of the Lavingtons, that the little rosy children may play round it, and the poor toil bent woman may wash and drink — Water!'

Another cause of rural misery, besides dirt, that Kingsley inveighed against in *Yeast* was poaching, or rather the preservation of game that led to poaching. Tregarva devoted some verses of his ballad to the subject:

> There's blood on your new foreign shrubs, squire;
> There's blood on your pointers' feet;
> There's blood on the game you sell, squire,
> And there's blood on the game you eat.

Lancelot then actually meets a poacher, a poor cringing creature whose head bobs up from under a river bank. Tregarva hauls him onto dry land and threatens to confiscate his night lines and his dog which are all that lie between him and the workhouse. 'Crawy' pleads effectually for a few months of fresh air before he goes back to 'prizzum'. We are also introduced to an organised gang of poachers who have come down from London by dogcart and are prepared to murder any keeper who comes between them and their sport.

Yeast is chiefly of interest to the modern reader for the self-portrait it contains of Kingsley as a young man. 'What a horrible ugly face!' says Argemone to herself after the meeting at the chapel, 'but so clever and so unhappy'. We are evidently being presented with the Kingsley of Cambridge days. 'Oh, I remember him well enough,' drawls Lord Vieuxbois, 'he was one of a set who tried to look like blackguards, and really succeeded tolerably. They used to eschew gloves and drink nothing but beer, and smoke disgusting short pipes. They used to make piratical expeditions down to Lynn in eight oars, to attack bargemen, and fen girls, and shoot ducks, and sleep under turf stacks, and come home when they had drunk all the public house taps dry.' We then see this rough-hewn character coming unwillingly under the influence of Argemone.

In the drawing room poor Lancelot, after rejecting overtures from several young ladies, set himself steadily against the wall to sulk and watch Argemone. She spied in a few minutes his melancholy moon struck face, swam up to him and said something kind and commonplace. She spoke in the simplicity of her heart but he chose to think she was patronising him; she had not talked commonplaces to the vicar. He tried to say something smart and cutting, stuttered, broke down, blushed and shrank back against the wall fancying that every eye in the room was on him.

Argemone then set about converting him to Christianity by the use of logic, and was thoroughly routed, as no doubt Fanny had been.

He flew at her as if she had been a very barrister, and hunted her mercilessly up and down through all sorts of charming sophisms, as she begged the question and shifted her ground, as thoroughly right in her conclusion as she was wrong in her reasoning, till she grew quite confused and pettish. And then Lancelot suddenly shrank into his shell, claws and all, like an affrighted soldier-crab, hung down his head, and stammered out some incoherencies, 'N-n-not accustomed to talk to women — ladies I mean! F-forgot myself.'

The last chapters of *Yeast* were written under great strain. During the summer of 1848 Kingsley was virtually doing four jobs simultaneously. Besides writing his novel, he was running his parish single-handed because he could no longer afford a curate. He had to make frequent trips to London in connection with *Politics for the People* and at the same time he was giving his weekly lecture on English Literature at Queen's College, which was no sinecure. His audience there was composed of young women and he welcomed the opportunity to teach them things that 'prudery and fanaticism normally forbade'. His subject was Early English Literature starting with *Beowulf* and his thesis that the Anglo-Saxon, a 'female' race, required impregnation by the great male race, the Norse, before it could produce the famous ballads of the border.

It was also at this time that Kingsley began his lifetime crusade to save the souls of strangers by post. After the publication of *Yeast* he became recognised as one of the few clergymen who, because he admitted to having had doubts himself, might be expected to understand them in others. As Fanny put it, even men of the world, 'fast men', dared to approach him. Defections to Rome were a cause of much concern at the time and clergymen wrote to ask him how to save members of their flocks from Popery; mothers to beg him to rescue their daughters from Romish confessors; while young women, hovering between the attractions of a nunnery and the monotonous duties of family life, laid their difficulties before the author of *The Saint's Tragedy*. One young lady even wrote for a cure for stammering. Some of the letters that reached him bore only the address 'Charles Kingsley, England'. Each received a lengthy and thoughtful answer and the direction of many lives was undoubtedly changed. But the writing of such letters was exhausting. 'One more thing done,' he would say, 'thank God,' as each was written. 'How blessed it will be, when it is all over, to lie down in that dear churchyard.' But it soon became obvious that he could not wait so long for his rest.

One Sunday evening, late in October, Kingsley fell asleep, having got through his two Sunday services with difficulty. He slept late into the next day and when he woke was so exhausted that his doctor ordered a month in Bournemouth in spite of the fact that he had already had two holidays that year, one at Ilfracombe in January and the other in the Fens in the summer with F. D. Maurice and Ludlow. Fanny went on ahead with the children while Charles stayed at Eversley to put his affairs in order. He wrote Fanny a letter in the almost illegible scrawl he adopted when deeply depressed. 'I am quite worn out with going round and seeing everyone today. I am trying to recollect and collect everything, but my brains are half addled. What would life be without you? What is it with you but a brief pain to make us long for everlasting bliss?'

The holiday at Bournemouth was not a success. Fanny put the blame for its failure on Henry, who had once more come to stay. He was now eighteen and it seems almost certain that he had been expelled from King's College School. This would explain why he was neither at school nor at university between 1848 and 1850, but receiving private tuition. Ludlow also hints as much in a letter: 'His family were in great trouble about him, he having got into bad courses while at King's College.' Henry had the black, button-bright eyes of his mother and wit and enthusiasm to match, but these attributes were trying to Charles in his run-down state, as Mansfield confirmed in a letter to Ludlow. 'It seems certain that his brother's presence causes him continual anxiety.'

Kingsley was obliged to continue work on *Yeast* during his stay in Bournemouth. In writing serially, he could never bring himself to get far ahead of the demands of the month, so that he had already published the middle of the novel before he knew how it was going to end. On his return to Eversley he worked in a state bordering on hysteria. It was his custom to write books by composing a paragraph at a time in his head while pacing his famous Quarterdeck and then rushing indoors and committing the paragraph to paper while standing at the shelf that served him as a desk. This method worked well enough when he wrote in the morning, which was the time of day he preferred to work. Now, for lack of time, he had to work far into the night and stride the Quarterdeck by moonlight. By December the book was finished and he was in a state of collapse.

CHAPTER 6

The Year of Collapse
1849

The prostration of Kingsley was complete. He could not write, talking became an effort and after an hour's reading, he told a friend, 'My poor addle brain feels as if someone had stirred it with a spoon'. The exertion of riding or even walking was beyond him. Mansfield who had acted as a companion and nurse while the last pages of *Yeast* were being written now decided that there was only one course left open. He despatched the author and his family down to the West Country.

The house that the Kingsleys took in Ilfracombe did not meet with Fanny's approval and, according to Mansfield she went out nesting and discovered Runnamede Villa, 'a perfect bijou of a place, having everything that could be wished for except a view of the sea'. Here Charles and Fanny and the 'infant pilgrims' as he called Rose and Maurice, settled down.

Kingsley had always been extraordinarily sensitive to the influence of surroundings and climate. It is true that on the first page of *Yeast* he mocked the man whose moral state depended on the barometer 'as if his soul, as well as his lungs, might be saved by sea breezes or his character developed by training him against a South wall', but he was such a man himself. His letters are full of allusions to climatic conditions and his response to them, and two of his most famous poems were written to the north-east and the south winds respectively. Now he was able to write and tell his mother 'a tremendous gale of wind has acted on me exactly like champagne and Cathedral organs in one, and restored my, what you would call *nervous*, and what I would call *magnetic* tone'. In fact it was the greater part of a year before his magnetic tone was completely restored.

When he first came to Ilfracombe Charles was obliged to keep to a strict regime. All mental exertion was forbidden and what letters he wrote were dictated to Fanny who saw that they were short. Fanny also insisted that he allocate a full hour to each of the four meals in the day, instead of jumping up from the table leaving half his food uneaten. 'I am leading a truly hoggish life,' he told his parents, '18 hours sleeping, 4 hours eating, 2 hours walking, 0 hours reading.' To induce eighteen hours' sleep he took a cold bath before going to bed.[1]

With this treatment his physical condition gradually improved and he began to take longer walks, 'although I get a strange swimming in the wits now and then, at seeing farm houses under my feet, and cows feeding like so many flies against a wall'. He even took to going for rides along Morte Sands although these were sad enough affairs, for he felt too close an affinity with his tired hired hack for comfort as he explained in a set of elegiacs he wrote at the time.

> Wearily stretches the land to the surge, and the surge to the cloud-land;
> Wearily onward I ride, watching the water, alone.
> No more on a magical steed borne free through the regions of ether,
> But, like the hack which I ride, selling my sinew for gold.

The last line of this poem contained a reference to F. D. Maurice, 'the oak of the mountain'. It was on Maurice's strength that he relied at this time, although Mansfield was more often with him.

Mansfield was convinced of the efficacy of the Mesmerism with which the two young men had experimented in their Cambridge days. His theory was that by making passes before the eyes of his patient he could hypnotise him and restore his 'animal magnetism'. The method was exhausting to the practitioner and eventually Mansfield had to return to London, having developed toothache and a swollen face after an exceptionally long session. Kingsley sent a letter after him blaming his weakness on his vegetarianism: 'If C. B. Mansfield had the share of beef-and-beer magnetism in him which God intended, he need not fear putting his hand on a fever patient's brow, or eating one either *si bon lui semblait.*' Kingsley now resorted to more conventional tranquillisers and admitted to Mansfield, 'I am being bedrugged. It is humiliating but it is the fashion. One shaves one's beard, one wears a hat, one goes to the university because Englishmen do, why not take medicine for the same reason?'

To health worries were now added money worries. The expenses of renting a holiday house, and paying the salary of a curate at home, were great, and Kingsley had lost the salary that went with his lectureship at Queen's College, while the £500 which he had borrowed from an insurance company had melted away. Nor could he any longer supplement his income with his pen. He did, it is true, write a review of Mrs Jamieson's *Sacred and Legendary Art* for *Fraser's Magazine*, but this

---

[1] ULF No. 103, 1849.

piece of work hung over him for many weeks before he felt strong enough to tackle it, and in several letters he mentioned the prospect of writing it with horror. He eventually started work one wet, windy Sunday in January, while Fanny was away visiting Caroline Warre. 'I have actually begun Mrs Jamieson's review. I am *quite well today*,' he wrote, 'I do not know why, but so it is.'[2] He was not proud of the finished result, dismissing it as 'the music of penny whistle and banjo' compared to the trumpet call of a fellow reviewer. Whatever its quality, it could not be relied on to bring in much money. The ninety-page article entitled 'North Devon' that he wrote for the same magazine, later in the year, only brought in £10.[3]

Finally Kingsley wrote to Ludlow in desperation.

> Can you as a lawyer, as well as a Friend, tell me of *any* means of borrowing £500 for, say, five years, at reasonable interest. By that time either my books may be selling well, or my house may have stopped falling about my ears, or — or God may think we have suffered enough. My father would, but cannot help me, and there-fore I dare not ask him: and as for certain rich connexions of mine, I would die sooner than ask them, who tried to prevent my marriage because forsooth I was poor.

When Mansfield saw the letter he suggested lending Kingsley £140 which was all he had, and promising the balance of the £500 in the near future. Ludlow, however, knowing Kingsley's pride, drew up a document in which the creditor appeared as H. N. Turnstiles. The arrival of Mr Turnstiles's letter at Ilfracombe was a cause of jubilation. Fanny wrote to Ludlow, 'Dear Friend, I believe you have saved my husband fm. going out of his mind and me fm. a broken heart. Yet I am not surprised, for my daring to propose to Charles to tell you our troubles came from a sudden inspiration in Church where I was praying (in quite an agony at the early morning service). Suddenly you came before me and I took courage.' 'Eventually,' wrote Ludlow, 'Mrs Kingsley twigged the trick, and there was a grand scene (of gratitude) though I am not sure that Kingsley quite relished my having been the means of humbugging him.'

Mansfield's attachment to Kingsley had become somewhat morbid since his return to the Church. He even considered taking orders and becoming his curate. There was, however, one obstacle to this; his private life. Many an evening at Eversley had he poured out his

[2] ULF No. 98, January 1849.
[3] ULF 1849.

matrimonial problems not only to Charles, but also to Fanny, who was surprisingly sympathetic and broad-minded in such matters. As a very young man he had been in love with a Miss Gardiner who would have none of him, perhaps because his parents had cut him off. On the rebound he married another woman who was constantly unfaithful to him and eventually eloped to Australia. From that time he started keeping mistresses. One of them was a woman of the lower orders whom he described as 'the Magdalen', another a Mrs Meredith, possibly the faithless wife of George. Whoever she was, her presence would certainly have been an embarrassment at Eversley and Mansfield eventually decided against ordination.

Another friend in trouble at this time was J. A. Froude, eventually to become famous as the historian. Froude was a Fellow of Exeter College and a brother of Richard Hurrell Froude, the short-lived but much-loved friend of John Newman. Kingsley had met him on a visit to Cowley Powles at Oxford. The two men had not taken to each other. To Kingsley, Froude seemed cold and remote, in spite of his charming manners and good looks, while Froude remarked of Kingsley, 'I wish he wouldn't talk Chartism and be always in such a stringent excitement about it all. He dreams of nothing but barricades and provisional governments and grand Smithfield bonfires where the landlords are all roasting in the fat of their own prize oxen.'

When disaster fell on Froude, however, Kingsley was the only man who would receive him. His novel, *Nemesis of Faith*, about a young clergyman with doubts, was condemned by William Sewell, the senior tutor of the college, as heretical. Sewell snatched a copy from an undergraduate during a lecture in the college hall, tore it to pieces and threw it in the fire. There was no alternative for Froude but to resign his Fellowship, and he now found himself penniless, for his father, the formidable Archdeacon of Totnes, had refused to admit his existence. The Kingsleys had moved, in April, to a house further east along the coast, at Lynmouth, in its deep wooded cleft. Charles, without hesitation, offered Froude a refuge in the house. Froude, with equally little hesitation, accepted.

Kingsley's friends were eager to meet the man who was the centre of so much controversy, and both Ludlow and Mansfield hurried down to Lynmouth, only to be disappointed. Mansfield quarrelled with Froude about fiction as a literary form, while Ludlow took against 'that horrible false laugh, which chills the blood in one's veins to hear, that foul sensual mouth and eyes, that made up voice of common talk'. There was one guest that summer, however, who did not find Froude unattractive, and that was Fanny's older sister, the intellectual Charlotte

Grenfell. Charlotte had gone over to Rome two years previously and had now been convinced by her Jesuit confessor, Father Brownhill of Hill Street, that she had a vocation to join the order of St Sepulchrens and become a teaching nun. The sight of poor young Mr Froude, deserted by the world and by his fiancée changed all that. Froude was strongly attracted by Charlotte and proceeded to pay her court. Even the sight of her being seasick all the way to the Island of Lundy on a day trip did not deter him.

Fanny was far from happy about the situation, as she confided in a letter to Ludlow. 'I *hope* I would rather see her in a convent even, than belonging to me again with poor dr. Mr F's views!' Fanny was not alone in deploring 'Mr F's views'. Association with him was doing her husband's reputation no good, and his parents wrote continually, imploring him to send him away. Finally, at the end of a long letter he agreed. 'Whatever may seem to me my duty to Froude, there can be no doubt of my duty to you. And therefore I solemnly promise to get rid of Froude or leave Lynmouth immediately.' But it was too late to save Charlotte. The following January she was married to Froude at St Peter's, Belgrave Square, and never darkened the door of a Catholic church again.

At Lynmouth Kingsley's chief pleasure was collecting specimens on the seashore. He threw himself into this occupation with the earnest enthusiasm he gave to everything he undertook. The successful bottling of a comatula, 'with his legs, by great dodging', ranked as high as the composition of a poem in his estimation. A sentence in a letter to his parents proves this. 'Where, oh where,' he cries, 'is the Venus Maidenhair gone? I have hunted every wet rock shute. Pray inform me; and pray don't say that *Yeast* is written by me.'

Rose and Maurice were still too young to accompany their father on these expeditions as they did in later years. Rose was only three, but we may be sure she was shown all the wonderful specimens her father brought home and preserved in basins of sea water. When Fanny went on a visit to Caroline Warre he was left in charge of the children. He wrote to report, 'Rose is gooder and gooder, and Maurice perfectly beautiful.' When it was Charles's turn to be away from home he wrote Rose long letters about the birds and animals he had seen. The only one that has been preserved he wrote during the Fenland holiday of the summer before his breakdown.

My dear Miss Rose,
    I am writing in such a curious place, a mill where they grind corn. And now I will tell you about the stork. He is called Peter and here

is a picture of him. See what long legs he has and a white body and black wings, and he catches all the frogs and snails and eats them, and when he is cross he opens his big bill, and makes such a horrible clattering rattle. And he comes to the window at teatime to eat bread and butter and he is so greedy, and he gobbled down a pinch of snuff out of Daddy's box, and he was so sick, and we all laughed at him for being so foolish and greedy.

Your own Daddy.

By June Kingsley felt strong enough to return to Eversley. On the way he stopped to see his London friends, and at once he was back on his magical steed, writing ecstatic letters home to Fanny in a huge euphoric hand. He breakfasted with de Bunsen the Prussian ambassador, he called on Carlyle and Francis Newman,[4] he took his brother George, now a medical student, to a soirée at Parker's, and told Fanny, 'George has never seen such *live* men before. He sees a new *avatar* opening before him. Ludlow thinks he has the most remarkable sardonic humour he has ever heard.'[5] He marvelled at F. D. Maurice's speech to a meeting of Chartists, and described him as 'inspired, gigantic, his head like some great awful Giorgione portrait. I will tell you all when I can collect myself.' He even spoke out at a meeting of workmen himself.

The occasion was a memorable one. The meeting had been called by the Christian Socialists who felt, quite rightly, that they were out of touch with the class they wanted to help. Soon several proletarian speakers began attacking the Church for its ineffectiveness, and the meeting seemed about to break up in disorder. It was at this juncture that Kingsley rose to his feet, folded his arms across his chest, and stammered out, 'My f-friends, I am a p-p-parson and a Ch-ch-chartist,' adding, almost in a whisper, 'Ch-church of England, I mean.' He instantly commanded silence and went on to explain how much he sympathised with the Chartists' sense of injustice, but how mistaken he thought their methods were. The men heard him through respectfully, and some were even won over to readiness to co-operate with the Church. The Scottish journalist, David Masson, who was present, reacted differently. He had never heard Kingsley speak and was unprepared for his stutter. Leaning over to a friend after the opening words of the speech he whispered, in broad Aberdonian, 'The man's drunk!'

At Eversley a low fever was brooding over the land, which people expected at any minute would flare up into a cholera epidemic. It was

[4] An Anglican theologian, brother of John Newman.
[5] ULF No. 91, 1849.

difficult to find nurses for the sick, and even with the help of a new curate, Percy Smith, one of the rector's Oxford admirers, the burden of work was heavy. Kingsley had never lost his horror of seeing others in pain. He could not even take his own children to the dentist. It can be imagined therefore what a toll on his strength was taken by long hours at the bedside of fever patients. As a friend pointed out, 'the sight of suffering, the foul scent of a sick room, would haunt him for hours. For all his man's strength there was a deep vein of the *woman* in him.'[6] After a night sitting up with a labourer's wife, the mother of a large family, giving her the nourishment every half hour on which her life depended, Kingsley broke down completely. After only two months the fiery steed was once more the hired hack.

Again Kingsley longed for the West Country, but this time he longed for something else also: to be away from Fanny. There can be no doubt that Fanny's presence was not always soothing. Deeply though the Kingsleys loved each other, their temperaments were profoundly different. Fanny, for all her good qualities, was bossy, bustling and anxious about appearances. Charles was impractical, forgetful and not much good with money. In many ways their natures complemented each other. There was a famous occasion, soon after their marriage, when Charles in church read the Apostles' Creed instead of the Athanasian, that was appointed to be read that Sunday. He disappeared from the church and, after a long interval, was discovered by Fanny sitting on a tombstone looking a picture of despair. 'Fanny, what shall I do?' he said. It seemed that the sermon he had prepared dealt with the problem of damnation raised in the Athanasian creed. Fanny, undismayed, procured the key of the rectory from a servant, selected an alternative sermon, and escorted her husband back into the church.[7]

But too often Fanny's desire to be helpful took the form of scolding. Even before they were married Charles had been obliged on one occasion to chide her for 'a very solemn old maidish attack on a poor lonely country curate for unpunctuality'.[8] After their marriage the scoldings had become more frequent. Charles lost tax returns, bills and letters. He forgot birthdays and, worse still, wedding anniversaries.[9]

[6] Letter from John Martineau.

[7] Violet Martineau, *John Martineau: Pupil of Charles Kingsley*.

[8] ULF No. 30, October 28, 1843.

[9] John Martineau bore this out in his memoir on Kingsley. He wrote of 'an impatience of petty matters of daily life which made him a bad guardian of his own interests, and, but for the tender assistance that was ever at his side, would almost have overwhelmed him with anxieties'. There is an amusing note written to Fanny in 1866 which simply runs, 'I have the most unpleasant feeling of having come away forgetting something. But I cannot recollect what it can be.'

Gradually Fanny had assumed control in practical matters. It will be remembered that Charles had insisted, at the time of their marriage, that she should have all but £100 a year of his income. As a result, appeals like 'I have but £3 of my £10 left. Please send me another cheque',[10] appeared frequently in his letters. From time to time he attempted to take a hand in his own financial affairs, always with disastrous results. There is a letter to Phelps, his wine merchant, preserved at Sackville College, East Grinstead, in which he admits, 'through pressure of business and Mrs Kingsley's illness', to having lost all his wine bills for the last three years and sends '26 pro tem'.[11] When called to account by Fanny to explain these confusions he would plead severe headaches: 'My head is swimming so, and aching, that I can hardly see my pen.'[12] To Alexander Macmillan, who was to become his publisher, he once wrote, 'I wonder whether I shall always be in Mr Micawber's purgatory — Income £20 p.a., expenditure £20.0s. 0½d, result total misery; or ever attain to his paradise — Income, £20 p.a., expenditure £19.19.11½d, result total felicity?'

Fanny was not unaware that she too had faults.

I chafe you with my Martha-ism and efforts after *Order*, you chafe me by little unpunctualities, and then comes the Wall and we must shout to hear each other. I will try to conquer my faults and not be angry when you remind me of them. I know I am ready to confess them in letters and yet get so angry if you try to do me good by my confession and use the power which I freely put into your hands — which you never do because of my odious temper. When we are out of debt, poetry will return. Then I will look, and speak and kiss as I once did.[13]

Charles, too, longed for an end to this bickering and on more than one occasion expressed the hope that 'one day we shall understand each other and grow closer as we grow older and *calmer*'.[14]

And so, for a real rest, he chose to go to Clovelly alone. He returned to it with the same joy that he had as a London schoolboy. 'I cannot believe my eyes: the same place, the pavement, the same dear old smells, the dear old handsome loving faces. It is as if I was a little boy again.' In a letter to his mother he wrote, 'This is the place. The wounded bird

[10] ULF No. 107, August 1849.
[11] April 26, 1853.
[12] ULF No. 127, June 1852.
[13] Unpublished letter from Fanny, March 14, 1854.
[14] ULF No. 122, 1850.

goes back to the nest; and I believe firmly in the *magnetic* effect of the place where one has been bred, not to mention that I am perhaps the only Englishman I ever met who has continually the true *heimweh* homesickness of the Swiss and the Highlanders. The very smell is a fragrance from the fairy gardens of childhood.'

He took lodgings with Mrs Whitehouse in a cottage on a terrace near the top of the steeply sloping street (now called Kingsley House), and spent his first evening 'running in and out of all the houses, like a ferret in a rabbit burrow'. For the next few days he was too prostrated to do anything but sit in his little first-floor room being visited by Old Wimble, a fisherman he had known as a child, 'who potters in, like an old grey-headed Newfoundland dog, about three times a day to look after me in all sorts of kind and unnecessary ways'. He wrote to tell Ludlow, 'I am as stupid as a porpoise, and lie in the window, and smoke and watch the clouds crawl across the bay, and draw little sketches of figures, and do not even dream, much less think'. The little sketches of which he spoke were a cause of some embarrassment to Fanny, judging by Kingsley's frequent requests for her approval of them. Remarks like 'I wonder whether you have looked at the drawings', and 'I wonder whether I shall displease you in sending you more drawings', occur frequently in his letters at this time and understandably. For these drawings were even more erotic than the illustrations for *The Life of St Elizabeth* into which he had poured the longings of a previous separation. The subjects in this series were a naked man and a woman. In one sketch they floated across the sea intertwined on a wooden cross. The couple was supposed to be the artist Claude Mellot and his wife Sabina, 'two of my most darling ideals with a scrap of conversation annexed to each, just embodying bits of my dreams about married love and its relations to art'. Kingsley always identified one side of himself closely with Mellot, and Sabina undoubtedly represented Fanny.

Without Fanny, he suffered from appalling loneliness and a sense of real physical deprivation.

These soft, hot, damp days fill me with yearning love; your image haunts me day and night as it did before we were married, and the thought of that delicious sanctuary . . . [the next words were scratched out by Fanny] . . . And yet you see I do not come home. I suppose I am a humbug, but I know both are true, my solitary enjoyment here, my yearning after you. I long, long, long for you, but I know that if I can keep from loneliness I am better away for a while.[15]

15 ULF Nos. 105 and 117, August 17, 1849 and May 23, 1850.

Fanny resented her husband's need to be without her. She could accept that he should be away from her in the course of duty but 'when you go away from self-inflicted absence I am in such a blind agony that I can see and learn nothing but that you are away and happy and I am left behind and miserable. Wicked of me!'[16]

Yet Charles proved to have been right in insisting on a separation. Strength now gradually ebbed back into his mind and body and on August 20th he felt able to undertake a memorable expedition to the Island of Lundy with his landlord, Mr Whitfield ('a reformed smuggler'), Mrs Whitfield ('a Wesleyan prophetess') and some 'Captains' daughters, as pretty, unassuming, well dressed a set of little things as you can see'. The crossing was no matter for weaklings. It started at six a.m. and the craft was a trawler 'with a huge boom swaying and sweeping backwards and forwards across the deck'.[17] Kingsley, however, revelled as much in the rough motion of a boat as that of a horse. 'There was all the wind as we could carry on full sail, and a sea not more than eight feet high. With the air, and the rush of the boat and the cliffs and the clouds it was perfect.' As the ship slipped away under the deer park cliffs of Clovelly Court Mrs Whitfield gave out the morning hymn,

> apparently as a matter of course. With hardly a demur, one sweet voice after another arose; then a man gained courage, and chimed in with a full harmonious bass, then an alto made itself heard, as it wandered in and out between the voices of men and women; and at last a wild mellow tenor, which we discovered after much searching to proceed from the most unlikely looking lips of an old mummified chrysalis of a man, who stood aft, steering with his legs and showing no sign of life except when he slowly and solemnly filled his nose with snuff.

A whole day was spent on the island. Kingsley recorded 'we dined at the Farmhouse, dinner costing me 1s 9d, and then rambled over the island. Oh that I had been a painter for that day at least!'[18] No doubt it was on this occasion that he saw 'the cyclopean wall of granite cliff which forms the western side of Lundy'. It was from this point, three hundred feet above 'the sapphire rollers of the vast Atlantic' that Amyas Leigh, the blinded hero of *Westward Ho!*, finally said farewell to the sea, and to his old enemy, Don Guzman, who sat eternally drinking

---

[16] Unpublished letter from Fanny, March 14, 1854.

[17] Charles Kingsley, 'North Devon' *Prose Idylls*.

[18] A. and M. Langham, *Lundy*, David and Charles.

wine in his cabin fathoms below. The journey back in the trawler was as gay as the one out, but the tone had deteriorated. Hymns were replaced by bawdy smugglers' songs.[19]

By the end of August Kingsley decided that the air of Clovelly was too relaxing and that he required the high winds that blow about the tors of Dartmoor. His need for a change of scene was intensified by his longing not only for Fanny, but for Rose and Maurice. 'How I long after them and their prattle,' he wrote. 'I delight in all the little ones in the street for their sake, and continually I start and fancy I hear their voices outside.'

On the way to Dartmoor he stayed with an old tutor of his Cambridge days, the Rev Thomas Drosier of Colebrook, near Crediton, where the troublesome Henry was being prepared for Oxford with two other boys. Drosier, who Kingsley described as 'the most angelic of men, with his handsome grey head and his imperturbable sweetness', was evidently getting on well with Henry 'whom he treated as a playfellow rather than a pupil'.

And so at last to the Moor. 'I am quite in spirits at the notion of the Moor. It will give me continual excitement and *it is quite new to me*',[20] Kingsley told Fanny rather puzzlingly, for it will be remembered he had spent several months there after coming down from Cambridge. He hit upon the idea of walking across Dartmoor from north to south, throwing a fly across any stream that should come his way. He started from Chagford and pursued the River Teign to its source at almost the highest point of the moor. On this part of the journey he was accompanied by Mr Perrott, the owner of the local fishing tackle shop.[21] Presumably here he and Mr Perrott parted company for, if not, the latter would have been more than a little surprised by the young Clergyman's behaviour as he marched jubilantly southward, covering twenty miles a day. So high were his spirits that in a Druid circle he broke into verse and, on top of a tor as big as a castle, he fell on his knees in prayer, 'for it seemed the only true state to be in in a place so primeval and so awful'. Wherever he went he gathered leaves, moss and fossil birch bark and stuffed them into his letters home, a sure sign of happiness. The finest moment of all was his first glimpse of Holne, after four silent hours of walking over 'the titanic ridges of Cater's Beam. It more than justified your praises and drawings,' he told his father, 'the first gleam of spires and woods and chequered fields, the

[19] Charles Kingsley, 'North Devon' *Prose Idylls*.

[20] ULF No. 107, August 1849.

[21] I am indebted for this information to Edgar Dodd who met Perrott seventy years ago. At that time he was over eighty, but still busy tying trout flies.

first creak of plough and murmur of the hidden Dart'. Drinking in all this beauty, he thought of those who never saw such sights, the Chartists and their families who lived in the evil, reeking alleys of London. As he strode across the Moor he composed one of the songs that appeared in his next novel, *Alton Locke*.

Weep weep weep and weep,
For pauper, dolt, and slave!
Hark! from wasted moor and fen,
Feverous alley, stifling den,
Swells the wail of Saxon men,
    Work! or the grave!

Down, down, down and down
With idler, knave and tyrant!
Why for sluggards cark and moil?
He that will not live by toil
Has no right to English soil!
    God's word's our warrant!

Up, up, up and up!
Face your game and play it!
The night is past, behold the sun!
The idols fall, the lie is done!
The Judge is set, the doom begun!
    Who shall stay it?

By September the 'joyous knight errant of God'[22] was home at Eversley and in the saddle once more, ready to tilt at a new monster, more terrible than any he had so far encountered.

[22] Charles Kingsley, *Elegy*, 1848.

CHAPTER 7

Alton Locke
1849–1851

Cholera was an ever present terror in the London of the 'thirties and 'forties, and two of the most severe outbreaks, those of 1832 and 1849, had started in Jacob's Island, a notorious area of Bermondsey, so-called because it was surrounded by tidal ditches. Immediately upon his return to Eversley, Kingsley read an article about this unsavoury place in *The Morning Chronicle*, describing it as 'the Venice of the drains'. The writer went into some detail about Mill Lane (now Mill Street), which formed its western boundary, telling of the 'wooden galleries and sleeping rooms which overhang the dark flood so that the place has positively the air of a Flemish Street flanking a sewer instead of a canal'. He went on to describe the water of that sewer which looked 'as solid as black marble, and yet we were assured that this was the only water the wretched inhabitants had to drink'.

Kingsley's blood was on the boil once more. He rushed up to London and, in company with Mansfield, insisted on a conducted tour of Jacob's Island. The area consisted of a rectangle of narrow streets to the east of St Saviour's Dock (an inlet from the Thames that may once have formed the estuary of the River Neckinger). Ten years earlier, in *Oliver Twist*, Dickens had described it as

the filthiest, the strangest, the most extraordinary of the many localities that are hidden in London, wholly unknown, even by name, to the great mass of its inhabitants . . . surrounded by a muddy ditch, six or eight feet deep, and fifteen or twenty wide when the tide is in, once called Mill Pond[1] but known in these days as Folly Ditch. It is a creek or inlet from the Thames, and can always be filled at high water by opening the sluices at the Lead Mills . . . At such times, a stranger, looking from one of the wooden bridges thrown across it at Mill Lane, will see the inhabitants of the houses on either side lowering from their back doors and windows, buckets,

[1] So called because it was once the mill pond of Bermondsey Abbey.

pails, domestic utensils of all kinds, in which to haul the water up; and when his eye is turned from these operations to the houses themselves, his utmost astonishment will be excited by the scene before him. Crazy wooden galleries common to the backs of half a dozen houses, with holes from which to look upon the slime beneath; windows, broken and patched; with poles thrust out, on which to dry the linen that is never there; rooms so small, so filthy, so confined, that the air would seem too tainted even for the dirt and squalor they shelter; wooden chambers thrusting themselves out above the mud, and threatening to fall into it — as some have done; dirt-besmeared walls and decaying foundations; every repulsive lineament of poverty, every loathsome indication of filth, rot, and garbage; all these ornament the banks of Folly Ditch.

It was to a rabbits' warren of houses in Mill Lane that Bill Sykes fled after murdering Nancy, and from a chimney of one of these that he hanged himself while attempting to escape.

Kingsley was to discover that neither Dickens nor *The Morning Chronicle* had exaggerated.

Oh God, what I saw! People having no water to drink, hundreds of them, but the water of the common sewer which stagnated, full of dead fish, cats and dogs, under their windows. At the time the cholera was raging, Walsh saw them throwing untold horrors into the ditch, and then dipping out the water and drinking it! And mind, these are not dirty debauched Irish, but honest hard-working citizens. It is most pathetic to see the poor souls struggling for cleanliness, to see how they scrub and polish their little scrap of pavement and then go through the house and see society leaving at the back poisons and filth such as would drive a lady mad with disgust in twenty-four hours. Talk of the horrors of the middle passage! Oh, that one tenth of the money which has been spent on increasing, by mistaken benevolence, the cruelties of the slave trade, had been spent on buying up these nests of typhus, consumption and cholera, and rebuilding them as habitations fit — I do not say for civilised Englishmen — that would be too much — but for hogs even.

He was soon snapping at the heels of those in authority, like a zealous collie attempting to move a herd of lethargic sheep. He sought interviews with the Prime Minister, Lord John Russell, and with Lord Carlisle, and obtained one with Bishop Samuel Wilberforce at Oxford.

He begged Sydney Osborne to fire one of his bombshells at *The Times* and Tom Taylor to bring the scandal to the notice of the readers of *Punch*. He urged Fanny, who was staying once more with Caroline Warre, to persuade her husband to bring up the matter in the House of Commons. He insisted that a public meeting be called as soon as possible. In the meantime, unable to wait even for this, he set about organising a water supply for Jacob's Island single-handed, or rather with the aid of a handful of friends. He bought a water cart, hitched a horse to it and from it filled great oak casks placed on the street corners. Mansfield and Ludlow shared the work with him until, after a few weeks, the inhabitants stole not only the brass cocks off the barrels, but the barrels themselves, and as a contemporary remarked, 'went back to drinking gin, which was no doubt healthier than ditchwater'.

It was several years, and another cholera epidemic later, that clean water eventually came to Jacob's Island. The water that the Southwark and Vauxhall Water Company had begun to supply by 1857 was neither constant nor pure, for some of it was drawn from the tidal reaches of the Thames, in contravention of an act passed in that year.[2] It was not until around 1860 that Folly Ditch finally went underground.[3]

Kingsley meanwhile set about writing a new novel, which was designed to portray, not only the dreadful living conditions of families in the East End, but also the appalling working conditions of tailors in the West End. He had already published a stirring pamphlet on the subject, *Cheap Clothes and Nasty*, the fruit of some extensive 'tailor hunting' in London. In this pamphlet he explained the sweating system by which a disreputable tailor, the owner of a 'plate glass palace' in the West End, instead of having his work done on the premises, sent it out to a series of 'sweaters' or middlemen whose employees worked in freezing attics on starvation wages. Alton Locke, the hero of Kingsley's novel of the same name, worked in such a place, in a room named by its inmates 'the Conscrumptive hospital — a'cause yer'll die here six months sooner nor if you worked in the room below. You get all the other floors stinks up here as well as your own.' Yet Locke did not fall as low as his colleague Bob Porter who literally became the prisoner

---

[2] Dr D. M. Connan, *History of the Public Health Department in Bermondsey*, 1936.

[3] The wide sloping pavement outside The Ship Aground in Wolsely Street is a reminder that the public house once stood beside Folly Ditch. Apart from this there are few remnants of the old Jacob's Island except for the name of the street that intersects it which is still Jacob Street. The area is now one of vast blocks of post-war council flats. Even the cliff-like Victorian warehouses lining St Saviour's dock are silent now, but fortunately no longer under the threat of demolition. They have recently been declared a conservation area as a result of the efforts of the Bermondsey and Rotherhithe Society.

of a sweater who took as much for the diet of bread, butter and tea, on which he fed his workers, as he gave in wages. Because the men had pawned even their communal coat, known as the 'releaver', not one of them had set foot outside the door for six weeks. It was from this place that stout Farmer Porter, shouting 'My barn, my barn', carried his son 'unwashed, unshaven, shrunken to a skeleton' in a famous scene from the book.[4]

During much of his year of illness Kingsley had been planning another novel. At first he had considered a second volume of *Yeast* (which he had originally envisaged as a trilogy) in spite of the fact that this would involve the resurrection of Argemone. But then a series of letters he had been receiving from Thomas Cooper took hold of his imagination, and complete scenes of *Alton Locke* began to flash upon his mind.[5] According to his younger daughter, Mary, 'it was always his habit to put down a scene, description or dialogue just as it occurred to him, leaving all linking up and filling in to a final rewriting of his book.'[6] A sentence from a recently discovered letter to Fanny shows the process at work. 'I have done his Conversion at the end, and today his becoming a poet towards the beginning.'[7]

The book that resulted from this method of writing was, as might be expected, good in parts; those parts that had come easily off the pen. Certainly it is the only one of Kingsley's novels that is still regularly read, apart from *The Water-Babies*, if only by students of Victorian social conditions. Within the last five years two new editions have appeared, each with a specially written introduction.[8] Carlyle, upon whom the character of Sandy Mackaye was probably based, summed it up best. 'While welcoming a new explosion of red hot shot against the Devil's Dung-heap I must admit your book is definable as crude. The impression is of a fervid creation left half chaotic.'

The plot of *Alton Locke* can be briefly summarised. Locke is the son of a poor Baptist mother who apprentices him to a tailor and then turns him out of the house for reading books in an attempt to improve

---

[4] Kingsley felt so strongly on this matter that he even established a tailor's co-operative workshop in Castle Street and persuaded Bishop Wilberforce to buy his servants' liveries there. The concern came to an abrupt end when Walter Cooper, the man in charge, absconded with the funds.

[5] Louis Cazamian, in *Kingsley et Thomas Cooper Etude sur une Source d'Alton Locke*, has proved almost conclusively that the character of Locke was based on that of Thomas Cooper, the Cockney poet.

[6] Lucas Malet, Preface to *The Tutor's Story*.

[7] ULF No. 110, 1849.

[8] Collins, 1967, with an introduction by David Lodge, and Everyman, 1969, with an introduction by Thomas Byrom.

himself. He takes refuge with Sandy Mackaye, the philosopher book-seller, who encourages him to write poems, and is for a time taken up by a Cambridge dean with whose daughter, Lilian he falls in love. However, he soon realises that his place is with his own class, becomes involved with a riot of Norfolk labourers, and does a spell in prison. After some harrowing experiences in Bermondsey he takes ship for an American Utopia but dies, a convert to Christianity, on the way.

In spite of the understandable anger that the book aroused, Kingsley claimed that its message was not a revolutionary one. 'The moral of my book,' he told a critic, 'is that the working man who tries to desert his class and rise above it, enters into a lie.' He considered the upper classes were those best fitted to govern, but they lacked a sense of responsibility towards the workers. The workers, meanwhile, should improve their own lot by education and co-operation, and not attempt to take over the government of the country.

Yet the savage picture that Kingsley drew of the sufferings of the hungry 'forties might certainly have aroused revolutionary sentiments in the breast of others, even if not in his own. The theme had already been treated in other recent novels of the time, notably in Disraeli's *Sybil* (1845) and Mrs Gaskell's *Mary Barton* (1848), which Kingsley had reviewed favourably.[9] Yet Mrs Gaskell's picture of artisan life in Manchester, pathetic as it was, could not touch Kingsley's lurid portrayal of the London scene.

Of that small band [wrote Frederick Harrison in *Forum* in 1895] Charles Kingsley was the most outspoken, and most eloquent and assuredly the most effective. When we remember how widely this vague initiative has spread and developed, when we read *Alton Locke* and *Yeast* again and note how much practically has been done in the last forty years to redress the abuses against which the books uttered the first burning protest, we may form an estimate of all that the present generation of Englishmen owes to Kingsley.

Alton Locke was a book of the 'tremendous school of literature, ever at the highest pitch', as John Brown, the gentle author of *Rab and his Friends*, put it, adding, 'The book is my especial horror.' Certainly not even a Dickens or a Harrison Ainsworth could have conjured up

[9] A letter has recently come to light that suggests that Kingsley called on Mrs Gaskell while attending a conference at Manchester about this time. On the same occasion he visited the famous shop in Toad Lane, Rochdale, where the Co-operative Movement had its beginnings. ULF No. 431, 1849.

more nightmarish slums than did Kingsley in the description of Jem
Downes' house on Jacob's Island.

What a room! A low lean-to with wooden walls, without a single
article of furniture; through the broad chinks of the floor shone up,
as it were, ugly glaring eyes ... the reflections of the rushlight in the
sewer below. The stench was frightful — the air heavy with pesti-
lence. The first breath I drew made my heart sink, and my stomach
turn. But I forgot everything in the object which lay before me, as
Downes tore a half-finished coat off three corpses laid side by side on
the bare floor.

There was his little Irish wife — dead — and naked; the wasted
white limbs gleamed in the lurid light; the unclosed eyes stared, as
if in reproach, and on each side of her a little, shrivelled, impish,
child corpse — the wretched man had laid their arms round the
dead mother's neck — and there they slept, their hungering and
wailing over at last for ever; the rats had been busy with them —
but what matter to them now?

Jem Downes saw that there could be only one fitting climax to such
a scene. He threw himself in Folly Ditch.

Locke rushed out on the balcony after him. The light of the police-
man's lantern glared over the ghastly scene — along the double row
of miserable house-backs, which lined the sides of the open tidal
ditch, over strange rambling jetties and balconies and sleeping sheds,
which hung on rotting piles over the black waters, with phos-
phorescent scraps of rotten fish gleaming and twinkling out of the
dark hollows, like devilish grave lights — over bubbles of poisonous
gas, and bloated carcasses of dogs and lumps of offal, floating
in the stagnant olive green hell-broth, over the slow sullen rows of
oily ripples which were dying away in the darkness beyond, sending
up, as they stirred, hot breaths of miasma — the only sign that a
spark of humanity, after years of foul life, had quenched itself at
last in that foul death.

After Jem's suicide Alton is struck down with brain fever and there
follows a long dream sequence which a critic[10] has described as 'one
of the strangest and most remarkable passages in nineteenth-century
fiction'. Not the least strange element in this fantasy was its foreshadow-
ing of the idea of evolution many years before the publication of the

[10] Naomi Lewis, B.B.C. broadcast, June 10, 1969.

Origin of Species. Alton dreams that he is 'a madrepore rooted to the rock, the lowest form of created life'. Gradually he crawls out on to the shore, as a crab, and into the forest as a prehistoric mylodon,

> a vast sleepy mass with elephantine limbs and a little meek rabbit's head . . . Intense and new was the animal delight, to plant my hinder claws at some tree-foot, deep into the black rotting vegetable-mould which steamed rich gases up wherever it was pierced, and clasp my huge arms round the stem of some palm or tree-fern; and then slowly bring my enormous weight and muscle to bear upon it, till the stem bent like a writhe, and the laced bark cracked, and the fibres groaned and shrieked, and the roots sprung up out of the soil: and then, with a slow circular wrench, the whole tree was twisted bodily out of the ground, and the maddening tension of my muscles suddenly relaxed, and I sank sleepily down on the turf, to browse upon the crisp tart foliage, and fall asleep in the glare of sunshine which streamed through the new gap in the green forest roof.

After many aeons the mylodon becomes a young ape, 'and as I looked down into the clear waters paved with unknown water lilies, I saw my face — a melancholy, thoughtful countenance, with large projecting brow — it might have been a negro child's. And I felt stirring in me germs of a higher consciousness.'

The dream has a faintly erotic tone, for throughout Alton's incarnations Lilian is present, although distant and unattainable. At one moment she becomes the flowers of a tree 'great sea green lilies, and nestled in the heart of each, the bust of a beautiful girl. Their white bosoms and shoulders . . . rosy white against the emerald petals.' At another she wanders, decked like Eve in bird's feathers, through the forest where Alton sits, now a mighty ape, lusting to tear her limb from limb. For, as the child-ape matured, he had become bestial once more, and the process of 'devolution' which Kingsley was to enlarge upon in *The Water-Babies*, took place. 'I saw year by year my brow recede, my neck enlarge, my jaw protrude, my teeth become tusks.'

In this portrait of an ape Kingsley in a sense saw himself. After five years of marriage he still felt himself to be foul, unclean: what he touched, he defiled. At the time of his wedding he had persuaded himself that, by mortification, his body could be made worthy of Fanny's. Now he wrote, in a wedding anniversary letter, 'I sometimes feel that I am a sham; that I am living with you on false pretences; that if you found me out you would hate me. I sometimes feel the highest form of love would be to love utterly the person who utterly hated and despised one.'[11] These feelings of guilt may have been increased by Fanny's growing lack of enthusiasm for love, no doubt induced by her poor health at this time. 'I long to be back in your arms,' he told her, 'while all you long for, you cruel, cold, darling beauty is, I find, to sleep by my side!'[12] Yet the couple were happy together, so happy that Kingsley felt, sooner or later, divine retribution would fall upon them, for such happiness must be paid for. 'When I look back upon the years since I married you, I see nothing but one steady current of prosperity, which frightens me. Much has been given and much will be required.'[13]

Life at the rectory ran smoothly in the early years of the 'fifties and a young boy, writing home to his mother, has left us a vivid picture of it. John Martineau, a cousin of the formidable lady author Harriet Martineau, was a boy of barely fifteen when he came to Eversley as a resident pupil. He died there, in what he called 'the enchanted place', sixty years later, still a devoted disciple, was buried at Kingsley's feet and commemorated his beloved master by endowing several ornately carved labourers' dwellings known as the Kingsley Cottages. Kingsley had been seeking a pupil for a year before he found Martineau but, in spite of Maurice's recommendations, he was offered 'only a dunce of sixteen, quite impossible'. Martineau's parents, however, were not put off by Kingsley's liberal political views, for they shared them. They entrusted their shy and silent son to him because he was too delicate for public school, but removed him after a year because he was becoming too attached to his master.

Martineau's first letter home gave a picture of several of the rectory's inhabitants.

Mr Kingsley is rather grave, and like me, never laughs; but he is very kind and I like him very much. His stammer is very unpleasant to listen to; it seems to be worse some days than others, and has been particularly bad today. He says he has not been quite well today, so that accounts for it. Mrs Kingsley is very delicate, I believe, and has had influenza for some time. She has only been out three times since Christmas. She is particularly kind and attentive; she insists on my having my fire lighted when I get up in the morning, and again to go to bed by. A broken brace end that I happened to leave on my

---

[11] ULF No. 114, January 1850.
[12] ULF No. 100, May 1849.
[13] ULF No. 114, January 1850.

table I found ready mended the next time I came into the room.
I have a nice large room but I am not to work (or, as Mr Kingsley
calls it, 'Grind') in my room at all. The dog Dandy has become
attached to me. He followed me to church on Sunday. I had just
opened the pew door when I looked down and there he was, somewhat to my horror, swinging his great tail and wriggling his body
about![14]

Dandy was a long-bodied, short-legged Dandy Dinmont Scotch
Terrier with brown eyes peering out appealingly through thick yellow
hair. A dog very like him had been Kingsley's constant companion at
Cambridge. Indeed it was by this dog that the cook at Magdalene remembered him: 'Mr Kingsley? I knew him. When it was time to pay
the bill for dog meat, he'd look down at the dog and say, "Gad sir,
why can't you go out and work for your living?"' Dandy used to
accompany his master on all his walks about the parish and never
missed a cottage lecture. A stone bearing the inscription *Fideli Fideles*
marked his grave on the lawn at Eversley, under the Scotch firs. It was
flanked by those of Sweep, a fine black retriever, and Victor, a dachs-
hund who was presented to Kingsley by the Queen and spent the
last two nights of its life in his arms.

Kingsley was exceedingly fond of animals. It was, after all, he who
first put into verse the suggestion that lame dogs should be helped
over stiles. Indeed he was far from sure that another life did not await
them beyond the grave. Of a swarm of bees he once wrote, 'How do
we *know* they have no souls?' and in a letter to Fanny before his
marriage he wrote, 'the dear dumb creatures who even now seek their
meat from God, are groaning and travailing with us for the day when
He shall in person renew the earth and make it all Eden!'[15] He was
particularly fond of cats. The stable always had its white cat, and the
house its black or tabby, and their master never tired of watching their
graceful movements. On the lawn dwelt a family of natter jacks (running toads), who lived on from year to year in the same hole in the
bank, which the scythe was never allowed to approach. The rector
also had two friends in a pair of sand-wasps, who lived in a crack of the
window in his dressing room, one of which he saved from drowning
in a hand basin. The fly catcher, who built its nest every year under his
bedroom window, was a friend of his, as was the slow worm in the

[14] Violet Martineau, *John Martineau, Pupil of Charles Kingsley*, 1909.
[15] It is true he once denied a soul to a tiny creature of the sea shore, *Nelicerta Ringens*,
but that was in a letter to Philip Gosse, whose stern Protestant theology he may have
feared offending.

churchyard which his parishioners were warned not to kill, from the mistaken idea in Eversley that slow worms were poisonous. All these tastes he encouraged in his children, teaching them to handle toads, frogs and beetles without a shudder. His guests were surprised one morning at breakfast when Rose ran up to the open window of the dining room holding a repulsive-looking worm in her hand. 'Oh daddy! Look at this *delightful* worm!' she cried. He was obliged, however, to admit to his children that he was terrified of spiders.

During the autumn of 1850 the country was in a state of unrest. Work was slack, and as winter approached, gangs of house-breakers and men who preferred begging and robbery to the workhouse, wandered about Hampshire, Surrey and Sussex. The rector of the nearby parish of Frimley was murdered in his garden and the foot-marks of a marauder were found in the flower-beds of Eversley. John Martineau wrote an excited letter home. Some of the servants, he explained, thought the footmarks had been made by the ghost of Cope's notorious bailiff, Clacy (lately dead) but Mr Kingsley knew better and had bolts put on all the doors. An ingenious system of strings attached to bells in the maids' rooms was constructed and at two thirty one morning all the bells started ringing. Kingsley, who slept with a gun and two pistols by his bed, rushed downstairs but Mr Lees, a young man he was preparing for ordination, was under the impression the murderer had reached the upper landing, and prepared to defend the bedrooms. 'He [Lees] looked immensely absurd,' wrote young John Martineau, 'with only a thin pair of trousers and slippers and a nightshirt on, crouching along through the doorway, presenting his pistol, expecting to have to shoot someone the next instant.' The rector meanwhile had rushed outdoors and emptied his gun at a point in the darkness above the head of the wildly barking Dandy. As no slug could be found on the ground the next day it was assumed it had found its mark, although evidently without fatal results.

After Kingsley's death John Martineau wrote a memoir of him which Fanny included in her book. Although it lacked the immediacy of his boyhood letters, it adds some interesting details about Kingsley and gives a vivid picture of his behaviour at table.

He ate hurriedly and it was an effort to him to sit still through a meal. His coat frequently had a white line across the back, made by his habit of leaning against the whitened chimney-piece of the dining-room during breakfast and dinner. Once, in the long summer days, we were condemned to a more than usually dull dinner-party at a neighbour's house, where the only congenial person was a young scientific doctor from the next parish. After dinner, it being broad daylight, we were all in the garden, and opposite to us were two high thick foliaged trees. I do not know which of the two suggested it, but in an instant his coat and the doctor's were off, and they were racing each other, each up his tree, like schoolboys, one getting first to the top, the other first down again to the ground.

Another first-hand description of life at the rectory at this time has been left us by Charles Kegan Paul, one of the group of young men who admired the author of *The Saint's Tragedy* at Oxford. He came originally to stay at the local inn as the guest of Kingsley's curate, Percy Smith. However, the morning after his first dinner with the Kingsleys, he received a note from the rector headed 'Bed, this morning', inviting him to come and stay. From then on Eversley became for him too 'the enchanted place'. Many years later he wrote:

The picturesque bow-windowed Rectory rises to memory, as it stood with all its doors and windows open on certain hot summer days, the sloping bank with its great fir trees, the garden — the sweep of drive before the drawing room and dining rooms, a grass plot before the study, hedged off from the walk — and the tall active figure of the rector, his complexion dark, his eye bright and piercing, tramping up and down one or the other. His energy made him seem everywhere, and to pervade every part of the house and garden. The manuscript of the book he was writing lay open on a rough desk in his study; his pupils were working in the dining room; his guests perhaps lounging on the lawn. And he had time for all, going from writing, to lecturing on a passage from Virgil, from this to a vehement conversation with a guest or tender care of his wife — who was far from strong — or a romp with his children. He would work himself into a sort of white heat over his book, till, too excited to write more, he would calm himself down by a pipe, pacing his grass plat with long strides. He was a great smoker, and tobacco was to him a needful sedative. He always used long clean clay pipes which lurked in all sorts of unexpected places about the parish. But none was ever smoked which was in any degree foul, and when there was a vast accumulation of old pipes, they were sent again to the kiln to be rebaked, and returned fresh and new.

When luncheon was over, a walk with Kingsley was an occasion of great pleasure. His delight in every fresh or known bit of scenery was most keen, and his knowledge of animal life invested the walk with singular novelty. I remember standing on the top of a hill with him when the autumn evening was fading, and one of the sun's latest rays struck a patch bringing out a very peculiar mixture of red brown colours. What were the precise plants which composed that patch? He hurriedly ran over the list of what he thought they were, and then set off over hedge and ditch, through bog and water-course, to verify the list he had already made.

During one of these afternoon walks he would visit one or another of his very scattered hamlets or single cottages on the heath. I was with him once when he visited a sick man suffering from fever. The atmosphere of the little ground-floor bedroom was horrible, but before the Rector said a word he ran upstairs, and, to the great astonishment of the inhabitants of the cottage, bored, with a large auger he had brought with him, several holes above the bed's head for ventilation.

Gestures like this did not make Kingsley universally popular with the working people in his parish. There were some who considered him 'nosey' (an adjective first applied to him in print by the Reverend R. S. Hawker[16]) and there is a man still living in Eversley who admits that his grandfather threw stones at Kingsley's carriage. But such incidents are hugely outweighed by the flood of affectionate anecdotes with which any visitor to Eversley will be regaled even today. Understandably they are mostly told by people whose parents knew Kingsley as children. There was old George Slyfield, gardener to a lady still living in Eversley, who declared that Kingsley said to him, ' "Garge! Be good" — and I 'ave been good!' There was George's younger sister whom Kingsley met on the long walk from school. 'And whose little maid are you?' he said, and when she told him he carried her home on his shoulders. The niece of a former huntsman with the Garth tells how her father came before Kingsley as a boy for smoking out a cottager by placing a turf over his chimney. At the end of the interview Kingsley patted him on the head and gave him a threepenny bit thereby winning the boy's undying devotion.

Kingsley's ability to get on with working men has already been mentioned. But he was equally understanding in his approach to their wives. In a lecture delivered at the Working Men's College in 1855 he warned his audience of philanthropic ladies against the dangers of taking a patronising attitude to the working mothers they visited.

Let your visits be those of women to women; instead of reproving and fault-finding, encourage. They scramble through life's rocks,

[16] John Lane, *The Life and Letters of R. S. Hawker*, Bodley Head, 1905.

bogs, and thorn-brakes, clumsily enough and have many a fall, poor things! But why, in the name of a God of love and justice, is the lady, rolling along the smooth turnpike road in her comfortable carriage, to be calling out all day long to the poor soul who drags on beside her, over hedge and ditch, moss and moor, barefooted and weary-hearted, with half a dozen children at her back. Why not encourage her, praise her, cheer her on her weary way by loving words, and keep your reproofs for yourself — even your advice; for she *does* get on her way after all, where you could not travel a step forward . . . Regulate your conduct to her . . . by the very same rules which apply to persons of your own class . . . All your piety may be nullified by simply keeping a poor woman standing in her own cottage while you sit, or entering her house, even at her own request, while she is at meals. And remember, a woman's heart is alike in all ranks, and the deepest sorrow is the one of which she speaks the least. We should not like anyone — no, not an angel from heaven, to come into our houses without knocking at the door, to say 'I hear you are very ill off — I will lend you a hundred pounds.'

The seed of Christian Socialism found fertile soil among these working people of Eversley. When, in a Whitsun sermon, the rector equated the Kingdom of God with the Socialist millennium, the two oboists and the horn-player who comprised the church band struck up *The Good Time Coming* and invited him to a dinner. The London Socialists were a less Godly lot and the newly established *Cooper's Magazine* was now strongly advocating the teachings of Strauss, the atheist, author of the controversial *Leben Jesu*. Kingsley felt the time was ripe once more to enter the lists of political journalism, and the second of the three short-lived Christian Socialist periodicals with which he was associated was launched in November 1850.[17] This successor to *Politics for the People* was called, unequivocally enough, *The Christian Socialist*. Ludlow was once more the editor and Lees, the young man who had so staunchly defended the bedrooms at Eversley, put up £100 for it. The aim of the periodical was to promote working men's associations, and Kingsley set to work eagerly on three articles on the Frimley murders (which Ludlow disliked) and nine on Socialism in the Bible, which Ludlow managed to stop before Parson Lot — once again his pseudonym, though few were now deceived by it — described the extermination of the Canaanites 'in a manner that would have shocked all but the most savage of his readers'. Ludlow

[17] The third was called *The Journal of Association*, but Kingsley contributed only three poems and an article to it.

now printed, somewhat unwillingly, the story called, *The Nun's Pool*[18] which he had turned down as editor of *Politics and the People*, but he absolutely refused to publish a letter against teetotalism written in what Tom Hughes used to call Kingsley's 'Pantagruelist mood'.[19] Indeed, Ludlow confided to a friend that he thought Kingsley 'must be ill to write such rubbish'.

In fact Kingsley had always disliked the principle of total abstinence, partly because of the holier-than-thou attitude it induced in its adherents, and partly because he enjoyed wine with his dinner himself. True, he was sometimes tempted to take too much port after it, if Fanny was not at home to discourage him, but he saw no reason why the working man should be deprived of his beer, provided it was home brewed, and not the adulterated stuff they sold in the public houses.

It was not easy for Ludlow to reject Parson Lot's work, for Kingsley was now his most influential contributor. The November 22nd issue contains proof of this. It carries an advertisement which announces that 'with the present No. of this journal is given away a correct Likeness in lithography of the Rev. Charles Kingsley (author of *Alton Locke*, etc.) with autograph on superior Plate Paper'. There were other indications of Kingsley's growing popularity by 1851. This was the year of the opening of the Great Exhibition (an occasion which moved Kingsley to tears) and many foreigners were in London. One of them, the distinguished Swedish novelist, Frederika Bremer, declared she would rather see the author of *Alton Locke* than the Crystal Palace and was invited to Eversley for the weekend. The diminutive old lady delighted Kingsley and amazed Rose and Maurice by falling on her knees in front of a gorse bush for, like Linneaus, she had never seen one.

Kingsley found another admirer in a lady novelist who lived nearer home, at this time. Mary Russell Mitford inhabited a leaking cottage, 'as rotten as an old cheese' and piled to the ceiling with books, in the neighbouring parish of Swallowfield. She had made a considerable amount of money with a series of sketches entitled *Our Village* which she contributed to a ladies' journal, but her father had gambled it all away and she spent the last years of her life bedridden as a result of a gig accident. She was enchanted with Kingsley and wrote of him, 'he is the most charming mixture of softness and gentleness with spirit,

[18] This story concerned the same Nun's Pool that was to 'wash Ashy clean again' in *Yeast*. In it Kingsley told how a curse was put on the pool when a prioress, pursuing a runaway nun and her lover, was drowned in it.

[19] Kingsley was a great admirer of the works of Rabelais and said of him 'were he seven times as unspeakably filthy as he is I wd. consider him priceless in wisdom'.

manliness and frankness'. Like Kingsley's daughter, Mary, she regretted that this gentleness was not conveyed by any of his portraits. Kingsley was equally enchanted with Miss Mitford, while confessing that, 'apart from the luminous intelligence of her eyes', she was very ugly. He wrote a sonnet to her praising her books rather than her person, and visited her until her last days, when she had to have her pen dipped in the ink for her to enable her to write.

Nevertheless at this stage in his life, the brickbats still came faster than the bouquets. John Parker had at last been persuaded to publish *Yeast* in book form, and its appearance was greeted with a deeply insulting review in *The Guardian*. Kingsley was accused of recommending profligacy of the kind indulged in by Lancelot at Cambridge, as an essential stage in the life of a Christian. But worse things were to follow. On June 22nd, 1851, he was invited to preach at St John's Church, Charlotte Street, on 'The Message of the Church to Labouring Men'. Most of his sermon was devoted to a fairly vague assertion of the principles of liberty, fraternity and equality which was quite in keeping with the creed of Christian Socialism. There was, however, an approving reference to the law of Moses which forbade the permanent sale of land and hence the accumulation of large estates. This could have been taken as an attack on the landed classes and was presumably so taken by the vicar of St John's, Mr Drew, for just as Kingsley was about to give the blessing, Mr Drew rose in the reading desk and declared that it was his painful duty to say that he believed much of what the preacher had just said was dangerous and untrue. The excitement of the congregation can be imagined. The working men who were present could hardly be kept quiet, and Kingsley himself had difficulty in maintaining a dignified silence. He only bowed his head, however, and passing straight through the crowd that thronged him with outstretched hands and cries of 'God bless you, sir!' went into the vestry, where his friends took the sermon from him that it might be printed exactly as it was written.

Kingsley returned to Eversley exhausted and depressed and paced his study all night, unable to sleep. It was during that night that he wrote the famous poem about the shipwrecks of his boyhood, *The Three Fishers*,[20] later successfully set to music. The London presses were also at work that night and another kind of storm burst in the morning. Several leading papers carried attacks on 'the Apostle of Socialism' and, under their influence the Bishop of London, Dr Blomfield, wrote to Kingsley forbidding him to preach in London. Kingsley replied respectfully, requesting his lordship to suspend

[20] This poem contains the line 'For men must work and women must weep'.

his judgment until he had read the sermon. Meanwhile letters of sympathy poured in from all quarters, from a few of the clergy, from many of the laity, and from vast numbers of working men. There was a meeting of these last on Kennington Common, and an expression of their allegiance and sympathy. In the meantime the sermon was printed, and a copy sent to the bishop, who wrote at once to ask Kingsley to come up and see him at London House, and withdrew his prohibition.

The excitement caused by this event shows how strong was the prejudice against a member of the upper classes, particularly a clergyman, who associated with his inferiors for their social advancement. The disapproval of his own class was something Kingsley always found it hard to bear, particularly as the 'inferior people' he was obliged to associate with were often repugnant to him personally. It was the members of the lower middle class, rather than the working class, to whom Kingsley objected. Meetings of the Promoters of Association in London were often attended by 'bearded men, vegetarians and other eccentric persons', as Tom Hughes put it, and on one occasion Kingsley was 'quite upset and silenced by the appearance of a member in a straw hat and blue plush gloves. He did not recover from the depression produced by those gloves for days.'[21]

It may have been depression from a similar cause that brought about another nervous collapse, in July 1851. Added to the work and controversy of the last eight months had been his ever-present money worries. It is true that *Alton Locke* had brought in £150 and quickly gone into three editions, and John Martineau's fees amounted to £250. To counterbalance this, however, Kingsley had given up the sinecure of Clerk in Orders at Chelsea, on principle, and reduced the tithes due to him at Eversley by a tenth to compensate for a poor harvest. In spite of painful economies, such as smoking the cheapest tobacco and keeping no horse, he had been obliged to ask his wealthy neighbour, Mr Parfitt[22] to stand surety for a loan a year previously, confessing to Fanny, 'it has been on my mind for *weeks and weeks*'.[23] Now he had to ask Tom Hughes to do the same for a sum of £500 which he was not able to repay until the publication of *Two Years Ago* in 1857. He had always hoped that matters would improve when Sir John Cope died, and it was in this year that Sir William, an heir who Kingsley had traced and brought to Sir John's notice, succeeded. Sir William was a canon at Westminster, but morally he proved little better than

---

[21] Tom Hughes, preface to *Alton Locke*.
[22] Mr Parfitt's house, called 'Parfitts', still stands at Eversley.
[23] ULF No. 110, 1849.

his predecessor. The best Kingsley could say of him was, 'poor man, he is very pleasant when sane'.[24] He refused to repair or rebuild damp low-lying cottages on his estate, or do what Kingsley considered his duty, live in Italy for seven years and so save something of the inadequate £3,000 a year which was the income the estate produced. He was also an extreme Puseyite ('why he stays in our church I cannot conceive') and accused Kingsley of neglecting his parish in favour of writing books.

And so, exactly two years after his last collapse, Kingsley once more found the burden of life had become intolerable. As so often in periods of stress, his digestion was suffering. It had never been strong since his attack of cholera at school. From time to time in his letters to Fanny he mentioned foods that had disagreed with him. There was the case of the pistachio nuts — 'Whether they suit the Turks or not they make me horribly bilious, and I never will no more never.'[25] But now he found difficulty in digesting even the rectory diet of 'plain mutton' washed down with a glass or two of wine. In a letter to Mr Lees he admitted the extent of his weariness: 'I wish I was in bed, which is after all the only place of rest on earth for a parson.' To a more intimate friend he yearned for a more permanent resting place 'whither I may flee away on the wings of a dove'. Another holiday away from Fanny was recommended and, as his parents and Henry were about to tour the German watering places, Kingsley agreed to accompany them, and 'cross the water' for the first time.

[24] ULF No. 158, July 17, 1855.
[25] ULF No. 152, March 24, 1855.

CHAPTER 8

Across the Water
1851-1853

Charles and Henry bought brown felt Mazzini wide-awakes with high crowns and wide brims for the journey. Henry had just completed his first year at Worcester College, Oxford, and had joined a set known as the Intellectual Bargees, notorious for the casual eccentricity of their dress. To the delight of the two brothers they found that Thackeray, also wearing a wide-awake and travelling with his family, was a fellow passenger on the little steamer moored at London Bridge. *Vanity Fair* had always been a favourite with Kingsley, and he claimed that he would rather have drawn Rawdon Crawley 'than all the folks I ever drew'.[1] When he was depressed and feeling 'stupid as a jug'[2] (usually when Fanny was away from home) he would read it over and over again for consolation. The two families now established themselves in deckchairs and fraternised until the roughness of the sea made polite intercourse impossible. Thackeray's thirteen-year-old daughter, Anne, recorded the occasion in her diary.

> It was a stormy crossing; the waves were curling unpleasantly round the boat; I sat by Mrs Kingsley [Charles's mother] miserable, uncomfortable, and watching in a dazed and hypnotised sort of way the rim of Charles Kingsley's wide-awake as it rose and fell against the horrible horizon. He stood before us holding on to some ropes.

She decided that Kingsley 'was a fine, honest, go ahead fellow who *charges* a subject heartily, impetuously, with the greatest courage and simplicity, but with little knowledge of the world'.

In spite of Kingsley's rooted objection to 'abroad', this, his first sight of it, was a cause of ecstasy. From Ems, where the family spent a fortnight, he wrote of stained-glass madonnas whose beauty had moved him to tears, of the 'vast, rushing, silent Rhine with its yellow vine

1 ULF No. 116, May 16, 1850.
2 ULF No. 115, May 16, 1850.

slopes and robber castles', of woods full of 'great orange slugs and great green lizards'. He scrambled up the face of the Lorelei and picked Fanny a bunch of flowers from the Nymph's seat; he found fifty plants unknown to him in a day, so many that keeping them was impossible; 'I just picked specimens, looked at them till I knew them, and went on regretful.' Poems, mostly to Fanny, poured out of him; *Oh, thou hadst been a wife for Shakespeare's self, Ask if I love thee* and *The baby sings not on its mother's breast* were all written at this time.

It was this yearning for Fanny that casts one of the few shadows over the happiness of this period. He wrote home to her constantly on letterheads which Fanny had prepared for him by writing in the names of the cities from which she expected notes. He was reminded daily of her because he was visiting the very places she had visited as a lovesick maiden ten years previously.

Oh that I were with you, or rather you with me here. The beds are so small that we should be forced to lie inside each other, and the weather is so hot that you might walk about naked all day, as well as night — *cela va sans dire*! Oh, those naked nights at Chelsea! When will they come again? I kiss both locks of hair every time I open my desk — but the little curly one seems to bring me nearer to you.[3]

A lesser but very real cause of unhappiness was the coldness with which his father treated his mother. 'I confess it is hard to keep one's temper, when one sees her so bullied, and yet slaving on. It makes my blood boil; but I have not had any unpleasantness as yet.' To compensate, he shared confidences with his mother, and was as attentive to her as possible, accompanying her on little expeditions into the town and, on one occasion, buying her a camp stool. He told Fanny, 'Except you, I know no human being to whom I dare say so much of my inner heart — about you, and poetry, and Popery, and the Old Saints, and all *the forbidden depths*.' He even showed her his letters to Fanny, to which she would add little postscripts such as, 'Charles is very flourishing, with the exception of occasional heart spasms when he thinks of you.' To one of his letters in which he described a certain Kurhaus, 'so lovely one longs to kiss it', his mother added, 'think of him kissing the curhouse! Don't be jealous!'

It may have been a feeling of exasperation with his father that now decided Charles to leave his parents for a fortnight and set off with Henry on a walking tour of the Eifel mountains. Certainly he was

[3] ULF No. 125, July 24, 1851.

anxious to avoid two stuffy days on the steamer going to Trier. The two men set off in high spirits with heavy packs on their backs, Charles's being considerably heavier than Henry's, 'for I am getting old and luxurious and cannot move without little comforts — which of course one's *non-taking friends* borrow after all'. Besides rods, pipes and letter-writing materials, he carried his beloved plaid and, suspended in a little bag round his neck, Fanny's two locks of hair.

As a result of walking fifteen miles a day under a load, and taking an evening sightseeing stroll as well, Charles's health was now completely restored. He had felt 'new nerves' ever since Cologne, although there had been a slight setback at Ems where an excess of the curative waters had brought on the colic and, by way of bettering matters, 'I nearly broke my nose in against the wall by jumping into bed in the dark'. But now he was able to report 'I am very well indeed and very strong. My limbs are all knots as hard as iron.' He was even able to survive a meal of 'raw bacon and hock at 9d. a bottle without an attack of katzenjammer' (indigestion) and declare, after a chat with the inn-keeper, that the Germans were fine people, 'although not members of the Church of England'.

Henry too, Charles was pleased to note, stood up well to the rigours of the journey. Although he was more than a foot shorter than his brother and had been puny as a boy, he had conscientiously developed his body by rowing at Oxford and had recently won a bet laid by a friend that he could not run a mile, row a mile and trot a mile in fifteen minutes.

The journey was full of wonders and Charles stood, but was sorely tempted to kneel in prayer, on the rims of many volcanic craters, some filled with 'ghastly blue lakes, some, quaintly enough, by rye fields and reapers', some apparently bottomless. Indeed in *Hypatia* he compared the face of St Augustine to one of these 'worn-out volcanoes, the earth-quake rents filled with kindly soil, and the cinder slopes grown gay with grass and flowers'. He filled his socks with rocks for Rose who, at eight, was evidently a keen geologist and his letters to Fanny crackled with botanical specimens. Twice the travellers were in serious danger.

We found ourselves about 8 p.m. last night at the top of a cliff 500 feet high, with a roaring river at the bottom, and no path. So down the cliff face we had to come in the dark, or sleep in the forest to be eaten by wolves, of which latter, one seen on our route yesterday was as 'high as the table'. And down we came, knapsacks, fishing rods, and all, which process must not be repeated often if we intend to revisit our native shores.

On the second occasion the brothers were arrested by the constable of the small town of Bitburg who, because of their unshaven chins, their strange hats and their foreign accents, took them for agents of Mazzini and assumed that their fishing rods were *todt instrumenten* — deadly weapons. Kingsley described the incident in his novel, *Two Years Ago*, published six years later. He changed only the victim's name (to Tom) and his death instrument (to a Colt revolver).

Prodigy on prodigy up the hill towards him charged, as he would upon a whole army, a Prussian gendarme, with bayonet fixed.

Tom sat down upon the mountain side, and burst into inextinguishable laughter, while the gendarme came charging up, right towards his very nose.

But up to his nose he charged not, for his wind was short, and the noise of his roaring went before him. Moreover, he knew that Tom had a revolver, and was a 'mad Englishman'.

Now he was not afraid of Tom, or of a whole army: but he was a man of drills and orders, of rules and of precedents, as a Prussian gendarme ought to be; and for the modes of attacking infantry, cavalry and artillery, man, woman and child, thief and poacher, stray pig, or even stray wolf, he had drill and orders sufficient: but for attacking a Colt's revolver, none.

Moreover, for arresting all manner of riotous Burschen, drunken boors, French red republicans, Mazzini-hatted Italian refugees, suspect Polish incendiaries, or other *feras naturae*, he had precedent and regulation: but for arresting a mad Englishman, none. He held fully the opinion of his superiors that there was no saying what an Englishman might not, could not, and would not do. He was a sphinx, a chimera, a lunatic broke loose, who took unintelligible delight in getting wet and dirty, and tired, and starved, and all but killed; and called the same 'taking exercise'.

The incident ended with a night in the prison at Trier 'among fleas and felons on the bare floor' and in the morning the mistake was discovered, the prisoners released and the constable returned to Bitburg with a reprimand. When the older Kingsleys arrived they found their sons being entertained royally at the town hall, 'the lions of Trier *pro tempore*, for the affair had made considerable fuss'.

For Mrs Charles Kingsley Senior the fortnight had not been without adventure. She had moved to Dresden and had been extremely terrified, when walking in the vicinity of the town, by the sudden appearance round a bend in the road, of a ruffianly young vagabond who, uttering a fierce exclamation, approached her with, as she had thought, a demand for alms; a close inspection had revealed that he was none other than her own son George returning literally from Bohemia, with his clothes in tatters, the remnants of his boots tied together with pieces of string, and his face burnt as brown as a gipsy's. George, who was at this time twenty-five, had qualified as a doctor in Paris, and was gratifying his passion for travel and female companionship by taking jobs as companion-physician to various great ladies on their travels. He was presumably between jobs at the time of this meeting.

The reunited Kingsley family now explored the Roman ruins at Trier. In the amphitheatre Charles felt he was standing over the skeleton of 'the giant iniquity, Old Rome', and he imagined all the hellish scenes of agony and cruelty that the place had witnessed. His horror of the late Roman Empire was extreme and the only word he would ever say in favour of the Roman Tyranny was that 'it provided free baths for its victims'. At Bonn he was in ecstasies over the fossils in the museum but regretted that his honeymoon study of the German language had not borne more fruit, for he could not communicate with the curator.

As the holiday drew to a close thoughts of a second honeymoon obsessed him increasingly and he wrote to tell Fanny he was bringing her home a special present, 'you will call it trumpery but I am determined to buy *one* piece of trumpery at least'.[4] He and Fanny planned to share the room in Chelsea where their first honeymoon had ended; 'I think the Chelsea plan is excellent, but we must sleep without a dressing room, which will of course make you blush very much and, as my mother expresses it, wallow in each others arms all night in a very narrow bed.' Fanny was concerned that she might not be well enough to welcome him properly but he brushed aside her pleas of ill health. 'As for you not being strong, you always look so much better after one of your bouts.'[5] He did, however, send one caution. He hoped at the hour of their reunion that Fanny would not be wearing spectacles. 'I do hate them so! I sat next to the first woman today I have seen in them, and behold she was an Englishwoman and I shuddered.'

Hypatia, Or New Foes with Old Faces, Kingsley's novel about the Ancient World, resulted from his visit to the Roman ruins in Germany. For two years he had been contemplating a book about Alexandria after the sack of Rome, depicting the clashes between Christians, Jews,

[4] ULF No. 125, July 24, 1851.
[5] ULF No. 126, July 25, 1851.

Greeks and barbarians in that dissension-rent city. For ten years he had been 'grubbing in Monk-Latin' and indeed he had been fascinated by the period ever since those boyhood days when he had peopled the 'Roman villa' at Hartland Point with Cornish concubines and been discovered reading the works of Porphyry and Iamblichus in his head-master's library. Now, fired by the amphitheatre at Trier and its ter-rible history of massacre, he set about portraying similar scenes in the amphitheatre at Alexandria, while admitting that the public slaughter of prisoners had been forbidden years before the period he was describ-ing and that the only gladiators likely to be found in 415 would have been elderly soaks in the wine shops.

Before embarking on *Hypatia*, Kingsley made a practice sortie into the past with a Socratic dialogue called *Phaethon, or Loose Thoughts for Loose Thinkers* (a sub-title on which the critics made unkind play). The plan of the pamphlet was for characters representing various schools of thought to demolish a Professor Windrush, who was to represent the 'Neoplatonic Anythingarianism' of Emerson. In *Hypatia* also, each of the characters represents a school of thought; Philammon, the hero, is a handsome but ignorant monk; Raphael, a cynical young Jew; Orestes, a decadent Roman prefect; and Amal, a barbarian warrior, anxious only for 'one hour's good hewing'. All, with the exception of Amal, are in love with Hypatia, a Greek philosopher who looks, and, alas, behaves, as if she had stepped off a Greek vase. Amal is in love with Pelagia, a coarser but more amusing beauty, who turns out to be Philammon's sister, thus giving an added twist to an already complicated plot. Suspense is supplied by the posing of three questions; will Philammon, the pupil of Hypatia, be won over to Neoplatonism, or will Hypatia become a Christian, or will they mutu-ally lose their virginity in each other's arms? All three seem about to happen at once in a scene intended as the climax of the book. By an admirable piece of stage management on the part of Miriam, an old Jewish sorceress, the godlike Philammon happens to be standing behind a curtain when Hypatia implores the help of Apollo before a votive fire. At the psychological moment the curtain is whipped aside, and there kneels Hypatia herself, stripped to the waist, 'her lips parted, her head thrown back, her arms stretched out in an agony of expecta-tion'.

> In an instant, before he had time to stir, she had sprung through the blaze and was kneeling at his feet.
> 'Phoebus! beautiful, glorious, ever young! Hear me! only a moment! only this once.'

Her drapery had caught fire from the tripod, but she did not heed it. Philammon instinctively clasped her in his arms, and crushed it out.

At that moment he caught sight of a negro slave holding up a crucifix, realised Hypatia's mistake, and fled.

From this moment the dénouement is swift. Hypatia is set upon by a Christian mob because of her association with the Roman prefect and hacked to death with oyster shells. Amal falls off the top of what appears to be the Pharos in a death grapple with Philammon and, being on the underside when they hit the rocks, goes to his fathers. Philammon returns to his monastery in the desert with the disgraced Pelagia and there brother and sister live out their days in prayer and mortification, finally to be buried in one grave.

In many ways this, the first of Kingsley's historical novels, was superior to the two he had already written with contemporary themes. The construction was more sophisticated than anything he had so far attempted and in some of the scenes, particularly the crowd scenes, he succeeded in giving a vivid picture of life in a civilisation that had been destroyed fifteen hundred years before his birth. Undoubtedly he was guilty of anachronisms. Only by Victorian standards could Pelagia have been considered totally disgraced because she danced (fully clothed) in the amphitheatre and one doubts whether Alexandrian ladies wore dresses that quite so strongly resembled the crinoline as the ones Kingsley describes 'stuffed out behind' in a manner to provoke 'ribald comments' from the gutter-snipes. Certainly Raphael Aben-Ezra, the most lifelike character in the book, bears a much closer resemblance to a world-weary undergraduate of nineteenth-century Cambridge than of fifth-century Alexandria. (Indeed Kingsley himself admitted he was based on the brilliant Alfred Hyman Louis, the twenty-year-old Jew who he was attempting to convert to Christianity at the time.) But in such matters Kingsley sinned no more than did Pater in *Marius the Epicurean* or Newman in *Callista*, published two years later with the intention of putting the record straight about certain practices attributed to the early Church in *Hypatia*.

In spite of its qualities, it is hard to imagine anyone reading *Hypatia* for pleasure nowadays. As a schoolgirl Una Pope Hennessy claims to have enjoyed the lush scenes of orgy and massacre (although Kingsley affirmed that they were unsuitable for young ladies) but one is tempted to suspect that even she skipped Hypatia's eight-page lecture on Neoplatonism or Abbot Pambo's equally lengthy defence of monasticism (lifted entire from the original Greek). It was the impropriety rather than the weightiness of the book that alarmed Kingsley's contemporaries. Tennyson objected to the final scene in the Caesareum where Hypatia rose 'for a moment to her full height, naked, snow white against the dusky mass around', before being overpowered by the mob. He disliked the use of the word 'naked' and said that he 'really was hurt at having Hypatia stript at her death'. To this Kingsley could well have replied that he was only relaying historical fact for it was thus that the real Hypatia died in 415. More serious charges were brought against him for the unflattering picture he drew of the early Christians. Lewis Carroll described as 'outrageous to taste' the sneers at Christianity which he puts into the mouths of some of the heathen characters. He was thinking of Hypatia's reply to the Roman prefect who declared that he expected every moment to have his brains knocked out by some mad monk. 'Why not?' said Hypatia. 'Why not? In an age when emperors and consuls crawl to the tomb of a tentmaker and a fisherman, and kiss the mouldy bones of the vilest slaves? Why not, among a people whose God is the crucified son of a carpenter?' Nevertheless many people liked the book, including Queen Victoria, Prince Albert and Baron de Bunsen, who invited the Kingsleys to spend a week at Carlton House Terrace on the strength of it.

To the biographer of Kingsley there is a character in *Hypatia* who is of special interest. Bishop Synesius does not play a large part in the story, apart from introducing Raphael to St Augustine during an ostrich hunt, but he bears a striking resemblance to Kingsley himself.

Up at four in the morning, always in the most disgusting good health and spirits, farming, coursing, shooting, riding over hedge and ditch after rascally black robbers; preaching, intriguing, borrowing money; baptising and excommunicating; bullying that bully Andronicus; comforting old women, and giving pretty girls dowries; scribbling one half hour on philosophy, and the next on farriery, sitting up all night writing hymns and drinking strong liquors; off again on horseback at four the next morning; and talking by the hour all the while about philosophic abstractions.

In describing Synesius Kingsley showed an extraordinarily acute perception of his own weaknesses. 'He lived in a whirlwind of good deeds, *meddling and toiling for the mere pleasure of action*, and as soon as there was nothing to be done, *paid the penalty for past excitement in fits of melancholy.*' (The italics are mine.)

In Kingsley's own life there were now fewer periods of meddling and toiling. With *Hypatia* he had abandoned the cause of Christian Socialism in fiction, and he was beginning to take a less active part in the movement in fact. He gave his reasons in a letter to Tom Hughes. 'I have seen that the world was not going to be set right in any such rose-pink way, excellent as it is, and that there are heavy arrears of *destruction* to be made up, before *construction* can ever begin.' But these were probably not the only reasons. With the passage of the *Industrial and Provident Societies Act* of 1852 the right of workmen to form associations was legally recognised and the fighting phase of the movement was over. It was fighting on which Kingsley throve. There may have been other less creditable reasons. Fanny's family was fast nearing the top rungs of the social ladder. Charles Pascoe Grenfell had recently bought Taplow Court from the Earl of Orkney and had rebuilt the old house with a roof of oak and plate glass and a large square centre tower which concealed a water tank. Riversdale Grenfell, known to the family as Riv, had an establishment almost equally large at Ray Lodge, near Weybridge. Kingsley was a frequent visitor at both houses and enjoyed a day out with the hounds on their splendid horses, particularly Riv's gelding, Crimea. This also was the year of F. D. Maurice's disgrace, a dreadful warning to his friends. Dr Jelf, principal of King's College, had set up a committee of enquiry to discover whether Maurice's *Theological Essays* were unorthodox. The committee had decided that his denial of the eternity of hell fire was indeed heretical and suspended him. But it was common knowledge that Jelf's real objection to his Professor of Divinity was that 'Mr Maurice is identified with Mr Kingsley, and Mr Kingsley is identified with Mr Holyoake[6] and Mr Holyoake is identified with Tom Paine. Thus there are only three links between King's College and the author of *The Rights of Man*.' Dr Jelf was in fact an hysteric and a coward and Kingsley thoroughly enjoyed his antics. He gleefully described a scene in which Jelf insulted a Mr P 'so brutally that he had to make an apology and then went into hysterics, and P had to throw water over him. What fun!' Such scenes might be fun, but they were not healthy for a man seeking preferment. And Kingsley had just been given an assignment which might lead to better things. On the strength of *Hypatia* he had been invited to go to Edinburgh to deliver four lectures on the Alexandrian schools to the Philosophical Institute.

Kingsley's thoughts at this time were turning increasingly towards poetry. His letters to Ludlow were now filled with discussions of metre rather than working men's associations. He told him, 'When I have

[6] Holyoake edited the *Leader*, a communist periodical to which Kingsley in fact never contributed.

done *Hypatia* I will write no more novels. I can write poetry better than any Englishman living. I don't say I have written it: but I know I can write it.'[7] It was probably two women who caused this temporary disillusionment with the novel form. One of them was Fanny, who had copied out *Hypatia* for him. Fanny was pregnant, a result of the rapturous homecoming from Germany, and far from well. He blamed her indisposition on too many hours spent working on his manuscripts. The other guilty woman was Harriet Beecher Stowe. It is hard to appreciate, at this distance, the phenomenal success of *Uncle Tom's Cabin* in the year of its publication. The book threatened the future of publishing itself in England, for no customer in any bookshop could be persuaded to ask for any other work. Unsold books piled up in the warehouses and publishers refused to accept manuscripts. 'Mrs Beecher Stowe', said Thomas Mozley, 'has entered the garden of Eden and has reduced it to a wilderness.' Kingsley was inclined to agree. He now set to work on two long poems with themes, like *Hypatia*, taken from the Ancient World.

The subject of Andromeda, a maiden exposed naked all night to the sea spray, was one naturally attractive to him. He had at first tried to express what he felt about 'that unfathomable myth' in a 'figure drawing', but was obliged to burn fifty attempts. 'If I conceive a thought I almost always begin by drawing it again and again,' he told Ludlow, 'and then the incompleteness of the pencil (for paint I can't) drives me to words to give it colour and *chiaroscuro*.' In the case of *Andromeda* the words fell into Homeric hexameters, which came so easily to Kingsley that he claimed he could rattle them off while dressing and breakfasting. Thus,

> They, on the sea girt rock, which is washed by the surges forever,
> Set her in silence, the guiltless, aloft with her face to the Eastward.

Andromeda was partly modelled on Tennyson's *Oenone* which Kingsley, on rereading, found 'more glorious than ever'. The same cannot be said about his own lines, in spite of the ease with which he claimed to have written them.

The subject of *Santa Maura*, set in the form of a dramatic monologue, was even closer to Kingsley's private fantasies. The speaker was a naked female saint hanging on a cross and dying slowly. She tells how, three months married and pregnant, she has refused to worship false

---

[7] These occasional outbursts of boasting were not untypical. When Kingsley met his old nursemaid, Annie Simpson, after a long absence, his comment to her was, according to her great-great-grand-daughter, Mrs Dawkins, 'You did not think I would make all this fuss in the world, did you, Annie?'

gods and, after being stripped and whipped, had been sent to join her deacon husband who had also been crucified. He, with both eyes gouged out, welcomes her with the words:

Come, come to thy bride bed, martyr wife once more!

And she replies:

I crawled to you, I kissed your bleeding feet and called aloud.
You heard me! You know all! I am at peace.
Peace, peace, as still and bright as is the moon
Upon your limbs, came on me at your smile,
And kept me happy when they dragged me back
From that last kiss and spread me on the cross.

Kingsley was deeply moved by the poem, which he wrote in a single day and a night. 'I can hardly bear to read it myself,' he told F. D. Maurice. 'It is the deepest and clearest thing I have yet done.' But the public thought otherwise and eventually Kingsley came to agree with them. 'Unrhymed blank verse is very bald in my hands,' he wrote, 'because I *won't* write "poetic diction" but only plain English — and so I don't get mythic grandeur enough.' Another fault in his long poems as in everything he wrote, was his tendency to preach. 'As a parson to the English public,' he told Ludlow, 'I am expected to point a moral.' In his shorter poems and ballads there was no room for sermons and it was this fact, combined with an innocent freshness of expression and a rollicking rhythm, that no doubt caused them to last and in some cases even become a part of the language.

Three years after the failure of *Santa Maura* he was so far disgusted with poetry as to write, to Archer Gurney:

I have deserted poetry as rats do a sinking ship. I have refused to publish my poems, actually ashamed of being called a poet, of being caught out in such a bad company (not yours of course,) and have taken to monosyllabic prose, as the highest achievement of man; considering modern taste so radically rotten, that I must unlearn almost all I have learnt from it and recommence with my alphabet and Mrs Trimmer. I can tell more truths in prose than I can in verse, and earn ten times as much money, wherefore Parnassus has seen my retreat, I doubt not, with dry eyes![8]

This was not, however, his final pronouncement on the subject.

[8] The letter is an unpublished one in the possession of the Rev. R. H. Gurney, to whom I am indebted for permission to reproduce.

(Kingsley seldom made final pronouncements on any subject.) Encouraged by the success of the publication of his poems in book form in 1858 he told Hullah, the composer, who wished to set some of them to music, 'poems are, after all, what I can do best. I am, like Camille Des Moulins, "*une pauvre créature, née pour faire des vers.*" '

Whatever his attitude to his own poetry, Kingsley's work as a reviewer for *Fraser's* brought him much into contact with the work of others and he became a friend of Tennyson, whose *In Memoriam* he regarded as 'the noblest Christian poem which England had produced in two centuries'. Kingsley had in fact first been introduced to Tennyson some years earlier, at the house of Macmillan. He was informed of the coming honour by telegram, which, he told Fanny, 'frightened me dreadfully. I was really quite ill.' In the event he found himself in sympathy with the great man and in 1851 Tennyson stayed at Eversley Rectory, for he was considering buying Brick Hill House, the handsome Jacobean farmhouse that still stands just up the hill from the church. Over a pipe in his study Kingsley regretfully advised the poet against the purchase, pointing out that the house faced north and was kept permanently damp by the springs draining into it from the hillside. There was later a temporary estrangement between the two, because Tennyson believed that the opium-eating poet, Elsley Vavasour, in Kingsley's novel *Two Years Ago*, was a caricature of himself. Critics have since expressed amazement that he could see any resemblance between himself and Vavasour, who was, it is true, much more like Shelley. They have, however, ignored the fact that, at the height of his madness, Vavasour dashed off forty verses of a poem that sounded remarkably like *The Charge of the Light Brigade* 'and forgot them the next minute'. Kingsley must have explained the matter away successfully, for in 1859 he and Fanny were invited to stay with the Tennysons at Farrington, on the Isle of Wight. On that famous occasion Tennyson read *Maud* in its entirety to Fanny, 'a never to be forgotten experience'.[9] An inscribed copy of *Maud and Other Poems* presented by Tennyson to Kingsley at the end of the visit has recently changed hands in a New York auction room. It had belonged to Kingsley's son Maurice, who emigrated to America.

Kingsley's appreciation of literature was somewhat limited by the fact that he demanded the writer to display 'manliness' both in his person and his work, and by 'manliness' he usually meant a proficiency

[9] Charles did not share Fanny's opinion of *Maud*. In an unpublished letter to Archer Gurney, which I quote with the permission of the present owner, the Rev. R. H. Gurney, he wrote, 'As for *Maud* — it is a sad falling off . . . but . . . I love and honour the man, as a private friend'.

in blood sports only attainable by the members of the upper classes. 'I have better hope of our class than of the class below,' he told Tom Hughes in a letter about *Tom Brown's Schooldays*. 'They are effeminate.' In a letter to another correspondent he said that the shopkeeping class were unable to stand pain; 'You seem to think them a hardier and less dainty class than our own. I find that even in the prime of youth they shrink from, and are often unable to bear (from physical neglect of training), fatigue, danger, pain, which would be considered as sport by an average public schoolboy.' People of a lower class were not only unfitted to write well, Kingsley even suspected they were incapable of appreciating what others wrote. In defending the melodramatic scene on the Glyder in *Two Years Ago* he wrote, 'I don't think the deer-stalkers of Park Lane and Belgravia will sneer, because they see such things in their field sports . . . but the true snubbers are the cockneys who write for the press, and who judge the universe from the experiences of the London suburbs, or a summer's watering-place trip.'

Many of Kingsley's fellow poets failed the blood sports test. Shelley failed it miserably not only because he was 'girlish' but because he dared to write an ode to the west wind without mentioning that it is the wind 'that blows the bait in the fishes mouth'.[10] Ruskin failed also, because he did not sleep with his wife and because there was something in his face that betrayed this fact and told Kingsley 'the first day I ever saw him, "that man and I, unless utterly changed, can never be friends" '.[11] Browning just passed muster, in spite of his lack of breeding, because of a certain raciness in his writing. Kingsley met the Brownings for the first time at the home of John Paine, a fishing friend, in Farnham. He recorded his impressions in a letter to Mansfield. '*He* won't wash; he is very clever, but low bred and effeminate, a man who fancies that a man can be a poet by profession and do nothing else, a wild mistake. *She* is wonderful; but very obstinate in her bad taste, and considers socialism is stuff, and competition as the Divine Cheese. Not that I argued with her. I never argue with anyone.' Years later Gerard Manley Hopkins saw much in Browning that reminded him of Kingsley, 'a way of talking (and making his people talk) with the air and spirit of a man bouncing up from table with mouth full of bread and cheese and saying

[10] Charles Kingsley, *Essay on Shelley and Byron*. In another unpublished letter to Archer Gurney, about the two poets, Kingsley referred to them as the leaders of 'the windbag-and-blasphemy school'.

[11] Dislike of Ruskin led to Kingsley's distant attitude to the Working Men's College, founded in 1854 by F. D. Maurice after his expulsion from King's College. He did however give them an occasional lecture, including a botanical one on the lawn of The Firs, the house that the Hughes and Ludlow families shared in Wimbledon.

that he meant to stand no blasted nonsense. There is a whole volume of Kingsley's essays which is all a munch and a not-standing-any-blasted-nonsense from cover to cover.'

Things did not go easily in the spring of 1852. Charles had not been able to find a pupil since his return from Germany and therefore could not afford a curate, and Fanny was pregnant and coughing. On one occasion Charles nearly caused her to lose the baby on his return from a country dinner party, by making her 'over-laugh' herself, but Dr Foster prescribed 'quinine and less baby' and disaster was averted. For Charles, not Fanny, a holiday was prescribed, for he was becoming increasingly hard to live with, and had been on the edge of another nervous collapse for weeks. In April he left for Wales to stay with the Froudes, aware that his wife was within six weeks of her confinement.

Anthony and Charlotte Froude had only just moved to Plas Gwynant, a little house at the foot of Snowdon. They had started their married life in Manchester where Froude had a job as a private tutor. Charlotte, however, was not at home in the circle of intellectual ladies such as Harriet Martineau and Mrs Gaskell who became their friends, and persuaded her husband to move to a house that Fanny described as 'ten miles from a butcher and 17 from the only rational doctor, the nearest being dead drunk from morng. till night'. From this 'perfect paradise' Kingsley wrote home letters filled with guilt.

I do so look forward to a long happy healthy summer with my darling beauty — we will be so loving and you will forgive me all my crossness. If I could possibly stop until the 19th June I should be very glad, for I am quite below any exertion either of body or mind. And yet I long already so intensely to be with you, so that between the two and the fear of your being lonely and above all the fear of you thinking me what I suppose I am, selfish and lazy, I don't know what to do.[12]

Gradually under the influence of fishing and otter-hunting, Kingsley's spirits revived. 'I am enjoying here a state of utter animalism,' he wrote to Ludlow, 'devoting myself to the comforting of my five senses, and taking care to go to sleep if I see any symptoms of the malady of thought approaching. There is a pool at the bottom of the garden into whose liquid ice Froude and I take a header every morning.' The request for an extension to his holiday, however, was not granted, and he was duly back at Eversley for the birth of his second daughter, Mary St Leger, on June 4th.

[12] ULF No. 127, June 1852.

The murder of Queen Gertrude of Hungary, mother of St Elizabeth, by her subjects.
Drawn by Kingsley to illustrate *The Life of St Elizabeth*, a wedding present for
Fanny.

BONUM EST HOMINI JUGUM IN JUVENTUTE FERRE

St Elizabeth carrying her cross with the inscription "It is right that a man should bear his yoke while he is young". Kingsley never denied that the naked woman who represented the saint was in fact Fanny. From *The Life of St Elizabeth*.

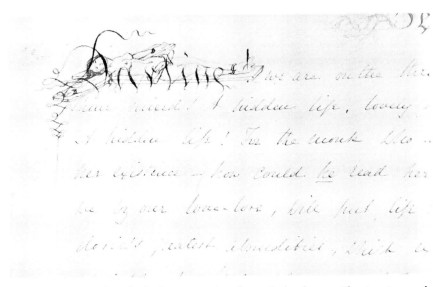

The crucifixion of St Elizabeth, representing, figuratively, the mortifications imposed on her by her monkish confessor. Used to decorate the first word of a chapter in *The Life of St Elizabeth*.

Written on the back of this drawing were the words "Charles's Fast! Every Friday at 10.0 o'clock. Eversley Cross. 1842–3." With the drawings that follow it forms a series made by Kingsley of himself and Fanny before their marriage.

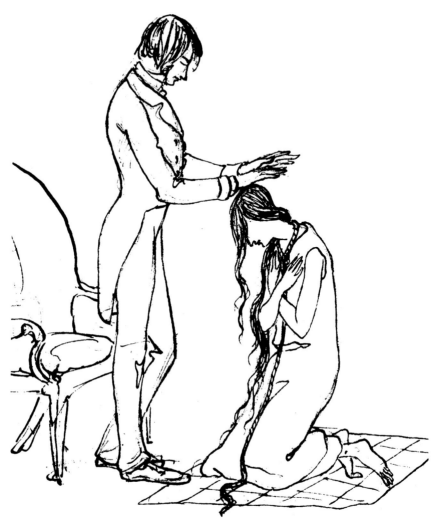

"I absolve thee from all thy Sin
In the name of the Father, the
Son & the Holy Ghost!"
Amen!

Charles forgives Fanny with the words "I absolve thee from all thy sin".

Kingsley entitled this drawing "The Thorn!" It is dated July 28, 1843.

The hallowed lovemaking of Charles and Fanny.

Kingsley wrote the words "The harvest truly is plenteous but the labourers are few"
on the back of this drawing.

Charles and Fanny ascend to heaven together.

Charles Kingsley.

Fanny Kingsley.

Helston Grammar School.

Henry Kingsley, brother of Charles Kingsley.   Mary Kingsley, mother of Charles Kingsley.

Eversley Rectory with Charles Kingsley in the foreground.

Rose Kingsley, the oldest of Charles Kingsley's children.

Maurice Kingsley.

Mary Kingsley.

Grenville Kingsley, the youngest, with his mother.

F. D. Maurice.

Thomas Hughes.

J. M. Ludlow.

Charles Mansfield.

Bramshill Park, home of Sir John Cope, Bart.

Jacob's Island, Bermondsey, about 1810.

Danae and her baby at sea in a chest.
One of Kingsley's own illustrations for
The Heroes.

Tom, the water baby, being
nursed by Mrs Doasyou-
wouldbedoneby. An illustra-
tion by Noel Paton for the
first edition of *The Water
Babies*.

Charles and Fanny Kingsley outside the study door at Eversley.

Charles Kingsley dressed to go fishing.

Charles Kingsley the year before he died. From a photograph taken in New York.

If Rose feared a rival in Mary she had no cause. Kingsley was overjoyed at her arrival and for several days after was 'too tired, confused and happy to work'. He was a loving father to the little girl he called Polly, but it is doubtful whether she ever held the same place in his affections as his beloved Miss Rose. Kingsley tried hard not to have favourites among his children, but in his letters remarks like 'love to Polly and my darling Miss Rose — not that Polly is not a darling too'[13] slipped out too often. Perhaps Polly was over-intelligent. In the Edwardian era she was to become a successful (and by no means negligible) novelist, writing under the name of Lucas Malet, but she was not, like her sister, a carbon copy of her father. Furthermore she was not pretty. Like Charles she had beautiful hands, but her teeth protruded and her chin receded. On these points the portrait painter Lowes Dickenson attempted to reassure her parents. 'He thinks the teeth and mouth will alter entirely as she grows up,'[14] Charles told Fanny when Mary was nine years old. But in fact she was never a beauty, although, according to her relations, she became 'the grandest thing that ever lived' in matters of dress and general turnout. It was Rose, and not Mary, who was chosen to accompany her father to California, a fact that Mary resented. As she pointed out, 'Daddy can never go to the United States for the first time again.'[15]

A legacy about this time contributed towards making life at Eversley more pleasant. Old Mrs Kingsley of Dulwich, the widow of a stockbroker cousin of Charles's father, died and left £500 each to Charles, George and Henry. The financial situation was further eased by the arrival of the Rt. Hon. Thomas Erskine in the parish. Erskine was a judge, and bought Fir Grove, a large house in the vicinity. Fanny went so far as to say that his presence ushered in a new era. He was a wealthy and godly man and contributed to parish charities that Kingsley had hitherto been obliged to support out of his own purse. He was also a valuable ally against the increasingly difficult Sir William, and his house became a second home to the Kingsley family.

After a lapse of two years Kingsley once more felt in a position to keep a horse, and Tom Hughes lent him a good one which gave him much pleasure. He had always found a stiff gallop over the common could rival a couple of hours with a fishing rod as a form of escape. 'Where could a man be better,' he wrote in *Hereward*, 'than on a good horse, with all the cares of this life blown away out of his brains by the keen air which rushed around his temples?' He hated to see a horse

13 ULF No. 259, 1871.
14 ULF No. 206, 1861.
15 Unpublished letter from Fanny, March 8, 1874.

6—TBATM * *

ill-treated. Indeed the first edition of *Black Beauty*, that famous equine autobiography, carried an introductory paragraph from Fanny's life of her husband describing how good he was to his horse. 'He was a perfect horseman and never lost his temper with his horse, talking and reasoning with it if it shied or bolted, as if it had been a rational being, knowing that, from the fine organisation of the animal, a horse, like a child, will get confused with panic fear which is only increased by punishment.' The sight of cruelty caused him real suffering. A coach journey across the Yorkshire dales was quite spoiled for him by the wretched condition of the coach horses 'for whom the knacker's yard cries out indignant', and he once devoted an entire afternoon to persuading a farmer to destroy a pitiful creature that was 'rotting alive' outside his gate. Finally he shot the animal himself.

With a good horse between his knees Kingsley was once more able to hunt. In the first flush of enthusiasm after his marriage he had foresworn the sport as a part of his base and animal past. Even as recently as June he had told a certain lord that he did not hunt because the slaying of animals, 'though delightful', was 'not a suitable occupation for a parson and anyway I am too proud to ride unless I am as well mounted as the rest'. Tom Hughes's mount was evidently up to scratch and Kingsley's scruples were overcome. In spite of his age (no horse that Kingsley owned was ever young) and his name (Puff), 'I will back him in a forest country with double banks against any horse of his size — and age.' To Tom Hughes Kingsley confided all his sporting exploits, for example the following:

Dinner was just coming on the table yesterday when the bow-wows appeared on the top of the Mount, trying my patch of gorse; so I jumped up, left the cook shrieking, and off. He wasn't there, but I knew where he was, for I keep a pretty good register of foxes (ain't they my parishioners?) and as the poor fellows had had a blank day, they were very thankful to find themselves, in five minutes, going like mad.

Kingsley's exploits in the hunting field were accompanied by a fair share of falls. He explained to a correspondent that he had found time to answer his letter only because he was fit for no other work, 'having been rolled into a pancake yesterday by a horse, who lay on me for five pleasant minutes at the bottom of a ditch'. One visitor to the rectory, however, was fortunately unaware of her host's sporting predelictions. When Mrs Beecher Stowe came to stay in 1856 the Bramshill hounds passed the rectory window during lunch and she cried out in horror that so barbaric a sport should have persisted into the nineteenth century. 'Hunting a man would be far better sport than a poor fox,' she declared. The children turned crimson and afterwards Maurice declared, 'I thought I should have thrown the water bottle at her head!' The creator of Uncle Tom never knew of her *faux pas*, but merely declared, 'How we did talk and go on for three days! I guess he is tired. I'm sure we were.'

Rose too now had her own pony and was able to accompany her father about the parish. Kingsley had bought it for £10, as soon as she could sit the brown donkey, Dicky, when he kicked. A year or two later, after a jaunt together over Bramshill Common, Kingsley wrote, 'Such a jolly ride! The dear child is most pleasant company and loves being with me so, that I must see more of her.'[16] Eventually she became a competent horsewoman and was able to endure eight hours in the saddle when touring the Yosemite mountains of California.

In the autumn of 1853 Fanny had a bad miscarriage, and a persistent cough was giving cause for concern. She had not rallied since Mary's birth and it was decided that she must leave the damp rectory for a long period. Charles also was approaching one of his periodic breakdowns, 'a combination of circumstances having, during the last year,' he wrote to a friend, 'so utterly exhausted me physically and intellectually, that I must lie very quiet for a time, and I look forward with dread even to the research necessary to make my Edinburgh lectures what they should be.' Eventually complete removal to the West Country was decided upon. It was a time of sadness for Kingsley, who was left behind to sell the cow and tidy things up in the parish. It was only eight years since he had arrived at the rectory so full of hope, and now he was leaving it for an indefinite period, in the hands of Lempriere, a new curate. 'Eversley', he told Fanny, 'feels like a grave, the grave of so many hopes of what the parish might have been.'[17] There was one achievement in that year, however, of which he could be proud. In November the first national school at Eversley was opened. It had been built with money contributed by Sir William Cope and Mr Stapleton and was later named after Charles Kingsley. It is in use to this day.

[16] ULF No. 159, 1855.
[17] ULF No. 144, summer 1854.

CHAPTER 9

Westward Ho!
1853–1855

Neither Charles nor Fanny bore separation well. Although Charles liked to go off on his own occasionally, he had a horror of being at Eversley without Fanny, and he was to be there often for the next two years, for it was hard to find curates, so many of the young clergymen he had known now being 'bechildrenned'. His letters were full of laments: 'I dread the days alone at Eversley',[1] 'I have never been into the drawing room. It seems quite ghastly and dead without its darling duck of a mistress',[2] 'I feel as stupid as a jug without you, and long to go to sleep in bed till you come home again.'[3] Furthermore he was seriously worried both about Fanny's bronchitis and about the expense to which it was putting him. One of the few sharp letters he ever wrote to her was on the subject; 'Do you have the oil rubbed in every morning over the whole of the upper part of your body by nurse or Susan? Don't neglect yourself and make all the expense null and void.'[4]

Fanny bore the separation equally ill; 'I am coughing today and am a poor creature', she wrote from Torquay. Twenty years later she claimed that her heart trouble started at this period though there is no mention of any such disability in the letters that have survived. She had, however, become convinced that complete rest was essential to her, and led a life of total idleness.

> Your daily letter is the moment I wait for — I enclose a cover so that you will not have the excuse of not having a stamp. Tell me many things, for I suppose I read each letter of yours 20 times, and if they are short it is not a satisfactory task to learn five lines by heart. My days are very weary, alternating between bed and sofa — neuralgia and influenza. Dear J. sends me *The Times* daily which is like a dose

[1] ULF No. 135, 1854.
[2] ULF No. 112, 1849.
[3] ULF No. 115, May 16, 1850.
[4] ULF No. 144, Summer 1854.

of Champagne. Even the advertisements are wonderfully *teaching* to anyone who thinks while they are reading them.[5]

With so many vacant hours to fill, Fanny relapsed into the morbidity of which Charles had accused her before her marriage. She was haunted by the fear of disasters that might befall him, and had only to hear of an accident in his vicinity to become convinced that he personally was involved. Years later, when a train crashed in New England, she waited weeks in suspense until a letter arrived from California to assure her her beloved had not been a passenger.[6] Now she dreamt that he was dead. 'I have had a horrible dream, that I was a widow. I shall not rest till I clasp you again.'[7] At other moments she feared that it was Charles who would be bereaved, and distressed him terribly by telling him he must marry again if she died. She declared that she longed to get 'rid of walls and roofs and all the chrysalis case of humanity and be with God'. Even when she sent news of the children it was usually bad news. 'Poor dear Rose's Princess of Wales doll, the one with real eyebrows, was killed by a railway accident yesterday, and when she arrived at Torquay Station her head was literally squashed. The anguish of dear Rose was piteous and all the Torquay dolls are hideous.'[8]

Mounting debts were a cause of anxiety to both Kingsleys. In endless letters Fanny bewailed the family's poverty and prophesied ruin. Charles wrote back, attempting to comfort her, although clearly worried himself. 'Of course I paid the money in, but pray don't be in a hurry to pay out. No one is dunning and Cope's tithe will come in in a week. There is plenty of money and no worry.'[9] Nevertheless, only a week or two earlier, he had written to say, 'Ridley duns for 23.16.9. Pray pay him at once,'[10] which suggests that Fanny's fears were not entirely groundless. At Christmas the Kingsleys were reunited and their anxieties were somewhat abated.

Charles found Fanny comfortably ensconced at Torquay, with a governess for the children and a nurse for Mary, in a large house on the front called Livermead. Torquay, in the 'fifties, was a fashionable watering place with London carriages and foreign aristocrats thronging

[5] Unpublished letter from Fanny, 1854. At Eversley the Kingsleys were not in the habit of taking a daily paper.

[6] Unpublished letter from Fanny, 1874.

[7] Unpublished letter from Fanny, March 14, 1854.

[8] Unpublished letter from Fanny, 1853.

[9] ULF No. 162, 1855.

[10] ULF No. 155, 1855.

its streets. It is quite possible that Fanny chose it in the hope that Charles might preach before people there who could be of use to him. If she had such hopes they proved groundless, for Henry, Bishop of Exeter, forbade the author of *Yeast*, *Alton Locke* and *Hypatia* to preach from any pulpit in the diocese. Such prejudice appears so extreme that many have doubted whether the bishop in fact ever delivered such a judgment, but a recently discovered letter written by Fanny, suggests that he did. 'As for Henry of Exeter,' she wrote to her sister, 'hanging is too good for him.'[11]

Deprived of all parish duties Kingsley was able to throw himself, with characteristic earnestness, into the task of collecting marine specimens. As he himself admitted, he was incapable of taking even his pleasures lightly. 'I go at what I am about as if there was nothing else in the world. That's the secret of most hard working men, but most of them don't carry it into their amusements.' Philip Gosse had recently published the first of the books on the fauna of the seashore whose fame led to the permanent denuding of the rock pools round our coasts. Kingsley offered to supply him with specimens and in reply Gosse sent down a hamper full of wicker-topped glass jars. Now the unemployed clergyman set to work to fill them. The search was organised like a campaign: 'This week I will manage a day at Petit Tor, a day at Tor Abbey and a day at Goodrington (whence come chirodata and the orange-mouthed actinia). Next week I hope to commence dredging.' Rose and Maurice were pressed into service as assistants, and pleased their father by 'running with proud delight to add their little treasure' to his stock and spending happy evenings releasing their catch into the vivarium beside Fanny's sofa and 'examining, arranging, preserving and noting down in the diary the wonders and labours of the long happy day'. The result of these labours also brought joy to the sad little house in Islington where the Gosses lived with their son Edmund. The arrival of a new set of jars in a hamper caused great excitement, and their contents 'were tipped into pans and bowls all over the house'. A year or two later, after the death of his wife, Gosse bought a villa at Oddicombe, near Torquay, and Kingsley was one of the few people who dared break in upon the privacy of this stern member of the Plymouth Brethren. His son, Edmund Gosse, recalled these visits in his book, *Father and Son*.

Charles Kingsley had reason to visit our neighbouring town rather frequently, and on such occasions he always marched up and attacked us. It was extraordinary how persistent he was. I vividly recollect

[11] Unpublished letter from Fanny, 1854.

that a sort of cross examination of would-be communicants was going on one weekday morning, when Mr Kingsley was announced; my Father in stentorian tones, replied; 'Tell Mr Kingsley that I am engaged in examining scripture with certain of the Lord's children.' And I, a little later, kneeling at the window, watched the author of *Hypatia* nervously careering about the garden, very restless and impatient, yet preferring this ignominy to the chance of losing my father's company altogether. Kingsley, a daring spirit, used sometimes to drag us out trawling with him in Torbay, and although his hawk's beak and rattling voice frightened me a little, he was always a jolly presence that brought some refreshment to our seriousness.

The friendship with Gosse lasted several years, but finally foundered on the rock of the *Origin of Species*. When the book appeared Gosse shut himself away for a year and wrestled with the problem of reconciling science with the literal interpretation of the Bible. He emerged with a book entitled *Omphalos* (the Greek word for a navel) in which he explained that, just as Adam, who had been created mature and without the assistance of a mother, had had a navel, so the rocks, which were created in a week, contained fossils which gave an *appearance* of great age. He had expected to astonish the learned world with this theory, and particularly Kingsley, but he was to be disappointed. After a careful perusal of *Omphalos* Kingsley wrote to say that he could not give up 'the painful and slow conclusion of five and twenty years study of geology, and believe that God had written on the rocks one enormous and superfluous lie'.

Kingsley, however, never lost his admiration for Gosse as a scientist and considered his own researches 'the mere pryings of an amateur' compared to those of Gosse. 'When I glanced my eye merely over your division of the *Actiniae*', he told Gosse, 'I felt that anyone who pretends to know even one corner of the Lord's world thoroughly must devote his whole mind to it, and not fancy he can pry into the doings of the Spirit, while he is frittering away his time on half a dozen other hobbies.' Kingsley did, however, have a gift for popularising science, and he first displayed it in a book written at this time, entitled *Glaucus, or the Wonders of the Shore*, a lengthened version of an article which originally appeared in the *North British Review*. *Glaucus* is chiefly of interest today as a less fanciful forerunner of *The Water-Babies*. It contains the same vivid pictures of underwater creatures, embellished by the same humour and marred by the same moralising. There is a memorable description of the sea worm:

Is it alive? It hangs helpless and motionless — a mere velvet string across the hand. You cannot tell where it begins or ends. It may be a dead strip of seaweed or even a tarred string. So thinks the little fish till he touches what is surely a head. In an instant a bell-shaped sucker has fastened to his side and slowly yet dexterously a curved finger begins packing him end foremost into the gullet, where he sinks, inch by inch, till the bulge which marks his place is lost among the coils.

But this delightful passage is, alas, followed by a disquisition about the place of ugliness in God's universe. Again, as in *The Water-Babies*, there are humorous passages. Kingsley was firmly convinced that certain animals were created to make men laugh and so we read of the antics of a pair of soldier crabs fighting for the same shell, and of the rare red-legged cockles 'snapping, starting crawling and tumbling wildly over each other' on the rocks of Torbay. The book eventually found its way into the royal nursery.[12]

In the summer the Kingsleys moved from the south to the north coast of Devon, to Bideford, just up the coast from Clovelly. Kingsley was already planning *Westward Ho!* and wanted to be within sight of the little port from which so many gallant ships had set out to rob the Spaniards of the Main. On the first page of *Westward Ho!* appears a description of Bideford which still holds true today:

All who have travelled through the delicious scenery of North Devon must needs know the little white town of Bideford, which slopes upward from its broad tide river, and many-arched old bridge toward the pleasant upland of the West. It stands where Torridge joins her sister Taw, and both flow quietly toward the everlasting thunder of the Atlantic swell.

The present-day traveller will find the famous stone bridge still there, though it now carries the ceaseless holiday traffic to Barnstaple; sea-going vessels are still moored beside the main street although their only cargo is gravel for the ever-turning concrete mixers of the coast, and the Ship Tavern, where the Brotherhood of the Rose was formed, still stands, although it is now the Rose of Torridge Café.

The Kingsleys rented Northdown House on the upper outskirts of the town. It was a large house of the type that Fanny now demanded. After the glories of her brothers' residences at Taplow Court and Ray Lodge, 'perfect little bijoux' of places would no longer satisfy her.

[12] Letter to Alexander Macmillan, May 19, 1856.

Northdown House now accommodates, admittedly with additions, a convent school of five hundred girls. It is an elegant cube-shaped house of the late eighteenth century whose ground floor comprises an entrance hall embellished by a wide curved staircase that appears to float down without visible means of support, and two reception rooms which, with their interconnecting door open, would be quite adequate for the holding of a private ball. From the window of the upstairs corner room where he wrote, Kingsley had a view over the park-like walled garden and, beyond it, to the distant shipyards of Appledore. In this peaceful place he brooded bloodily upon war.

In the summer of 1854 Britain was in the grip of the fever of hate against Tsar Nicholas I which precipitated the Crimean War. Kingsley was as incensed as anyone. He longed for 'an hour's skirmishing in those Inkerman ravines and five minutes with butt and bayonet as a *bonne bouche* to finish off with'. Tom Hughes suggested he should release his pent-up feelings in a patriotic ballad but he replied

as for a ballad — oh! I tell you, the whole thing stuns me, so I cannot sit down to make *fiddle* rhyme with *diddle* about it, or *blundered* with *hundred*, like Alfred Tennyson. He is no Tyrtaeus, though he has a glimpse of what Tyrtaeus ought to be. But I have not even that; and am going rabbit shooting tomorrow instead. Would that the Rabbits were Russians, tin pot on head and musket in hand!

In the end he put his aggression into words in the form of a tract entitled *Brave Words for Brave Soldiers*. In it he assured the boys at the front that the British Army was God's Army. When the tide of victory turned in the winter of 1854, and the British Army, instead of following up the success at Alma by seizing Sebastopol, proceeded to spend the winter freezing outside its walls, he wrote a second pamphlet, in the form of a letter to Hughes and Ludlow. Unlike the rest of the nation, he had no pity to spare for the three miles of living corpses at Scutari. What he was concerned to know was why a new army was not sent out. 'Why was Lord Raglan kept idle at Balaklava?' He claimed to know why.

Because a certain Prince keeps him there. Because a certain Prince must at all hazard to the nation, swamp the war for fear of those petty bankrupt German princes being crushed by it, as God grant they may be. But no one dares say so. *The Times* dare not. Who dares? Everyone knows it but everyone knows too that if you begin at the beginning, you may end up at the end — and what that end would

be they don't (I'm sure I don't) like to know. 1688 was all smooth
sailing because you had William of Orange to fall back on: but
now —.

Such thoughts were too treasonable to publish. Indeed the pamphlet
appears in print for the first time as an appendix to the present volume.
Frustrated of an audience, Kingsley had to content himself with bringing the nation's blood to the boil with what he himself described as 'a
most ruthless, bloodthirsty book, *Westward Ho! Or the voyages and
adventures of Sir Amyas Leigh*[13] *Knight, of Burrough in the County of
Devon, in the reign of Her Most Glorious Majesty Queen Elizabeth.
Rendered into modern English by C.K.*'

The tone of *Westward Ho!* was set, before even a line had been
written, by the dedication which was to Rajah Sir James Brooke, and
George Augustus Selwyn, Bishop of New Zealand, two peculiarly
ferocious gentlemen. The choice of Brooke was a strange one, for he
was a controversial figure in 1855. As a young man he had fitted out a
140-ton schooner and set about slaughtering the pirates off the coast of
Borneo with such vigour that he had ended by routing the sultan and
being declared rajah of the province of Sarawak. So great was the
carnage involved that he was tried by a Royal Commission at
Singapore in 1851 for gaining the unheard of sum of £20,000 in head
money from the British Government, and although the case was declared 'not proven' he was deprived of the governorship of Labuan and
the granting of head money was discontinued. Bishop Selwyn's war-
like operations were not on such a scale but, during the Maori wars, he
spent days and nights in the saddle, sometimes swimming broad rivers,
and was rumoured, perhaps wrongly, to have taken part in the fighting
on both sides. If he had he would have won nothing but approval from
Kingsley who had a liking for fighting clerics, as he states on several
occasions in *Hereward the Wake*.

It is hard to believe today that *Westward Ho!* was originally intended
for adults. Certainly it contains much that is unsuitable for children, in
the form of lengthy discourses about Elizabethan hexameters and the
relative merits of Lyly's *Euphues* and Sydney's *Arcadia*. But the wise
child of an earlier day no doubt discovered that he had but to follow
Kingsley's advice and 'turn the leaf till he found pasturage which suited

[13] The Leighs were a real family, and did indeed live at Bardon Hall until the
beginning of this century. Kingsley, however, did not model his story on any particular member of the family, although an Amyas Leigh does appear in their family
Bible. Mrs Glover is the only surviving member of the family. I am indebted to
Geoffrey Gilbert for this information.

him better'. And rich pasturage it was with such splendid set pieces as
the battle with the Spanish treasure fleet, the ambush in the South
American jungle and the rout and wrecking of the Armada in the
storm off Lundy. With so much excitement the thinness of the plot,
concerned chiefly with the attempt to rescue the beautiful Devonshire
maiden, Rose, from Don Guzman, seems hardly to matter.

As a book for adults *Westward Ho!* is today harder to stomach.
Lacking as we do Kingsley's conviction that England alone has the
privilege of 'replenishing the earth and subduing it for God and the
Queen', and that all Catholics are 'Jesuitical plotters' and all negroes
'ant-eating apes', we cannot view their slaughter with the enthusiasm
expected of us. To us, but evidently not to Kingsley, the extermination
of seven hundred Spaniards in Ireland is somewhat repugnant.

It was done. The shrieks and curses had died away, and the Fort del
Oro was a red shambles, which the soldiers were trying to cover
from the sight of heaven and earth, by dragging the bodies into the
ditch, and covering them with the ruins of the rampart. It was done;
and it never needed to be done again. The hint was severe, but it was
sufficient. Many years passed before a Spaniard set foot again in
Ireland.

After such a scene one is inclined to quote W. R. Greg:

What unspeakable relief and joy for a Christian, like Mr Kingsley,
whom God had made boiling over with animal eagerness and fierce
aggressive instincts, to feel that he is not called upon to control these
instincts, but only to direct them; and that once having, or fancying
he has, in view a man or an institution that is God's enemy as well as
his, may hate it with a perfect hatred, and go at it *en sabreur*! Accordingly he reminds us of nothing so much as a war-horse panting for
the battle; his usual style is marvellously like a neigh — a 'ha! ha!
among the trumpets'; the dust of combat is to him the breath of life.

Yet there were gentler passages of what the Victorians called 'word
painting' in the book. Many have admired the descriptions of the Devon
coastline, but few have drawn attention to the dream-like quality of
some of his pictures of South American jungle scenery. In one we see
Amyas and his men paddling up the glassy River Meta 'between two
green walls of forest, while a long procession of monkeys kept pace
with them along the tree tops, and proclaimed their wonder in every
imaginable whistle and grunt and howl'. In another, two escaped

sailors find a tropical paradise beside a waterfall overhung with orchids: 'the air was heavy with the scent of flowers, and quivering with the murmur of the stream, the hum of the colibris and insects, the gentle cooing of a hundred doves, while now and then, from far away, the musical wail of the sloth, or the deep toll of the bell bird, came softly to the ear.'

It is always said that the book contained portraits of Kingsley's friends. Some have even suggested that Amyas Leigh, the hero, was based on Kingsley himself but this is manifestly untrue, for Amyas was a bluff, games-playing extrovert whose first act, on attaining adolescence, was to bring his school slate down on the bald coxcomb of Sir Vindex Brimblecomb, his schoolmaster. Kingsley himself firmly declared that Amyas was based on his Cambridge friend, Frank Penrose, and that his courtly, intellectual brother, Frank, 'as delicately beautiful as his brother was huge and strong', was Charles Mansfield. There have been suggestions that Amyas's mother was based on Kingsley's own, but there seems little resemblance between the melancholy lady of Bardon Hall and the brisk mistress of St Luke's Rectory.

Kingsley did not offer *Westward Ho!* to Parker. Relations with the editor of *Fraser's* had been strained since an anonymous article against Christian Socialism had appeared in the same issue as the second instalment of *Hypatia*. In the end it was offered to the Macmillans who had published *Cheap Clothes and Nasty* and several other non-fiction works. Daniel and Alexander Macmillan were an enterprising pair of brothers from Scotland who had started their own publishing firm and quickly become publishers to the University of Oxford. Daniel, in particular, had been a personal friend since the days of *Politics for the People* and Kingsley sometimes stayed at his house in Wandsworth and took his 'lovely little girl' for walks on the Common. The two men were in correspondence during the seven hectic months of *Westward Ho!'s* composition. On November 11th, 1854, Kingsley wrote to say that the book was two-thirds finished and would be longer than planned (it in fact ran to three volumes and 250,000 words). He added that he was willing to make it one-third longer or shorter than originally envisaged, whichever his publisher preferred. In another he asked for a loan of £40 to keep him going for a month or six weeks.

Westward Ho! put Macmillan on the map as a publisher, and earned Kingsley £400, more than he had ever earned from a novel; so much in fact that he wrote to Ludlow asking whether he should not perhaps declare it to the income tax authorities! It was a book that was in tune with the times. Caroline Fox described it as 'a fine foe exterminating book of Elizabethan days written in the religious spirit of Joshua and

David. For Spaniards read Russians'. Most people agreed with her but there were a few dissentient voices. Henry Crabb Robinson confided to his diary, 'Now that I have finished Kingsley's *Westward Ho*, I will say that it is one of the least agreable, to my taste, of any I have read by him. The incidents, if invented, are disagreable; if copied, ill-managed. I fear it has been produced by the wish to induce a vulgar hatred of Popery.' George Eliot, summing the book up in a few well-chosen words for the *Westminster Review*, probably made the fairest comment. 'Kingsley,' she wrote, 'sees, feels and paints vividly, but he theorises illogically and moralises absurdly.'

Among the book's critics were the inevitable quibblers about its historical accuracy. Two Barnstaple historians pointed out that Kingsley had given Bideford too large a share of the credit for supplying the ships that defeated the Armada. Kingsley wrote back humbly enough pointing out that his main source had been 'my old Hakluyt' and admitting that he had no access to state papers or town records. But as regards the Barnstaple tourist trade, the damage was done. In the popular view Bideford is the home town of the great Elizabethan sea-dogs and a statue of Kingsley, professorially robed, stands on the quay to prove it. Westward Ho!, a new resort, succeeded entirely because of the name,[14] said to have been suggested to its developer by Kingsley personally.

While he was living at Bideford Kingsley complained bitterly that he lacked male companionship. 'Here I am,' he wrote, 'an old Jeremiah with my Elizabethan papers.' He did in fact make one lifelong friend there, in the person of W. H. Ackland, a philanthropic doctor who lived in a bow-windowed house in Bridgeland Street. Ackland shared Kingsley's interest in social reform and often took him on his rounds. He would stop his gig at the corner of Northdown House and signal to Kingsley, who would leap from his desk to join him with long strides across the lawn. It was probably with Dr Ackland that Kingsley first visited the Braunton Hills beyond the Torridge, from which he could see the green panorama of the Devon countryside stop abruptly hundreds of feet above the Atlantic. He declared it the finest view in the kingdom. Later he became godfather to Ackland's son and presented him with a set of his sermons on his second birthday.

Another distraction at Bideford was a drawing class for the young men of the town who Kingsley saw hanging about 'wasting their hours in worse than wasting'. He brought flowers from his conservatory

[14] Probably only students of Elizabethan drama are aware that Kingsley in turn cribbed the title *Westward Ho!* from the play *Eastward Ho!* written jointly by Ben Jonson, Chapman and Marston in 1605.

for the young men to draw and amazed them with his anatomical sketches on the blackboard. In later years, when lecturing, he often found the easiest way to make a point was literally to illustrate it. At home he was constantly making little sketches for his children and friends and he had not lost his Cambridge habit of doodling. His sermon book was filled with the unattractive heads of 'bigoted shavelings' and 'Puseyite fanatics' and at a Social Science Congress that he chaired at Bristol the pages that he appeared to be covering with notes were in fact filled with caricatures of the audience. When the room was cleared, his subjects would return, unknown to him, and beg to have them.

In June Kingsley made the long journey to London in search of society, and arrived safely, 'save that the toothpowder was taken ill all over the inside of my bag'.[15] At first he stayed at Chelsea and delighted his mother by preaching to the little maids in her Sunday School. While he was there, he told Fanny, 'who should break into my slumbers but George, looking better than I ever saw him before, having travelled all night from Paris'. George, who was also a keen zoologist, had brought fireflies for the children from Nice, and together the brothers spent 'a happy microscopic evening' and read the last chapter of Gosse's new book which contained descriptions of the specimens Kingsley had sent him. They also went to see 'a sweet picture' of Fanny at the Royal Academy Exhibition, and admired it, although Charles secretly wished she had been painted as Eve, 'so that I might have a likeness of *all* my treasure!'

In July Kingsley was a guest at a large house in Belgrave Square and had his first taste of that lionisation that was soon to become so familiar. His letters home were now sprinkled with the names of the great. 'To Lincoln's Inn with Lord Goderich, where was everybody on earth.'[16] 'Bulmer Lytton was here, to whom I was introduced, and who has a devilish face.'[17] 'I was at Monckton Milnes' last night and went home with *Mecca* Burton and sat till 3 a.m. with him. A splendid little fellow — just off to find the Mountains of the Moon.'[18] 'Dickens was at dinner and he and I fraternised. He is a really genial lovable man, with an eye like a hawk. Not high bred but excellent company, and very sensible. But Mrs Dickens! Oh the fat vulgar vacancy!'[19]

People were beginning to pursue Kingsley, particularly women. 'I

[15] ULF No. 148, June 1854.
[16] ULF No. 142, June 12, 1854.
[17] ULF No. 143, 1854.
[18] ULF No. 147, 1854.
[19] ULF No. 225, April 1855.

was taken possession of by a Baroness Von Weser. Oh, the flattery! Reading *Hypatia* had saved her life after her last confinement, and she needs must come down to Bethnal Green and hear me preach — wanted to take me in her carriage.' Kingsley was shy of female admiration and was particularly alarmed by women who were beautiful as well as predatory. He made a point of evading a certain Mrs Hyford Burton who made a dead set at him at a house party in Hampshire. 'She has a beautiful face and figure,' he told Fanny, 'though the complexion a little helped, and teeth too regular to be *all* alive. But her eye! Furtive, wanton, rolling, ugh! I won't go near her if I know it.[20] On another occasion, after a sermon at the Chapel Royal, he told Fanny, 'Two Yankee women, one a pretty girl, rushed into the vestry to have "the honour of shaking me by the hand", which I did, and fled.'[21]

He was equally shy of corresponding with women. He made a point of not replying to letters from ladies to whom he had not been introduced. Such letters were passed on to Fanny with comments like the following. 'Will you look at this old cat's letter? What a hand she writes! I won't help her a bit — and think it best not to answer her till it is too late. But just advise me by return of post.'[22]

He seldom admitted to admiring a woman. Only one letter exists in which he is openly appreciative of beauty other than Fanny's: 'Mrs Senior came and lunched here. Oh, what a glorious creature, and what glorious hair, the very ideal of a rich blonde!' Even this outburst was followed by an assurance that he would drive any jealousy out of Fanny's head when he got home, 'by means best known to myself and not unknown to my pretty Fanny'.[23] Normally a complimentary remark about a lady was immediately followed by another that contradicted it. 'Mrs Marx is certainly one of the most clever, agreable, well-read women I have ever met. But she weighs 16 stone and has a moustache like a man,'[24] was typical. One of the reasons for this was, no doubt, Fanny's feeling of insecurity. In spite of his constant declarations of love she felt unsure of his affection and on one occasion rather pathetically begged him to promise he would still love her when she had grey hairs. He only admitted once to love for another woman, and that was love of a wholly blameless variety, for the object of it was a consumptive girl named Emma Home who lived in one of the cottages

20 ULF No. 201, 1860.
21 ULF No. 180, 1859.
22 ULF No. 221, 1862.
23 ULF No. 164, 1855.
24 ULF No. 213, 1862.

at Eversley. 'How one does love a girl in a consumption,' he told Fanny.

In the summer of 1855 Kingsley was again in London. Cholera was once more stalking the land, and to Kingsley's satisfaction Palmerston had refused to allow a national fast day which, in his view, would suggest that God was responsible for the disease instead of 'man's selfishness, laziness and ignorance'. Kingsley now led a deputation to the Prime Minister. The interview was evidently satisfactory: 'I had an opportunity of telling Lord Palmerston a great deal, which I trust may save many lives,' he told Fanny. 'Remember, it is now a question of blood guiltiness. *That is all.*'

One friend he had planned to see in London that summer was Charles Mansfield. But since February he had known that Mansfield would never again 'flash down over the glebe at Eversley, with his knapsack at his back'.[25] He had been badly burnt in a laboratory accident and on the very day that Kingsley wrote his letter-pamphlet to Hughes and Ludlow about the Crimean War he died.

Mansfield's erratic career was in the ascendant at the time of his death. He had published a book on his travels in Paraguay, Brazil and the Plate (which no doubt supplied Kingsley with local colour for *Westward Ho!*) and another on aeronautics, and had been asked to supply a sample of his famous Benzol for the Paris Exhibition. It was during the preparation of this sample that the accident occurred. A naphtha still, under the supervision of a boy assistant, boiled over, and in an effort to save the boy and the house in St John's Wood where he rented a room, Mansfield picked up the still and ran to the window with it. Before he could throw it out his hands were flayed. He ran into the street with his clothes on fire, rolled in the snow, and walked a mile before he could find a cab to take him to the Middlesex Hospital. There he died an agonising death ten days later.

Kingsley was too distressed by Mansfield's death to attend his funeral at Weybridge. He wrote to Ludlow: 'To him and to Frank Penrose what do I not owe. They were the only two heroic souls I met during those dark Cambridge years. They alone kept me from sinking into the mire and drowning like a dog. And now one is gone and I shall cling all the more to the other. Tell Frank Penrose so.' And yet he claimed to have had foreknowledge of Mansfield's approaching end. 'I have had a feeling, as I have had in the case of others, that he would go. His image, as others have, grew fainter and more distant. There was a great mist just beyond him and he was fading away into it.' It is certainly strange that Kingsley should have killed off Frank Leigh

[25] Charles Kingsley's introduction to Mansfield's *Paraguay, Brazil and the Plate.*

(Mansfield's fictional counterpart) in the prime of life only a few months earlier.

In the beautiful autumn of 1855 the Kingsleys returned to 'dear old treacherous Eversley'. The long rest and the mild Devon climate 'where the flowers of autumn meet the flowers of spring',[26] had cured Fanny's bronchitis, but with the onset of the autumn rains it showed signs of returning and once more she insisted on moving out of the rectory. Again, nothing less than a mansion would suit her, and the house she now chose, Farley Court in the neighbouring parish of Swallowfield, was so vast that in recent years it has been divided into several flats. It is a handsome Georgian brick house standing at the end of a drive that winds its way through several acres of woodland. The expanse of gravel in front of it would accommodate twenty visiting carriages without difficulty. Here Fanny expressed her intention of staying until a new rectory was built.

At first Sir William Cope seemed sympathetic to the plan of building a new house on the Mount on condition that Kingsley contributed £200 of his own money and secured a loan of a further £1,000 from Queen Anne's bounty. Kingsley hired an architect, Mr Habershon, to draw up successive plans, all of which were turned down by Sir William, who finally declared he would consent to the new house only if it were an exact replica of the old. At the same time he declared that he thought the old rectory

a pretty looking house, and all accounts agree (for I have never been over it) that it is roomy and convenient. I cannot help regretting (if I may say so without offence) that you did not postpone the rebuilding until a larger sum was at your disposal. I certainly do not feel at all called upon to contribute to that object where the living already possesses a sufficient and commodious house and where the change is not one of necessity, but of convenience. The house is a good house as it stands and has been sufficient for many Rectors, and indeed for yourself for many years.

This letter put an end to the project, and Charles now tried to convince Fanny that the existing building could be made tolerable with alterations. It is a measure of his unselfishness, or possibly of his desperation, that he was even prepared to abandon his beloved study, and move into the dining room, to appease Fanny, although he admitted to regrets,

[26] Charles Kingsley, *Glaucus or The Wonders of the Shore.*

for it would mean the carriages driving in front of my window. However it does not matter. One cannot always have sugar to one's bread and butter. The place will be an Elysium, if we will only be good and serve God in it. All my love for the place is coming out again. Was it not the place where you and I began, and our children were begotten and born? And I never wish to leave it as long as I live.

Fanny was not appeased, the alterations were never carried out, and instead it was decided that Charles must make an all-out effort to obtain preferment. What he most wanted was a canonry in one of the cathedrals which would demand only three months' residence in the year. In such a post he could retain the living at Eversley and have somewhere dry to migrate to with his family in the winter.

The first vacant stall for which he tried was at Hereford, but although the dean came to London to hear him preach, the stall was evidently left vacant. Next he attempted St Paul's, but was beaten to the post by the popular preacher Henry Melvill, Principal of the East India College at Haileybury. Now it was decided that all possible guns must be brought to bear on Palmerston for the vacant stall at Westminster. Charles Pascoe Grenfell had already promised to help, but, as Kingsley pointed out to Hughes:

> Charles Grenfell would principally urge his own claim — as the head of a great Whig family, who have worked for the party for 60 years. What is wanted is someone besides to make Lord Palmerston aware of what few claims I have *personally*, and what effect on the working men's mind and their feeling toward the Church the government's patronising me would have. Now do you think that Mr William Cowper[27] would do this? He has always been civil enough to me: But I don't know him well enough to ask him or even to 'aborder' him on the point. Do you, and if not, who does? I am much too proud to blow my own trumpet, or state my own doings. But you know, and others ought to know, what I have done, and what I might do, were I in such a post.

The faithful Hughes enlisted not only Cowper, but also two members of Parliament and Lord Goderich, a peer with radical views who was already a friend of Kingsley. All in vain however. The next Westminster stall to become vacant remained unfilled until 1860, and Kingsley had to wait until 1873 before he achieved a canonry there.

[27] William Cowper was the stepson and heir of Lord Palmerston.

The Years of Drought
1856–1858

During the autumn of 1855 Kingsley wrote *The Heroes*, his first children's book. He had a poor opinion of many of the children's books that were being produced at the time, whose chief intention was to inculcate good morals. In *The Water-Babies* he was to express his dislike of books with names like *Squeeky*, *The Pumplighter*, *The Narrow World*, *The Hills of the Chattermuch* and *The Children's Twaddeday*. He considered 'a jolly good fairy-tale' superior to any such works. Now he set about retelling some of the 'old Greek fairy-tales' as a Christmas present for his three children, Rose, Maurice and Mary. The impulse to rewrite the Greek myths came from a reading of Hawthorne's *Tanglewood Tales*, which Kingsley found 'distressingly vulgar'. Characteristically, as the title suggests, Kingsley chose fighting men for his subjects, 'men who killed fierce beasts and evil men'. The book was divided between three of them, a section each being allotted to the adventures of Perseus, Jason and Theseus. Invited to criticise the manuscript, Ludlow said that Kingsley should have told the stories 'as if from himself', but Kingsley pointed out to 'old hole-picker' that, in order to capture the spirit of the Greek original, he had adopted 'a sort of simple ballad tone', and tried to make the prose 'as metrical as possible'. He was equally determined to avoid the Gothic excesses of Hawthorne, and in this he was successful, for the book has the same direct appeal as *Lamb's Tales from Shakespeare*. It was extremely successful, being brought out in many editions, and eventually even being translated into Greek, a fact which would have delighted its author. Kingsley himself illustrated the book with simple outline drawings looking like tracings. Among them was one of the fifty sketches of Perseus and Andromeda he had made a few years previously. In consideration for the age of his readers, Andromeda, on this occasion, was decently clad.

No sooner had Kingsley finished *The Heroes* than he set to work, in his study at Farley Court, on the third of his novels about contemporary life, *Two Years Ago*. The book was so named because it dealt with the period of the Crimean War, a war which was supposed to have had a regenerative effect on several of its main characters, including Tom Thurnall, the hero. Tom, like Lancelot Smith of *Yeast*, was muscular and well-bred and, like him, only converted to Christianity in the last chapter, as the result of unrevealed experiences in a Russian prison. He was almost certainly based on Kingsley's brother George. Like George, Tom was a cheerful weatherbeaten cynic although he lacked 'George's awful temper'. Like George he had trained to be a doctor in Paris where he 'became the best pistol shot and billiard player in the Quartier Latin'. Like George, he had then wandered 'round the world and back again', collecting scars from Indian tomahawks, Russian sabres and Australian pickaxes. Like George, too, he was probably a womaniser, although this side of his character is hinted at so delicately that it would pass unnoticed but for a reference that Kingsley made to it in a letter.

> I fear you take Tom Thurnall for a better man than he was, and must beg you not to pare my man to suit your own favourable conception; but consider that that is the sort of man I want to draw, and you must take him as you find him. My experience is, that men of his character (like all strong men till God's grace takes full possession of them) are weak upon one point — everything can they stand but *that*; and the more they restrain themselves, from prudential motives, the more sudden and violent is the temptation when it comes. I have indicated as delicately as I could the world-wide fact, which all know and all ignore; had I not done so, Thurnall would have been a mere chimera fit only for a young lady's novel.

The story begins when Tom is shipwrecked at Clovelly (thinly disguised as Aberalva) and the plot, such as it is, revolves round the loss of a belt full of money which he suspects the heroine, Grace Harvey, of stealing. A sub-plot, concerning the beautiful quadroon, Maria, saved from slavery by Tom and destined to become a famous singer, appears to have no connection with the main events. No doubt the author intended to imply that Tom had had an affair with the voluptuous *diva* before the story begins but no hint of such an impropriety appears in the text.

The book is, in fact, like *Yeast*, chiefly a vehicle for the prejudices of the author, but the prejudices have changed since 1849. Apart from a description of a cholera epidemic at Aberalva (based on a similar one that George Kingsley had combated in Flintshire in 1849) there is little mention of the condition of the working classes. High Anglican clergymen and dissenting ministers come in for their usual share of fire, but the main volley is reserved, surprisingly, for a poet, Elsley Vavasour, author of *The Soul's Agonies*. Elsley is an effete creature in a wide-awake hat and a cloak, who would rather stand on the cliffs composing a poem about a shipwreck than go down to the beach to help the survivors. In the book Kingsley sets forth the view that no man can be a great poet whose private life is not blameless and whose chief aim in writing is not to improve the lot of humanity. Elsley does not live up to either of these maxims. Morally, he is a weak selfish creature who neglects his wife, and the subject of his poetry is not, as it should be, 'needlewomen and ragged schools, dwellers in Jacob's Island and sleepers in the dry arches of Waterloo Bridge' but the woes of faraway Italy. Worse still, as he grows older, his poems cease to have any subject at all. 'Manner takes the place of matter' and the poetry becomes 'full of mere sensuous beauty, mere word-painting'. As 'a vigorous moral purpose' vanishes from Elsley's work, so a decline in his character sets in, and, ignoring Tom Thurnall's advice to use the dumb-bells twice a day, he takes to the opium vial. The climax of the book is reached when Elsley runs amok at midnight in the Snowdon area. He calls at Mrs Owen's farmhouse at Pen-y-gwryd, where his strange behaviour leads two stout-hearted public schoolmen on a fishing holiday to suppose he must have been 'taken ill with a poem'. They follow him into the night, whooping and baying, and the hunt is on. Critics at the time questioned the probability of the storm that followed, with thunder bouncing like a ball of fire from one black peak to another. More improbable seems the course of Elsley's flight, which is upwards to the very peak of the Glyder Vawr. A man who had practised so little with the dumb-bells would have been more likely to run downhill. Be that as it may, the scene on the top of the Glyders is fine gothic stuff, and the best thing in the book:

An awful place it always is; and Elsley saw it at an awful time, as the glare unveiled below him a sea of rock waves, all sharp on edge, pointing toward him on every side. Terrible were those rocks below; and ten times more terrible as seen through the lurid glow of his distempered brain. All the weird peaks and slabs seemed pointing up at him; sharp toothed jaws gaped upward — tongues hissed upward — arms pointed upward — hounds leaped upward — monstrous snake heads peered upward out of cracks and caves. Did he not see them move, writhe? or was it the ever-shifting light of the flashes? Did he not hear them howl, yell at him, or was it the wind, tortured in their labyrinthine caverns?

The strong anti-intellectual bias of the novel was reiterated in the poem which contains the famous line 'Be good, sweet maid, and let who will be clever', which appeared for the first time in its pages. The poem had in fact been composed some months earlier by Kingsley as a farewell to his wife's niece, Charlotte Grenfell, and appears in the collected poems in a slightly less philistine version: 'Be good, sweet maid, and let who *can* be clever.'

But if poets and intellectuals are held up for derision in the book, naturalists are singled out for admiration. Indeed, so obsessed does Kingsley appear to have become with the subject of natural history, that an interest in zoophytes in a character is all but equated with moral goodness. When a rather wooden colonel called Campbell is introduced, we know at once that he is a goody, for his face 'worked with almost childish delight' at the prospect of a specimen of *Zoanthus Conchii*. Tom Thurnall's good old father, on meeting his son who has returned from Australia after many years, immediately enquires, not after his health, but about certain rare antipodal fauna. And Tom Thurnall himself is, of course, an amateur naturalist, as was his prototype, George Kingsley. Indeed there is a portrait of Tom Thurnall at work at low tide that could stand equally for George or for Charles himself as, 'with an old smock over his coat and a large basket on his arm', he 'comes hopping towards you, dropping every now and again on hands and knees, and turning over on his back, to squeeze his head into some muddy crack, and then withdraw it with the salt water dripping from his nose'.

Apart from Tom Thurnall and Elsley Vavasour and some Aberalva worthies, the characters in *Two Years Ago* are a wooden collection. Certain stock personalities from *Yeast*, such as Lord Minchampstead, the reforming landlord, and Claude and Sabina Mellot, those artistic lovebirds from 'the wilds of Brompton', are resuscitated but hardly given new life, while the virtuous heroine, Grace Harvey, a nonconformist Aberalva schoolteacher, is altogether too good to be true. The book was nevertheless well received in its day and Kingsley wrote home triumphantly to Fanny, 'Macmillan is going to print 3,000 and make it a 7/6 book, and give us for the edition — will you believe it? — between £100 and £150, he thinks nearer the latter sum. So we shall get on well this winter, thank God. It seems *Westward Ho!* and *Glaucus* have put my name up so that anything I write will sell.'[1] The book in fact sold well. Mudie alone ordered 1,200 copies for his lending library and eventually Kingsley almost certainly made £1,000 out of it. He was at last able to repay Hughes the £500 he had borrowed in

[1] ULF No. 172, 1857.

1851, declaring to him, 'I am better off than I have been for years.' Froude firmly declared, 'Charles has written his best book and all the world knows it', but Kingsley probably gained more satisfaction from the knowledge that 'a distinguished member of one of our universities' was converted on his deathbed by the scene of Elsley's madness.

The Welsh mountain scenes in *Two Years Ago* were inspired by a memorable holiday in what Kingsley called Snowdonia, which took place while he was writing the book. Once more Fanny was not of the party, but Tom Hughes and Tom Taylor (the popular playwright and contributor to *Punch*[2]) were, and in their company the rector of Eversley was transformed once more into a boisterous schoolboy. Hughes once said that Kingsley reminded him of 'a great Newfoundland yearling dog out for an airing, plunging in and out of the water, shaking himself over the ladies' silks and velvets; and all with the rollicking good humour that disarmed anger'. It was in one of these playful moods that he wrote a letter in doggerel and left it in Tom Hughes's chambers when he found him not at home.

> Come away with me Tom,
> Term and talk is done;
> My poor lads are reaping,
> Busy every one.
> Curates mind the parish,
> Sweepers mind the Court,
> We'll away to Snowdon
> For our ten days sport,
> Fish the August evening
> Till the eve is past,
> Whoop like boys at pounders
> Fairly played and grassed.
> Down, and bathe at day-dawn,
> Tramp from lake to lake,
> Washing brain and heart clean
> Every step we take.
> Leave to Robert Browning
> Beggars, fleas, and vines;
> Leave to mournful Ruskin
> Popish Apennines,
> Dirty stones of Venice
> And his Gas-lamps Seven;

[2] Tom Taylor invented the character called Dundreary after whom the whiskers were named. He appeared in a play called *Our American Cousin*.

We've the stones of Snowdon
And the lamps of heaven;
See in every hedgerow
Marks of angels' feet
Epics in each pebble
Underneath our feet;
Once a year, like schoolboys,
Robin-hooding go,
Leaving fops and fogies
A thousand feet below.

The holiday was a success in spite of the torrential rain that made Kingsley's plan for fishing all through the short summer nights impractical. They stayed, not at fashionable Beddgelert, that 'Babylon of guides, cars, chambermaids, tourists, artists, and reading parties,'[3] but at a remote inn at Pen-y-gwryd, where three of the mountain valleys meet. Their hostess was the hospitable Mrs Owen (who, with the name unchanged, had sheltered the mad Elsley Vavasour) and their fare 'braxy mutton, young taters, Welsh porter (which is the identical draining of Noah's flood turned sour) and brandy of more strength than legality'. They rose early, walked and climbed all day, and revelled in the air and the grandeur of the scenery. One day they conquered Snowdon before lunch and killed a dozen trout before evening. 'I never was so well in all my life,' wrote Charles to Fanny.

As a rule the three adventurers made the haven of Mrs Owen's kitchen by nightfall. They must have looked a villainous gang as they sat round the table in the evenings in the 'low room, ceiled with dark beams from which hung bacon and fishing rods, harness and drying stockings, and all the miscellanea of a fishing inn kept by a farmer'.[4] Tom Taylor was bearded and wearing a red flannel shirt, his breeches being patched across behind with a piece of red and blue Welsh flannel petticoat. Hughes was also wearing ragged trousers and over them a boating blazer.

Kingsley [Hughes wrote] was stealing everybody's paper to dry plants in and jogging of the table in an unchristian way so that parties can't write a bit; his neck half broken by a rock in the stream where we bathed this morning, and otherwise but struggling into respectability by reason of the common domestic linen collar and a clean shave.

[3] Charles Kingsley, *Two Years Ago*.
[4] Ibid.

There was only one cloud on the horizon of Charles's happiness: the letters he was receiving from home. Fanny had deeply resented his abandonment of her, and at this time her habitual morbidity seems to have been moving towards a pathological state of depression. Her letters are lost, but Kingsley's reply to one gives sufficient indication of their contents.

Why will you write me letters that only pain me, about crimes which you have never committed, and of which I never dreamt? If you write two more such I shall come strait (sic) home to you to find out if you are in your right senses or not. You are the dearest, sweetest, wisest creature on earth. I am a foolish careless man who will never grow old, and who vexed you treasonably by foolish crowing over going up Snowdon, and I am wrong and you are right and for God's sake say no more only love me, love me, love me.[5]

No sooner had he returned to Eversley than Kingsley's spirits plunged almost as low as Fanny's. In recent years his depressions were taking the form of a deep dissatisfaction with the course that the whole of the first half of his life had taken. On his thirty-fifth birthday, two years earlier, he had written to Fanny, 'It is a very solemn thought that half one's career is over, perhaps more. God grant the next thirty-five years may see more work and less folly come out of me than the last thirty-five. I hate the remembrance of it, except what has been spent in your beloved arms.' What merit, he now asked Ludlow, had there been in his work for Christian Socialism? Had not even his outspokenness brought him fame and money? 'I've often thought what a dirty beast I was; I made £150 by Alton Locke, and never lost a farthing by anything — and I got, not in spite of, but by the rows, a name and a standing with many a one who would never have heard of me otherwise.' And what merit was there in speaking out anyway?

I see clearly that I have given the devil, and bad men, a handle, by not caring what people would say and by fancying that I was a very grand fellow, who was going to speak what I knew to be true, in spite of all fools, and really did intend so to do, while all the while I was unaware of the proud, self-willed, self-conceited spirit which made no allowance for another man's weakness or ignorance; nor again, for their superior experience on points which I had never

[5] ULF No. 169, August 1856.

considered: which took a pride in shocking and startling, and defying, and hitting as hard as I could, and fancied, blasphemously, as I think, that the word of God had come to me only, and went out from me only.

To F. D. Maurice he revealed even more distressing doubts, doubts indeed of the very existence of God.

A period of collapse has come upon me. I live in dark nameless dissatisfaction and dread. My dear Master, terrible and sad thoughts haunt me, thoughts which I long to put away. But meanwhile comfort yourself on one point, that I am humbled and have had a peep or two down through the sea of glass and seen the nether fire within half an inch of my feet. Everything seems to me not worth working at, except the simple business of telling poor people, 'Don't fret, God cares for you', and that I can't tell fully, because I daren't say what I think, I daren't preach my own creed, which seems to me as different from what I hear preached and find believed, everywhere, as the modern creeds are from Popery, or from St Paul — and as St Paul — horrible thought — seems to me at moments from the plain simple words of our Lord. When one's trust in the Bible seems falling to pieces one feels alone in the universe, at least alone among mankind, on a cliff which is crumbling beneath one, and falling piecemeal into the dark sea.

For a time he suffered a revulsion even from Carlyle. A session with him about this time drove him almost to frenzy.

I was with him, with Froude and Parker, [he told F. D. Maurice] and I never heard a more foolish outpouring of Devil's doctrines, Raving Cynicism which made me sick. I kept my temper with him: but when I got out I am afraid I swore with wrath and disgust, at least I left no doubt on my two friends' minds of my opinion of such stuff. All the ferocity of the old Pharisee without Isaiah's prophecy of mercy and restoration, the notion of sympathy with sinners denounced as a sign of innate scoundrelism, a blame I am very glad to bear: I must tell you all *viva voce*. If I can temperately. I never was so shocked in all my life, and you know I have a strong stomach, and am not easily moved to pious horror. Meanwhile his wife is pining, poor creature, for want of sympathy and attention from him, and very ill. Whatever her faults may be, *he* has no right to neglect her.

During this period the springs of creativity dried up, and it was six years before they began to flow once more, suitably enough, with *The Water-Babies*. Several works were commenced and then put aside, for huge financial inducements were being offered. Macmillan was prepared to pay £2,000 for his next novel. In 1858 he spent a few weeks in Yorkshire collecting material for a book about the Pilgrimage of Grace, but abandoned it in favour of a contemporary novel with a Yorkshire setting, *Alcibiades*.[6] This novel he also left unfinished on the grounds that it was libellous. 'I have been too much behind the scenes of court, fashionable and intellectual circles,' he explained to Macmillan, 'and would introduce personal portraits.' He turned once more to historical fiction, this time choosing the period of Wellington's campaign in the South of France. 'I have had an inspiration,' he told Fanny, 'about a book which will be a refreshment and change to my mind, and will not cost me another long visit to York.' But again the inspiration failed.

It must have been trying for Kingsley that, during this period of drought, two people very close to him, neither of whom he had suspected of literary ability, published first novels. It was a measure of his generosity that he welcomed both books and 'puffed' them wherever he could. In the spring of 1857 Tom Hughes had sent him the almost completed manuscript of *Tom Brown's Schooldays*. Kingsley read it with care, suggested minor alterations, and advised his friend 'to finish the book in your own original way, and never mind Ludlow'. A year later another book, almost equally successful in its day, appeared. Its title was *The Recollections of Geoffrey Hamlyn* and its author was none other than Henry Kingsley.

Henry had had a somewhat chequered career since the German walking tour seven years earlier. He left Oxford without a degree and there is a strong suspicion that he was sent down for homosexual practices. Certain aspects of his behaviour at the University would lead one to imagine this, for he was a founder of the Fez Club, members of which were vowed to celibacy and who met monthly (suitably fezzed) to denounce womankind in all its forms. There were also overtly homosexual references in several of his books. To take but two random examples: one short story (*Jackson of Paul's*)was about a man who marries the sister of his boy-love (killed in battle). 'My love lies dead,' he declares, 'I only loved her through him.' And in the novel *Stretton*, Allan fondles 'the very small hands of Eddy' in their 'beautifully made lemon-coloured kid gloves'.

[6] His daughter Mary completed the story and published it after his death, under the title *The Tutor's Story*.

After leaving Oxford Henry took ship for Australia and was not heard of for six years. He followed the gold rush to Victoria and sank very low, digging and washing for gold dust 'until it was a toss up whether he would die first of disease or starvation'. Then he worked as a painter of inn signs, a trooper in the Sydney mounted police and a stock driver. Finally he sunk to the ignominious position of a sundowner, that is to say a tramp who knocks at the door of a lonely farm in time for the evening meal and leaves at dawn, before he has paid for his night's shelter with a day's work. It was at this stage that a gentleman farmer at Langa-Willi took pity on him, lent him a shack and gave him the six months' leisure he needed to turn his experiences into a book.

When Henry finally returned to England he made straight for the rectory in Chelsea, and hesitated for an hour before he could summon up courage to ring the bell. When he eventually did, it was only to discover that his parents had just moved to Eversley. He followed them there and found them, much aged, living in a charming cottage called Dressors, which still stands, surrounded by a large garden, at Eversley Street. The next day he walked the shady mile that separates Dressors from the rectory, and laid the manuscript of *Geoffrey Hamlyn* before the brother for whom, he claimed, his love only grew stronger as he grew older. Charles was impressed with the novel and persuaded Macmillan to publish it.

The Recollections of Geoffrey Hamlyn is the original of all the bush-ranging tales of adventure and excitement, and was regarded by Ralph Bolderwood,[7] who knew Henry at Langa-Willi, as 'the best Australian novel, and for a long time the only one.' Some critics have suggested that Henry was a better writer than Charles; certainly his brother George was of that opinion. Alexander Macmillan went only so far as to praise his ability to describe landscape; 'it is wonderfully quiet and yet powerful; it has a kind of lazy strength which is very charming'. Encouraged by his success Henry decided to become a writer, and settled, in a cottage next door to Dressors, with a close male friend called Campbell, spending his afternoons gardening[8] and fishing and his nights writing, with frequent assistance from the jug of rum and water he always kept on his desk.

In 1858 Eversley had become almost a Kingsley enclave. Besides the five Kingsleys at the rectory and the three at Dressors, Charlotte, also a novelist, had come on a long visit to her parents from Ilfracombe where

[7] Author of *Robbery under Arms*.
[8] Henry, like his niece Rose, was a keen gardener and introduced some of the first roses into this country including La France and Souvenir de Malmaison.

her husband, the Rev J. M. Chanter, was vicar. And in this year a fourth and last baby was born to Charles and Fanny. Grenville Arthur, named after his mother's ancestor, Sir Richard Grenville and Arthur Penryn Stanley, Dean of Westminster, was a much-wanted child. When Charles heard that Fanny, now over forty, was once more pregnant, six years after the birth of her last child, he wrote — 'And now — what shall I say of my delight at your news. It seems too good to be true.' Unfortunately, because Grenville was the youngest child by so far, and a boy, Fanny spoilt him outrageously and Charles did little to redress the balance.

By Victorian standards Kingsley was a remarkably indulgent father to all his children. He did not beat them for fits of inattention or temper as his nurses and tutors had beaten him, but held the latest view that children 'have their hours of rain, when the quicksilver falls', and parents should pass lightly over them 'by supplying a change of occupation'. He loved to romp with the little ones, and games of cricket in the hall and practical jokes at breakfast were the breath of life to him. He hated to see children forced into tight uncomfortable clothes, 'as we wretched boys used to be forty years ago, frill collar, and tight skeleton monkey jacket, and tight trousers buttoned over it — and a pair of low shoes — which always came off if one stept into heavy ground.'[9] In *The Water-Babies* Mrs Bedonebyasyoudid devised special punishments for 'foolish ladies, who pinch up their children's waists and toes . . . and she laced them all up in tight stays, so that they were choked and sick, and their noses grew red, and their hands and feet swelled; and then she crammed their poor feet into the most dreadfully tight boots, and made them all dance, which they did most clumsily indeed.'

Kingsley's son, Maurice, looking back on his childhood, said he remembered it as a time of 'perpetual laughter'. Sundays, which were days of gloom in so many Victorian homes, were days of particular enjoyment at Eversley.[10] There was church in the morning of course and the decorating of the graves in the churchyard, but in the afternoon there was the much-loved walk across the Common to the service held in the schoolroom at Bramshill and, best of all, in the

[9] Charles Kingsley, Lecture given at Wellington College, June 25, 1863.

[10] Kingsley was never a Sabbatarian, and allowed the village boys, although not his own, to play cricket on the green at Eversley on Sundays. The landlord of the Chequers (which is still a pleasant place to stop between Reading and Guildford) used to say, 'Eh, Parson, he doan't objec' — not ee — as loik as not 'e'll coom and look on, and 'ee do tell 'em as it's a deal better to 'ave a bit o' 'elthy play o' a Sunday evenin' than to be a-larkin' 'ere and a-larkin' there hall hover the place a-courtin' and a-drinkin' hale.'

evenings the Sunday picture books were brought out and each child chose a subject from them for his father to draw.

Yet, in a circle of so many indulged children, Grenville (who was called 'Baby' or 'My Lord Grenville' till he was five) was selected for special indulgence. For Rose, Maurice and Mary their father might draw pictures, but for Grenville he made a train of nine carriages, still preserved at Eversley school. Considering that he was a man whose practical gifts lay, as he himself, admitted in the arts of destruction (sport) rather than construction, the making of this train must have involved no small effort. A recently discovered letter suggests that he was driven to the bench by the sight of his youngest son's inept attempts at making a train for himself. 'I found Baby today working hard with George White[11] at the back garden gate. He ran up to me in great excitement — "I've been making a steam train and I've painted it" — and he had got two great logs and laid them across, and painted one brown with George White's paintbrush and was boring a hole in the other with his great auger, just like a train.'[12] Throughout his childhood Grenville was treated as a delicate child of whom no great effort must be required. In a letter to Fanny, Charles wrote, 'If ever you see that prognathous, drooping look, about the outside of G's upper lip (which he has had more than once since he was born) he should have idleness and food and fresh air at once, and nothing else.'

In this year the Kingsleys lost a son as well as gaining one. The time had come for Maurice, now nine years old, to be sent away to school. Charles hated the idea of him leaving home and as for Fanny, she regarded the isolation of her firstborn son in some distant institution as nothing less than catastrophic. Indeed, only two years previously the couple had decided that Maurice should be educated entirely at home, like his sisters.

You are right, [Charles wrote to Fanny]. He shall not go to school to be made a beast of. I will work with him and for him, so help me God. I have just been talking over the very same thing with Mrs Senior, and she vows *her* boy shall not go to school. She says that even in Tom Hughes it begot a hardness which it took years to cure. No, nature must be right, and if home education is not natural what is? As for polish, our boy will not need to go to school for that. And I will restrain my temper.[13]

[11] The gardener and man-of-all work at Eversley.
[12] ULF No. 183, 1865.
[13] ULF No. 163, June 15, 1856.

Unfortunately Kingsley was not a hard enough taskmaster and Maurice, although physically active, was mentally lazy. When he was finally handed over to professionals, they found his ignorance on almost every subject complete.

The school chosen for Maurice was a small preparatory school at 9 Eliot Place, Blackheath, run by Cowley Powles. In the past the school had numbered Disraeli among its pupils, and in the future it was to have the doubtful distinction of harbouring the latest candidate for the role of Jack the Ripper among its masters.[14] Kingsley accompanied the boy there with strict instructions from Fanny that he was to stay with the Powles family for four nights and nowhere else. Powles benefited by the arrangement (Kingsley made him laugh 'which he has not done for weeks') and Maurice seemed happy enough. Indeed, according to Kingsley, the chief danger was that he would 'get too *much* petting and pampering from Powles'. But Fanny at Eversley was half frantic. 'We have been married fourteen years and this is my first real grief and trial. I cannot tell you what I suffered. I felt in the night, as I lay praying and crying, that it was almost unbearable parting with that boy. The feeling he was unhappy, perhaps crying in his little bed among strange boys, seemed more than I could bear.'[15] Nor did Kingsley feel she was exaggerating, for he too solemnly declared, 'this is indeed a crisis, the beginning of a new life for us.'[16] He visited the school assiduously, on one occasion delivering a lecture on coconuts. An old gentleman, who was ninety-two in 1949, recalled those visits in a letter to *John O'London's Weekly*. 'Kingsley was very good to us boys, taking us about the commons and teaching us about birds and nature. We remember pleasing him by killing a snake which was a very poisonous one from the West Indies, evidently hidden in fruit. I do not remember that he stammered then.'

Several of Kingsley's letters, addressed to 'My dear Morry' have been preserved. Most deal with the correct behaviour required of 'a gentleman and an officer' who does not go in for 'swopping which is a dirty business, like horse dealing', does not run away from school and does not fight fellows smaller than himself. Maurice evidently took his father's advice only too literally on this last point for Kingsley had

[14] According to Daniel Farson, author of a recent book on the subject, the Ripper was a barrister called M. J. Druitt who taught at the school for a year in 1888 before drowning himself in the Thames. If Druitt was indeed Jack, he must have been a man of remarkable stamina, for he played for The Blackheath Cricket Club barely six hours after the brutal murder of Annie Chapman in the East End (*The Cricketer Magazine*, January 1973).

[15] Unpublished letter from Fanny, 1858.

[16] ULF No. 176, 1858.

to write restraining him. 'Dad is so pleased at your defending the weak from the strong, but I advise you not *to throw boys downstairs*, for fear they should arrive at the bottom with their skulls cracked.' By way of consolation, the letters also contained promises of sporting treats in store for the coming holidays — a fishing trip to Newbury, a larger cricket bat, a new saddle for the hunting season, 'which will give you a firm seat'. And there was always news of the horses, often accompanied by drawings. 'The grey is lame, and Mamma had to hire Marlow's horse to go to Reading, and he stopped at every public house on the road. Oh ho, ho, says your Ma, that vulgar conduct won't do for me. So she got out and walked past the publics!'

After a year at Eliot Place Maurice was sent to the newly founded Wellington College, of which his father's friend E. W. Benson was headmaster. Kingsley took a keen interest in the school, although he disapproved of it architecturally, saying the two towers joined by an attenuated middle section reminded him of a wasp. Wellington was only a few miles from Eversley, and he lectured and preached there frequently. He also helped to found the school museum.

Kingsley's mood in the closing years of the 'fifties was one of unwonted calm and contentment. Even his indignation at the Indian Mutiny would not draw him into the public arena. He refused several invitations to London concerts to hear Miss Dolby sing his poems set to music by Hullah. Almost his only excursions from home were for the purpose of giving lectures in the provinces. One of these, delivered to the Mechanics Institute in Bristol, contained the famous plea for washing.

The poor man's child [he declared] has no means of washing himself properly; but he has enough of the innate sense of beauty and fitness to feel that he ought not to be dirty. In all the ragged schools and reformatories, so they tell me, the first step toward restoring self-respect is to make the poor fellows clean. From that moment they begin to look on themselves as new men. Not for nothing was baptism chosen by the old Easterns as the sign of a new life. That morning cold bath, which foreigners consider as Young England's strangest superstition, has done as much, believe me, to abolish drunkenness, as any other cause whatsoever. With a clean skin and nerves and muscles braced by a sudden shock, men do not crave artificial stimulants. I have found that, *caeteris paribus*, a man's sobriety is in direct proportion to his cleanliness.

A lady who Fanny described as 'a highly cultivated woman of the world' was present at this lecture and was deeply impressed by the earnestness and intensity with which these words were spoken, although she could not suppress a smile at the suggestion 'that if you only wash your bodies your souls will be all right'.

Kingsley's brief holiday in the Yorkshire dales collecting material for a projected book has already been referred to. He stayed at Malham Tarn House, near Skipton, the home of the enlightened Walter Morrison, and fished Malham Tarn, 'a lake a mile square, and simply the best trout fishing I ever have seen'. Although the book on the Pilgrimage of Grace was never written, the background was not wasted, for Malham Tarn House[17] with its mixed architectural styles, was the original of Harthover Place, the house where little Tom the sweep got lost in the chimney. Likewise the cliff down which he ran before he plunged into the river to become a water-baby was the nearby Malham Cove, a great limestone cliff curved like a natural amphitheatre, its walls two hundred and fifty feet in height. Tradition has it that the little black marks made by lichen on the cliff face first gave Kingsley the idea of *The Water-Babies*. A friend asked him what caused the marks and he replied that they might have been made by the sooty feet of a little chimney sweep as he climbed down from the top.[18]

Kingsley's only other excursion from home at this time was for the purpose of consulting Dr James Hunt, the speech therapist, whom he visited both in London and at his house in Swanage. Although at times Kingsley claimed to thank God for 'this paralytic *os hyoides* of mine, which makes me refrain my tongue when I try to be witty and eloquent under, the penalty of stammering dumbness,' at others he declared that 'a man has no more right to go among his fellows stammering than he has stinking'. Hunt diagnosed improper breathing as the basic cause of the trouble, as Kingsley explained in a letter to a friend.

My defect came from an under jaw contracted by calomel, and nerves ruined by croup and brain fever in childhood. That prevented me opening my mouth; that gave me a wrong use of the diaphragm muscles, till I got to speak inspiring, and never to fully inflate my lungs; and that brought on the last and worst, yet most easily cured, spasm of the tongue. All the while, I could speak not only plain but stentorially, while boxing, rowing, hunting, skating, and doing anything that compelled deep inspirations.

By training his patient not to speak while inhaling, Hunt partially cured the stammer, although Kingsley continued to 'hesitate'. One young

[17] Now a field study centre.
[18] R. and L. Hinson, *Wharfedale*, Dalesman Publishing Company, 1970.

lady who heard him at this time found the hesitation more trying than the stammer. 'In ordinary conversation Mr Kingsley stammers a good deal,' she commented, 'but, being conscious of it, he has taken pains to overcome the defect by speaking very slowly — almost too slowly — for when we heard him make a speech on one occasion, we felt inclined to goad him on, it became so tiresome.'

Kingsley's new mood of stay-at-home contentment was admirably summed up in an article entitled 'My Winter Garden' contributed to *Fraser's* in 1858. In it he claimed (inaccurately) to be now on the wrong side of forty, and to have had his share of travel and the world of affairs.

The time has come [he wrote] when the first grey hairs begin to show on the temples, and one can no longer jump as high as one's third button, scarcely, alas, to any button at all — and what with innumerable sprains, bruises, soakings and chillings ones lower limbs feel, in a cold thaw, much like an old post-horse's.

Now, he declared, the moors round Eversley were more to his liking than the Alps or even the Himalayas, for he had struck root there

as firmly as the wild fir trees do. I learn more, studying over and over again, the same Bagshot sand and gravel heaps, than I should by roaming all Europe in search of new geologic wonders. Fifteen years have I been puzzling at the same questions and have only guessed at a few of the answers. What sawed out the edges of the moors into long narrow banks of gravel? What cut them off all flat atop? What makes *Erica Tetralix* grow in one soil, and the bracken in another? How did three species of Club-moss — one of them quite an Alpine one — get down here, all the way from Wales perhaps, upon this isolated patch of gravel?

He now felt truly part of the parish, for he knew not only every living soul in it, but, in many cases, their fathers and grandfathers. As the hunt passed by he would declare, 'That huntsman I have known for fifteen years, and sat many an hour beside his father's death-bed. I am godfather to that whip's child. I have seen the servants of the hunt, as I have the hounds, grow up round me for two generations.'

Kingsley was a familiar figure during the autumn that this article was written, striding about the parish with a large stone bottle of gargle under his arm, a preventative measure against a new disease, diphtheria, which was carrying off children all over the country. To see him on his parish rounds nobody would have guessed he was a clergyman, for, according to G. W. E. Russell, who met him about this time, he never dressed like one. 'One of Kingsley's peculiarities was that, except on Sundays, when he wore a black coat and a white neckcloth, he always dressed as a layman, and in his grey breeches and gaiters, thick shooting boots, and parti-coloured tie, he might have passed for a farmer, a gamekeeper or a country gentleman.'[19] For fishing he sometimes wore an even stranger garb, a Scots shepherd's plaid worn crossed over his chest in the traditional manner.

Throughout his life fishing remained Kingsley's favourite sport for he found half an hour 'whipping the water' was the perfect antidote to a vigil at a death-bed although, if the death had been a hard one, 'the dreadful agonised face' of the sufferer would sometimes come between him and the river. 'For the fisherman,' he once wrote, 'the twelve foot rod is transfigured into an enchanter's wand, potent over the unseen wonders of the water-world, to call up spirits from the vasty deep.'[20]

This year he wrote Tom Hughes many letters about the odd day's sport he cadged from water-owning friends (for he despised waters that were 'clubbate, clubbified, or beclubbed, by too many of the respectable-of-the-town-of-Farnham-gents-continually-and-with-thumping-brass-and-other-minnows-becoopered'. He uses a jocular schoolboy slang when writing to his old friend which, at times, amounted to a secret language. Remarks like 'Am froze, coughing in limbo, and every soul in the parish in the flenzies,' alternated with minute descriptions of fishing flies: 'If you get free, get half-a-dozen smallest governors, but with pale partridge wings, and pale HONEY-coloured tails; pheasant wings and orange tails are fit only for cockneys to catch dace at Hampton Court.' But the letters also contained descriptive passages about the world of the river bank that were amongst the best things Kingsley ever wrote.

It was in this year also that Kingsley contributed an article called 'Chalk Stream Studies' to Fraser's, which is still regarded as something of a classic in the fly-fishing world. A touching memento of the former rector's passion for fishing is still preserved at the rectory in the form of a leather fly-wallet. It is very like a needle book, with a carefully stitched leather cover and pages made of cream-coloured flannel, stuck with flies. No doubt it was the loving work of Rose, or some other female member of the family.

[19] G. W. E. Russell, *Afterthoughts*, 1912.
[20] Charles Kingsley, *Yeast*.

During this period of rustic retirement Kingsley embarked upon the only piece of original scientific work he ever undertook. He started to classify a species of water gnat known as the Phryganae with a view to becoming a member of the Linneaan Society, but the task was never completed, for the world was once more about to break in upon him. It was paradoxical that, just when he had ceased to seek for fame, fame should beat a path to his door. The first signs of the approaching accolade were far from welcome, for it was in this year that the term Muscular Christianity was first applied to Kingsley, probably by a contributor to the *Saturday Review*. The label stuck, for it so exactly described the athletic, upper-class young men who were the heroes of Kingsley's books. At first he was far from pleased by it, and described it as 'a painful, if not offensive term', but eventually, and somewhat characteristically, he began to trade on it. In a sermon on David, delivered to the undergraduates of Cambridge six years later, he drew a round of applause every time he used the phrase, in spite of the fact he was in church.

Another sign of approaching fame was the increasing number of officers from the newly established camp at Aldershot who were attending Eversley Church, for Kingsley's reputation as a preacher was fast growing. Officers often joined the family at the rectory for lunch, and the rector, in turn, was invited back to the mess at Aldershot, where efforts were made to maintain a conversational tone suitable for a gentleman of the cloth. He had always said, 'I like to have men of war about me', and never allowed his children to forget that they were descended from the general whose portrait now hung in St Luke's rectory. He had spent much time as a boy drawing plans for fortifications and there was scarcely a hill within twenty miles of Eversley whose strong features, from the point of view of defence, he had not worked out.

In after years one of these officers recalled Kingsley's manner in the pulpit. 'He always spoke in a strange rich high-pitched musical monotone which filled the church and commanded fixed attention even from the most ignorant of the congregation.' According to Fanny,

when preaching he would try to keep still but as he went on, he had to grip and clasp the cushion on which his sermon rested, in order to restrain the intensity of his emotion; and then, in spite of himself, his hands would escape, and they would be lifted up, the fingers of the right hand working with a peculiar hovering movement, of which he was quite unconscious. His eyes seemed on fire, and his whole frame worked and vibrated.

These performances were now destined for the ears of the highest in the land. In an unpublished letter to Macmillan, Kingsley casually announced, '*Two Years Ago* has done its work in one direction. The Prince has got hold of it, likes it very much, and has sent for me to preach before the Queen.'

PART III

Canon Kingsley

CHAPTER 1

Royal Favour
1859–1860

Kingsley preached at Buckingham Palace for the first time on Palm Sunday 1859. He knew that Her Majesty liked a sermon that was short and Protestant and did not wander from the text, a copy of which she held in her hand. The one he preached was barely a thousand words long, and like those he had given at Eversley, colloquial and simple in style. The queen liked its directness and the feeling with which Kingsley spoke, and appointed him there and then Chaplain in Ordinary with a brief to preach once a year at the Chapel Royal, St James, for a salary of £30. A greater honour was in store, for in the autumn Kingsley was invited to preach at the private chapel at Windsor Castle, and was afterwards presented to the Queen and the Prince Consort, and to the Crown Prince and Princess of Prussia.

Gone now were all traces of the anti-royalist feeling the rector had expressed so vehemently four years ago. To Charles and Fanny this association with the Royal Family was infinitely precious. As the widowed Fanny explained to the widowed Queen, fifteen years later, Charles would come back stimulated by his visits to Windsor, but would confide what had passed there to none but herself. 'It was all too sacred and yet like a fairy tale. And we rejoiced together in secret.'[1] All letters connected with the Royal Family were preserved in the little red despatch box and the most revealing of them, the one that describes the first meeting with the Queen at Windsor, has only recently come to light. Kingsley had been in a great state of trepidation about the meeting: 'And now I have to dine with her glory great Queen Victory in a pair of tights wh. Wellesley[2] has lent me which I hope won't pop in the middle of the Ceremony, or get covered with hot soup, for they are very thin.' Neither of these fearful predictions were fulfilled and Kingsley was able to write afterwards to Fanny,

[1] Unpublished letter from Fanny, February 8, 1875.
[2] Kingsley was staying with his old friend and neighbour, Gerald Wellesley, now Dean of Windsor.

stop in the Middle of the
Ceremony; or got corered with
hot Soup; for they are very true.

Oh dear to think that I shd
come to this!

Thank Heaven it is all over. And very like a dream it was, although not an unpleasant one. After dinner I was to be presented and we all stood near the door talking quite freely. Presently She came up and I was taken straight up to her. I had to kneel and kiss hands and I didn't like it. (Colonel Liddell said I did it marvellously.) Then she began to talk and I to funk. They had had great delight in my books (accent slightly foreign). Then she stopt to think in the shy way she had, between each speech, which makes one in a more awful funk than ever, but she has the dearest sweetest smile woman could have. Then she liked *Hypatia* best of all. Then what was I going to make Maurice? I said a soldier, that I could see nothing better than that he should serve her and die for her if need be, and she bowed and smiled much.

Then the princess wanted me and I had to go to the middle of the floor and bow to her (accent quite foreign). She said the Prince had read nothing but my books all through her honeymoon. She was more difficult than the Queen, she was so set-speechy. A very common looking person, she might be anybody's daughter of the town middle class, or farmer's, but a nice honest happy face. Then the Prince Consort came up to me and talked for I should think half an hour, about St Elizabeth who is an ancestress of his. I cannot repeat or remember all the handsome things he said to me. I can't see any coldness in him. I should say his face is rather mobile and impressionable.[3]

Heaven knows how I got on. I seem to myself to have made great mistakes.[4]

Evidently he did not make great mistakes, for from that day the sun of royal favour never ceased to shine upon him, and the course of his life, as Fanny pointed out in a letter to the Queen, was changed.

When you first took notice of him he was a strange position; a devoted parish priest sought out by men of the world, 'fast' London men to whom the clergy had not a word to say, because his books made them feel they dared. At that time he was hated and suspected by all parties in the Church, High and Low, and considered by the majority of the world a dreamer and revolutionist. My heart was often bitter. Then Your Majesty chose to notice of him, he preached

[3] Kingsley's admiration for Prince Albert continued to grow. 'I am quite in love with that man', he declared a few weeks later.
[4] ULF No. 181, November 14, 1859.

at Buckingham Palace, visited Windsor, and at once the tide turned in his favour.[5]

Fanny spoke truly. It is a temptation for the biographer to select certain dates as turning points in his subject's life, but the Palm Sunday of 1859 surely deserves to be considered such a date. On that day Parson Lot bowed himself off the stage, and Canon Kingsley, the darling of the Establishment, took his place. From then on there were no further outcries against the government and the landowners, and the canon's championship of the working class, already half-hearted, ceased almost completely. He had already declared himself against associations, 'because the working men are not fit for them, I confess.'[6] By 1862 he had revised the portion of *Alton Locke* that dealt with his hero's treatment at the hands of the Cambridge hierarchy, and written a new preface to the fourth edition of *Yeast*. In it he declared:

The labourers during the last ten years are altogether better off. Free trade has increased their food, without lessening their employment. The politician who wishes to know the effect on agricultural life of that wise and just measure will see it in the faces and figures of the school children. He will see a rosier, fatter, bigger-boned race growing up which bids fair to surpass the puny and ill-fed generation of 1815–1845.

The first concrete sign of royal favour was the offer of the chair of Regius Professor of Modern History at Cambridge, recently vacated by Sir James Stephen. There was neither faculty nor students in Modern History in Cambridge, and it was hoped that Kingsley would start a movement in this direction. He had recently been moving in historical circles at Oxford, since Max Müller, Taylorian Professor of Modern European Languages, had married his niece, Georgina Grenfell, 'next to my own beloved so long'.[7] The young couple had borrowed the rectory for their honeymoon and through Müller Kingsley met Ranke and many distinguished Germans. Nevertheless he, understandably, had grave doubts about accepting a professorship for himself, partly because he was in the throes of yet another breakdown,[8] partly because he was unsure of his qualifications, and partly because of strong opposition from some of those closest to him. John Parker, the

5 Unpublished letter from Fanny, February 8, 1875.
6 Letter to John Bullar, November 26, 1857.
7 Charles Kingsley, *To G.A.G.*, Poem, 1856.
8 Letter to John Bullar, November 19, 1859.

editor of *Fraser's*, objected, for he feared the Cambridge salary of £371 would be earned at the expense of Kingsley's writing. Kingsley attempted to reassure him on this point. 'The money will not be so hard earned to me, because I have already made up my mind to devote myself to the study of history[9] and the lectures when published will bring me in a certain yearly income. In any case I would have taken the post, even at a loss, because it connects me with the Prince, who recommended me for it, and it may lead to something better.[10]

The other objection came from an unexpected quarter. Fanny was absolutely against Charles accepting the professorship. It has always been assumed that she was in favour of it; some have even suggested that she engineered it. But recently discovered letters prove that, ambitious though she was for her husband, the honours she required for him were ecclesiastical. She refused to join him in Cambridge in May, using ill health was an excuse, and remained unmoved by such letters of entreaty as the following:

Our residing in Cambridge will allow us to get first rate masters for the girls: I will never be there during Maurice's holidays. I do entreat you to put out of your mind fear and forecastings, and consider *the noble honour of the thing* and the status it will give me and you and the children henceforth — besides relieving me of the need of writing. God help you, my own darling, I feel now that my work for the rest of my life is clear before me. Only I am unhappy at your seeming frightened and low about it. But you are not well; and when you get strong, that will wear off. Think of the noble work among the young men and take heart.[11]

Kingsley did indeed feel that a new era in his life was beginning.

I feel much older, anxious, and full of responsibility; but more cheerful and settled than I have done for a long time, [he told Fanny]. All that book writing and struggling is over, and a settled position and work is before me. Would that it were done, the children settled in life, and kindly death to set one off again with a new start somewhere else! I should like the only epitaph on our tomb to be Thekla's

> We have lived and loved,
> We live and love.

[9] Kingsley was contemplating writing a *Child's History of England* at the time.
[10] Unpublished letter to Parker, May 11, 1860.   [11] ULF No. 192, 1860.

There was a full-scale row at Eversley on the day of the professor's departure, and as soon as he arrived at Cambridge he wrote begging forgiveness 'for being cross that last day. All this is so very awful and humbling to me.' Fanny took her revenge by becoming very ill; for weeks afterwards Charles's letters were filled with references to her health. 'I cannot bear the thought that I have left you ill and in such pain. I will do anything to make you happy; and only entreat you — Trust me for everything. (I suppose you will be able to read at least these few lines.)'[12] To placate her he promised to write daily, but at times the strain was too much and there would be abject apologies. 'I was ready to cry last night when I came in and found I had never posted my letters. I love you so much but I really have not *time* to look after you as I should like to.'[13]

Under these inauspicious circumstances Kingsley went to stay at Trinity College as the guest of the master, Dr Whewell,[14] for the purpose of taking his M.A. degree which he had previously neglected to do, and was immediately uplifted by the beauty of the place. 'It is like a dream, most beautiful. London being the only buildings I have seen for several years, I am struck with the richness of the stone-work and the clearness of the atmosphere. My windows look into Trinity Walk, the finest green walk in England, now full of flags and tents for a tulip show.'

Although 1860 was a year of achievement in Kingsley's public life, it was a year of sadness in his private one, for in it two people very close to him died. The first to go was his father. Old Mr Kingsley had been much enfeebled physically and mentally for two years, and during that time his son had had to carry the load of his clerical correspondence as well as his own. As early as 1855 Charles had written to Fanny, 'My father is very poorly. He clings to me and you and the children very much.' From that time onwards the rector of Chelsea was a gentler character; 'I have never known my father so reasonable,' wrote Charles in 1858. The two men were probably closer to each other in those last few years than they had been at any time in their lives.

Old Mr Kingsley died at Chelsea Rectory with Charles at his side. The death was a slow one, and deeply distressing, as Kingsley explained to an old college friend, James Montagu.

Miserable to see life prolonged when all that makes it worth having *physically* is gone, and never to know from day to day whether the

12 ULF No. 198, 1860.
13 ULF No. 196, 1860.
14 Dr Whewell was the man who invented the word 'scientist'.

end is to come in six hours or six weeks. James Montagu, never pray for a long life. Better die in the flower of one's age, than go through what I have seen him go through in the last few days.

To F. D. Maurice he wrote:

How every wrong word and deed towards that good old man, and every sorrow I caused him rises up in judgment against one, and how one feels that right-doing does not atone for wrong-doing. I have this comfort, that he died loving me and satisfied with me and my small success, and happy in his children, as he said again and again. But if death — at least the death of a rational human being — be not an ugly damnable solecism, even in a good old age, then I know not what is.

Charles Kingsley Senior was buried in Brompton Cemetery under an epitaph composed by his son.

Here lies
all that was mortal
of
Charles Kingsley
Formerly of Battramsley House, in the New Forest, Hants,
And lately of St Luke's Rectory, Chelsea
Endowed by God with many noble gifts of mind and body
He preserved through all vicissitudes of fortune
A loving heart and stainless honour
And having won in all his various Cures
The respect and affection of his people,
And ruled the Parish of Chelsea well and wisely
For more than twenty years,
He died peacefully in the fear of God and in the faith of Christ
On the 29th February, 1860
Aged 78 years
With many friends, and not an enemy on earth
Leaving to his children as a precious heritage
The example of a Gentleman and a Christian.

The obituary in the *West London Observer* of March 3rd, also emphasised the qualities of the deceased as a courteous gentleman, but devoted rather more column inches to an appreciation of 'the benevolent exertions of Mrs Kingsley to alleviate the sufferings of the sick and afflicted and to impart instruction to the children of needy parents.'

Old Mrs Kingsley, after 'breaking down frightfully' at the funeral, survived her loss better than had been expected. Charles took her to stay with old friends in Wales just before beginning his summer residence at Cambridge, and reported, 'Grandmamma bore the journey very well, and seemed more and more amused and cheerful the further we went.'[15] But Grandmamma, as Kingsley called his mother from this time onwards, was to survive her husband by a further thirteen years, and she was not always cheerful. In her last years she went to live at the rectory at Eversley and began to show the family tendency to lapse into periods of deep depression. Charles always adopted 'a light hearted boyish air' in her presence, however low his own spirits, which, according to Fanny, had a 'wonderfully uplifting effect' on hers.

When he returned from his summer term at Cambridge Kingsley found himself with another bereaved relative on his hands. Charlotte Froude had died suddenly at Torquay, after twelve years of marriage. She left several children and a distraught husband, all of whom came to stay at Eversley, where she was buried. The churchyard had recently been expanded (at the expense of the rectory garden) and Charlotte's was the first grave to be dug under the three famous firs on the rectory lawn, where Charles and Fanny now lie. Charles took a great pride in the new churchyard and spent many hours in the spring with Bannister, his faithful farmer churchwarden, planting it with evergreens, for it had long been his ambition to make his churchyard an arboretum. During the planting he had selected the site for his own grave and, as he explained to Fanny, had promised adjoining sites to several of his old retainers.

> I comforted old West by telling him I would put Mrs West near me, in the corner of the new ground, just under our great fir tree which I have always marked out for us. He agreed: but I found a new competitor in dear old Bannister who had been telling Fred that he would like to be buried close to me. So we have kept a corner for ourselves, and then Bannister comes at my feet, Mrs West next, and by our side Betsy Knowles,[16] insists on lying.[17]

Charlotte had been Charles's favourite among Fanny's numerous sisters, ever since the days when, as a curate, he had tried to impress her

---

[5] ULF No. 186, May 14, 1860.

[16] Kingsley's old nurse.

[17] ULF No. 185, March, 1860. The only grave remaining of all these neighbours of Kingsley is that of old Bannister who lies, as he wished, at his rector's feet.

with his knowledge of theology. After her marriage and her return to the Anglican fold, he had established an excellent relationship with her. According to Fanny her grave was to him, during the remainder of his own life, 'a sacred spot, where he would go almost daily to commune in spirit with the dead and where, on Sunday mornings, he would himself superintend the decorations'. If Charles was upset by Charlotte's death, however, Anthony was little short of frantic, and it was with a view to assisting the bereaved husband that Kingsley set off for Ireland in pursuit of his first salmon that July. From one point of view the holiday was a success. He found the excitement of killing salmon 'maddening . . . I have done the deed at last!' he wrote, 'killed a real actual live salmon, over 5 pounds weight . . . another huge fellow ran right away to sea, carrying me after him waist deep in water and was lost by fouling a ship's hawser. There is nothing like it. I am going to sleep for two hours.' There were, however, two clouds on the horizon of that Irish holiday: the condition of Froude and that of the Irish peasantry. Of Froude he wrote, 'I am anxious about him, he is quite broken down and won't fish.' And of the peasants, 'I am haunted by the human chimpanzees I saw along that 100 miles of horrible country. To see white chimpanzees is dreadful; if they were black, one would not feel it so much. But their skins are as white as ours.'

There was one Irish peasant with whom Kingsley got on well, however, and that was a gamekeeper. He recounts a delightful conversation with him in *The Water-Babies:*

'Is there a salmon here, do you think, Dennis?'

'Is it salmon, thin, your honour manes? Salmon? Cartloads it is of thim, thin, and 'ridgmens, shoulthering ache other out of the water, av' ye'd but the luck to see thim.'

Then you fish the pool all over, and never get a rise.

'But there can't be salmon here, Dennis! and, if you'll but think, if one had come up last tide, he'd be gone to the higher pools by now.'

'Shure thin, and your honour's the thrue fisherman, and understands it all like a book. Why, ye spake as if ye'd known the wather a thousand years! As I said, how could there be a fish here at all, just now?'

'But you said just now they were shouldering each other out of the water.'

And then Dennis will look up at you with his handsome, sly, soft, sleepy, good-natured untrustable Irish grey eyes, and answer with the prettiest smile:

'Shure, and didn't I think your honour would like a pleasant answer.'

The days of dossing down in country inns and farmhouses were now over. As a royal chaplain and a Cambridge professor Kingsley was inundated with invitations to stay at great houses, and while he was in Ireland he stayed with the Coopers at Markree Castle in Sligo. Future summers saw him as a guest at even more exalted homes, such as The Grange where Lady Ashburton gathered round her a brilliant circle, and the Duke of Argyll's place in Scotland, Inverary Castle. When staying at country houses Kingsley always sent home meticulous descriptions of the arrangements made for his personal ablutions. He liked a 'sponge bath' provided in his room (bathrooms were still a rarity in British country houses) and at Markree Castle he found the size of the tub and the quantity of hot water supplied particularly to his liking.

But the time had come to pack up the salmon tackle and prepare for the inaugural lecture at Cambridge.

CHAPTER 2

The Water-Babies
1860–1863

On November 13th, with a strange half-frightened look on his face, Kingsley took his place at the desk in the Cambridge Senate House to deliver a lecture on 'The Limits of Exact Science applied to History'.[1] As a lecturer he was always unsure of himself, and indeed he admitted to Fanny that before the first of the four Edinburgh lectures he had been asked to give some years earlier, 'I was so dreadfully nervous, I actually *cried* with fear up in my own room beforehand'. When a lecture was over he needed constantly to reassure himself that it had been a success, and his letters were filled with such phrases as, 'Had a *very* successful lecture', 'Never spoke better in my life', 'Received 90 cards'.[2]

Certainly there was one person present at the inaugural lecture who did not consider it a success. Justin McCarthy described the impression made by the new professor in the following words:

Rather tall, very angular, surprisingly awkward, with thin staggering legs, a hatchet face adorned with scraggy whiskers, a faculty for falling into the most ungainly attitudes and making the most hideous contortions of visage and frame; with a rough provincial accent and an uncouth way of speaking which would be set down for caricature on the boards of a theatre.

McCarthy was equally unimpressed by the content of the lecture. Kingsley's thesis was the Carlylean one, that history is made by great men and not by economic forces. He was attempting to refute the positivist view of history held by most of the advanced thinkers of the day, Comte, Mill, Darwin and, in particular, Buckle, but, according to McCarthy, he did not know what these authors professed to teach.

[1] Published with other lectures in *The Roman and the Teuton*, 1864.

[2] ULF No. 218, November 2, 1863. It was the custom for those attending lectures to hand in their card before leaving. These cards were normally collected by a 'gyp' but Kingsley preferred to gather them himself from the rostrum.

'That an impulsive, illogical man should on the spur of the moment talk nonsense even from a professor's chair is not wonderful', McCarthy concluded, 'but it does seem a little surprising that he should see it in print, revise it, and publish it, without ever becoming aware of its absurdity'.[3]

There were others who found fault with the new professor of history. William Stubbs, whose charters are still the Bible of the modern history school, raised his head briefly from the study of monastic chronicles to lampoon him.

> Froude informs the Scottish youth
> That parsons do not care for truth.
> The Reverend Canon Kingsley cries
> History is a pack of lies.
>
> What cause for judgements so malign?
> A brief reflection solves the mystery
> Froude believes Kingsley a divine,
> And Kingsley goes to Froude for history.[4]

But where senior members of the university scoffed, junior ones worshipped. Kingsley was immensely popular with the undergraduates of his day and undoubtedly had the most vital of all gifts in a teacher, the ability to inspire genuine enthusiasm. His lectures were better attended than any in Cambridge and, as he reached the climax of some tale of Teutonic heroism in the face of Roman tyranny, a spontaneous cheer would break out from his audience. On these occasions, according to one of his young admirers, 'He would beckon for quiet, and then, in a broken voice, and with dreadful stammering say, "Gentlemen, you must not do it. I cannot bear it". But it was no good — we did not mean to cheer — we could not help it'.

Perhaps one of the reasons for his popularity with the young was his own innate boyishness. He regarded himself as one of them, and did not maintain the dignified distance of most of his colleagues. He joined in their play as well as their work, as one of them recalled years later:

How well I remember how one dull February afternoon, at Baitsbite Lock — willows bare — river swollen — time about four o'clock — the light failing — a few enthusiastic undergraduates in

---

[3] Justin McCarthy, *Reminiscences*, Vol. II.
[4] The verses were written after Froude became Rector of St Andrews.

peajackets and comforters, waiting for a long training grind down to Ely to return. Through the deepening twilight come two figures; one tall, felt-hatted, great coatless, with a white comforter, swinging along at a great pace . . . Then the sound of thrashing oars — out comes the boat . . . As she passes him he throws his cigar in the river, and begins to run too. I'll never forget it. I remember the boat stopped for an 'Easy all', and his short comment, 'I'm afraid that won't do, gentlemen' and it didn't do.

Cambridge lost the boat race that year.

News of Kingsley's success with undergraduates evidently reached royal ears, for barely three months after his arrival in Cambridge, he received what he considered the greatest honour ever conferred upon him; he was appointed history tutor to the Prince of Wales and given the right to bear the Prince's feathers embossed upon his notepaper (a right he made full use of). The future Edward VII had had a stern upbringing. Although not of an intellectual disposition, from an early age he had been obliged to study for six hours a day six days a week under a tutor, and was forbidden even the novels of Walter Scott by way of recreation. He had already attended the University of Oxford for a year, but had resided outside the town, away from other undergraduates. Now a similar arrangement was made for him at Cambridge. He was to live at Madingley Hall and ride in twice a week for a class with Professor Kingsley, composed of specially picked undergraduates, and then go through the week's work each Saturday at his tutor's house at 3 St Peter's Terrace.

Kingsley was understandably somewhat alarmed at the responsibility of the task that had been set him, and spent most of the vacation preparing a course in German history for the Prince. He was even more alarmed when he was informed by the Prince's private tutor, Mr Herbert Fisher, that the area in which the young man most needed instruction was not German history but English history, from William III onwards. In the event, however, his fears proved unfounded; he found the prince 'very jolly' and his letters were full of accounts of him. Writing to Mr Augustus Stapleton, Kingsley said: 'The Prince is very interesting, putting me in mind of his mother . . . free and everything. I had him in private today and we had an interesting talk on politics, old and new, a free press and so forth'.

The Prince and the professor met on many social occasions and Kingsley enjoyed the sight of his fellow academics angling for invitations to dine with the youth whose guest he so often was. In one letter to Fanny he wrote, 'Dinner party at Madingley with the Prince of Wales. Old Barns of King's sat next to him, having come all the way from London, and told him hunting stories without end, and was evidently in an ecstasy of bliss'. In another he described a garden party at which the Prince was present: 'Prince was awfully mobbed by the country folk of all ranks. He entered with a body guard of six, arm in arm to keep off the mob, which had a grand and decided effect as to his flanks, but his rear suffered severely from the enemy.' (This letter was accompanied by a drawing of a row of pin-men, with arms linked, wearing top hats.) The Prince evidently regarded his tutor as a friend, for, on one occasion at least, he pressed him to accompany him to the races, 'which being forbidden by the authorities I couldn't well do'.

It is perhaps surprising, in view of the suggestions of this sort made by the Prince, that Kingsley never suspected the weakness in his character that was to lead to the abrupt severing of their academic association at the end of the year. On November 25th the Prince Consort heard of his son's involvement with the Irish actress, Nellie Clifden, and visited him at Cambridge. Within a fortnight Prince Albert had died of typhoid. Edward, although as deeply distressed as his mother, was blamed by her for the disaster and sent abroad. A year later he was married to Princess Alexandra of Denmark, in the hope that a settled home life would cure him of his taste for ladies. The Kingsleys were invited to the wedding, which Charles described as an occasion of 'fairy tale splendour', and continued to be on close terms both with the Prince and his mother. He was often included in house parties at Sandringham, and became almost as familiar a figure in the royal nurseries as in his own.

Throughout all these years his misplaced faith in the Prince's purity of character remained unshaken. In the year of the famous Mordaunt scandal (1871) when Edward had actually to appear in the witness box and refute the imputation of having fathered Lady Mordaunt's child, Kingsley wrote to him declaring, 'I do not believe a quarter of what I have heard about you. At Madingly you seemed to me far more virtuous than most young men of your age'.[5] He did, however, advise the Prince to regard his near-fatal attack of typhoid as a sign that 'we cannot afford to be merely amusing ourselves'. He suggested sanitary reform as a suitable occupation for 'a gallant and earnest prince' and indeed the Prince did eventually sit on a committee concerned with the housing of the working classes, but that was not until thirteen years later.

Kingsley was at this time much interested in Darwin's theory of evolution, recently proclaimed to the world with the publication of

[5] Unpublished letter to the Prince of Wales, 1871.

the *Origin of Species* in 1859. Unlike most churchmen, he readily accepted the possibility that man was descended from the apes, and that the world was not thousands, but thousands of millions, of years old. He was eventually publicly to declare his views in two lectures given at the Royal Institution, entitled 'Science and Superstition'.[6] He corresponded with Darwin about the migration of the eye in the flat fish and indeed conferred on him the title of Master that had for so long been the exclusive property of F. D. Maurice. He also wrote letters to Sir Charles Lyell, the father of modern geology, on the subject of his beloved Bagshot sands. He met these men, and many others almost as distinguished, at the home of the enlightened Sir Charles Bunbury. Sir Charles lived at Barton Hall, Suffolk, and Kingsley spent many weekends with him while he was at Cambridge. It was Sir Charles who proposed him as a Fellow of the Geological Society; with Sir Charles Lyell as a second he had no difficulty in being elected.

Social problems were again exercising Kingsley's mind at this time. Although he had ceased to be an active Christian Socialist, the Lancashire Cotton Famine[7] of 1861 to 1863 had brought the problem of life in an industrial society once more to the attention of the public and he wrote a letter to *The Times* inveighing against the Manchester mill-owners who had 'collected vast heaps of people from every quarter, without the least care as to their housing, education, Christianizing or anything else, and now left them, penniless, to live off the charity of school children robbed of their little saving, and delicate ladies starving themselves into illness, to save here a shilling and there a shilling'.[8]

Kingsley was appalled at the best of times by the thought that so large a proportion of his fellow men were obliged to spend their lives in the slums of industrial cities, manipulating machines in dark unhealthy factories.

I conceive it to be a very great evil that large bodies of men should be employed in exclusively performing day after day, the same minute mechanical operation, till their whole intellect is concentrated on it, and their fingers kept delicate for the purpose. I would gladly see such men emigrate, even though they fared badly at first, because the life of a colonist would, by calling out the whole man, raise them in body and mind enormously.

[6] Printed in *Fraser's Magazine*, June and July 1867.

[7] The famine was caused by the American Civil War which cut off Lancashire's supply of cotton and left half a million people unemployed and destitute.

[8] At this time the schoolchildren of Eversley, and many of the poor, brought their money weekly to the rectory to be forwarded to the North.

He called the victims of this system 'human soot', explaining, in a sermon to the Kirkdale Ragged School, 'Capital is accumulated more
rapidly by wasting a certain amount of human life . . . by producing
and throwing away a regular per-centage of human soot — of that
thinking and acting dirt which lies about, and alas! breeds and per-
petuates itself, in foul alleys and low public houses and all and any of
the dark places of the earth'. It was just such an atom of this human
soot, one of 'those children in your streets, ragged, dirty, profligate,
untaught, perishing' that was to play the central part in the book he
now embarked upon.

The story of how the first chapter of *The Water-Babies* came to be
written is well known. On a fine spring morning in 1862 Fanny
reminded Charles of an old promise: 'Rose, Maurice and Mary have
got their book,'[9] she said, 'and baby must have his.' Kingsley made no
answer, but barely stopping to finish his breakfast, he locked himself in
his study and returned half an hour later with the first chapter of *The
Water-Babies* complete.

It is strange to consider that this book, which cost him so little effort,
was to outlive the many tomes over which he laboured so long, and to
fulfil his own prophecy about his work, made many years before, that
his was 'the music of the penny whistle and banjo' and not the loud
trumpet call. The success of *The Water-Babies* was instant, and thirty-
five years later it was still listed by the *Pall Mall Gazette* as the sixth most
popular children's book in England.[10] Today, over a hundred years
after it was written, it is still available in nine editions and is familiar to
children in almost every part of the English-speaking world. Only
recently a government clerk wrote to me from Ceylon assuring me
that, like Edward Lear, 'I firmly believed it to be all true.'[11] As early as
1907 a film was made of it and since then dramatised versions have been
broadcast and televised. As recently as the summer of 1973 a musical
version was staged at the Royalty Theatre with Jessie Matthews in a
leading role. Strangely enough, however, few Americans appear to
have heard of it apart from Mary McCarthy.[12]

It is not difficult to understand why the book has had such a success
with children. The first chapter bears the mark of the inspired mood in

[9] She referred to *The Heroes*.

[10] *The Heroes* took seventh place in the list.

[11] Unpublished letter from Edward Lear to Charles Kingsley, 1871, in the possession
of Florida State University, Tallahassee.

[12] 'His mother had read him a book called *The Water-Babies*'. Mary McCarthy,
Birds of America, Weidenfeld and Nicolson, 1971.

which it was written, and the first paragraph is a masterpiece of conciseness and deserves quoting:

Once upon a time there was a little chimney-sweep and his name was Tom. That is a short name, and you have heard it before, so you will not have much trouble in remembering it. He lived in a great town in the North country, where there were plenty of chimneys to sweep, and plenty of money for Tom to earn and his master to spend. He could not read nor write, and did not care to do either; and he never washed himself, for there was no water in the court where he lived. He had never been taught to say his prayers. He had never heard of God, or of Christ, except in words which you never have heard, and which it would have been well if he had never heard. He cried half his time, and laughed the other half. He cried when he had to climb the dark flues, rubbing his poor knees and elbows raw; and when the soot got into his eyes which it did every day in the week; and when his master beat him, which he did every day of the week; and when he had not enough to eat, which happened every day in the week likewise. And he laughed the other half of the day, when he was tossing halfpennies with the other boys, or playing leap-frog over the posts, or bowling stones at the horses' legs as they trotted by, which last was excellent fun, when there was a wall at hand behind which to hide.

As the story opens, early one morning, Tom and his master Grimes are on their way to Harthover House, where Tom gets lost in one of the chimneys and lands on the hearth in little Ellie's spotless white bedroom. She arouses the household with a shriek, Tom jumps out of the window and the hunt is on, and a very humorously described hunt it is, with everybody on the estate dropping their tasks and joining the hue and cry, sometimes with embarrassing results. 'Only my lady did not give chase; for when she put her head out of the window, her night-wig fell into the garden, and she had to ring up her lady's maid, and send her down for it privately; which quite put her out of the running, so that she came in nowhere, and is consequently not placed.'

Meanwhile Tom had 'paddled up the park with his little bare feet, like a small black gorilla fleeing to the forest', pushed his way through a wood, over a wall, and burst out upon Harthover Fell. The description of the chase across the great grouse moors, sparkling with dew under the morning sun, comes as close to poetry as prose can, and the repetition of the phrase 'and he never saw the Irishwoman coming down behind him' gives it almost the quality of a ballad. At last Tom reaches the very edge of Lewthwaite Crag and looks down into Vendale,

> a deep green and rocky valley, very narrow, and filled with wood; but through the wood, hundreds of feet below him, he could see a clear stream glance. Oh, if he could but get down to that stream! Then, by the stream he saw the roof of a little cottage, and a little garden, set out in square beds, And there was a tiny little red thing moving in the garden, no bigger than a fly. As Tom looked down, he saw that it was a woman in a red petticoat!

He performs the unheard of feat of scrambling down the face of the crag, flings off his filthy clothes, and crying 'I must be clean' disappears into the brook.

Although Tom's life above water was undoubtedly lived in Yorkshire, some of his underwater adventures probably took place in the Itchen, for it was on the banks of this 'loveliest of vale rivers'[13] where it meanders through watermeadows near Winchester, that Kingsley settled to finish his book. He could hardly have chosen a better stream for his purpose for, as he pointed out in *Hereward the Wake*, the waters of the Itchen were 'so clear that none could see where water ended and where air began'. He was a guest of Mrs Marx of Alresford at the time (the lady whom he described to Fanny as 'one of the most agreable women I have ever met, but she weighs 16 stones and has a moustache'.) When the Marxes moved to London he transferred to the Plough Inn at Itchen. As he passed days gazing into the clear depths of the river (sport was poor that year) he imagined what life would be like in it for a four-inch eft[14] which was what Tom had become. These middle chapters are among the most magical in the book although there is in fact little 'magic' in them. Kingsley described with scientific accuracy all the creatures that Tom met in the underwater world, but to that accuracy he added a touch of humour that made them delightful. His description of the caddises was typical.

> Very fanciful ladies they were; none of them would keep to the same material for a day. One would begin with some pebbles; then she would stick on a piece of green weed; then she found a shell, and stuck it on too; and the poor shell was alive, and did not like at all being taken to build houses with, but the caddis did not let him have any voice in the matter, being rude and selfish, as vain people are

13 ULF No. 214, June 1862.
14 Newt.

apt to be; then she stuck on a piece of rotten wood, then a very smart pink stone and so on till she was patched all over like an Irishman's coat. Then she found a long straw, five times as long as herself, and said, 'Hurrah! my sister has a tail, and I'll have one too!' and she stuck it on her back and marched about with it quite proud, though it was very inconvenient indeed. And, at that, tails became all the fashion among the caddis-baits in that pool, as they were at the end of the Long Pond last May, and they toddled about with long straws sticking out behind, getting between each other's legs, and tumbling over each other, and looking so ridiculous, that Tom laughed at them till he cried.

It is only when Tom reaches the sea that the tenor of the story changes. Kingsley can no longer resist the urge to mount the pulpit, and the tale becomes a moral one. 'If I have wrapped up my parable in seeming Tom-fooleries,' he declared to a friend, 'it is because so only could I get the pill swallowed,' and a bitter pill it is at times. Tom now meets Mrs Bedonebyasyoudid, an ugly old woman in a black bonnet and green spectacles. It is her role to devise a series of punishments to fit his crimes; thus when he feeds the sea anenomes with stones she pops a pebble into his mouth instead of a lollipop, and when he steals sweets from her underwater cupboard he finds himself 'all over prickles like a sea egg'. There follows a long redemptory journey to find and forgive Mr Grimes frozen into a chimney pot like one of the lost souls in Dante's *Inferno*. During the course of this journey Tom learns the positive virtues and is fitted to spend Sundays in heaven with little Ellie, the girl into whose bedroom he burst in Chapter One.

It is a measure of the book's power that it can carry what one critic has described as the 'inchoate mass' of the second half,[15] for the tale now becomes not only moral but muddled. Anyone who has read it aloud to small children knows that the passages that must be skipped become longer and more numerous as the book progresses. Few can inflict upon a five-year-old of the 1970s the references to obscure scientific and political controversies of the 1860s[16] or can chant the list of remedies tried on Professor Ptthmllnsprts to cure him of his belief in water-babies, a list which is written in the style of Rabelais and runs

[15] Gillian Avery, *Nineteenth Century Children*, Hodder and Stoughton, 1965.
[16] 'If you will go to Nice, you will find the fish-market full of sea-fruits, which they call "frutta di mare": though I suppose they call them "fruits de mer" now, out of compliment to that most successful, and therefore most immaculate, potentate who is seemingly desirous of inheriting the blessing pronounced on those who remove their neighbours landmark.'

to four pages. The joke about evolution going backwards was hailed with delight by Kingsley, who wrote to Fanny, 'I have invented a wonderful waterproof picture book in which Tom sees how a race of men in time become gorillas by being brutish.'[17] The joke is less well received by the modern child, and caused the book to be banned from certain convent libraries in the early years of this century.

Nevertheless *The Water-Babies* rises above all these shortcomings because it has in it the elements of an archetypal myth which can be read at many levels. When Kingsley wrote it he dived deep into his own unconscious, although he was probably quite unaware of the fact, and the book has been a happy hunting ground for amateur psychologists ever since. In 1969 a correspondent to *The Times* described it as 'a great eschatalogical parable', while Maureen Duffy in her recently published *The Erotic World of Faery*[18] positively runs amok amid the sexual symbols. Tom's descent of Ellie's chimney while she is asleep is attempted rape; with his plunge into the water world he becomes at once 'the questing penis' and 'the unborn foetus in its amniotic fluid'. Yet in one of her interpretations of the story Miss Duffy falls not so far short of the target. *The Water-Babies*, she declares, is a fable about masturbation. Tom is a little boy with nasty habits who must be purified before he is fit to enter heaven with Ellie. He must learn to leave the hidden sweets alone, declares Miss Duffy, for they will make him grow prickles. The book's ethic, she points out, 'is concerned with how a boy may resist temptation and grow up pure to marry'.

Miss Duffy may be over-specific in her interpretation, but *The Water-Babies* probably does mirror Kingsley's sense of guilt about sex and his consequent obsession with washing. Tom, the dirty little sweep, has come down Ellie's chimney uninvited, and now he must be purified by water before he is fit to be her mate. At once all the references to beautiful women beside or in water in Kingsley's works, come to mind; the maiden who sat by Trehill Well, in the poem he wrote when he was sixteen; the heroine of his first novel, *Yeast*, who was called Lavington and died burbling of clean water; Andromeda washed all night by spray; the golden hair of Mary among the nets on Dee;[19] the list is endless. And one remembers all the references to washing in his love letters to Fanny; his anxiety after first making love to her, to 'wash off the scent of her delicious limbs', his plans to build her a rustic bath in the garden and his constant admonitions to her to

[17] ULF No. 214, June 1862.
[18] Hodder and Stoughton, 1972.
[19] Charles Kingsley, Poem, *The Sands of Dee*.

kiss herself all over *in the bath* on his behalf. In *The Water-Babies* itself there is the beautiful earth mother, Mrs Doasyouwouldbedoneby surrounded by babies and, of course, water:

She was the most nice, soft, fat, smooth, pussy, cuddly, delicious creature who ever nursed a baby; and she understood babies thoroughly, for she had plenty of her own, whole rows and regiments of them, and has to this day. And all her delight was, whenever she had a moment to spare, to play with babies. And therefore when the children saw her, they naturally all caught hold of her, and pulled her till she sat down on a stone, and climbed into her lap, and clung round her neck, and caught hold of her hands; and then they all put their thumbs into their mouths, and began cuddling and purring like so many kittens . . . And Tom stood staring at them, for he could not understand what it was all about.

Safely surrounded by the pure element of water, Tom feels able to abandon himself to her embrace: 'She took Tom in her arms, and laid him in the softest place of all, and kissed him, and petted him, and talked to him, tenderly and low, such things as he had never heard before in his life; and Tom looked up into her eyes, and loved her, and loved, till he fell fast asleep from pure love.'

From this obsession about washing no doubt grew some of Kingsley's most marked characteristics. He was constantly preoccupied with personal cleanliness, and could not bear to wear clothes that were dirty. 'If I have a spot on my clothes,' he wrote to Ludlow, as a young man, 'I am conscious of nothing else the whole day long, and just as conscious of it in the heart of Bramshill Common, as if I were going down Piccadilly.' From this preoccupation with personal cleanliness grew his absurd conviction that a man has only to take a cold bath every morning to become morally good, a conviction for which generations of English public schoolboys have had reason to curse him. No doubt his lifelong passions for fishing and sanitary reform had a similar root.

But the overt theme of *The Water-Babies* is of course straightforward and philanthropic. Kingsley wanted to better the lot of sweeps' boys. Kingsley was by no means the first Victorian to be scandalised at the exploitation of these unhappy children, who not infrequently suffocated in the chimneys up which they were forced by means of burning straw. In the eighteen-forties Anna Sewell's mother was already going from door to door collecting the £10 necessary to buy a set of sweep's brushes which would rescue one boy from his foul calling. At about the

same time her brother, John Wright, discovered how they were procured for the trade. He was visiting the workhouse at Buxton, near
Norwich, when a sweep arrived in search of an apprentice. He picked
out several successively as likely to suit him, but, in each case, their
parents objected; at last a little boy was pointed out to him who had
no friends or relations to care for him, so the master sweep was told he
would have no trouble about him; no one would enquire what had
become of him. It will be remembered that young Oliver Twist only
just avoided the dreadful calling.

Kingsley's book, however, did more than the work of such philanthropists to better the lot of sweeps' boys. So horrified was the public
by the story of Tom that, within a year of the publication of the book,
the Chimney Sweepers Regulation Act was put on the Statute Book.
This act forbade the use of children for sweeping chimneys and was
only repealed three years ago. The announcement of its demise appeared under the headline 'Sweeping away the last of the Water-Babies
Act' in the *Daily Telegraph* for February 3rd, 1971.

Until recently there was an old man living in Wokingham who
claimed to be the original Tom. His name was James Seaward, and he
was eventually elected mayor of Wokingham. On this occasion a local
paper interviewed him and described him as a fine-featured, fresh-
complexioned, elderly man with keen grey eyes and a commanding
voice, who had always swept the rectory chimneys at Eversley. He
admitted to having met the canon only once, and stated that the story
of his early sufferings was told to Kingsley by a lady who had taken
an interest in him.

Another lady, still living, who knew James Seaward when she was
a child, has confirmed that he was indeed the original Tom.

He was the local chimney-sweep for Wokingham and district in my
childhood, a familiar sight driving round in his little dog cart drawn
by a white horse. My personal encounter was when I was about
seven or eight. I ran into my neighbour's home to watch him at
work. He asked me if I had read *The Water-Babies* and on hearing I
had said, 'Well, I'm Tom.' I think I must have looked very sceptical,
for his next remark was 'Mr Kingsley told a lie when he turned me
into a water-baby.'

An interesting point about *The Water-Babies* that seems to have
escaped the eye of previous commentators is that it contains what must
surely be a self-portrait of Kingsley. He appears in the last chapter as a
giant in pursuit of the crazed inhabitants of the land of Hearsay.

And running after them, day and night, came such a poor, lean, seedy, hard-worked old giant, as ought to have been cockered up, and had a good dinner given him, and a good wife found him, and been set to play with little children; and then he would have been a very presentable old fellow after all; for he had a heart, though it was considerably overgrown with brains.

He was made up principally of fish bones and parchment, put together with wire and Canada balsam; and smelt strongly of spirits, though he never drank anything but water; but spirits he used somehow, there was no denying. He had a great pair of spectacles on his nose, and a butterfly net in one hand, and a geological hammer in the other; and was hung all over with pockets, full of collecting boxes, bottles, microscopes, telescopes, barometers, ordnance maps, scalpels, foreceps, photographic apparatus, and all other tackle for finding out everything about everything, and a little more too. And, most strange of all, he was running not forwards but backwards, as fast as he could.

At first the giant attempted to collect Tom in one of his bottles, but in the end he relented, for, like his creator, he was kind at heart. A recently discovered letter written to a little girl[20] shows just how gentle and charming Kingsley could be to children.

My dear little girl,
  Looking today among some old papers I found a letter from you, which must have been hidden away, I do not know how, or how long. I am very sorry I have not answered you: for I am never rude to anyone, least of all to little girls: so you must forgive a stupid careless old fellow, whose table is covered with heaps of books and papers, till he hates the sight of them, and longs to throw all into the garden and play with all the little children he can find.
  Every yours vy faithful and very sorry I mislaid your letter
                                         C. Kingsley.

[20] The letter was written to Agnes Rebecca Augusta Alleyne in 1868. I am indebted to Mrs M. A. Bowdler, her grand-daughter, for bringing it to my attention.

CHAPTER 3

'And all the wheels run down'
1863

The year that *The Water-Babies* was published in book form saw
Kingsley once more fishing a chalk stream, this time the meandering
Test in its wide water meadows near Whitchurch in Hampshire. Again,
the experience produced a lyrical mood in him, so lyrical in fact that
a letter written home during a wet afternoon at the White Hart is
something of a minor masterpiece and deserves quoting:

> White Hart, Whitchurch, May 26, 1863
> 6.30. I reopen this, having been driven off the water by real rain
> — rain which is raining grass and gold. So I am settled down, and
> can do nothing better — indeed, nothing else — as there are no
> books in Whitchurch, than sit and twaddle to you. I like this place,
> and that is the truth. It is old without being decayed. This low room
> has a beautiful Queen Anne's ceiling, and could, by withdrawing
> the partition, be enlarged from the club room into a ball-room, in
> which three belles and one and a half beaux of Whitchurch would
> have full room to dance. Opposite me, across a street rather wider
> than the room, is a chemist's shop, which is also a post office. How
> quietly and gracefully here the new invades the old, without dis-
> possessing or confusing it. The two storeys are rather lower than one
> of an average London house, so that we all hope the folks inside are
> not tall; but there is a grand peaked roof with dormers, in which
> I suppose servants are stuffed away but I hold my nose at the thought.
> In the window are a dozen bottles, some near a hundred years old,
> with drugs of ditto age. One hopes they are all labelled right. The
> only one I can answer for is one of poppy-heads; so I suppose tooth-
> aches are known here. There are also two plaster of Paris horses,
> indicating that horse-balls may be had within; a cabinet of scents;
> an accordion; two framed prints — one seemingly of a military, the
> other of a fox-hunting nature, evidently by a French artist; a bottle
> or two filled with what looks humiliatingly like *lollipops;* and a blue

tablet bearing a golden inscription, in the very centre of the window, which I must examine tomorrow and report to you. In front, instead of pavement, are great flints and a row of posts, which prevent the carriages of Whitchurch from rushing into the house windows, and drunken men thereof from losing their way home. There are also two gutters down which are running now gallons, ay, tons, of true London milk — chalk and water, with a slight tinge of animal matter. The population are 'understood but not expresst', like words in the Latin grammar which don't appear. I know there was a Methodist parson walked up to the station an hour ago, and came back again worse luck for the place; and there was a shepherd came and stood in the exact centre of the town, of course with an umbrella (all Chalk shepherds have umbrellas), and has been doing nothing in particular, certainly for an hour, in pouring rain. Also a groom boy went by, who looked as if he had been expelled from Lord Portland's stables for dirt. And there you have the Whitchurch news.

Nobody reading this letter would imagine that it was the work of a man in declining health whose most constant wish was to die. Yet so it was. Fanny always said *The Water-Babies* was the last book (except his West Indian one, *At Last*) that he wrote with any real ease, 'for his brain was getting fatigued, his health fluctuated, and the work of the Professorship, which was a constant weight on his mind, wore him sadly'. Certainly when he returned to Cambridge in the autumn he was far from well. He claimed that the climate did not suit him: 'I cannot live in that relaxing air, and the malaria of the river acts as poison on my insides.' It was, however, not relaxing air that was troubling him when T. G. Bonney met him in the King's Parade that winter. 'He approached me, his shoulders up to his ears, his attitude and face expressive of acute discomfort. As we met he ejaculated, "What a miserable day!" "But, Professor," I returned, "it is a north-easter." "Ah, my dear fellow," he replied with a characteristic stutter, "I was young and foolish then."'[1] Bonney added that Kingsley's conversation at this time was frequently interrupted by fits of coughing and expectoration, after one of which he exclaimed that 'Satan had got into his lungs'.

---

[1] Bonney was of course referring to the famous *Ode to the North-East Wind* which contained the lines:

> Welcome, wild North-easter!
> Shame it is to see
> Odes to every zephyr;
> Ne'er a verse to thee.

Fanny must undoubtedly take some of the blame for the decline in her husband's health. Although she eventually agreed to come and live in the house he took in St Peter's Terrace for the first two years of his tenure of the professorship, she then decided that even the dampness of Eversley Rectory was preferable to the climate of Cambridge which, she said, made her ill. Unable to afford two residences, Kingsley was forced to part with his Cambridge one, and to go up twice a year only, once to deliver his lectures (twelve to sixteen in number) and once for the examination of his class for degrees. He regretted this necessity, for it prevented him knowing the men in his class personally, which he had made a point of doing during his first two years, when they often came to his house in the evening and talked to him on equal terms.

Kingsley was now obliged to spend his periods of residence either in college or in lodgings, and this autumn lodgings were not easy to find. 'At last I have found rooms at Peck's the chemists, opposite the Fitzwilliam, the quarter I like best,' he wrote on October 20th, 'a ground floor sitting room, and only a little bedroom since you will not share it, alas.'[2] His letters were full of anecdotes about the misfortunes that befall temporary bachelors. 'I got home about half past ten last night,' he told Fanny on one occasion when living in college, 'and burnt my fingers and nearly set the college on fire with an Etna, making myself some coffee. Then I sported myself out of my own rooms and could not get the door open again for an hour !'[3] He might make light of such accidents, but he admitted to missing the comfort of home life. 'I cannot live without having you to vex and torment, as I do,' he wrote on one occasion. 'I wish I was home.'[4] After twenty-two years of marriage he was still deeply attracted to his wife and found the nights almost intolerable without her. When he forgot her birthday he wrote fervently thanking God for the day she was born:

> Benedetta sia la madre
> Che ti fece cosi bella
> Benedetto sia il padre
> D'una si gentil donzella[5]

Not only nights, but evenings too were comfortless without his *gentil donzella*. It was delightful to dine out occasionally, and enjoy the company of brilliant men, but to dine out nightly, from loneliness and the need to economise, was another matter. 'My cold is gone,' he wrote

[2] ULF No. 217, October 20, 1863.
[3] ULF No. 209, 1861.
[4] ULF No. 239, July 15, 1867.
[5] ULF No. 227, 1866.

in one letter, 'but there was a great deal of stuff in my throat this morning. The continual wet and being out at night causes this.'[6] In the next, intended to be reassuring, he added, 'Paget says there is no *malignant* disease.'[7] This suggests that he was beginning to fear some more deep-seated cause for the frequent congestion of his lungs. Fanny also, in her biography, spoke of 'chronic illness' at this time, and implied that this was something distinct from her husband's periodic nervous breakdowns. The symptoms of these were now familiar, and Kingsley had learnt the cure for them — the complete cessation of mental work. Leaving his brain alone, however, could produce no cure for this new illness, and a strain of deeper sadness began to enter his letters from this time onwards. Although he was only forty-four in the winter of 1863, he seemed to be fulfilling the prophecy made when he was an undergraduate, that he would be old before he was forty. The second verse of the poem *When all the world was young lad*, again so reminiscent of Housman, seems symbolic of his mood at this time:

> When all the world is old lad
> And all the trees are brown;
> And all the sport is stale lad
> And all the wheels run down,
> Creep home and take your place there,
> The spent and maimed among
> And God grant you find one face there,
> You loved when all was young.[8]

To more serious disorders at this time was added the minor one of toothache. We tend to overlook the agonies our great-grandfathers suffered from decaying molars, but to them they were real enough. It would be interesting to know on how many occasions the course of history was changed by 'an awful sleepless night of toothache'. Certainly the course of the latter half of Kingsley's life was not eased by such nights, and he frequently referred to dental treatment that makes even toothache seem preferable. 'My teeth do not ache but are so sore from filing that I cannot bite anything. Rogers says they will harden in a few days.'[9] On more than one occasion he wished that he had no teeth. 'Oh dear, why wasn't I born an edentate like one of those porcupines in Sir C. Bunbury's diary which have no teeth to ache! That's why they get so fat.'[10]

[6] ULF No. 194.   [7] ULF No. 195.
[8] This poem was specially written for *The Water-Babies*.
[9] ULF No. 446.
[10] ULF No. 190, 1862.

During his third year at Cambridge, Kingsley was clearly not only missing his wife and his home, but also the countryside round Eversley. His love affair with the architecture of Cambridge was over, and he had always found the Cambridge landscape ugly. He wrote home nostalgically about his native commons. 'This is but a doleful spot and when I look at it I thank God for dear Eversley, though it is in a hole.'[11] He spoke nostalgically of Stapleton's pond and Wellington's bog[12] and even considered writing a book about the Vale of Blackwater that would be 'a humble imitation of White's *Selbourne*'.[13] This mood of depression was not improved by the very considerable snub Kingsley received at this time from the University of Oxford. His name had been put forward as a candidate for the honorary degree of D.C.L. and he fully expected to receive it, for he had many supporters at the university including Max Müller, the Professor of Modern Languages. At the last moment, however, Pusey, who disapproved of *Hypatia*, announced his intention of calling out '*Non Placet*' when the voting took place. To avoid a public scandal Kingsley stood down, but the wound went deep. Three years later, when he was invited by Bishop Wilberforce to preach at St Mary's he replied, 'I do not think it stands with my honour to appear publicly in Oxford till some public retraction and apology has been made'. No apology was forthcoming so Kingsley never preached at St Mary's.

In this state of mental depression and physical debility he now took on the most formidable opponent of his life, a man who had preached very frequently at St Mary's.

[11] ULF No. 204.
[12] ULF No. 205. The duke was a neighbour at Eversley.
[13] Unpublished letter to C. A. Johns.

CHAPTER 4

The Newman Controversy
1864

In January 1864 Kingsley reviewed Volumes VII and VIII of Froude's *History of England* for *Macmillan's Magazine*, no doubt with a view to giving his brother-in-law a 'puff'. The volumes dealt with the Elizabethan period and must have revived in his breast the anti-Popish feelings to which he had given such free rein in *Westward Ho!* for he allowed the following paragraph to slip into his article: 'Truth for its own sake has never been a virtue of the Roman clergy. Father Newman informs us that it need not, and on the whole ought not, to be; that cunning is the weapon which Heaven has given the saints wherewith to withstand the brute male force of the wicked world which marries and is given in marriage.'

The statement to which Kingsley referred was supposed to have been made by Newman in a sermon entitled 'Wisdom and Innocence', published in 1844. What the sermon actually said was that the weapons with which the Church defends herself, prayer, holiness, and innocence, are to the world of physical strength so incomprehensible that it must believe that the Church conquers by craft and hypocrisy. 'The words "craft" and "hypocrisy" are but the versions of "wisdom" and "harmlessness", in the language of the world.'

Newman was not a subscriber to *Macmillan's Magazine*. He was at that time leading a life of seclusion with the Oratorians at Birmingham and, like Kingsley, was far from well. An anonymous well-wisher, however, saw to it that he received a copy of the magazine with the offending passage marked. He wrote a letter of gentle protest to *Macmillan's*, denying that he sought either reparation or even an answer to his letter: 'I do but wish to draw the attention of yourselves, as gentlemen, to a grave and gratuitous slander, with which I feel you will be sorry to find associated a name so eminent as yours.' There followed a lengthy exchange of private letters between the two clergymen and Kingsley printed an apology in the February issue of *Macmillan's*:

In your last number I made certain allegations against the teaching of Dr John Henry Newman which I thought were justified by a Sermon of his, entitled 'Wisdom and Innocence'. Dr Newman has by letter expressed, in the strongest terms, his denial of the meaning which I have put upon his words. It only remains therefore for me to express my hearty regret at having so seriously mistaken him.

At this point the matter might have rested had not Newman suddenly decided to publish his correspondence with Kingsley with a final section entitled 'Reflections on the Above'.[1] The most significant passage of the 'Reflections', which took the form of a mock-dialogue between the two contenders, ran as follows:

Mr. Kingsley exclaims: 'Oh, the chicanery, the wholesale fraud, the vile hypocrisy, the conscience-killing tyranny of Rome! We have not far to seek evidence of it! There's Father Newman to wit; — one living specimen is worth a hundred dead ones. He, a Priest, writing of Priests, tells me that lying is never any harm.'

I interpose: 'You are taking an extraordinary liberty with my name. If I have said this tell me when and where.'

Mr Kingsley replies: 'You said it, Reverend Sir, in a Sermon which you preached when a Protestant, as vicar of St Mary's, and published in 1844, and I could read you a very salutary lecture on the effects which that Sermon had at the time on my opinion of you.'

I make an answer: 'Oh not it seems as a Priest, speaking to Priests, but let us have the passage.'

Mr Kingsley relaxes: 'Do you know, I like your *tone*. From your *tone* I rejoice, greatly rejoice — to be able to believe you did not mean what you said.'

I rejoin: '*Mean* it! I maintain I never *said* it, whether as a Protestant or a Catholic!'

Mr Kingsley replies: 'I waive that point.'

Newman's dialogue was considered 'famous sport' by the periodicals of the day. 'How briskly', wrote the editor of the *Athenaeum* ,'do we gather round a brace of reverend gentlemen when the prize for which they contend is which of the two shall be considered the father of lies'. Even R. H. Hutton of the *Spectator*, a friend and admirer of Kingsley, applauded Newman's wit:

[1] J. H. Newman. *Mr Kingsley and Dr Newman: A Correspondence on the Question oj Whether Dr Newman Teaches that Truth is No Virtue.*

A more opportune Protestant ram for Father Newman's sacrificial knife could scarcely have been found; and the thicket in which he caught himself was, as it were, of his own choosing, he having rushed headlong into it quite without malice, but also without proper consideration of the force and significance of his own word. Mr Kingsley made a random charge against Father Newman in *Macmillan's Magazine*. The sermon in question certainly contains no proposition of the kind to which Mr Kingsley alludes. Mr Kingsley ought to have said, what is obviously true, that on examining the sermon no passage will bear any colourable meaning at all like that he had put upon it.

Thus provoked, Kingsley all too hastily snatched up his pen and dashed off the pamphlet *What Then Does Dr Newman Mean?* 'I am answering Newman now,' Kingsley told a friend, 'and though I give up the charge of conscious dishonesty, I trust to make him and his admirers sorry that they did not leave me alone. I have a score of more than twenty years to pay, and this is an instalment of it'. The person who was made to feel sorry, however, was not Newman, for the pamphlet was a disastrous failure. Having already accepted Newman's explanation of the meaning of 'Wisdom and Innocence', Kingsley could now only appeal to the lowest prejudices of his readers by showing that no man could be honest who believed in such things as monks, nuns, miracles, stigmata, the virginity of Christ's mother and, of course, celibacy.

Kingsley did not wait for Newman's reply to his pamphlet. One of his periodic 'brain storms' was upon him which, added to an ulcerated bowel was a cause for real alarm. There is a panicky little note in Fanny's hand among the Macmillan papers which runs: 'Sir James Clarke insists that he leaves at once for Spain. Nothing less will renovate his mind and body.' Froude was planning to go to Madrid to consult manuscripts for his History and had invited Kingsley at the last minute to accompany him. Kingsley had accepted with alacrity and even suggested prolonging the voyage as far as Gibraltar and returning by sea; 'I have always felt that one good sea voyage would add ten years to my life,' he told Froude. 'Remember that I can amuse myself in any hedge, with plants and insects and a cigar and that you may leave me anywhere, any long, certain that I shall be busy and happy. I cannot say how the thought of going has put fresh life into me.'

Kingsley left in such a hurry that he did not even stay to conduct the Easter services at Eversley that were so dear to him, but was in Paris to witness strange 'idolatrous' rites in Notre Dame by Good Friday.

Apart from these, he declared, 'These Frenchmen are a civilized people. The splendour of this city is beyond all I could have conceived, and the beautiful neatness and completeness of everything delights my eyes'. Nevertheless he did not at first abandon himself to France with quite the enthusiasm with which he had given himself to Germany in 1851. In the intervening thirteen years he had grown more insular, and was inclined to make remarks like, 'The Landes are not unlike Hartford Bridge Flat', 'Pau is a mixture of Bath and Edinburgh' and 'Biarritz is just a cross between Bude and Scarborough'. Biarritz took its revenge on him for this last calumny, for he fell ill there and was unable to accompany Froude into Spain. (One wonders whether some embarrassment at his treatment of Spain and the Spaniards in *Westward Ho!* did not also have an inhibiting effect.) He was content instead to gaze at 'the awful Pyranees' from his bedroom window.

In other respects too this Charles Kingsley on holiday was not the one who had humped a knapsack twenty miles a day over the Eifel, but an altogether gentler character who

> lounged about on the rocks, watching the grey lizards (I haven't seen any green ones yet) smoking penny Government cigars, which are very good . . . and luxuriating in the blessed, blessed feeling of having nothing to do! I start sometimes and turn round guiltily, with the thought surely I ought to be doing something, I have forgotten something, and then feel there is nothing to do even if I wanted.

Sometimes he fell asleep for two hours at a time on the sand.

He was enchanted by the little long-woolled sheep of the Basque peasants and 'the cows you could put under your arm'. Their owners, he told Fanny, 'put brown holland pinafores on their backs, and persuade them, as a great favour to do a little work. But they seem to get so fond of them that the oxen have much the best of the bargain'. He spent much time with the six-year-old daughter of a chemist living opposite and wrote to tell Mary (now twelve years old) 'She knits all her own woollen stockings and we have given her *Mlle. Lili,* and she has learnt it all by heart, and we have great fun making her say it'.

At last he tore himself away from the seashore and made for Pau, 'that beats all cities seen for beauty'. In spite of an internal upset which he put down to the water, 'which is horrible, I suppose from the great age of the town', he now felt strong enough to tackle the Pyrenees and surprise the 'Mossoos, who can't walk you see, and think it an awful thing', by strolling up, in an hour, to a plateau from which the magnificent Pic du Midi could be viewed. Evidently the locals regarded this as an expedition that required horses and guides. (It did not occur to Kingsley that they might hold this view for economic reasons.) 'A Wellington College boy,' he declared in a letter to Grenville, 'could trot there in three-quarters of an hour'. Nevertheless he did not linger amid the eternal snows, but succumbed quickly to the lure of the warm, lazy, pleasure-loving South.

Near Béziers he had his first glimpse of the Mediterranean.

There it is, — the sacred sea. The sea of all civilization, and almost all history, girdled by the fairest countries in the world; set there that human beings from all its shores might mingle with each other and become humane — the sea of Egypt, of Palestine, of Greece, of Italy, of Byzant; the sea, too, of Algeria, and Carthage, and Cyrene, and fair lands now desolate. Not only to the Christian, nor to the classic scholar, but to every man to whom the progress of his race from barbarism toward humanity is dear, should the Mediterranean Sea be one of the most august and precious objects on this globe; and the first sight of it should inspire reverence and delight as of coming home — home to a rich inheritance in which he has long believed by hearsay, but which he sees at last with his own mortal corporal eyes.[2]

Kingsley's immediate reaction, on seeing the sea, was to get into it. 'We ran literally through it for miles between Agde and Cette.'

At Arles he admitted to admiring the beauty of 'those Arlesiennes whose dark Greek beauty shines, like diamonds set in jet, in the doorways of the quaint old city'.[3] At Nîmes he basked in

the mere pleasure of existence in this sunny South. I am sitting, after a café-au-lait at 8.30 at an open window. Gardens, trees, flowers, fountains, outside, with people sitting out on the benches already, doing nothing but simply live; and more and more will sit there, till late tonight; from 7 to 10 the whole population of this great city will be in the streets, not sunning but mooning themselves, quite orderly and happy, listening to music, and cutting their little jokes, along the boulevards, under the beautiful trees these French have the sense to plant. I understand them now. They are not Visigoths, these fellows. They are the descendants of the old Roman Gauls, the lovers of the town, and therefore they make their towns

[2] Charles Kingsley 'From Ocean to Sea', *Prose Idylls*.
[3] Charles Kingsley, *Hereward the Wake*.

livable and lovable with trees and fountains, and bring the country into the town, while the Teutons take the town out into the country, and love each man his own garden and park.

Once more he allowed himself a delicious *frisson* at the massive monuments that the 'giant iniquity' had left behind, in this case the Pont du Gard, 'that *thing*, hanging between earth and heaven, the blue sky and green woods showing through its bright yellow arches, and all to carry a cubic yard of water to Nîmes, twenty miles off, for public baths and sham sea-fights in the amphitheatre.' In true Kingsley fashion he could not resist the urge to walk across it: 'one false step and one was one hundred feet below, but that is not my line'. Once more he admired the Roman baths, repeating that with all their sins their creators were the cleanest people the world has ever known. 'The remarkable thing was the Roman ladies' baths in a fountain bursting up out of the rock, where, under colonnades, they walked about, in or out of the water as they chose. All is standing, and could be used tomorrow, if the prudery of the priests allowed it.'

An ecstatic day was spent roaming the countryside round Nîmes. Kingsley wrote home to Fanny,

I was in a new world; *Genista Anglica*, the prickly needle furze of our commons (rare with us) is in great golden bushes; and box, shrubby thyme, a wonderful blue lily, bee orchis and asters, white, yellow, purple (which don't dry, for the leaves fall off). Then wild rosemary, and twenty more plants I never saw. We went . . . into a natural park of ilex and poplar (two or three sorts,) and watched such butterflies till Case said, 'This is too perfect to last', which frightened me and made me pray; and there was reason; for such a day I never had in all my life of beauty and wonder.

Strangely enough Newman had fallen under the spell of the Mediterranean in just the same way some years earlier. But whereas in Kingsley the voluptuousness of the South induced a sense of guilt that now decided him to turn his steps for home, instead of joining Froude in Barcelona, Newman had stayed on in Sicily after his companion returned to England.

Kingsley now started on the long journey back to Eversley, wearing a beard ('If I am laughed at, I shall cut it off') and carrying striped Basque stockings for the girls and red Basque berets for the boys. As he travelled north he wondered idly 'if Newman is answering again', and whether he was 'returning to fresh trouble and battle'. Fanny in her letters had not announced the appearance of the *Apologia*, but when her husband returned it was to find the completed work on his table, waiting for an answer.

The *Apologia pro Vita sua* was originally published in weekly instalments by Longman. It consisted of three sections, the first two of which were entitled 'Mr Kingsley's Method of Disputation' and 'True Mode of meeting Mr Kingsley'. It was only the third section, the autobiography, that was eventually published in book form. In it Newman explained, with deep and moving sincerity, the whole course of his religious life, and explained, step by step, how he came to the brink of the abyss from which the next logical step must be Rome.

Kingsley could not bring himself to open the *Apologia* for some days after his return. 'I shall not read him yet,' he told Macmillan, 'till I have recovered my temper about Priests — which is not improved by the abominable idolatry which I have seen in France.' This idolatry had undoubtedly banked the fires of battle while he was abroad. From Paris he had written to his curate Frederick Stapleton, 'When I get back, I will tell further volumes as to what I have seen of the Mariidolatry of France. I could not have conceived such things possible in the 19th Century. But I have seen enough to enable me to give Newman such a *revanche* as will make him wince, if any English common sense is left in him, which I doubt.'

In the end Kingsley decided not to reply to the *Apologia* at all. This could have been because he had at last recognised that theological controversy was not his strong point. He had once explained to a Wesleyan opponent, 'My business is attack, and not defence. If I cannot make myself understood the first time of speaking, I am not likely to do it by any subsequent word splitting explanations.' More likely, it was because he was not well enough to write. As he explained to F. D. Maurice, 'I am come back from France better not but well, and unable to take any mental exertion.' Instead he wrote Macmillan a letter 'which you may show to anyone including Mr Hutton'.[4]

I have determined to take no notice whatever of Dr Newman's apology.

1) I have nothing to retract, apologise for, explain. Deliberately, after 20 years of thought, I struck as hard as I could. Deliberately I shall strike again, if it so pleases me, though not one literary man in England approved. I know too well of what I am talking.

2) I cannot trust — I can only smile at — the autobiography of a man who (beginning with Newman's light, learning, and genius)

[4] R. H. Hutton of the *Spectator*.

ends in believing that he believes in the Infallibility of the Church
and the Immaculate Conception. If I am to bandy words, it must be
with sane persons.

3) I cannot be weak enough, to put myself a second time, by a
fresh act of courtesy, into the power of one who, like a treacherous
ape, lifts to you meek and suppliant eyes, till he thinks he has you
within his reach, and then springs, gibbering and biting, at your
face. Newman's conduct in this line has so much disgusted Catholics
themselves that I have no wish to remove their just condemnation
of his doings.

In the opinion of his contemporaries, Newman undoubtedly emerged
victorious from the contest. Few men have had the misfortune to be so
utterly and publicly confounded as was Kingsley in 1864. Even the
faithful Fanny admitted that 'he had crossed swords with one who was
too strong for him'. From that day to this, however, there have been
people who have insisted that Kingsley was, after all, not so completely
wrong. As recently as 1969 Mr Egner published a book entitled *Apologia
Pro Charles Kingsley* in which he pointed out that 'Kingsley courted
disaster by gratuitously insulting Newman in the first place, but his
accusations themselves were far more substantial than Newman
allowed'.

It only remains to enquire why Kingsley permitted himself the
'gratuitous insults' that provoked the *Apologia*. The answer lies, of
course, in his strong personal antipathy to Newman, whom he had
never met. Newman stood for the things that Kingsley most disliked
and feared in himself. He was a Catholic and he was effeminate.
We have already seen how close to Roman Catholicism Kingsley had
come himself as an undergraduate, a fact that he admitted in the first
letter he wrote to Newman in the course of the controversy: 'It was
in consequence of that Sermon that I finally shook off the strong
influence which your writing exerted on me.' That Kingsley regarded
the cat-like Cardinal as effeminate he had freely admitted in a letter
written twelve years earlier: 'In him and all that school, there is an
element of foppery — even in dress and manner; a fastidious, maunder-
ing die-away effeminacy, which is mistaken for purity and refinement;
and I confess myself unable to cope with it.' In the same letter he told
his correspondent, 'I have been through that terrible question of
"Celibacy versus Marriage" once already in my life. And from what
I have felt about it myself, and seen others feel, I am convinced that it
is the cardinal point.'

In his muddled way Kingsley connected the honouring of the Virgin with this effeminacy. In another letter, written about the same time, he poured scorn on the advice of a Roman Catholic priest who had said to one of his female correspondents, 'Go to the Blessed Virgin. She is a woman, and can understand all a woman's feelings.' 'Ah! thought I. If your head had once rested on a lover's bosom, and your heart known the mighty stay of a *man's* affection, you would have learnt to go now in your sore need, not to the mother, but to the Son — not to the indulgent virgin, but to the strong man, Jesus Christ.'

Looking back one feels that little purpose was served by the spectacle of two such eminent men sparring in public. Certainly the cause of truth did not benefit, though that hardly concerned those at the ringside, as Monckton Milnes admitted at the time of Kingsley's death. 'How preferable was Newman's gentlemanlike falsehood to his [Kingsley's] strepitose fidgety truth.' Newman's career undoubtedly benefited from the contest. As a result of it his star, which had grown increasingly dim since his exile from Oxford, was once more in the ascendant, and indeed one suspects that he may have prolonged the controversy for this purpose. At the Provincial Synod of the Birmingham clergy that summer he was publicly thanked, although he still had many years to wait before he received his cardinal's hat. The one unquestionably good result of the row was that it produced the *Apologia*, one of the major works of nineteenth-century literature. It was Kingsley's misfortune to be the fly embedded in the clear amber of his antagonist's apology.

CHAPTER 5

Hereward the Wake
1865–1866

Kingsley was ill for a year after the Newman controversy and seriously considered resigning his professorship. He was still afflicted with an ulcerated intestine and 'utterly worn out with influenza and coughing and sp - ing' (*sic*), as he explained to C. A. Johns. By the end of the winter he was so weak that he was obliged to leave home with his family and settle on the coast for three months. For reasons not known, he chose the East Coast and not the West, and indeed he seems to have had a premonition that he would never visit his beloved West Country again for he said as much in the letter to Dr Ackland which now hangs in the little museum at Bideford. Before he left Eversley, he wrote a letter to Hughes which lacked all the bounce of his usual effusions to the author of *Tom Brown*. 'I am getting better after fifteen months of illness, and I hope to be of some use again some day; a sadder and wiser man, the former, at least, I grow every year. I catch a trout now and then out of my ponds. I am too weak for a day's fishing, and the doctors have absolutely forbidden me my salmon.'

Not only was he physically ill, but mentally depressed. He had been shaken by the early death of his neighbour Henry Erskine ('a nobler, honest kindlier man never lived') within weeks of his father, Thomas the judge, and began to be haunted by thoughts of mortality. His mood was summed up in the poem *Drifting Away* written in 1867:

> I watch them drift — the old familiar faces,
> Who fished and rode with me by stream and wold,
> Till ghosts, not men, fill old beloved places,
> And, ah! the land is rank with churchyard mold.

A strange poem for a man of forty-eight to write.

His doubts about the existence of God once more returned. To F. D. Maurice he wrote, 'I feel a capacity of drifting to sea in me which makes me cling nervously to any little anchor. I feel glad of aught that says to me, "You must teach this and nothing else; you must not run riot in your own dreams!" ' Fanny knew well enough what dreams these were, for she added, after quoting the above letter, 'This may be a comfort to troubled souls, when they remember the calm assured faith with which he faced life and death.' Perhaps George Fox's words best expressed his attitude, 'And I saw that there was an Ocean of Darkness and Death: but an infinite Ocean of Light and Love flowed over the Ocean of Darkness.' Yet visions of that ocean *unlit* would keep returning.

It is worth dwelling upon the nervous collapse of 1864 because it was the first that Kingsley had had for five years, and the last that he was ever to have. Between the ages of thirty and forty he had suffered a breakdown almost every year.[1] So regular, indeed, were his collapses, that he might, with accuracy, have been described as a manic-depressive at this period, oscillating regularly between moods of high euphoria and deep melancholy.[2] During his manic phases he embarked on fresh philanthropic ventures, founded periodicals, dashed off novels. During his depressive ones, he was incapable of any activity, either mental or physical: 'I can't think; I can't write; I can't run; I can't ride — I have neither wit, nerve nor strength for anything, and if I try I get a hot head, and my arms and legs begin to ache . . . When I tried to work, and yet could not, I had, over and above, a nasty craving for alcohol.'[3]

Why, one asks, did the breakdowns suddenly cease in 1859, with the single recurrence in 1864? Perhaps the explanation is not far to seek. It was in 1859, as we have already pointed out, the tide of Kingsley's life turned. In that year he was noticed by the Queen and given the chair of history at Cambridge. He began to be an accepted, even admired member of society instead of an outcast. From that time on his reputation only suffered one serious reverse; the defeat at the hands of Newman. It was this defeat that brought on the isolated breakdown of 1864.

In the late spring of 1865 health did, however, begin to return, and by July Kingsley felt strong enough to offer hospitality at Eversley to Queen Emma of the Sandwich Islands, who had come to England to make arrangements for an Anglican mission to her people. Kingsley had first met the dusky sovereign while visiting Ely and, knowing she had wanted her son to attend a British public school, had he lived, suggested she might be interested to visit Wellington. He implied that

---

[1] Kingsley suffered from breakdowns in 1848, 1849, 1851, 1852, 1853, 1855, 1856 and 1859.

[2] There is a high probability that Kingsley's youngest son, Grenville, committed suicide at the age of forty at his home on the Logan River in Queensland.

[3] Letter to John Bullar, November 19, 1859.

such a visit would please Queen Victoria because of the connection of the school with the Prince Consort.

Her Majesty graciously accepted the invitation and an account of her twenty-eight hours at Eversley can best be left to the pen of Fanny. Kingsley had offered the Queen a view of the menage of a 'plain country clergyman, living in a quiet parsonage, where no footmen are kept or grand dinners given, but people eat plain mutton, and enjoy music and good talk'.[4] Fanny saw to it that she received quite another kind of hospitality, as she told her sisters:

Dear Queen Emma's visit has been one of the most interesting passages of one's life, and will ever remain in our memories as a very perfect and most strangely interesting event — perfect because everything went well and smoothly, — strange — because the feeling of having a Queen civilised and yet of savage, even cannibal, ancestry sleeping under one's roof in Charlie's and my room — eating at one's table — talking of Tennyson and *Tom Brown School Days* (!) of the delight with which she and the late King, her dear Husband, had read *The Water-Babies* to their little Prince; strange — it was passing strange, and made me feel that we had been living for 28 hours in a dream!

It was only on Friday that we knew she was coming, so we busied ourselves all Saturday in preparing for her that we might not have anything to disturb our minds on Sunday . . . Susan plunged into the Plate Chest, out of which all the old Kingsley silver-handled knives and forks and dishes and cream jugs and candlesticks were rapidly exhumed. Rose and I plunged into the China Cupboard. Mrs Hedges, the old fat cook, assumed a royal air, and stepped into a small pony cart, at the risk of her neck, to have a private interview with the Butcher and sit with him upon saddles of Mutton and joints of Beef (which I vainly endeavoured to persuade her would not appear as it was to be strictly a Russian Dinner). The Fishmonger was ordered to procure a Turbot or a Whale if he could get one; Lord Eversley was written to for Fruit. Everybody who came into the Kitchen received a hint, that Game wd. be acceptable and each of us assuming an air and step of Majesty endeavoured calmly to suppress our strong emotion; and not to be upset even by a Queen in this well regulated Parsonage. Old furniture was humped into cupboards, windows cleaned, pink calico and white muslin were cut up regardless of expense — and the Queen's room (Charlie's and mine) soon looked very pretty. Bedrooms were prepared for the

4 Unpublished letter to J. H. Friswell, 1867.

Black Chaplain (a delightful man), the Lady-in-Waiting, the Aide de Camp, a Footman (English) who had lived with the Queen 9 years, and a French Lady's Maid.

Fanny then described how the Queen was duly met at Wokingham Station.

As we got into the carriages the rain began to pour down and continued in such a deluge that no one could see an inch of Country from the Windows. It was despair! but Queen Emma cd. just see enough of the Fern and Heather and Fir Trees by the road side to interest her ... and in ½ an hour we arrived at the Great Gates of the Wellington, where the Head Master in his gown, Mrs Benson and the servants all in the old Duke's liveries, were ready to receive us. The Great Gates were thrown open, Mr Benson walked with the Queen, and I, with matchless presence of mind, marshalled the procession, sending Charles with the Lady-in-Waiting, (such a huge gentle savage,) the Aide de Camp with Mrs Benson, etc etc. The rain poured down in torrents, the boys swarmed after us — but we were happily under the corridor. Queen Emma asked the most intelligent questions about everything — then the Boys were to be seen in Hall at dinner. This was most interesting. Queen Emma stood at the high Table and asked in a low voice for a half holiday — upon which Ponsonby [the head boy] said in a loud voice 'Three Cheers for Queen Emma'. It was the first time she ever heard English boys cheer — and you may imagine her amazement.[5]

It can only be taken as proof of Kingsley's inconsistency, or of his now overriding love of royalty, that within a year of entertaining the black queen he had joined the Governor Eyre Defence Committee whose war-cry was 'Down with nigger philanthropists'. In the autumn of 1865 Edward John Eyre, governor of Jamaica, had put to death six hundred natives including a leader named Gordon, in an attempt to quell a riot in which some twenty Europeans had perished. Eyre had been commended by a royal commission for his promptness in stopping the riot, but reprimanded for unnecessary vigour and disregard of individual rights. At this stage the Jamaica Committee was formed by those who considered that the reprimand was too mild and that the governor should be tried for murder. The members of the committee included John Stuart Mill, Huxley and Tom Hughes. Ludlow

[5] Tradition has it that the Queen was, for a moment, so terrified by the din that she made a rush for the window in an attempt to escape.

was among its most active supporters. Two months later, an equally strong committee was formed for the defence of Eyre, headed by Carlyle, Tennyson and Ruskin. Henry Kingsley, who admired Eyre's work as a protector of natives in Australia, rallied to its support. Charles at first hung back but then, rather surprisingly (for it was usually he who led and Henry who followed) also took up arms in his support.

Kingsley's dislike of negroes was of long standing. He had always been deeply convinced that the negro race was an inferior one and once marvelled, in a sermon, that out of sticks and stones, yea, out of Hottentots, could the Lord raise up worshippers. He was convinced that the wrong side was victorious in the American Civil War and felt so strongly on the subject that, while the war was being fought, he devoted his Cambridge lectures to American history. Lincoln, he told his audience, was but 'a poor cute honest fellow', fit only for splitting rails and responsible for a proclamation that made secession inevitable. Slavery, although an abomination, was probably the best method of ruling a people incapable of self-government. When asked for a subscription to help the freed slaves, he had refused, saying, 'The negro has had all I ever possessed; for emancipation ruined me. I am no slave holder at heart. But I have paid my share of the great bill, in Barbados and Demerara.' Presumably he referred to the Lucas estates in the West Indies inherited by his mother and long since sold.

The results of the fracas were unfortunate not only for Eyre who, although not hanged, was condemned to a life of poverty, but also for Kingsley who lost two of his best friends because of it. From this time on the frequent letters to Ludlow and Hughes ceased. The friendship with Ludlow had been wearing thin for some time. Ludlow wrote about its demise when, as an old man who had survived all his friends he declared:

> I continued corresponding with him till the time of the Jamaica Committee, tho' not with the same fullness as before, as I had to crush a plan which he proposed to me, after the stoppage of the *Journal of Association*, for setting up a new party, and I do not think he liked this. Again, as time went on, I found that he no longer cared to receive from me criticisms of his writings, unless purely eulogistic. Then when the Jamaica massacres took place, and T. Hughes and myself joined the Jamaica Committee, I was amazed to hear that, without saying a word to either of us, he had himself joined the antagonistic organisation, the Eyre Defence Fund. I wrote to him to say that our paths now ran so divergent that it was useless to cor-

respond any longer. From that time we neither corresponded nor met each other until Mr Maurice's funeral, when we met, I am glad to say, on perfectly friendly terms.

Kingsley's last years at Cambridge were brightened by the presence of both Maurices at the university. In 1866, using his professorial influence as an elector, he had succeeded in getting F. D. Maurice presented to the chair of Knightsbridge Professor of Casuistry, Moral Theology and Moral Philosophy, in spite of his many enemies. He attended Maurice's lectures (which were always delivered with tightly closed eyes) assiduously and was deeply moved by the series on 'Conscience'. A clergyman, who sat next to him while Maurice was discussing the inadequacy of Bain's theory of conscience, says, 'Professor Kingsley's fighting blood was evidently roused when Nelson's famous signal was referred to. I had to shrink into very small compass, for a strong right hand shot out straight from his shoulder, passed quite as near as was pleasant to my face. I looked and saw that Professor Kingsley could not see for tears.' Kingsley often brought undergraduates to meet Maurice in the evenings. There are several contemporary accounts of the care he took to distract these young men's attention from him until the shy Master felt sufficiently relaxed to exert his charm.

In 1865 Kingsley's son Maurice had entered Trinity College, Cambridge, as an undergraduate, somewhat against his will, and indeed it was for this reason that his father had decided not to resign his professorship in that year. The handsome boy had shown no more academic ability at Wellington than he had at his preparatory school, although he was capable of considerable feats in the hunting field. Like his father, at the same age, he was showing a strong desire to give it all up and become 'a wild prairie hunter', an urge which his father had curbed with a stiff letter written on December 12th, 1864.

My dearest boy,
    A letter came tonight for Fanny. I opened it of course, she being away. Don't try to hide anything from me, for you will find me — not as reasonable as she is — but quite reasonable enough for a fellow who has a skin and can stand a pin prick.
    All I say is do what you like, only do it. India is a very fine opening. So is Queensland, though I should prefer India for you, though I will be fair on your side, there are no convicts in Queensland, and therefore no fear for you or your children's morals on their score. Before you go to any place you will go to Cambridge. And there

you will stay till you take your degree. On that point there will be *no* change of purpose. And by that time *you* will have changed your mind three or four times, and no blame to you. If you qualify yourself for the Indian Civil Service, you will qualify yourself for half-a-dozen things.

In fact Maurice's stay at Cambridge was a happy time, for his father at least, although the young man was often in academic difficulties. For the first time in many years Kingsley was able to enjoy his son's company, and announced proudly, 'Maurice walks everywhere with me, like a dog, of his own accord.'[6] In another letter he wrote of Maurice, 'He has been regretting that he has read so little and yearns, for the first time in his life, after art. Oh, what a blessing to see him grow under one's eyes — and to be able to help him at last by teaching him something oneself. It is quite right that the schoolmasters have the grounding and disciplining, but the father who can finish his boy's education ought to be thankful.' So pleased was he with his son's progress that he announced, 'I am going to give him a pair of *breeches* for a birthday present, he deserves it.'[7]

During his last years at Cambridge Kingsley gave up attempting to write the *History for Children* that he had planned for so long; (only three chapters were ever completed). He now often made excursions into the Fens and the spell of their beauty (which had captivated him in childhood) was once more upon him: 'a beauty as of the sea, of boundless expanse and freedom ... Overhead the arch of heaven spread more ample than elsewhere ... and that vastness gave, and still gives, such cloudlands, such sunrises, such sunsets as can be seen nowhere else in these isles.'[8] Now he conceived the idea of writing a novel about a fenland hero, Hereward the Wake, using Cambridge as a convenient base from which to do research. He wrote to Fanny, 'I have found treasures about Hereward worth thousands to me. I believe now I shall make it the best thing I ever did.' When the book appeared a year later some critics regarded this estimate as somewhat optimistic. The general opinion was that the book lacked the liveliness of *Westward Ho!*, perhaps because it was written with great effort and under the need for money, and not, like its predecessor, under the lash of a strong emotion aroused by a national event. The modern reader, however, might consider this absence of boisterousness and bombast an advantage.

Hereward the Wake; last of the English, to give it its full title, is a

[6] ULF No. 237, February 11, 1867.   [7] ULF July 15, 1867.
[8] Charles Kingsley, *Hereward the Wake.*

carefully researched historical novel. Kingsley's years in the chair of modern history had given him some respect for accuracy, and, as he tells us, perhaps once too often, he knew the relevant parts of the *Anglo-Saxon Chronicle* backwards before he set pen to paper. As a result he is able to give us a vivid picture of what life was like in England in the dim and distant year of the Norman Conquest, when vast areas of the land were still under virgin forest and men invoked fen-fiends and wood-fiends as often as Christian saints.

Hereward, called 'the Wake' because he was never caught unawares, was a hero after Kingsley's own heart, although almost completely forgotten at the time that the book was written. He symbolised the spirit of bulldog English resistance to the French invaders and their monks. He was the typical Viking hero of the old sagas, 'the Berserker, the brain-hewer, the land-thief, the sea-thief, the feeder of wolf and raven' whose ambition was to make many women widows, and at last mount Odin's horse

> With heroes hot corpses
> Heaped high for my pillow.

In him Kingsley saw reflected the spirit of the schoolboy of his own day; 'Hard knocks in good humour, strict rules, fair play and equal justice for high and low; this was the old outlaw spirit, which has descended to their inlawed descendants; and makes, to this day, the life and marrow of an English public school!'

Such absurd comparisons fortunately do not detract from many lively episodes, particularly in the second half of the book, when Hereward, isolated in East Anglia by the Conqueror's castle at Lincoln, makes his last stand. The outlaw's sacking of Peterborough is fine rumbustious stuff, and better still is his defence of the Isle of Ely. While his wife Torfrida stands, with manacled arms aloft, invoking St Sexburga, he watches the Conqueror's causeway slowly subside until at last 'one sideway roll it gave, and then, turning over, engulfed in that foul stream the flower of Norman chivalry; leaving a line — full quarter mile in length — of wretches drowning in the dark water, or, more hideous still, in the bottomless slime of peat and mud'.

Like all Kingsley's novels, *Hereward* has faults. It lacks form and suspense, and tends to consist of a series of episodes strung loosely together in the manner of *The Adventures of Robin Hood* which it at times resembles. This may be partly due to the professor's anxiety to stick closely to historical facts, and partly to his failure to produce a strong character to be a worthy opponent to Hereward. The 'half savage hero' himself is real enough. We see him in youth as a long-haired and bearded gang-leader, terrorising the neighbourhood of Peterborough; we see him in his prime coming under the civilising influence of his French wife, Torfrida, and rising to heroic stature; we feel the tragedy of his downfall when, abandoning both cause and wife, he becomes King William's man, falls for the seductions of Alftruda, and loses his self-respect; we rejoice to see him blot out his disgrace at last by dying a hero's death. But where is the heroic opponent for this hero? William the Conqueror, 'the Mamzer', was a character who Kingsley felt unable to describe. He dubbed him an 'unfathomable master-personage' and abandoned the attempt. Instead he turned to a minion, Ivo Taillebois, 'brutal, ignorant, profligate', and pitted him against Hereward. But Ivo proves unworthy of his role, for he never develops into a real character. Nor indeed does the other main character in the book. Torfrida, like all Kingsley's heroines, is too well endowed with the virtues of Victorian womanhood to be real. 'Oh, woman, woman!' cries Hereward in despair, 'I verily believe that God made you alone, and left the devil to make us butchers of men.' He speaks only too truly. Torfrida, like Grace Harvey, of *Two Years Ago*, is altogether too good to be true.

The style of the book is also uneven. Sometimes it is epic, as when Hereward is described as a 'lightning brand, flashing into the fens and out again causing the birds upon the meres to cry "The Wake is come!"' At others it is consciously archaic: a character will be 'cloven to the chine' or cry out, 'Pish! It fell not upon that wise!' At other times again it is prosaic and even abrupt; a monk is described as talking 'some such bombast' and the chapter on Hereward's campaign in Holland is limited to half a page on the excuse that it was a 'weary business' and could all be found in Richard of Ely anyway.

Few people probably read *Hereward* for pleasure nowadays. Dent's popular edition (like that of *Westward Ho!*) comes complete with a list of questions and exercises at the end which suggests that the average reader is a captive of the schoolroom. Nevertheless there are worse ways of picking up background information about the state of England in the eleventh century. The book contains lively descriptions of the everyday life of the time; how it felt to eat reeking cormorant pie at the rough wooden tables of one of the stone barns that passed for castles in those days; the sensation of a Norman knight in armour waiting in ambush on a frosty morning 'with freezing iron feet in freezing iron stirrups'. Certainly it makes more lively reading than its predecessor, Bulmer Lytton's *Harold*.

Kingsley's novels were now in great demand. The editors of *Good Words* and *Macmillan's Magazine* almost came to blows over the question of who should serialise *Hereward*. Fanny favoured the claims of *Good Words*, a magazine to which she was in the habit of sending her husband's lectures and sermons on the quiet. Charles wrote to her pointing out that Macmillan had the first right:

> I do not see how I can refuse Mac *Hereward* for the magazine, if he pays as much for it as the Scotchman.[9] Moreover I shall not get the money from *Good Words* till it is finished, whereas I can draw on Macmillan when I like. Now he has got me it is worth any money to him to keep me and he knows it. I told him some weeks ago of having refused Mc L's offer of £1,500, and he opened his eyes and said he was exceedingly obliged and I should never have to repent it.[10]

In the event, Fanny won. Kingsley's last novel appeared serially in *Good Words* in 1865, and was then published in book form by Macmillan. It was through her business acumen that her husband made a further large sum with *Madam How and Lady Why*, a series of papers on land formation written with the intention of arousing an interest in geology in Grenville and other boys of his age.[11] It was she who encouraged him to write the book and she who negotiated the £1,000 he was paid for it. 'What a wise woman you seem, to have set me writing about physical science!!!' he told her. In deference to the 'wise woman' he gave up an attempt to write another historical novel set in the South of France. At the beginning of 1868 he sent Macmillan

> the plan of a novel, or Romance. The autobiography of a poor English Scholar from about 1490 — and going on to about 1530-40 — who should see the outburst of the Reformation, know Erasmus, Rabelais, etc. be at the Sack of Rome in 1526 — at Marguerite of Navarre's court at Pau, and generally about the world. I have sketched the man and much of the scenery and incident, in my head; and I can't help feeling that people might like it. The man would be a simple miller's son out of my own parish, and come back to end his days here.

A few days later Fanny wrote, 'He is so *overdone* that I shrink from the novel. I believe it will just finish him!' Kingsley took her advice, and never wrote another work of fiction.

[9] The editor of *Good Words* was a Scot to whom Kingsley often referred as Mc L.
[10] ULF No. 231, 1865.
[11] One present Fellow of the Geological Society assures me his interest in the subject was first aroused by this book.

CHAPTER 6

Exit the Professor
1867–1869

Kingsley's thoughts now turned once more to science. While Froude was in Spain in the spring of 1867 he took his place for a few months as editor of *Fraser's Magazine* (John Parker having died, much mourned by his friends, in 1860). During his tenure he tried, not very successfully, to turn the magazine into a scientific periodical. He approached several eminent scientists for contributions but the amiable Sir Charles Bunbury was the only one who obliged. At this time Kingsley was also in correspondence with Huxley and put forward to him the view that all young men should have some knowledge of science before they left school, an excellent idea that was not, alas, to be realised for many a long year. In a lecture entitled 'The Theology of the Future' he declared, 'I sometimes dream of a day when it will be considered necessary that every candidate for ordination should be required to have passed creditably in at least one branch of physical science, if it be only to teach him the method of sound scientific thought.'

While he was discussing education in science with Huxley, the volume of derisive cries against his own teaching of history was becoming deafening. The historian Freeman, who no doubt considered *he* should have had Kingsley's job, had never been kind to him. Some of the things he said in a prolonged campaign in the *Saturday Review* would surely be grounds for libel in our gentler age. In a review of *The Roman and the Teuton*[1] he wrote:

> Of all the strange appointments ever made, that which turned Mr Kingsley into a Professor of History seemed, at the time, to be the very strangest. Other Professors, whether competent or incompetent, had at least some outward and visible connexion with the subject which they undertook to teach ... But the appointment of Mr Kingsley seems a mere inexplicable freak. There was apparently no more reason why he should be made a Professor of History than why

[1] A collection of Kingsley's history lectures published in 1864.

he should be set to command the Channel Fleet. The thing seemed a joke. Mr Kingsley once could, and still can by an effort, write good sense and good English, but there are pages and pages of these lectures which are simply rant and nonsense — history, in short, brought down to the lowest level of the sensation novelist . . . Mr Kingsley is a clever man, a warm hearted man, and an honest man; but of all men living he is the least qualified to undertake the work of an historian or an historical Professor. He confesses that his Lectures are not. in the popular sense, history at all, and it is beyond our power to find out any more esoteric or recondite sense in which they deserve the name.

In November 1867 came criticism of a more serious kind, for it appeared not in an 'obscure print', as Macmillan described the *Saturday Review*, but the august columns of *The Times*. In a review of Kingsley's *Three Lectures on the Ancien Régime* appeared the following paragraph:

We cannot say that it [the volume under review] will silence the calumnies of the uncharitable persons who have insinuated that the appointment of Mr Kingsley to the chair of Professor of Modern History at Cambridge was a sign that the University despised the subject or knew little about it . . . Mr Kingsley has repeatedly shown that he cannot grasp the whole of a subject, examine it thoroughly in all its bearings, and form a judicial estimate of it; his opinions are sometimes hasty and crude; his manner vehement, illogical, and discursive; and these defects, we regret to say, are not absent from the present volume.

Kingsley was deeply wounded by the attack which hit him squarely on what F. D. Maurice called his 'inferiority complex'. He now wrote a letter to the Master, full of self-abasement. 'I feel more and more my own unfitness for the post,' he wrote. 'My memory grows worse and worse, and I am only fit for a preacher or poetaster; not for a student of facts (moral and historical, at least).' Both Maurice and Fanny advised him against resigning at once. Fanny gave her views to Maurice in the following letter.

Charles, you see, is quite ready to wait till he sees you and the Vice Chancellor. I have long wished him to give up the Professorship, simply because it is too much for his brain! The responsibility and the work, which are so heavy now, would not weigh upon him so, if he had nothing else to do — but the Parish work and the writing besides, is too much for any man of his organisation — and if I had not felt he wd. so like to be at Cambridge while our dear boy Maurice was there, I shd. have persuaded him to give it up 3 years ago, and so I think would Sir James Clark.[2] But I quite agree with you that *this* is a most unfortunate moment — and I wd. not yield to that insolent *Times* for the world! Especially as I believe the article to have been written by a certain Mr Woodham, a *Times* writer, who was trying for the Professorship when Charles got it, and he has never forgiven him getting the post he coveted himself. I feel, with you, that if people succumb to this Tyranny of the Press, it will end by swallowing up all free action and free speech — so I am glad to have this move delayed, though I long to have Charles relieved from the fearful responsibility of his Cambridge work. It is a great and noble work and I believe him to be so *morally* fitted for it — independent of all intellectual power — but he *could* not give up his Parish work and the wretched necessity of writing for the children's sake. Combined together they are too much for him and will kill him, unless he is relieved from a great deal of the work by the Queen's giving him a Canonry which I am sure she will do when she can.

In her heart of hearts Fanny knew there was another reason for her husband's exhausted state — her own refusal to live with him at Cambridge. She gave some somewhat lame excuses for this at the end of her letter. 'We are so hampered, too, just now by having his Mother living with us, and the difficulty it is to leave her and go to Cambridge together — also by his idea that Cambridge disagrees with me. It is true that I have been very ill there, but that would not dissuade me from going, in order to be with him.' Fanny's refusal to leave home was now reaching pathological proportions. She would not even join her husband on his summer visits to great houses, no doubt secretly fearing their grand ways, for although she often harped upon the splendid social life of her girlhood, she appeared shy of mixing with illustrious strangers outside her own home. Charles's letters often contained gentle reproofs for her embarrassing refusal to accompany him on visits. From Mountfield Court, Hurst Green, he wrote 'They do entreat that you will stay here coming back — and so do I. *Why not? Why not?*' From another country house he wrote, 'Why will you not come? Everyone thinks it is so strange.' She was beginning to refuse social engagements even within driving distance of Eversley, claiming that she could not stand 'the racket' of the 'Innumerable Croquets' that were then the fashion, and that she preferred to stay at

[2] Kingsley's physician.

home 'brooding upon theology'. This tendency towards theological speculation, that Charles had found so attractive in Fanny as a young woman, he now tended to decry. In several letters he chided her gently for some new theory she had expounded. 'I do so enjoy your thoughts, when you have time for them. But I don't care for rationalising away the dear old Bible stories,' he wrote in one such letter. In another he firmly ordered her to read no more books by a modern theologian whom he considered 'dangerously perverse'.

There were several great houses in the neighbourhood of Eversley at which the Kingsleys were welcome visitors. There was Strathfield Saye[3] where the Duke of Wellington ('that old noodle') kept an elephant in special shoes to mow the lawn, and Bear Wood, the home of John Walter, proprietor of *The Times*. Kingsley particularly enjoyed evenings 'politicking' at Heckfield Place, the home of Lord Eversley, a former Speaker of the House of Commons. After his wife died, her place as hostess was taken by his eccentric daughter, Miss Shaw-Lefevre, who occasionally gave tea parties on the roof. She disapproved of railways and, when eventually obliged to use one, had her brougham strapped to a flat truck to ride up to London in the only manner that she considered genteel.

Perhaps it was just as well that Fanny was not with her husband when he was the guest of the Prince of Wales at Abergeldie Castle in September 1867. For while the gillie was celebrating Kingsley's catch by taking an enormous bagpipe, and 'booming like an elephantine bumble bee all round the dinner table', Grenville was running away from his first preparatory school.

Grenville was always supposed to be a delicate child who suffered from a liver and could not stand the heat. There had been the usual heart searchings about sending him away to school, and eventually Winton House, the young gentleman's academy that Kingsley's old master, the Rev C. A. Johns had recently established at Winchester,[4] was chosen. The place was said to have a waiting list of hundreds, and father and son went to inspect it together. Charles wrote home a glowing letter to Fanny: 'Nothing can have gone better than our day. I left Grenville playing with the boys by himself, and I *ran in the sack race*. He was happy, and good and quite well. The place is delightful — high and healthy — and the arrangements for the boys perfect. They are a nice looking set — rosy and jolly. Mrs Johns is like a mother to them all.'[5]

[3] Opened to the public for the first time in the summer of 1974.
[4] The school, in Andover Road, is now an Approved School.
[5] ULF No. 244, 1867.

On September 19th, Grenville, aged nine, was duly packed off for his first term and Charles wrote a letter of sympathy to the bereaved Fanny:

I am quite unhappy today thinking of your parting with the dear boy, for I can understand, though my man's coarser nature cannot feel as intensely the pang to you of parting with a bit of yourself. More and more am I sure, and the physiologists are becoming more sure also, that the mother is the more important, and in the case of the boy, everything. The child *is* the mother, and her rights, opinions, feelings, even fancies about him, ought to be first regarded. I suppose you will write to me all about his starting; but I have no fear of him being anything but happy, and Madame V. says that boys are always so much *healthier* as soon as they go to school.

Within a week Grenville was reunited with his mother, and his father was engaged upon the embarrassing task of excusing the behaviour of 'my little renegade' to his headmaster.

I am sure this is merely the first struggle of a child who has never met his equals and been much petted and spoilt. But he is really perfectly hardy, strong and bold, because he has never been bullied — and quite shrewd, not to say clever, as I suspect him to be. My own belief is — that if we can only keep right the *liver* which he inherits from both parents — he will be a fine, frank, forward lad, and a credit to us both.
P.S. I long for you among these wonderful deer forests.

The weather was too hot that summer for good salmon fishing and Kingsley, with his inexhaustible thirst for chatting with his inferiors, encouraged his gillie to tell him stories of the Celtic hermits who had once lived in that part of Scotland. These he decided to collect into a book entitled *The Hermits,* adding to them the stories of the North African penitents that he had unearthed while working on *Hypatia* and winding up with St Guthlac, over whose body rose the Abbey of Crowland amid the watery wastes of the fens.[6] Having filled a hundred and ninety-five pages with tales of wonders and miracles, including the story of how lions dug the grave of St Anthony (aged a hundred and thirteen) for St Paul (aged eighty-seven), Kingsley proceeded to inform his readers that he himself did not believe a word of them:

[6] Kingsley was thoroughly familiar with Crowland Abbey, for it was here that Torfrida took refuge when Hereward abandoned her.

'the hermits worked no real miracles and saw no real visions. They had merely managed, by continual fasts and vigils, to work themselves up into a state of mental disease.'

Because of Fanny's refusal to accompany her husband, Rose, now twenty-three years old, often took her place. In future years, when chained to the side of a bedridden mother at Leamington Spa[7] she must sometimes have looked back wistfully to those glamorous visits to the great houses of the land, and to a certain party given by the Vice-Chancellor at Oxford, where she was introduced to Lord Palmerston and Jenny Lind, and stood modestly aside while her father had 'a long and most interesting religious talk with the Swedish nightingale'.[8] She was also beginning to take over her mother's duties as secretary, and remarks like 'Rose wrote for me for an hour or two capitally', began to appear in the letters of this period.

Rose was an accomplished young woman, a keen amateur historian and natural scientist, and a fair performer on the piano. Although neither she nor Mary was ever sent away to school, good masters were hired for their education at home and Rose eventually became the author of several history books for children, and an expert whose name is still remembered in the world of rose-growing.[9] As she grew older, her manner became somewhat domineering, as a lady still living in Eversley, to whom she attempted to teach English and History, recalls. She was a pioneer in the controversial matter of making secondary education available to girls, and is still remembered as the founder of Leamington High School for Girls.

It is hardly a surprise, therefore, to discover that Kingsley was at this time a supporter of the campaign for the education of women. In acknowledging the receipt of a copy of John Stuart Mill's book, *The Subjection of Women*, Kingsley wrote;

I beg you to do me the honour of looking on me, though I trust a Christian and a clergyman, as completely emancipated from those prejudices which have been engrained in the public mind by the

[7] After her mother's death in 1888, Rose built a house for herself at Eversley, called Keys, and wrote a book about the place called *Eversley Gardens*.

[8] ULF No. 225, 1867.

[9] According to C. H. R. Morris, in an article in the magazine, *The Rose*, printed in the spring of 1969, Rose Kingsley's book, *Roses and Rose Growing*, published in 1908, is among the most reliable records of the rose-scene from 1860. He describes her grasp of pruning and propagating as surprisingly modern, and sufficiently different from the official attitude at the time to suggest that she was relaying her own thought and practice.

traditions of the monastic or canon law, about women, and open to any teaching which has for its purpose the doing woman justice in every respect. Mrs Kingsley begs me to add the expression of her respect for you. Her opinion has long been that this movement must be furthered rather by men than by the women themselves.

Dr Elizabeth Blackwell, one of the first women to qualify as a doctor, became a frequent visitor to Eversley, and used to take long walks through the fir woods, engaged in earnest conversation with the rector. 'Only a few weeks before his death,' wrote Dr Blackwell, 'although his health was broken, and he was suffering from overwork, he agreed to become chairman of a committee for securing medical degrees for women'. He was less active, however, in supporting a campaign for votes for women. As had happened in the case of Christian Socialism, although he found the cause good, he often found its supporters repugnant. In a long letter to Mill he explained that the cause was 'not well served by foolish women, of no sound or coherent opinions, and of often questionable morals . . . who are smarting under social wrongs. These women', he explained, 'would swamp the movement with hysteria, which I define as the fancy and emotions unduly excited by suppressed sexual excitement.'

Kingsley drew an even more vivid picture of the emancipated women he so detested when he described 'that ghastly ring of prophetesses in the Hatchgoose drawing-room', in *Two Years Ago*.

Strong-minded and emancipated women, who prided themselves on having cast off conventionalities, and on being rude and awkward, and dogmatic and irreverent, and sometimes slightly improper; women who had missions to mend everything in heaven and earth, except themselves; who had quarrelled with their husbands, and had therefore felt a mission to assert women's rights and reform marriages in general; or who had never been able to get married at all, and therefore were especially competent to promulgate a model method of educating the children whom they never had had; women who wrote poetry about Lady Blanches whom they never had met, and novels about male and female blackguards whom (one hopes) they never had met, or about whom (if they had) decent women would have held their peace; and every one of whom had, in obedience to Emerson, 'followed her impulses' and despised fashion, and was accordingly clothed and bedizened as was right in the sight of her eyes, and probably in those of no one else.

Rose naturally shared her father's views in this matter as in most others. Not without reason was she once described as 'Charles Kingsley in petticoats'. This filial adoration was to have unfortunate consequences, for it tended to discourage suitors, and Rose never married. In *Hereward* Kingsley inveighed against fathers who were jealous of their daughters' lovers. 'There is no dog in the manger so churlish on such points as a vain man. There are those who will not willingly let their own sisters, their own daughters, their own servants marry.' Yet he was just such a jealous father, as a letter written in 1863[10] proves.

> I say nothing about Rose, but don't suppose I don't think about her. If this fellow doesn't settle the matter right away, I will punish that man. I will do it and find out how to do it. If a man hurts me, I will die sooner than hurt him. If he hurts my child, I will die but what I will avenge her. So Rose, for her gentleman's sake, had better act once and for all. For he is running up an ugly score with me. I am giving communion somewhere every day this week.

Some years later, while on a visit to America, Rose fell in love with Captain Howard Schuyler, a man of whom her father might have been expected to approve, for he was a hero of the Civil War and a noted fighter in the wars against the Indians. He had, however, a fatal flaw: he was an American. Kingsley thanked God with profound gratitude when he married another.

In the last years of the 'sixties, Kingsley's letters began once more to be filled with references to money, or rather the lack of it. Remarks like 'I expect the tithe in a few days, and money from Macmillan' or 'I have written to Macmillan to find what money he can',[11] appear frequently, in spite of the fact that his income had been practically doubled by the professorship, and he had published six books in four years.[12] One cause of financial embarrassment was certainly the cost of educating his children. Kingsley was now supporting a young man at university and a boy at school, while at the same time paying salaries to tutors for his girls at home. But another cause was, undoubtedly, Fanny's extravagance. We have seen, from her letter about Queen Emma, that she was eager to ape a standard of living that was above

[10] ULF No. 228.

[11] ULF No. 239, July 15, 1867.

[12] 1866 *David and Other Sermons*, 1866 *Hereward the Wake*, 1867 *The Ancien Régime* (Lectures), 1867 *The Water of Life and other Sermons*, 1869 *The Hermits* 1869 *Madam How and Lady Why*.

her husband's means. Now she insisted on installing central heating at
the rectory, an operation which, to judge from a letter from her husband
written at the time, involved pulling down most of the back of the
house.

> I wish you would send Grenville to the cottage on Saturday.[13] All
> the back of the house is open. He will as surely catch a cold as can be.
> Moreover it would be physically so dreadfully dangerous. No floors,
> open rafters, no stairs, open pits everywhere and bricks and wood
> continually dropping. And if he was kept away from the work it
> would be a perpetual irritation to him. We have settled all the pipes.
> We are going to take them into the W.C. and warm it thoroughly.
> I believe more colds and sciatica are caught there than anywhere.
> I know how a cold W.C. affects *me*.[14]

Once more Kingsley mounted a campaign for the ecclesiastical
preferment that he believed would solve his financial problems and at
the same time free him from his professorship. He had every reason
to expect a post, for he had remained in high favour with the monarchy,
in spite of his somewhat frank choice of texts for royal sermons. (In
1867 he chose a quote from *Euphues* that ran, 'Tis virtue, gentlemen,
that maketh the poor rich, the baseborn noble, the deformed beautiful,
the subject a sovereign.') He was often a guest in the bachelors' quarters
at Sandringham, where he was treated as one of the family. Letters
about his visits were still preserved reverently in the despatch box:

> Up till two this morning playing bowls with the Princess, but that
> did not prevent my being in the garden with Carmichael a few
> minutes after 9 and settling about the seeds. The fool's cap was a
> great success yesterday (I got in just in time for tea). The little Princes
> and Princesses played with it, and Princess Victoria insisted on
> putting it on me, and then smoothing my hair with her own hands
> because she had rumpled it.[15]

But tangible proofs of favour were limited to gifts of pheasants,
including one parcel which arrived with a note, in Kingsley's hand,
instructing Fanny that they were all to be cooked except 'a most beauti-

---

[13] Fanny, who was staying at Bournemouth, was sending Grenville home because
the sun on the beach was too much for him. 'The Cottage' was his grandmother's
house, Dressors.

[14] ULF No. 228, 1865.

[15] ULF No. 252, 1870.

ful pheasant wrapt apart, which He gave me to have stuffed'.[16] In 1868 the Queen had suggested that her chaplain should be appointed to a vacant canonry at Worcester, but was informed that 'the preferment of Mr Kingsley just now would be seriously prejudicial to Mr Disraeli'.[17] When Disraeli was defeated by Gladstone in the autumn, Kingsley made a determined attempt to secure, not a mere canonry, but the deanery of Durham (a fact not previously known). Although he dreaded the responsibility of managing a cathedral, and often declared that he required no such honours, these declarations usually came after he had failed to secure them. With Fanny's ever-increasing demands, the prospect of an income of £3,000 a year was too tempting. The post, however, went to someone else, and Kingsley wrote to Fanny consoling her with the thought that 'the Bishop of Salisbury's death and the Bishop's Retirement Bill will make plenty of vacancies, and then our turn will come'.[18] There was a rumour widespread at the time that Kingsley had been offered the deanery of Rochester, although he firmly denied it in a recently discovered letter to the Bishop of Limerick.

In the Lent term of 1869 Kingsley delivered his last series of lectures at Cambridge. Their theme was similar to that of his inaugural lecture, delivered eight years previously: the course of history is decided not by economic laws but by individual heroic men. To substantiate his thesis he contrasted the works of Comte, who believed that society was regulated by laws as immutable as those of Newtonian physics, with three books that put forward the opposite point of view, F. D. Maurice's *The Kingdom of Christ*, Carlyle's *The French Revolution* and Bunsen's *God in History*. The painstaking study of twelve volumes of Comte proved a burdensome task. At the end of it Kingsley concluded that he must resign his professorship, in spite of the fact that no alternative post had been offered him. On April 1st he wrote as follows to Dr Thompson (Whewell's successor as Master of Trinity):

I have obtained leave from the Queen to resign it at the end of the academic year, and have told Mr Gladstone as much, and had a very kind reply from him. My brains, as well as my purse rendered this step necessary. I worked eight or nine months hard for the course of twelve lectures which I gave last term, and was half-twitted by the time they were delivered; and as I have to provide for children

[16] ULF No. 203, 1867.
[17] Letters of Queen Victoria.
[18] ULF No. 245, summer 1869.

9—TBATM * *

growing up I owe it to them not to waste time (which is money)
as well as brain, in doing what others can do better.

After delivering his last lecture Kingsley sat down and wrote a letter
to Fanny, telling her, 'I can't help hoping it is the last I shall ever give.'[19]
It might have consoled him to know that his successor, the distinguished
J. R. Seeley, did not receive much kinder treatment when he delivered
his inaugural lecture. As he left the lecture hall Dr Thompson declared,
'Dear, dear, who would have thought that we should so soon have
been regretting poor Kingsley!'

Within four months of his resignation news of a canonry at last
arrived. It was worth only £500 a year, and Kingsley's friends, such
as Macmillan, considered he 'deserved better', but Fanny was delighted.
She wrote her good news to a friend, Miss Bulteel.

The Queen has most kindly given him the vacant canonry at Chester
which lapsed to the crown by the Elevation of Dr Moberly to
Salisbury. It is not a *rich* canonry, being £500 a year, but it enables
us to remain at Eversley, and to have a nice change once a year for
3 months without giving dear Charles very heavy work. The Dean
(Dr Howson) is an old friend of his, and a very energetic man who
is trying to make the Cathedral do a real work, and has services in
the Nave ... at which he and the resident Canon preach every
Sunday, and the Bishop once a month. There is a very good furnished house, which the 4 Canons inhabit by turns, which does not
sound comfortable, but it will save us a great outlay of furnishing,
which would have absorbed a year's income, so we are well satisfied,
and very thankful — and feel that we can go on in our own quiet
way — and not alter our mode of life at all, in a nice old fashioned
town like Chester, which is *Everything to Me*. It will indeed be
a blessed rest, after the heavy work and responsibility of the
Professorship, which Charles gave up in June.

[19] ULF No. 248, spring 1869.

CHAPTER 7

The Tropics at Last
1869-1870

It had been a lifelong ambition of Kingsley to visit the West Indies where his mother had been born, and an invitation to stay with Sir Arthur Gordon, the governor of Trinidad, whom he met at Miss Shaw-Lefevre's dinner table, supplied the opportunity. In December 1869, during the interval between leaving Cambridge and going to Chester, he set sail, with Rose, in the mail steamer *Shannon*. He planned to emulate Darwin and bring back a collection of flowers, skeletons and bird skins that would astonish Sir Charles Bunbury. Rose intended to import a live monkey, an ant-eater and a parrot: 'I hope she will not carry out the threat,' her father confided to Sir Charles.

The money for the venture was to be raised by sending a series of articles home to *Good Words*, later to be published in book form under the title *At Last: A Christmas in the West Indies*. The book, Kingsley's last,[1] is strangely disappointing. In it Kingsley is constantly telling us how overpowered he is by the richness and variety of the vegetation around him, and then proceeding to catalogue that vegetation item by item. At one point he pauses to comment, 'If the reader cares nothing for botanical and geological speculations he will be wise to skip this chapter.' It would be perilously easy to skip a large part of the book, but in so doing we would miss descriptions of many picturesque adventures, not to mention 'delightful mishaps', as Kingsley sportingly described them.

The first island at which the *Shannon* docked was St Thomas in the Virgin Islands, and there the behaviour of the negroes who were shovelling coal on board from barges confirmed all his prejudices against their race. It was, he said, 'a scene which we would fain forget. Black women on one side were doing men's work, with heavy

---

[1] Five further books by Charles Kingsley appear in the British Museum catalogue under the title 'Supposititious Works'. They consist of messages purporting to have been 'transmitted clair-audiently' from the spirit of Kingsley through 'Crusader', pseudonym of Charles D. Boltwood. See Appendix 2.

coal-baskets on their heads, amid screaming, chattering, and language of which, happily, we understood little or nothing. On the other, a gang of men and boys, who, as the night fell, worked, many of them, altogether naked, their glossy bronze figures gleaming in the red lamp-light.' The fact that these barbarians were singing work songs for which a modern collector would no doubt give an arm and a leg only increased the disapproval of the rector of Eversley: 'A lad, seeming the poet of the gang, stood on the sponson, and in the momentary intervals of work improvised some story, while the men below took up and finished each verse with a refrain, piercing, sad, running up and down large easy intervals. The tunes were . . . all barbaric, often ending in the minor key, and reminding us much, perhaps too much, of the old Gregorian tones. The words were all but unintelligible.' Worse was to follow for when the musicians on board struck up a waltz, they set 'the negro shoveller dancing in the black water at the barge bottom, shovel in hand; and pleasant white folks danced under the awning, till the contrast between the refinement within and the brutality without became very painful. For brutality it was, not merely in the eyes of the sentimentalist, but in those of the moralist; still more in the eyes of those who try to believe that all God's humans may be somewhen, somewhere, somehow, reformed into His likeness.'

Eager to escape from such sights, Kingsley espied an unspoilt beach round the point and called for a bum-boat to 'get into that paradise'. The chief officer obliged, four British tars were set to the oars, and Charles and Rose shortly found themselves on the white sand, over-powered by exotic sights and sounds. Here were the pink-lined shells he had admired behind the glass of his mother's 'West India cabinet' at Barnack Rectory, lying in profusion at his feet; here were the shiny black seeds she had preserved so carefully in a little box at home, and, ballooning from the trunk of a tree, the great green calabashes whose dried up ancestors he had played with in his mothers' drawing room at Clovelly. Father and daughter revelled in 'the drooping boughs of the shore grape with its dark velvet leaves and crimson midrib and the Frangipane, and the first coco-nut, and the mangrove swamp and above, sailing overhead, flocks of brown and grey pelicans'. The sailors also were observed to derive great benefit from the experience.

Charles and Rose now proceeded, with only tantalisingly short stops at Antigua, Guadeloupe, St Lucia and Grenada, to Trinidad, the most southerly of the islands, where they were to spend the main part of their holiday. Here they were welcomed by the governor, Sir Arthur Gordon, and comfortably installed in a 'cottage ornée' in the garden of his country residence outside Port of Spain. The garden was a romantic place, tended by a handsome Indian prisoner with the word 'felon' printed on his shirt, and Kingsley sent home a description of the view from the bathroom window:

the scene that first proved to me that we were verily in the tropics. To begin with, the weeds on the path, like and yet unlike all at home ... then the rattle of the bamboo, the clashing of the huge leaves of the young fan palms. Then the flower-fence, the guinea grass, the sand-box, the hibiscus, with its scarlet flowers, a long list; but for the climax, the groo groo palms, a sight never to be forgotten — the immovable pillar-stem, looking the more immovable beneath the toss, the lash and flicker of the long leaves, as they awake out of their sunlit sleep, and rage impotently for a while before the mountain gusts, to fall to sleep again.

He, however, was not content to relax beneath the groo groo palms, and, with Sir Arthur (who evidently shared his taste for adventure) and four gentlemen of the governor's suite, he set off in search of the rare Guacharo bird among the offshore Bocas Islands. Kingsley had longed to find the Guacharo bird (pronounced Huacharo), for it was his ambition to bring a live specimen back to the London Zoo, or at least a dead one to the Cambridge Museum. The bird, however, was not an easy one to find for, in spite of being frugivorous (feeding chiefly on very hard fruits) it was nocturnal, and spent the hours of daylight in the farthest recesses of sea caves situated on the windward side of the islands. In Humboldt's day the Indians ventured into these caves only once a year, at midsummer, and braved the hideous echoing cries of the birds for the sake of capturing their young. These they secured by knocking down their nests with sixty-foot poles, and rendered into the finest butter in their clay cooking pots.

Kingsley and his companions set off at dawn in a boat rowed by four stalwart negroes, admiring, as they passed along the north shore of Trinidad 'the coco-palms hung double reflected as in a mirror not of glass but of mud'. Soon the morning sun sucked up 'the malarious fog', and smote, with its perpendicular rays, the backs of the heads of the travellers as they sat beneath the awning, making them envy the long locks of 'our old cavaliers', for, as Kingsley observed, 'in the West Indies, as in the United States, the early morning, and the latter part of the afternoon are the times for sunstrokes'.

After spending the day among the smaller islands they docked at Mono, the home of the Guacharo bird, and were welcomed by the coastguard, 'a gallant red-bearded Scot' who was to be both their host and their guide on the island. Not for the only time in the West Indies did Kingsley envy what he described as 'The Gentle Life' of this man, who proved that it was possible to be 'high-minded, industrious, athletic, even in the most primitive surroundings'. This Scot, Kingsley wrote, had all that could be desired in life:

> a handsome Creole wife, and lovely brownish children, with no more clothes on than they could help . . . The sea gives him fish enough for his family, and for a brawny brown servant. His coco-nut palms yield him a little revenue: he has poultry, kids, and goat's milk more than he needs; his patch of provision-ground gives him corn and roots, sweet potatoes, yam, tania, cassava, and fruit too, all the year round. He needs nothing, owes nothing, fears nothing. News and politics are to him like the distant murmur of the surf at the back of the island; a noise which is nought to him. His Bible, his almanac, and three or four old books on a shelf, are his whole library. He has all that man needs, more than man deserves, and is far too wise to wish to better himself.

A first attempt to enter a Guacharo cave was made the following day, but one look at the wild sea that beat against its mouth discouraged the adventurers, and instead they spent an idyllic afternoon in a sheltered cove nearby, collecting shells among the fallen leaves of the giant Matapalos.

The night, in the Scottish coastguard's hut, was passed less idyllically, for, as Kingsley recalled:

> shortly after I had become unconscious of the chorus of toads and cicadas, my hammock came down by the head. Then I was woke by a sudden bark close outside, exactly like that of a clicketting fox; but as the dogs did not reply or give chase, I presumed it to be the cry of a bird, possibly a little owl. Next there rushed down the mountain a storm of wind and rain, which made the coco-leaves flap and creak, and rattle against the gable of the house and set every door and window banging, till they were caught and brought to reason. And between the howls of the wind I became aware of a strange noise from seaward — a booming, or rather humming, most like that which a locomotive sometimes makes when blowing off steam. It was faint and distant, but deep and strong enough to set one guessing its cause.

In the morning the noise was traced to nothing less than the famous 'musical or drum fish; of whom one had heard, but hardly believed, much in past years'.

The following day a second and final attempt was made on a Guacharo cave:

But alas, the wind had chopped a little to the northward; a swell was rolling in through the Boca; and when we got within twenty yards of the low browed arch our crew lay on their oars and held a consultation of which there could be but one result. They being white gentlemen, and not Negroes, could trust themselves and each other, and were ready, as I know well, to 'dare all that became a man'. But every now and then a swell rolled in high enough to have cracked our skulls against the top, and out again deep enough to have staved the boat against the rocks. If we went to wreck the current was setting strongly out to sea; and the Boca was haunted by sharks, and (according to the late Colonel Hamilton Smith) by a worse monster still, namely the giant ray . . . and, on the whole, if Guacharos are precious, so is life. So, like Gyges of old, we 'elected to survive', and rowed away with wistful eyes determining to get Guacharos from one of the limestone caverns of the northern mountains.

In fact this plan was never carried out and Kingsley had to content himself with 'a list of seeds found in the stomachs of Guacharos by my friend Mr Prestoe of the Botanical Gardens, Port of Spain', which he printed as an appendix to the first edition of At Last. His publisher, perhaps understandably, omitted it from subsequent editions.

Kingsley's remaining adventures with the energetic Sir Arthur and his aides-de-camp took place on the mainland of Trinidad. On four or five occasions the party set out beneath the Southern Cross, mounted on stout cobs and mules and armed with 'cutlasses and umbrellas', for it was the rainy season and at any moment 'two or three warm buckets full of water' would be emptied upon the traveller's head. The mud was appalling and on one occasion a member of the party almost disappeared into it: 'As we rode, M—— the civiliser of Montserrat[2] and I side by side, talking of Cuba and staring at the Noranteas overhead, a dull sound was heard, as if the earth had opened; as indeed it had, engulfing in the mud the whole forehand of M——'s mule; and there *he* knelt, his beard outspread upon the clay, while the mule's visage looked patiently out from under his left arm.'

[2] Montserrat is a region in the centre of Trinidad.

Under the stimulus of travel and adventure Kingsley's health seemed completely restored. 'I have not been so well this seven years,' he told Fanny. 'I have been riding this week six to eight hours a day, through primeval forests, mud, roots, gullies, and thickets such that, had I anticipated them, I would have brought out breeches and boots . . . It is so wonderful to be my old self again, to see . . . the darkies nearly dying with heat and go along myself with a light heart and step.' To his mother he wrote, 'We shall come home, please God, all the wiser but none the fatter for I distil a couple of pints of pure water out of each joint every day, and am grown hard as whipcord in consequence.'

Such letters evidently provoked a warning from Fanny, for in his next Charles wrote, 'I assure you I am very careful. I had to lie off a mangrove swamp in burning sun, very tired, after having ridden four hours and been shoved over the mud in a canoe among the calling crabs, by three niggers, and I did not feel it the least, though the mud stank, and the wind was off shore, because before I got into the canoe, I took a good dose of quinine, which I always carry.' There were some comic elements in the incident of the canoe which Kingsley suppressed in his letter to Fanny but he gave them in full in *At Last:*

I got without compunction into a canoe some three feet wide; and was shoved by three Negroes down a long winding ditch of mingled mud, water, and mangrove roots. To keep one's self and one's luggage from falling out during the journey was no easy matter; at one moment indeed, it threatened to become impossible. For where the mangroves opened on the sea, the creek itself turned sharply northward along shore, leaving (as usual) a bed of mud between it and the sea some quarter of a mile broad, across which we had to pass to reach the boat, which lay far out. The difficulty was, of course, to get the canoe out of the creek up the steep mud-bank. To that end she was turned on her side, with me on board. I could just manage, by jamming my luggage under my knees, and myself against the two gunwales, to keep in, holding on chiefly by my heels and the back of my neck. But it befell, that in the very agony of the steepest slope, when the Negroes, (who worked like really good fellows,) were nigh waist-deep in mud, my eye fell, for the first time in my life, on a party of Calling Crabs, who had been down to the water to fish, and were now scuttling up to their burrows among the mangrove-roots; and at the sight of the pairs of long-stalked eyes, standing upright like a pair of opera glasses and the long single arms which each brandished, with frightful menaces, as of infuriated Nelsons, I burst into such a fit of laughter that I nearly

fell out into the mud. The Negroes thought for the instant that the
'buccra parson' had gone mad: but when I pointed with my head
(I dare not move a finger) to the crabs, off they went in a true Negro
guffaw . . . So all the way across the mud the jolly fellows, working
meanwhile like horses, laughed for the mere pleasure of laughing;
and when we got to the boat the Negro in charge of her saw us
laughing and laughed too for company, without waiting to hear the
joke; and as two of them took the canoe home, we could hear them
laughing still in the distance.

Perhaps this happy experience with male West Indians helped to
wipe out memories of less happy ones with females. There was, for
instance, the occasion when Rose had asked one to attract the attention
of another for her: after pretending not to hear, the woman finally
bawled to her friend, 'You coloured lady! You hear did white woman
a wanting of you?' Nevertheless Kingsley was inclined to be tolerant,
pointing out, 'We white people bullied these black people quite enough
for three hundred years, to be able to allow them to play (for it is no
more) at bullying us.' He even forgave the negro women their splen-
didly robust bodies and their obvious enjoyment of life, pointing out
'we have at home tens of thousands of paupers, rogues, whatnot, who
are not a whit more civilised . . . than the Negro, and are meanwhile
neither healthy nor comfortable. The Negro may have the *corpus
sanum* without the *mens sana*. But what of those whose souls and bodies
are alike unsound?' More to his own taste however were the wives of
the Indian coolies, whom he admired for some time on a roundabout
('a huge piece of fool's tackle') at the races. 'The Hindoo women,
though showing much more of their limbs than the Negresses, kept
them gracefully together, drew their veils round their heads, and sat
coyly, half frightened, half amused, to the delight of their 'papas' or
'husbands'. On the other hand, 'The Negresses, I am sorry to say,
forgot themselves, kicked up their legs, shouted to the bystanders,
and were altogether incondite.'
    After seven weeks on the island Kingsley was obliged to return
home, for part of his purpose in making the trip had been to prove that
the West Indies could be enjoyed within the space of three months.
He left Trinidad full of regrets, for the 'westward fever' was upon him
and he longed to take a steamer across the narrow straits that separate
Trinidad from Venezuala and up the delta of the Orinoco. He had
failed also, somewhat strangely, to visit Barbados, his mother's birth-
place, in spite of the fact that the island is no great distance from Trinidad. He had in fact been invited to stay there by a man he had met on

the way out, but he appeared satisfied by a conversation with this Trinidad planter, who had once managed Clapham, one of his grandfather's estates, and who assured him that the old fig tree[3] at Harmony Hall, of which his mother had recently dreamt, was still standing.

Collecting plants had also proved harder than Kingsley had expected and of bird skins and skeletons we hear nothing, although there was a snake, the dreaded *fer de lance*, preserved in a jar of spirits and 'many curious nuts'. He wrote to Sir Charles Bunbury explaining the difficulties:

> I have found collecting plants, riding through the forest, to be almost impossible; and yet I did my best always remembering you, and hoping that my specimens would find their way to your herbarium. But damp and mishaps made me lose so many specimens, that I at last gave up in despair; and all the more as, most of the plants not being in flower, I could identify hardly any. Still a few I have brought home and will send you if you will accept them.

Rose was more successful. When father and daughter went on board the *Neva* at the end of February they were accompanied by a vulturine parrot and a kinkajou. The kinkajou, Kingsley recalled,

> got loose one night and displayed his natural inclination by instantly catching a rat, and dancing between decks with it in his mouth: but was so tame withal, that he let the stewardess stroke him in passing. The good lady mistook him for a cat, and when she discovered next morning that she had been handling 'a loose wild beast', her horror was as great as her thankfulness for the supposed escape.

As the ship slipped past Land's End, Kingsley, for nearly the last time, saw his beloved West Country:

> We could see up the Looe Pool to Helston Church, and away beyond it, till we fancied that we could almost discern, across the isthmus, the sacred hill of Carnbrea ... and regrets for the lovely western paradise were all swallowed up with bright thoughts of the cold northern home. With what joy did we round the old Needles and

[3] Probably one of the few remaining Bearded Fig trees from which Barbados is said to have taken its name. In early times these trees formed part of the primeval forest that covered the island. They were so named because their roots hung like bead curtains from their trunks and branches. One can still be seen at Welchman Hall Gully, an area of forest preserved by the National Trust of Barbados.

run past Hurst Castle, and with what shivering too . . . At first an English winter was a change for the worse. Fine old oaks and beeches looked to us, fresh from ceibas and volayas, like lifeless brooms stuck into the ground by their handles; while the want of light was for some days painful and depressing. But we had done it, and within the three months, as we promised. As the king in the old play says, 'What has been, has been, and I've had my hour.' At least we had seen it, and we could not unsee it.

CHAPTER 8

A Canon at Chester
1870–1873

Another returning traveller suffering from the cold that winter, at Eversley, was Maurice Kingsley. After leaving Cambridge without a degree he had studied agriculture at Cirencester and set off in search of employment on a ranch in the Argentine, a country of which his father had little opinion, since it was governed by 'a bunch of ruffianly Spaniards'. He had now come home to collect £2,000 of his mother's money, which, at the last minute, her third trustee ('who I am afraid I should like to poison or drown or something dreadful', she commented) refused to release. Father and son now proceeded to enliven the lives of the people of Eversley with Penny Readings about their foreign adventures.

It is hard now to imagine the dullness of the life of an English agricultural labourer in the last century. For men and women the day was a period of unremitting drudgery to supply the food for a meagre evening meal which was, as often as not, followed by bed, either from sheer exhaustion or from boredom. Most of them could not read, and if they could, they had only the glimmer of a farthing dip candle to read by. Many of them had not travelled beyond the next village so that subjects for conversation were limited. For such people the sight of a well-lighted schoolroom alone was worth a two-mile walk on a wet night. Kingsley was one of the first to institute those fortnightly readings which became so popular in the mid-Victorian period. At them his daughters and their London friends played the piano and sang to 'a low hum of appreciation', and he himself told tales of heroism and gave simple lectures on hygiene. Encouraged by the success of these meetings Kingsley also established a working men's club in the village by providing a room where they could drink light beer and read the newspapers. For this club he collected books, organised readings, and set up a bagatelle board. All went well at the beginning, but eventually the attraction of the seven pubs of the parish proved too strong and the club had to be closed.

Eversley was no longer the remote undiscovered place it had been when Kingsley first saw it thirty years previously. There had been many changes. Aldershot was now a flourishing military centre and there were frequent attacks of what Fanny called scarlet fever in the parish when the Prince of Wales would encamp with his regiment, the Tenth Hussars, on Bramshill Common, and half the village would decamp thither to watch the goings-on of the red coats. Great was the excitement when the Prince himself, mounted on a black charger, would ride over to pay a call at the rectory. Mary, who could not bear curtseying, would absent herself on these occasions, but her uncle Henry must have been present on at least one of them, for he inserted a description of the Prince at this time in his novel *Oakshot Castle*, 'a bull-necked, bull-headed young man', who liked to perform as an amateur fireman, 'but looked as if he could love, fight and die like a gentleman'.

With a growing number of visitors came an increase in forest fires. Kingsley took a characteristic pleasure in organising bands of fire-fighters to put these out.

At such a time [wrote a friend] the Rector was all activity. On one occasion the fire began during the time of divine service. A messenger posted down to the church in hot haste, to call out the men, and Mr Kingsley, leaving a curate to finish the service, rushed to the scene of action, taking a flying leap, surplice, hood, and stole, over the churchyard palings. The fire was an extensive one; but he, armed with a bill-hook, and now divested of everything ecclesiastical, was everywhere, organising bands of beaters and, begirt with smoke and flame, resisting the advance of the fire at every advantageous point. For many nights subsequently watchers were placed in the woods and at a late hour (between 11 p.m. and 2 a.m.) Mr Kingsley would sally forth and go the rounds, carefully inspecting the country, cheering the watchers with hearty words of encouragement — himself intensely interested in the general picturesqueness of the event, and excited by the feeling that the alarm might be given at any moment, and the firs which he loved so deeply be wrapped in flame.

Another undesirable result of progress was the enclosure of Eversley Common, bitterly resented by Kingsley. According to Fanny he was 'really distressed' over the matter from the aesthetic point of view, since he felt that the characteristic beauty of the parish he loved so well would be destroyed and that old associations and old cricket grounds might be broken up. That Kingsley was a keen conservationist his latest curate, William Harrison, also bore out. He described how, on one occasion, seeing that an ancient tree had been cut down, his rector burst into tears exclaiming, 'I have known that tree ever since I came to the Parish.'

William Harrison was to play an important part in the lives of the Kingsleys, for, a year after Kingsley's death, he married his daughter Mary. The couple in fact separated amicably after a few years, probably because Harrison, although well disposed, was rather a dull young man. Mary may also have found his excessive admiration for her father trying, for she was somewhat of a rebel by nature, and regarded Charles as naïve and old-fashioned. We must be grateful to Harrison, however, for his description of an evening of conversation with Kingsley in his study after the family had gone to bed, for it is the last picture we have of the rector at Eversley.

Surely if ever a room was haunted by happy ghosts it would be his study at Eversley, peopled as it must ever be with the bright creations of his brain. There every book on the many crowded shelves looked at him with almost friendly eyes. And of the books what were there not? — from huge folios of St Augustine to the last treatise on fly-fishing; and of what would he not talk? — classic myth and mediaeval romance, magic and modern science, metaphysics and poetry, West Indian scenery and parish schools, politics and fairyland, and of all with vivid sympathy, keen flashes of humour, and oftentimes with much pathos and profound knowledge. As he spoke he would constantly verify his words. The book wanted — he always knew exactly where, as he said, it 'lived' — pulled down with eager hands; and he, flinging himself back with lighted pipe into his hammock, would read, with almost boylike zest, the passage he sought for and quickly found. It was very impressive to observe how intensely he realised the words he read. I have seen him overcome with emotion as he turned the well thumbed page of his Homer, or perused the tragic story of Sir Humphrey Gilbert in his beloved Hakluyt. Nor did the work of the study even at such moments shut him in entirely, or make him forgetful of what was going on out-side. 'It is very pleasant', he would say, opening the door which led on to the lawn, and making a rush into the darkness, 'to see what is going on out here.' On one such occasion, a wild autumnal night, after the thrilling recital of a Cornish shipwreck he had once witnessed, and the memory of which the turbulence of the night had conjured up, he suddenly cried, 'Come out! come out!' We followed him into the garden, to be met by a rush of warm driving rain before a south-westerly gale, which roared through the branches of the neighbouring poplars. There he stood, unconscious of personal discomfort, for a moment silent and absorbed in thought, and then exclaimed in tones of intense enjoyment, 'What a night! Drenching! This is a night on which you young men can't think or talk too much poetry!'

Another man who met Kingsley for the first time at this period was equally impressed by the brilliance of his conversation. G. W. E. Russell had also spent evenings in the famous study.

A strong beam ran across the ceiling from which a cord hammock (South American I think) was suspended. Into this he got, lit a long clay pipe and began to talk, wandering from topic to topic. I have never known so interesting and delightful a talker as Charles Kingsley. He had an enormous deal to say on every conceivable subject, and longed to say it. But his stammer was always checking him. He gurgled, and gasped, and made faces, and would sometimes break off a conversation or a meal, rush out into the open air, and liberate his suppressed emotions by rapid exercise or physical exertion.[1]

Russell has left a description of Kingsley's appearance in these, his last years:

He was not, I suppose, above middle height, but his extreme attenuation made him look taller. There was not a superfluous ounce of flesh on his bones, and he seemed to be compact of wire and whipcord. His features were strongly marked, trenchant nose and prominent chin; his eyes bright and penetrating; his skin furrowed and weather-beaten; his abundant hair and bushy whiskers, originally dark but now tinged with grey.

In spite of his advancing years and accumulating dignities, Kingsley still had a liking for gossip, and it is worth quoting a letter here which shows him as a parish priest going about his ordinary duties but not above taking an interest in local scandals at the same time:

All well here, and jolly. Grenville did his Latin nicely this morning. I have just come in from my cottage lecture and from burying old Sims. Poor Haynes of Hollybush went off suddenly yesterday afternoon with a heart complaint. He had eaten a good luncheon of

[1] G. W. E. Russell, *Afterthoughts*, 1912.

chicken and soup and drunk some beer, when he turned black in the face, and said he was going.

I met Mr Stapleton today, of course full of enclosure. But when I could get in a word, I talked to *him* about Lady Rodney. He said, frankly he did not consider her in her right mind when he saw her 3 or 4 months ago. He says that while she was nursing Lord Rodney (which she did for 3 years) she took a great deal too much stimulant — Eau de Cologne and salvolatile and whatnot — just what one would believe of her. I shall hear more tonight — for I am going in after dinner to Warbrook to avoid sitting alone, reading my eyes out and smoking too much.[2]

In an equally light-hearted mood are the answers he wrote in an autograph book at Ray Lodge:

Favourite character in history? David.
Favourite kind of literature? Physical science.
Favourite author? Spenser.
Favourite artist? Leonardo da Vinci.
Favourite composer? Beethoven.
Favourite dramatic performance? A pantomime.
Favourite kind of scenery? Wide flats or open sea.
Place at home and abroad you most admire? Clovelly.
Favourite reminiscence? July, 1839.
Favourite occupation? Doing nothing.
Favourite amusement? Sleeping.
What do you dislike most? Any sort of work.
Favourite topics of conversation? Whatever my companion happens to
    be talking about.
And those you dislike most? My own thoughts.
What do you like most in woman? Womanliness.
What do you dislike most? Unwomanliness.
What do you like most in man? Modesty.
What do you dislike most? Vanity.
Your ambition? To die.
Your ideal? The One Ideal.
Your hobby? Fancying I know anything.
The virtue you most admire? Truth.
The vice to which you are most lenient? All except lying.
Your favourite motto or proverb? 'Be strong'.

[2] ULF No. 232, 1866.

On May 1st the entire Kingsley family moved into The Residence in Abbey Square, Chester, for three months. There were to be three of such periods of residence and they proved among the happiest times in Kingsley's life. Fanny was with him and, after Cambridge, it was a relief to be once more a large fish in a small pond. He loved the quaint old city with its girdle of walls and towers and its modest little cathedral, as he explained to the members of the Archaeological Society a few days after his arrival. He felt that in coming to Chester he was coming back to the home of his ancestors. He confessed to a feeling of pride in his connection with Cheshire, and in the mention of his name in the old Tarporley Hunting Song:

> In right of his bugle and greyhounds to seize
> Waif, pannage, agistment, and wind-fallen trees;
> His knaves through our forest Ralph Kingsley dispersed,
> Bow-bearer-in-chief to Earl Randall the First.
>
> This Horn the Grand Forester wore at his side
> When'er his liege lord chose a-hunting to ride —
> By Sir Ralph and his heirs for a century blown,
> It passed from their lips to the mouth of a Done.[3]

Dean Howson had been somewhat apprehensive about his new canon, explaining, in a letter to Fanny after Kingsley's death. 'There seemed to me an incongruity between the author of *Alton Locke* and cathedral life' (he no doubt recalled that Kingsley had once suggested that the cathedrals of England should be turned into winter gardens). But his fears proved groundless. The Christian Socialist canon was far from arrogant. 'That he was far my superior in ability and knowledge made no difference. I happened to be Dean, and he happened to be Canon; and this was quite enough.'

Kingsley had always loved architecture, and he found constant diversion in the richly decorated interior of the cathedral. Dean Howson described how once, in the midst of Divine Service, his new canon started with surprise on observing that there were monkeys in the midst of the crockets of some of the canopies. Ornate choral services had previously repelled him because of the slovenliness of those who took part in them, but at Chester the reverent attitude of all, from the bishop down to the smallest choir boy, impressed him deeply. Although he was not particularly musical he came to love the sung services and to look forward to certain canticles and anthems. The daily morning service was his great refreshment and he spent many peaceful moments

[3] The bugle alluded to was included in the Kingsley coat of arms.

in the old chapter house, before the 8 a.m. service. At this hour he was presumably safe from tourists. At other times of the day there was a danger of invasion from parties of Americans. As Fanny explained: 'their first act, when disembarking at Liverpool, is to come over to Chester and see the oldest thing they can — i.e. a Cathedral — and then the Old Verger who unfortunately is a great Hero worshipper, invariably tells them who the Canon in Residence is, and asks if they would not like to see him too! They are all paraded into the Chapter room too suddenly for Mr Kingsley to make his Exit'.

Kingsley became enormously popular at Chester. It is said that people queued outside the cathedral for his sermons on Sunday evenings. Not content with his cathedral duties, he determined to do something that would bring the cathedral clergy and the townspeople together, and to this end he started a small class to keep the young men of the town from mischief on the long summer evenings. Although the subject he chose was botany, one of the first lectures he gave was entitled 'The Rain and the Wind'. He wrote to tell Fanny, 'I really believe that last night's lecture was a great success, at least so everyone thought. And it will, I think lead to the forming of a natural history club among the journeymen. I have determined not to let in rich folks and fine ladies to take me away from my own dear fellows and throw them into the background.' In this ambition he failed for in a short time half the élite of Chester had joined. His botanical class of 1870 became the Scientific Society of 1871, and developed into the Chester Natural Science Society, with Lyell and Huxley as honorary members.[4] He had started off in a small room belonging to the city library but the class soon increased so much in numbers that he had to migrate to a larger room. A weekly walk and a field lecture were instituted and one of these gatherings was so large that a man who met them in a country lane supposed them to be a congregation going off to the opening of a Dissenting chapel. Eventually special trains had to be laid on. Fanny describes how, 'at the appointed hour a happy party, numbering sometimes from sixty to a hundred, would find the Canon and his daughters waiting for them on the platform, he with geological hammer in hand, botany bag slung over his shoulder, eager as any of his class for the holiday.'

At Chester, Kingsley was able to indulge to the full his pleasure in teaching, without the discomfort of jealous academics breathing down his neck. Once more he proved his power to arrest the attention of the young and ignorant, even if he failed to impress their masters. A cartoon

[4] The Chester Society of Natural Science, Literature and Art has just celebrated its centenary.

drawn at the time can be taken to make this point, although no doubt it was intended to make a less kind one. It shows Kingsley sitting on a stile reading *Westward Ho!* to a besmocked peasant boy. The boy stands entranced, with mouth agape. Another charm of Chester was fishing for the Dee salmon upstream from where Mary met her fate.

It was twenty years since Kingsley had written his poem, *The Sands of Dee*, but the river still held a romantic charm for him. As he paced its banks the words of that most anthologised of all his poems may well have run through his head:

'O Mary, go and call the cattle home,
    And call the cattle home,
    And call the cattle home
  Across the sands of Dee;'
The western wind was wild and dank with foam,
  And all alone went she.

The western tide crept up along the sand,
    And o'er and o'er the sand,
    And round and round the sand,
  As far as eye could see.
The rolling mist came down and hid the land:
  And never home came she.

'Oh! is it weed, or fish, or floating hair —
    A tress of golden hair,
    A drowned maiden's hair
  Above the nets at sea?
Was never salmon yet that shone so fair
  Among the stakes on Dee.'

They rowed her in across the rolling foam,
    The cruel crawling foam,
    The cruel hungry foam,
  To her grave beside the sea:
But still the boatmen hear her call the cattle home
  Across the sands of Dee.

The Franco-Prussian War of 1870 broke in upon these peaceful reveries and brought Kingsley out in a fever of excitement, although on the German side. To Sir Charles Bunbury he wrote;

I confess to you, that were I a German, I should feel it my duty to my country to send my last son, my last shilling, and after all, my own self to the war, to get that done which must be done, so that it will never need doing again. I trust that I should be able to put vengeance out of my heart, to forget all that Germany has suffered for two hundred years past, from that vain, greedy, restless nation.

The Kingsley family were peripherally involved in the war, for not only did Rose, who had trained briefly as a nurse at Chester Infirmary, volunteer to go out and tend the wounded with her cousin Mary Grenfell (as far as is known they never went), but Henry went out as a war correspondent for the *Edinburgh Daily Review*, a paper he had been unsuccessfully editing for some months. With a glengarry on the back of his head (it will be remembered that he affected strange headwear), a Norfolk jacket and a knapsack, he cadged lifts from one battlefield to the next, in hourly danger of being arrested and shot as a spy. There is something slightly unpleasant about his descriptions of the great golden Prussian Hussars sprawled at leisure beside their tethered horses, and something positively ghoulish about his descriptions of the French dead. The large bullets of the new Prussian *Zundnadelgewehr* wreaked horrifying havoc among their ranks. Henry congratulated himself at being first on the scene after Sedan, 'the grandest slaughter which the world has ever seen'. With horrid enthusiasm he described the sun-blackened faces of the corpses, and the red cloth of trousers blended with bleeding entrails. 'Forty thousand men of that pretty French army lie out on the hill-side, a mere heap of rags, bones, entrails, and brains.' And yet, he declared, 'the sight of it is immensely beautiful: the dead men look so pretty from a little distance. They group themselves as they fall, and even when they crawl away to die, they look well, for death is generally beautiful.'

When Henry came home he found himself discharged by his paper and penniless. His financial affairs had been far from satisfactory since he had married in 1864 and set up a home of his own in a *cottage ornée* at Wargrave in Berkshire. His marriage took place after Campbell, his close friend and secretary, had gone home to Australia. Deeply lonely, he took to visiting the Rev and Mrs Blunt, his parents' successors at St Luke's Rectory, with the result that he fell in love with Sarah Kingsley Hazelwood, a second cousin, who was the children's governess there. Sarah was a dark, high-complexioned young woman, who even her friends could only describe as 'boisterous'. She proved an expensive acquisition, for not only was she penniless, but she brought with her a penniless mother and an undisclosed history of ill health, requiring frequent medical attention.

Henry's books had proved increasingly unsuccessful. Although his second novel, *Ravenshoe* (which was concerned with the Crimean War) was well reviewed in places, by the time his fourth novel, *Silcote of Silcotes*, appeared, the critics were prepared to hurl themselves upon it in a body, denouncing it as a series of 'rubbishy love stories' whose 'characters were puppets as active as fleas'. Shortage of money, however, did not curb Henry's style of living. He regarded it as his right as a gentleman to inhabit an elegantly furnished house and give large dinners to famous men (Swinburne and Dodgson were both guests at Wargrave, the latter newly famous as the author of *Alice*). Meanwhile his unfortunate wife continued to have miscarriage after miscarriage and somebody had to pay the bills.

It was after his return from the war that the begging letters started, first to Macmillan his publisher, and when that source had dried up, to his brother Charles. These letters, which were often written by Henry's wife, caused great embarrassment, and were known and dreaded as 'Sarah's money letters'. Worse was to follow, for Henry began writing to Charles's distinguished acquaintances for money, assuring them that he would inherit £12,000 from his mother on her death[5] and entreating them not to mention these applications to Charles. There was great confusion when he applied to Lord Houghton both for a personal loan and for support for an application to the Royal Literary Fund. On hearing of it Charles, greatly concerned, wrote as follows to Lord Houghton:

I have reason to believe that my brother's wife, Mrs Henry Kingsley, has been in communication with you on a subject on which she is wont to have communications with many persons, and that you have behaved with your accustomed kindness and generosity. If this be so, let me entreat you not to do so again, or to entertain any proposal either from her or her mother Mrs Hazelwood (who is equally likely to trespass on your good nature) without referring to me, who am intimately acquainted with the true state of my most industrious, but most unhappy brother's affairs, and also have known all about these two women for some 20–30 years.

In 1872 Henry moved into a house at 24 Bernard Street, Bloomsbury, and the spate of letters increased, with the expense of furnishing and decorating. His literary output in other directions was decreasing, he was constantly late with his copy, and he spent much of his time in

---

[5] Henry in fact added a nought to the sum his mother intended to leave him. And anyway, as a codicil to her will points out, in 1869 he had 'borrowed' the £1,200 she had hoped to leave him and so had nothing further to expect.

Bohemian haunts or 'anywhere where there were boon companions and the right kind of liquor to keep good wit rolling'.[6]

Two years later he was obliged, by poverty, to move to Kentish Town, then little better than a slum. During these years he often took refuge from the racket of barrel organs and watercress women at his brother George's small house at Highgate, with its one front window and its lone strip of garden behind. It was here that George's daughter Mary Kingsley, the future African explorer, kept her fighting cocks as a girl. George himself was almost always away on his travels, but his wife, who had been left to manage as best she could with her two small children, always made Henry welcome. Many of his increasingly desperate begging letters to Charles were no doubt written from the attic of this house, which was regarded as Henry's sanctuary.

The effect of all this on Charles was disastrous. We shall never know all the scandals in which Henry involved him, for the Victorian propriety of Fanny saw to it that almost all trace of them was erased, but he hinted at them broadly enough in an unpublished letter to C. A. Johns: 'What I have suffered, and what work I have had, with rogues and fools for two months (and Mrs Kingsley far more so) would make a whole sensation novel.'[7] It was to Henry that he referred in the last two lines of a poem about Grenville's first day out with the Bramshill Hounds, written on November 6th, 1872. The poem is worth quoting in full, not on account of its literary merit, which is slight, but for the picture it gives of the Kingsley home life.

THE DELECTABLE DAY

The boy on the famous grey pony,
    Just bidding goodbye at the door,
Plucking up maiden heart for the fences
    Where his brother won honour of yore.

The walk to the Meet with fair children,
    And women as gentle as gay, —
Ah! how do we male hogs in armour,
    Deserve such companions as they?

The afternoon's wander to windward,
    To meet the dear boy coming back;
And to catch, down the turns of the valley,
    The last weary chime of the pack.

[6] S. M. Ellis, *Henry Kingsley 1830–1876. Towards a Vindication*, Grant Richards, 1931.

[7] Unpublished letter to Johns, July 27, 1873.

And at night the septette of Beethoven,
   And the grandmother by in her chair.
And the foot of all feet on the sofa
   Beating delicate time to the air.

Ah, God! a poor soul can but thank Thee,
   For such a delectable day!
Though the fury, the fool, and the swindler,
   To-morrow again have their way!

It is tempting to pause for a moment and consider the relationship between these two brothers, so alike in so many ways, so utterly unlike in others. Both upheld the ideal of muscular Christianity in literature and emulated it in the field, both had a love of nature and poetry, both had a strong feminine streak in their character and both were strangely in love with death and destined to die early. Yet while the one was a man with high ideals and a genuine concern for his fellow men, the other was frankly a bounder. The socially unacceptable tendencies, which in Charles were present but under control, in Henry flourished unchecked. He was almost certainly bisexual, he was wildly irresponsible with money, he lied, drank too much and smoked so excessively that he died of cancer of the tongue at the age of forty-six. If Charles was the stone saint on the façade of the cathedral, Henry was the gargoyle who caricatured him and spouted foul water from the cornice above his head, and the saint did not escape without a sprinkling. Henry was a burden to his brother throughout his life. His impositions began with his visit to Eversley rectory in 1844, when the young couple had only just moved in. In 1848 he helped to precipitate Charles's most serious nervous breakdown by moving in on him again, this time at Bournemouth. But these impositions were as nothing to the financial ones of 1872 and 1873. His constant demands for money must have contributed to the financial crisis that led Kingsley to abandon his congenial post at Chester and seek employment of a more exhausting nature that led to his death within two years.

Henry alone, however, cannot bear the responsibility for Kingsley's increasing expenses. Fanny's demands for her children were becoming ever more excessive. After Grenville left Winton House with low marks, a young German tutor, who quickly fell a victim to the rector's charm, was employed to prepare him for public school. The child expressed repugnance at the idea of going to Winchester which had the convenience of being near Eversley, and it was decided he should go to Harrow. 'I am sure this is best with a melancholic boy like him,' wrote Kingsley to C. A. Johns, his headmaster. Fanny, however, would not consider abandoning her darling completely to 'that sea of vice'.[8] She became hysterical in her insistence that the family should leave Eversley completely and buy a house at Harrow, to be near him. Kingsley compromised by renting 2 Woodside, in that exclusive part of Harrow known as Harrow-on-the-Hill which stands almost in the school grounds. He used his own and his family's health as an excuse to Sir William Cope for leaving his parish for a year. It was at this house that he had the deep sorrow of seeing his mother die after a long illness, at the age of eighty-six. It is curious that Fanny, who had refused to move old Mrs Kingsley to Cambridge when in perfect health, was prepared to convey her, dying, to Harrow.

Kingsley did not benefit under his mother's will, as he had already had his share of her money during her lifetime and he now had the expense of running three houses (including the one in Chester) added to public school fees. Also Rose was developing expensive tastes in travel. Since her trip to the West Indies she had visited Maurice in Colorado where he was working on the mountain railway between Denver and Colorado Springs, and performed amazing feats of endurance in the saddle while prospecting with him to carry the line into Mexico. Maurice too continued to be a financial liability, for the Mexican job was only a temporary one, and by the spring of 1873 he was home, in time to bid his grandmother farewell. Although by all accounts a charming young man, who had inherited some of his father's gifts as an artist and a naturalist, he still lacked the power of steady application. Kingsley wrote to Sir Charles Bunbury offering his son's services as an explorer on a scientific expedition, but six months later the boy returned to Mexico with nothing arranged, and no doubt at his father's expense.

With so many financial obligations to meet, there was no alternative but to set in motion once more the machinery that would lead to advancement in the church. Yet it was with regret that Kingsley started to write the necessary letters. 'Had I been an old bachelor,' he confided to a Chester friend, 'I would never have left Chester. My eyes fill with tears when I think of it.' He was once more unwell and he dreaded the exertions that a more responsible post would involve. He had recently been shocked by the loss not only of his mother, but of the man who had taken the place of his father, F. D. Maurice. When he heard of the death of another friend, Norman McLeod, he could not keep from saying: 'Ah, he is an instance of a man who has worn his brain away, and where he is gone I am surely going.' He had

[8] Unpublished letter from Fanny, May 8, 1874.

always held the opinion that 'a man brings into the world with him a certain amount of vital force, in body and soul; and when that is used up, the man must sink down into some sort of second childhood'.[9] The young Maurice, on his return from his three-year absence, had been horrified at the change in his father's appearance, and recommended a long sea voyage at once, but Kingsley felt he must put it off for a year.

The deanery at Winchester had just come vacant, and Kingsley went to stay with C. A. Johns to be on the spot for his campaign to secure it. Yet it was but a half-hearted campaign, for even as he walked on those 'delectable' chalk downs he knew that he was 'not worth much to last'.[10] He explained in a letter to a friend that he only persisted because Fanny was making herself 'ill with anxiety about the matter'. An interview with the Prince of Wales, recently recovered from his terrible bout of typhoid, was sought and gained, and Charles sent home a description of the appearance of the convalescent.

After luncheon at Marlborough House, the Prince sent down word he could not see me, but after sent word he could. So as soon as the Italian minister went, I went up. I found him pale but well furnished in flesh. His hair is growing again. He was very lame. The leg suffers all down from retarded circulation. He lies on a sofa with his foot up, and evidently has to shift it often from discomfort. He was most courteous and affectionate.[11]

Lord Portman, the patron of Sydney Godolphin Osborne, was also approached, but his influence evidently had no more effect than that of the Prince, and Gladstone gave the post of dean to Lord Lyttleton. When Johns wrote to condole, Kingsley replied that he had no regrets: 'I should have taken Winchester with a heavy heart, as a duty to my wife and children, not as a rest to myself. I also always feared that Fanny would find the Deanery even more relaxing than Eversley.' To the disappointed Fanny he explained that the post would have required hard work and the heavy expense of keeping open house. 'Powles says that a canonry of £1,000 would be a hundred times better for us.' Such a canonry had just come vacant at Windsor, and Kingsley's old friend Gerald Wellesley the Dean of Windsor advised him to try for it rather than the deanery at Winchester. 'Of course I had far sooner be Canon of "W" than Dean of the other "W",' wrote

[9] Charles Kingsley, *Hereward the Wake*.
[10] ULF No. 265, 1872.
[11] ULF No. 263, October 13, 1872.

Charles in a footnote to Wellesley's letter, which he forwarded to Fanny. At this moment a letter concerning a third 'W' put both the others out of his head. The letter was from Gladstone: proposing 'with the sanction of Her Majesty, that in lieu of your canonry at Chester, you should accept the vacant stall at Westminster Abbey. I am sorry to injure the people of Chester; but I most sincerely hope your voice will be heard within the Abbey, and in your own right.'

Kingsley naturally accepted the honour which, he imagined, would free him forever from the necessity of earning his living by his pen, and would provide him with a vast congregation for his sermons. 'It was,' he said, 'like coming suddenly into a large inheritance of unknown treasures. The congregations in the autumn are chiefly of middle and working class men: if I find I can get the ear of that congregation it will be a work to live for, for the rest of my life. What more can a man want?' The City of Chester seems to have fallen into a state of mass mourning at the news of the canon's departure if the letters he received from his friends there are to be believed. One rather emotional lady went so far as to speak of 'the distress of the old city' and added, 'You would have been both glad and sorry if you had been at the cathedral last night, and could have seen the sorrowful little groups all discussing the news, which I for one steadfastly refused to believe till the dear Canon's letter yesterday took away our last little hope.'

CHAPTER 9

The American Lecture Tour
1873-1875

Kingsley preached for the first time from the pulpit of Westminster Abbey in April 1873, although he was not due to take up his residence until September. The subject of his sermon was, rather surprisingly, temperance, although he admitted, 'I am not a total abstainer; but that does not prevent my wishing the temperance movement all success, and wishing success also to your endeavour to make people eat oatmeal.' In the same sermon he advocated, with Dean Stanley's permission, that the British Museum should be opened on Sundays. The Abbey was filled for the appearance of so famous a man, and in September he was installed at 'a very impressive ceremony'[1] again before a large congregation.

While he was at Westminster Kingsley held to his resolution of giving up writing entirely and devoting himself to sermons and sanitation. His enthusiasm for cleanliness among the working classes burned as strongly in this, the last year of his ministry, as it had in the first. In recent years he had been an ardent supporter of the Women's Sanitary League and had made passionate appeals to its members personally to visit the hovels of the poor and prevent 'the massacre of the innocents' within. On one occasion, fixing the ladies with burning eyes he said, 'It is in the power of every woman in this room to save three or four lives during the next six months.' In the cold and rain of the autumn in Westminster he did not hesitate to venture forth to lecture on hygiene in halls that were often almost as insanitary as the homes he was fulminating against. 'The atmosphere of the room was disgusting,' he told Fanny on one occasion; 'and I told them so. It was enough to make people ill. But I am all right this morning.'[2]

Living in London did not suit Kingsley. Number 6 Little Cloister, his house overlooking a charming private cloister beyond the main

[1] ULF No. 270, September 1873.
[2] ULF No. 268, 1873.

cloister of the Abbey[3], could appear light and cheerful on fine autumn days, but when the fog descended on it, it descended on its tenant's spirits as well. Fanny, who was now sixty, had refused to join her husband on the plea of ill health, once more preferring damp Eversley to 'the London crossings which would have killed me'.[4] As usual, Charles missed her desperately, although he had Rose as a companion for his walks along the embankment, and he claimed that his happiest day that autumn was a visit to Eversley: 'I must write and tell you that my day with you was the happiest I have had for months. The fresh air and sun and sky which I had not seen for days made a new man of me. But the cold of Willesden and Kensington when I had to wait, and the fog here, which is infernal, are a little depressing.' Furthermore, the two Sunday sermons, before vast congregations, beneath the echoing vaults of the Abbey, were an alarming experience, and he was haunted by the fear that he was not 'getting hold of the people.[5] The responsibility is too much for me. I am glad I have only two months residence,' he told Fanny towards the end of his first autumn at West-minster. 'I do not think I could have stood the intense excitement of the Sundays much longer.'

Yet there were compensations. As he told Fanny, who had given 'lack of society' as one of her reasons for not joining him, 'You would not find this place so very secluded. We see only too much of society.' Kingsley was now a famous man and much sought after. Many memoirs of the time give us glimpses of the canon at the more amusing dinner tables of London. Shirley Brooks, the editor of *Punch*, noted in his diary of March 25th, 1873:

To Crowdy's to meet, first time, Canon Kingsley; very delightful — very like Gladstone. His stammer not much at dinner, but in the evening, when he naturally sought to speak more eagerly, it was marked. Says he had made himself a voice — speaks from his lower depth, and holds his upper lip tightly down, working with the under one — so does the Bishop of Winchester.

[3] A later tenant of this Queen Anne house, F. R. Barry, declared that it was ex-ceptionally light and one of the most beautiful in London, overlooking as it did the fountain on one side and the Abbey Garden on the other. The drawing-room was famous for its Grinling Gibbons ceiling. F. R. Barry, *Period of My Life*, Hodder and Stoughton, 1970. A new house now stands on the site of Kingsley's House, which was destroyed by bombs during the last war.

[4] Unpublished letter from Fanny. April 26, 1873.

[5] Kingsley was not alone in finding preaching in the Abbey an ordeal. F. R. Barry has declared he never ceased to find it 'extremely terrifying'.

Another dining companion was W. P. Frith who declared that Kingsley and Mark Twain were two of the liveliest men he knew. He met them both on the same night at Brooks, and recalled 'the former with the drawback of a slight stutter, delighting us with his bright talk; and the latter with his quaint humour'.

The real deprivation he now suffered was a lack of intimate friends. Mansfield and F. D. Maurice were dead, Ludlow and Hughes estranged, and there was a new family at St Luke's Rectory. As at Cambridge, Kingsley was once more obliged either to dine out or alone. The end of the year saw him in a state quite unfit to embark upon that most exhausting of all undertakings, a lecture tour of America. It has always been assumed that Kingsley undertook the voyage that led to his death for the sake of his health. A member of his family, however, has assured me that he went for the same reason as any other transatlantic lecturer goes — for the money. The canonry at Westminster which was supposed to solve all the Kingsley financial problems had solved none. As Kingsley's income increased, so did Fanny's wants. She now insisted that the houses at Eversley and Westminster needed repairing and decorating throughout, and it was at her suggestion that Kingsley set sail in mid-winter. She had heard that $300 could be asked for a lecture and, in a good week, $1,000 could be earned.

Within seven weeks of her husband's arrival in the United States Fanny was demanding more money, having already received £100 from him.

Painting and repairs are essential, so a little of the money you are so laboriously earning will come in a wonderful help. The £100 came and is gone nearly in bills. And if you can let me have a little more before June, I shall be very thankful. I am so grateful for what you *have* sent, dear good husband. In your absence I have time to reflect on your goodness. When we are together we can only rush along with the crowd.[6]

Kingsley had never cared for the idea of America, and considered little could be expected of a country which had 'exterminated their southern aristocracy' and forced their 'northern hereditary aristocracy, the Puritan gentlemen of the old families, to retire in disgust from public life'. He had almost made a visit there with Mansfield many years before, but had been 'frightened off' by his parents who told him he would miss Fanny too much. On this occasion he took Rose with

[6] Unpublished letter from Fanny, April 1874.

him to allay loneliness, but a letter he wrote to Fanny in a huge exhausted hand just before he embarked suggests that he entered upon the
venture in low spirits. 'I have done most of my packing and all my
writing and now I should like to spend a week in bed at Harrow with
you, but it cannot be. Ah, when I get back we shall have both got our
health again, please God, and be able to sit down and grow old hand
in hand.'[7]

The voyage in fact turned out to be a comfortable one, in the
White Star Line's new high speed *Oceanic*, and a reception fit for a
celebrity, at New York, quickly revived the lecturer's spirits. He was
escorted through the customs shed without having his baggage in-
spected and taken to stay with wealthy people in Staten Island where,
he told Fanny, 'the air is like champagne and the days already an hour
longer than in England, and a blazing hot sun and blue sky. It is a
glorious country and I have met with none but pleasant, clever,
well-bred people.'

One of his first lectures was to the Lotos Club of New York where,
he claimed, he was a greater success than had been expected. 'I draw
not the mob, but the educated, and R.[8] confesses that none of his men
ever had such high toned audiences. Moreover, they are finding out
that I can speak, which no Englishman of late has been able to do; and
I was expected to mumble and hesitate like the rest.' There were,
however, other opinions on his performance, as the review of the
lecture in the *New York Daily Tribune* for February 28th suggests.

Canon Kingsley's presence is not what one expects in a public
speaker; he looks only a shy gentleman, embarrassed at finding
himself famous, and only half at home behind the slim music stand
that he wishes were a lectern. While the Rev Mr Potter is introducing him he shrinks, covered with confusion, blushes in his
arm-chair, and, when the time comes, rolls himself off his cushion,
seizes his manuscript as a sheet anchor, fumbles off his last kid glove,
straightens himself up, and launches out with a voice that sounds
like the wail of miserable sinners in his own Abbey service. For an
hour and a half this mournful cry keeps on, with scarcely a change
of note, with hardly a dying fall, and with such wide mouthed
rolling vowels and outlandish accent that many a time what he is
saying might as well be Greek for all that can be made of it. There
is but one gesture — the right elbow supported by the left hand,
and the right hand, or its forefinger, waving like a pennon, appealing,

[7] ULF No. 343, January 1874.
[8] Redpath, a veteran lecturer who had befriended him.

threatening, emphasizing, doing all the work of two hands and answering the awkward angularity of the body's swaying back and forth.[9]

From New York he moved down the coast to Boston where his hostess was the indefatigable Annie Fields of Beacon Street, wife of the head of Ticknor and Fields, his American publisher. There was a rumour that Mrs Fields had fallen in love with Charles Dickens during his visit to her house in Boston. She certainly showed him great kindness when he was ill and within months of his death. There is no suggestion that she was similarly affected by her new guest but she did remark that Kingsley reminded her 'in his nervous unrest somewhat of Dickens'. He hardly returned the compliment when he informed Mrs Fields that he thought her countrywomen very ugly because they failed to use their lips sufficiently: 'They are often pretty enough until they begin to talk and then it is not only impossible to understand them but they lose all flexibility of mouth and lips and pick the words out instead of playing with them and singing them.'

Kingsley found both New York and Boston 'a great rattle — dining, and speechifying and being received'. That these excitements had overstrained him is obvious from a photograph he had taken in New York which shows him with tense jaw and staring eyes. The portrait shocked Fanny who claimed it was not 'a satisfactory likeness' and added, 'I am afraid you are overdoing yourself. You must have a real holiday in the Far West, away from cities.'[10]

It was a relief to leave Boston, cross the Charles River and enter what was then the quiet little town of Cambridge. 'Here is a little haven of rest,' Charles told Fanny. 'Longfellow came to dinner last night and we dine with him tonight. Yesterday dear old Whittier[11] called on me and we had a most loving and like-minded talk about the other world. He is an old saint. This morning I have spent chiefly with Asa Gray and his plants, so that we are in good company.' Yet the arctic cold of the New England winter appalled him.

New England [he wrote] is, in winter at least, the saddest country, all brown grass and ice polished rocks . . . an iron land which only iron people could have settled in. But though it is hard frost under foot, the sun is bright, and hot and high, for we are in the latitude of Naples! I feel better than I have felt for years; but Mr Longfellow

[9] Quoted from R. B. Martin's *Dust of Combat*.
[10] Unpublished letter from Fanny, April 3, 1874.
[11] The celebrated Quaker.

and others warn me not to let this over-stimulating climate tempt me to overwork. One feels ready to do anything, and then suddenly very tired.

If Kingsley had minded Longfellow's advice, all might have been well, but he persisted in talking himself into a state of exhaustion on and off the platform as he zig-zagged between Philadelphia, New York and Boston. Worse still, in Washington he developed the dangerous habit of opening his window at night when the mercury was well below zero, claiming, 'my dreams are more pleasant now I sleep with my window open to counteract the hideous heat of these hot-air pipes'.

In Washington, where he was advertised as 'Sir Canon Kingsley', he did a mammoth day's sightseeing, ending up in the Senate House where he had the satisfaction of meeting Charles Sumner an hour before he dropped dead of a heart attack. His lecture halls continued to be thronged. In Philadelphia he addressed a crowd of four thousand, although one suspects that most of them merely came to say they had been. His most popular lecture was one entitled 'Westminster Abbey' which he had given so many times that as early as his second visit to Boston he said that he sometimes felt like stopping in the middle and telling the audience to collect their money at the door and leave quietly without making him finish. Not everyone admired the Abbey lecture. Mr Hurlbert, editor of *The New York World*,[12] wrote to Lord Houghton:

Kingsley's lecture here ought to make a temperance man even of his mad novelist brother. He is all tear-mists and winds of God and gushing to that degree that women cry out for a cockfight as an alternative. He has openly yearned for a dead American to bury in Westminster Abbey and I go in fear of having him propose Chiffinch, or some other easily spared corpse from the Abbey, for Sumner's embalmed remains.[13]

Whatever the reception of his lectures, 'the filthy greenbacks' continued to roll in satisfactorily. By the time Kingsley and Rose set off on the long rail trek westwards ('Don't frighten yourself at our

[12] Kingsley had met Hurlbert when the latter had stayed rather longer than was convenient with Tom Hughes in 1856. His name had been changed from Hurlbut and it is thought that he was the original of Mr Stangrave, Maria's lover in *Two Years Ago*.

[13] Quoted from R. B. Martin, *Dust of Combat*.

railroads', he told Fanny, 'they seem utterly safe') he had earned close on $3,000 and had had few expenses owing to the hospitality of the American people. In the Middle West they were to meet a party of friends who would take them on a free tour of California. There was, however, no hurry, and on the way Kingsley stopped off in Canada to see the Niagara Falls. He stayed with an old friend, Colonel Strange, who related how he conducted him to a little platform over the abyss looking down at the boiling cauldron with its cone of frozen foam, and how he left him in silence to commune with the Nature he loved so well. 'I was afraid somebody would shout above the roar of the torrent how many cubic feet of water per second went down or something of that sort. A little time afterwards Kingsley said, "Thank you, you understand me. I would as soon a fellow talked and shouted to me in church as in that presence." '

It was while enveloped in the freezing fog of Niagara that Kingsley caught what he took to be a cold, until he found that he could not shake it off. At St Louis, on the banks of that 'huge rushing muddy ditch, the Mississippi' the mid-western summer hit him without any warning of spring, and for three days he could 'neither eat nor sleep for the heat'. The hundreds of miles of prairies, 'mostly tilled, a fat, dreary, aguish, brutalising land' had depressed him, and suddenly he began to 'wish already that our heads were homeward, and that we had done the great tour and had it not to do'.

No doubt the fact that, as he moved westward, the enthusiasm of the people for being lectured at decreased, did not help matters. The letters he was receiving from Fanny were also far from encouraging. Without consulting her husband she had taken Grenville away from Harrow and was back at Eversley with him. 'If you saw the boy's exhausted look and poor small face, you would agree he is wholly unsuited to public school', she wrote in two disjointed letters on May 7th and 8th. 'He is growing so fast and developing neither muscle nor flesh. He hates the place for its wickedness which is indeed surpassing!!! It is of course vexatious to think of that nice house at Harrow standing empty. I am so thankful we did not give up Eversley. You were so wise to wait. For it is salvation for Grenville to be here.'[14] Grenville in fact now ended his education on the grounds of ill health at the age of sixteen. It is worth noting, however, that when he left for Australia a few years later, as a result of an entanglement with a married woman, he worked as a drover and proved capable of spending 'eighteen hours a day in the saddle and night watches besides'.[15]

[14] Unpublished letter of Fanny to Charles, May 7, 1874.
[15] Unpublished letter of Fanny to Macmillan, June 15, 1888.

If Kingsley had turned homeward at St Louis, as he had wished, the approaching collapse might yet have been avoided. But, ignoring his 'cold', he and Rose pressed on to Omaha and their appointment. Here, the 'glorious air rushing down, down in a gale five hundred miles from the Rocky Mountains'[16] had a renovating effect upon the pair and revived in Kingsley memories of the days when he had planned to be a 'wild prairie hunter'. He wrote joyously home to Fanny:

And we are at Omaha! a city of 20,000, five years old, made by the railway, and opposite to us is Council Bluffs!! Thirty years ago the palavering ground of trappers and Indians (now all gone), and to that very spot, which I had known of from a boy, and all about it, I meant to go in despair as soon as I took my degree, and throw myself into the wild life, to sink or swim, escaping from a civilisation which only tempted me and maddened me with the envy of a poor man!

On May 14th the party of friends the Kingsleys were awaiting arrived at Omaha. The group which now numbered eleven Americans and five English, 'quite filled, but did not crowd, the magnificent Pullman car which was our home for the next fortnight'. The first halt of the Pullman party was Salt Lake City where Kingsley was both fascinated and repelled by the achievement of Brigham Young, who had taken the same route westward as he, leaving the trail 'fat with Mormon bones'. 'The City is thriving enough', he wrote. 'But, ah! what horrors this place has seen!' He referred, of course, to the Mormon habit of plurality of wives, and confidently prophiesed, 'It is all breaking up fast. The tyrant is 70, and must soon go to his account, and what an awful one.' He naturally did not deign to reply to Young's offer of the Mormon temple as a place in which he might lecture or preach and, on leaving the city, was pleased to be shown the army guns that were kept permanently trained on the city in case of a Mormon rising.[17] Rose in her diary noted that 'General Moreau, at his station at Camp Douglas on a hillside above the city, had one of the Gatling guns fired for our amusement. On our remonstrating against such a waste of ammunition, he said that he was glad sometimes to show "those rascals in the city"

[16] Rose Kingsley's diary.
[17] The Mormons at this time were considered a serious threat to the United States government. When they were settled at Nauvoo on the Mississippi, before the murder of Joseph Smith and the persecution, it was said that their private army was larger than the national one, and their leader had plans to make himself president by force.

how straight his guns fired, and that if they gave him any trouble he could blow the city to pieces in an hour.'

When the party reached the magnificent mountains of Yosemite in California Kingsley forgot his afflicted lungs in his anxiety to prove that an Englishman could stay longer in the saddle and scale greater heights than an American. Rose described a typical day:

At 6 we started, and my father said he felt a boy again, and thoroughly enjoyed the long day in the saddle, which many of our friends found so tiring. We chose a new and unfrequented route, and we had to climb two mountains and ride along precipices and ford four rivers in flood in 29 miles. But rough as the ride was, it surpassed in beauty anything we had ever seen before, as we followed the windings of the Merced river between pine-clad mountains, still white with snow on their highest points, till we reached the mouth of the valley itself, emerging from a thicket of dogwood to see the Bridal Veil Fall rushing in a white torrent, 900 feet high.

After the dry desert heat of Salt Lake City, the high sierras, still under snow, were bitterly cold, but Kingsley continued to insist on throwing the window of his log cabin wide open at night to the horror of his 'unhealthy' American hosts. A week later, in the fogs of San Francisco, he paid the price, for his lungs became so congested that he could barely draw breath, and was ordered to leave the city instantly by a local doctor. After a very trying journey of four days the party reached Denver in the Colorado Rockies, and providentially met with the ubiquitous George Kingsley, who diagnosed a severe attack of pleurisy and advised a stay at Dr Bell's house at Colorado Springs. The move involved a further journey of seventy-five miles on the narrow gauge railway that Maurice had helped to build four years before, but at the end of it the patient, for whom every breath was an agony, found himself in a charming English house at the foot of Pike's Peak. His host, Dr Bell, was an old friend, who had also welcomed Maurice when he first came to Colorado.

For six weeks Kingsley lay and gasped for breath in the little town that stands where the Rockies rise from the great middle-western plains. In those days the place was a noted resort for tubercular patients and many a pale young pioneer gasped his last looking towards the magnificent peaks of Bergun's Park. Kingsley was more fortunate, but he well knew how close he had come to the other Great Divide. When he was well enough to write once more to Fanny he told her, 'I must live, please God, a little longer, for all your sakes.' But during those long hours of semi-consciousness he dropped the burden of worldly ambition for the last time, as if he knew that it was with another world he must now concern himself. 'Please God I shall get safe and well home, and never leave you again, but settle down into the quietest old theologian, serving God, I hope, and doing nothing else. God has been so gracious that I cannot think that he means to send my grey hairs down in sorrow to the grave, but will, perhaps, give me time to reconsider myself, and sit quietly with you, preaching and working, and writing no more.' He rejoiced that only the Mississippi and the eastern hills now lay between him and his beloved Eversley. 'Yes! We shall rest our weary bones there before kind death comes, and, perhaps, see our grandchildren round us there. Ah! please God that!'

While he was at Colorado Springs he heard the good news that Maurice, who had recently married an American girl called Marie Yorke, had arrived safely in New York with her from Mexico. A few months later the couple's first child died at birth, as Kingsley himself lay on his deathbed. Fortunately he never knew it.

Before he left Colorado Springs, Kingsley wrote a sad little ballad about the English turf, induced no doubt by the homesickness that most travellers feel when they are ill and far from home. It had a curious repeated chorus which was supposed to represent the thud of a horse's hooves on turf.

'Are you ready for your steeple-chase, Lorraine, Lorraine, Lorree?'

Barum, Barum, Barum, Barum, Barum. Barum, Baree.
'You're booked to ride your capping race today at Coulterlee,
You're booked to ride Vindictive, for all the world to see,
To keep him straight, and keep him first, and win the run for me.'
Barum, Barum, etc.

She clasped her new born baby, poor Lorraine, Lorraine, Lorree,
'I cannot ride Vindictive, as any man might see,
And I will not ride Vindictive, with this baby on my knee;
He's killed a boy, he's killed a man, and why must he kill me?'

'Unless you ride Vindictive, Lorraine, Lorraine, Lorree,
'Unless you ride Vindictive today at Coulteree,
And land him safe across the brook, and win the blank for me,
It's you may keep your baby, for you'll get no help from me.'

'That husbands could be cruel,' said Lorraine, Lorraine, Lorree,
'That husbands could be cruel, I have known for seasons three;

But oh! to ride Vindictive while a baby cries for me,
And be killed across a fence at last for all the world to see!'

She mastered young Vindictive — Oh! the gallant lass was she,
And kept him straight and won the race as near as near could be;
But he killed her at the brook against a pollard willow tree,
Oh he killed her at the brook, the brute, for all the world to see.
And no one but the baby cried for poor Lorraine, Lorree.

Kingsley returned to Eversley to hear that many people in the parish had died of fever and that his old schoolmaster, C. A. Johns, had passed away suddenly at Winchester. He was shocked and grief-stricken and wrote to Mrs Johns ,'I had planned to bring home for him a whole collection of U.S. Lepidoptera. At least I can hope to meet hereafter somewhere, that brave, able and beloved spirit to whom I have owed so much on earth.'[18] He now set about nursing those who were still sick in the parish, an exhausting business in the sultry August weather, for one who himself had been ill so recently. His curate was away on holiday and his joy at being with his people again made him plunge too eagerly into work, before he had regained his own strength. When he went up to Westminster in September, he suffered a severe attack of congestion of the liver, which prevented his preaching in the Abbey on the first Sunday of his residence. The illness shook him gravely, and from that time he was unable to preach more than once a day on Sundays during his residence.

Fanny had agreed to accompany him on his second term of residence at Westminster, claiming in a letter that she was getting stronger and could 'walk about London (only short distances) unterrified'.[19] In October, however, she developed angina. Perhaps it was an unconscious protest at being obliged to live in London. When she was out of immediate danger, Kingsley, who had had another liver attack, was persuaded to take a brief holiday with friends in the country, but his appearance before a large congregation in the Abbey in November alarmed his friends. 'I went back', wrote one, 'sad at the remembrance of the bent back and shrunken figure, and grieved to see one who had carried himself so nobly, broken down by illness.'

In spite of his ill health Kingsley could not desert his post for, during Dean Stanley's absence on urgent family business in Paris, he was expected to take his place at the Abbey. On Advent Sunday, November 29th, he preached his last sermon during a violent thunderstorm. He

[18] Unpublished letter to Mrs Johns, 1874.
[19] Unpublished letter from Fanny, April 26, 1874.

finished with Fanny's favourite text, 'Come as thou seest best, but in whatsoever way thou comest, even so come, Lord Jesus,' took a side door out of the Abbey and went straight through the cloisters to his house, where Fanny was waiting for him. 'And now my work here is done, thank God!' he exclaimed, as he collapsed exhausted into a chair.

The next day he dined at the Deanery to meet Dr Caird, before attending his lecture at the Abbey at a special evening service. The night was damp, and coming out afterwards into the cold cloister he caught a fresh cold and coughed all through the night; but he made light of it, for he could think of nothing but returning to Eversley for a peaceful Christmas with his family. On December 3rd he conveyed Fanny, with many rugs and footwarmers, by train to Wokingham, where the brougham was waiting for them. But the journey had proved too much for her. In the night she had another of her attacks, and although, to Charles, she did not seem so very ill, Dr Heynes, the family doctor assured him that she could not recover. 'My own death warrant', he said, 'was signed with those words'.[20] Telegrams were sent to Windsor Castle excusing Kingsley from attending the Queen that Saturday, and to Maurice in New York summoning him home at once.

At last the terrible moment had come, the moment he had dreaded for thirty-five years, the moment of separation from Fanny. It was a bitter winter, with the snow lying for two months, and for three weeks Kingsley barely left his wife's side. In the large bow-windowed bedroom, that he had planned to paint with arabesques so many years ago, and from which he had planned to exclude even the servants, he sat crouched beside the bed, while maids tiptoed in and out with hot-water bottles and trays. The cold in that room was intense, for Dr Heynes had ordered that all the windows be kept open in order that Fanny could get her breath during her attacks.

As Fanny lay, terrified at the one journey that could not be put off, she asked Charles if she was being very cowardly. 'Cowardly!' he said. 'Don't you think I would rather someone put a pistol to my head than lie on that bed there, *waiting*?' Together they went over the whole of their life together, and favourite poems were read for the last time: Wordsworth's *Reflections on the Intimations of Immortality*, Milton's *On Time*, Matthew Arnold's *The Buried Life* and certain passages from Shakespeare. Together they planned every detail of Fanny's funeral, for which her pencil directions have recently been

[20] It is probable that Fanny was suffering from angina minor, which, although painful, never causes sudden death. She was in fact to survive another sixteen years.

discovered. There were to be 'no hatbands or shams', no undertakers, not even a carriage. Local worthies, including George Chaplin the groom and handyman, were to carry the plain wooden coffin made by the village carpenter. They were 'to carry it *low*, not on their shoulders', and be paid a guinea each for their pains. 'Let us be so still', wrote Fanny. Together they agreed on an epitaph — *Amavimus, amamus, amabimus* — and inside the cover of a diary Kingsley sketched the tombstone Fanny wanted, a circle representing eternity, enclosing a spray of passion flowers, representing their love.

For three weeks Kingsley lived entirely forgetful of himself, caring little for a future that seemed to hold only lonely years. The charm of life for him was over, and he spoke the truth when he said his heart was broken. He coughed continually, but took no care of himself. Inevitably his cough became bronchitic and three days after Christmas he took to his bed with the dread symptoms of pneumonia. For a month husband and wife lay in bedrooms at opposite ends of the house, able to communicate only by pencilled notes, for Charles was ordered to remain in a constant warm atmosphere. After a week the notes ceased for they became 'too painful and too tantalising'. Unable to resist the temptation to see his beloved once more, Charles escaped his trained nurse (brought down specially from the Westminster Hospital) and made the journey through the cold bedrooms that separated him from Fanny. For a few moments he sat by her bed holding her hand and gazing into her eyes. 'This is heaven,' he said. 'Don't speak.' Almost at once a severe fit of coughing came on, he could say no more. They never met again.

Kingsley was now kept constantly under opiates to quiet the cough and keep off haemorrhage, and often he lost all sense of time and place and imagined he was back in his sickbed at Colorado Springs or travelling through the jungles of Trinidad. In his lucid moments he could still feel a detached scientific interest in his condition, and told his nurse that, if he survived, he would write a book about the 'singular experience' he was undergoing. A visiting specialist was struck with 'his brilliancy in describing his symptoms and his splendid fight for life'.

On January 20th the Prince of Wales, concerned about the condition of his old tutor, requested the royal physician, Sir William Gull, to go down and examine the patient. On returning to London, Sir William wrote an optimistic note to the Prince, reporting that although the patient was 'severely prostrated from a recent attack of extensive inflammation of the right lung (pleuro-pneumonia) the acute symptoms are diminishing and there is at present a fair chance that the strength will rally'.[21] Even as the physician penned his optimistic prognosis, Kingsley started to cough up blood once more. 'Heynes!' he cried. 'I am hit; this last shot has told.' He asked whether Fanny knew, and when Rose told him, 'She knows all', he assumed that she had already gone and that his dearest wish, that they should die together, had been granted. For two days he lay, mostly in a coma, constantly repeating the phrase 'It is all right — all *under rule.*' On the night of the 22nd he repeated the burial service to himself, turned on his side and never spoke again. The following afternoon a garden boy on 'the famous grey pony' made his way through the deep snow to John Martineau's house. As soon as Martineau saw 'the pale horse' he recognised the messenger of Death and so the boy proved. Kingsley had breathed his last, without a sigh or a struggle, just before noon.

The tables were now turned and the funeral that was to be Fanny's became Charles's. Dean Stanley telegraphed to say that the Abbey was open to the Canon and the Poet, but the family knew that a grave in Eversley churchyard was what the rector had desired. On January 28th Eversley witnessed a funeral the like of which it had never seen. Even the staid gentleman from *The Times*, who came down to report on it, was carried away.

> Though the funeral was, by special desire of the deceased, conducted privately, the occasion was made such an exhibition of sympathy and respect as is rarely witnessed. As the distance from the rectory to the churchyard is only some 50 yards the road was nearly blocked by carriages. Shortly before half-past 2, the time fixed for the ceremony, a large assemblage of clergymen and mourners appeared on the broad gravel road facing the rectory. Eight villagers carried out the coffin into the open, and then the procession formed. Besides the relatives and friends of the deceased there was present Mr MacMillan, Sir Charles Russell, Professor Max Müller, the Deans of St Paul's and Chester, and Colonel the Hon. A. Fitzmaurice, representing the Prince of Wales. At the grave, Dean Stanley read the whole of the service, evidently deeply affected. The Bishop of Winchester gave the benediction. By special desire of the deceased the grave was not bricked, his wish being that his body might be committed to mother earth without that formality.

The Times reporter omitted to mention that, among the throng at the graveside, one of the saddest was Charles's younger brother Henry, already smitten with cancer of the tongue and aware he must

[21] Unpublished report from Sir William Gull.

soon, as always, follow where his elder brother had led. The reporter also failed to mention the throng beyond the churchyard wall, which included not only most of the gypsies of the common, but the servants of the Bramshill Hunt complete with their horses and hounds.

In London the bells of the Abbey tolled, and the following Sunday Dean Stanley preached a sermon about the late canon. He rightly picked upon the one consistent feature in a seemingly inconsistent character, the endless striving to improve the lot of his poorer brothers. With tears in his eyes he recalled a sentence from one of Kingsley's last sermons. 'To be discontented with the divine discontent and be ashamed with the noble shame, is the very germ and first upgrowth of all virtue.'[22] To this he added a remark that Kingsley had made ten years earlier at Windsor Castle: 'The age of chivalry is never past, so long as there is a wrong left undressed on earth, or a man or a woman left to say "I will redress that wrong, or spend my life in the attempt." ' As Stanley had gazed upon the still face of Kingsley at Eversley on the day of the funeral he had felt that he was looking at a crusader struck down in battle; the features were those of 'the stone effigy of an ancient warrior'. It was at Stanley's suggestion that a marble bust of Kingsley was placed in the Abbey, to commemorate a man who was a national figure then and is not forgotten today.

[22] Charles Kingsley, *Health and Education*, 1874.

Letter-pamphlet on the Crimean War
February 25th, 1855

(Fanny included only one paragraph from this letter in her life of her husband, the paragraph referring to Christian Socialism, printed here in italics. The original was discovered recently accompanied by a note in Fanny's handwriting saying 'Do not publish this — it would be misunderstood, grand though it is.')

My dearest Friends, both Ludlow and Hughes,

Many thanks for two delightful letters which I answer as one to save time. Thanks for the account of C.M.[1] I have, I confess, still fears for his life but we will not anticipate. Would we not *both* nurse him were we in Town!

As for my tract, now you have found it out (I can't conceive how) I will tell you that I wish it kept a secret, from private reasons which I cannot explain to you, as they relate to folk you don't know. Do keep my name back or you will spoil its sale in the very quarter I want it most spread.

And now Ludlow calls Palmerston my idol. He really is not. When all we wanted was pluck I looked to him with immense hope, because he had it, I thought. But we are now come to a point where nothing but a righteous man can steer us round — and I certainly never took Pam for that. And even in point of pluck he failed from the moment when he reconstituted the ministry out of its identical successors. Don't hang him because he must be premier for a while; but after that, let him go to the union workhouse. I shan't stop him.

Next, Hughes asks me to cry aloud and spare not. So can a cat in a gutter, but a cat can be repaid by a jug of cold water and therefore had better have held its tongue like me. For if I cry I shall cry to a tune for which the English people is not ready, nor will be till they have lost another army or two, to judge by any signs I see.

For though I think reform more possible now than ever, and nearer,

[1] Charles Mansfield, who in fact died on the day this letter was written.

I see no real turn of the tide. I see none in the ministry, they first reconstitute themselves, then try Baring, Wood, etc. etc. as if Fiddle Major and Faddle Major being licked, should put into the ring Fiddle Minor and Faddle Minor and then Fiddle Minimus and Faddle Minimus, to see if they can lick the boy their elders couldn't. My children, the English nation is simply insulted and humbugged, by a show of reform that means nothing at all. Lagard, Lazy and Lowe are to be taken in, eh? So is the British public. Each of them is to be taken into the ministry as soon as they have made themselves formidable, for the purpose of stopping their mouths. Lord Goderich is to be taken, to silence his Army Reform Motion. My dear men, if any real reform had been intended, would the ministry be talking now, as I know they talk, about the war as a game of chess? Would they, as I know they do, ignore the very existence of the Crimea? Would they keep not only Lord Raglan at Balaklava, but Lord Hardinge at the Horse Guards. And why? Because a certain Prince keeps him there. Because a certain Prince must at all hazards to the nation, swamp the war for fear of those petty bankrupt German princes being crushed by it, as God grant they may be. But no one dares say so. *The Times* dare not. Who dares? Everyone knows it but everyone knows too that if you begin at the beginning, you may end up at the end — and what the end would be they don't (I'm sure I don't) like to know. 1688 was all smooth sailing because you had William of Orange to fall back on, but now! Let it alone: but don't fancy in the meanwhile that your lawyers are going to set this matter right with pen and parchment, acts of Parliament and the rest of our tackle for voting things strait that are crooked, and even, which are odd. We have thrown away the Gospel and put ourselves formally under the Law. And what says the Law? Without shedding of blood there is no remission of sin. And who so sheddeth men's blood, by him shall men's blood be shed. And the blood of that Crimean Army cries from the ground — I know not whom: but God knows: and God will demand that blood. Don't ask me to say whose blood because there is no use recommending the fellows till one has settled a little who should be hanged. Sidney Herbert and Gladstone, I do see my way toward hanging but no further, for Gladstone has lied more than ever. He lied when he stated in Parliament that the Crimean Army was 30,000 for he knew that it was not half that. Sidney Herbert lied, and blasphemously too, when he dared, in his canting speech, to throw on God the blame for what he knew was due to Lord Hardinge's misrule — but it was better to blame God than a German prince.

And so on, and so on. And Ludlow says there is something grand in the prelates standing out against this commission even though wrong. Things are grand when done by grand men and for grand purposes. I can only see in it one more cant, one more shuffle, one more reckless venture on the laziness of England, which will let by-gones be bygones and agree that just because the thing is so bad the least said soonest mended. And as for any grandeur in the House of Commons, what grandeur is there in the sight of six hundred men, who have everyone a lie in his hand, kicked by the force without into pretending to do what they don't intend to do — six hundred men who are said to represent England and who represent no more than my dog, but have to be driven to do anything real by the fear of the very men who never voted for or against them (rich and poor) and don't care sixpence if they were transported tomorrow. What grandeur in the sight of these wretched men keeping up Carlyle's soubriquet of 'the laughing House of Commons' by forgetting England's disgrace and the fearful Question which God will ask when man is tired of asking in vain — 'Where are the 40,000?' in giggling like girls at every petty distress of their opponents, as shallow and mean as themselves. There: that is what I think. Will you have me print that in a pamphlet? *You may have fancied me a bit of a renegade and hanger back of late. Still in our ashes lie their wonted fires, and if I have held back from the Socialist movement it has been because I have seen that the world was not going to be set right in any such rose-pink way, excellent though it is, and that there are heavy arrears of destruction to be made up before construction can ever begin; and I wanted to see what those arrears were. And I do see a little. At least I see that the old Phoenix must burn before the new one can rise out of its ashes.*

Next, as to our army, I quite agree with you both — if it existed to agree about. But the remnant that comes home, like gold tried in the fire, may be the seed of such an army as the world never saw. Perhaps we may help it to germinate. Don't compare the dear fellows to Cromwell's Ironsides. There is a great deal of personal religion in the army no doubt, and personal religion may help a man to endure, and complete the bulldog form of courage: but the soldier wants more; he wants a faith that he is fighting on God's side, he wants military and corporal and National religion, and that's what I fear they have to get, and what I tried to give in my tract. That is what Cromwell's Ironsides had and by it they conquered. That is what the Elizabethans had up to the Armada, and by it *they* conquered.

And if you try to raise that among our troops, you will find the authorities, at home, and *The Times* too, try to quash it. Macmillan sent a copy of *Brave Words* to each of the ministry. I fear the comment of two out of three of them, if they looked at it, would have been

'Whe-eugh! Here's a man trying to turn the war into a religious war. Why, he is as bad as the Czar! It is quite bad enough to have to carry on the war, or be carried on by it, already, without fanaticism added to the stimulants. If we once let the people fancy that it is God's cause and not diplomacy's and ours, God only knows where it will all stop.' The same covert atheism, which has put down duelling, put down drawing lots, and is trying to put down taking oaths, will put down all attempts to acknowledge a Divine Ruler or Arbiter in war. In all the prayers put out by High Church and Low, I see this cardinal defect; they will pray for the sick, wounded, nurses, everyone but the fighting men as fighting men, everything but the war itself — they carefully abstain from pronouncing any opinion on the justice of the war. And there perhaps they are right. It is not a just war. It began in a lie and cant. We pretended to go to war for liberty; if we had we should have armed Hungary and Poland long ago. We went to war because the ministry wanted to keep in by yielding to the popular cry and hoped that all would be over in six months and behold it is grim earnest and we are in it and for it and shall have to carry on the war honestly and call in America to help us, if we have not already alienated her as we have the Continental Democracies. But as long as the war remains a mere struggle of half a dozen small mammonite tyrannies against one huge grey one, God's blessing will not be on it, and the eternal laws will fight against it, the covenant of lies will not stand, the European nations will break up, as Greece did before Macedon.

Shall I print this? No, let us bide our time.

Supposititious Works of Charles Kingsley

In August 1932 a medium known as Crusader was sitting at home with his wife and a close relative when he felt a pressure on the nape of his neck and began to speak with the voice of Charles Kingsley.

From that day forward the life of Crusader, whose real name was Charles D. Boltwood, was changed. He was commanded to give up his employment as a traveller for Eucryl and establish the 'Kingsley Mission'. His wife received orders to change her name to Sunbeam and rename their house at Thorpe-le-Soken 'Sunbeam's Healing Centre'. A few years later she received a further message telling her she must leave her husband and take up residence at a bungalow near Aberystwyth called Demonstrable Heights. Here, withdrawn from earthly vibrations, she became the 'Cell Nucleolus' of the movement.

Crusader meanwhile was persuaded by his followers to publish the revelations about the Bible that he had been receiving from Kingsley. These appeared in six slim volumes, privately printed around 1940, entitled *Logic of Eternal Life, Spirit Revelation Unveils the Bible, Exaltation of Woman, Messages of Charles Kingsley, Spirit Sermons of 1940* and *Deathless Freedom*. The books dealt with such matters as the creation of man and his fall and included diagrams captioned 'The Influence of the Zodiac on Mortal Life', and 'The Polarised Man of Immortality Standing Square on the Twelve True Foundation Stones of the New Jerusalem'. Neither the style nor the subject matter of the books are particularly reminiscent of the earthly Charles Kingsley, although there is one mention of Fanny's biography and one of a madrepore, a coral-producing animal Kingsley once wrote about. Certainly *Exaltation of Woman* dealt with a subject dear to Kingsley, that of the spiritual equality of man and woman. It is doubtful however whether he would have gone as far as Boltwood, who attacked 'Protestantism, Calvinism and Nonconformitism [*sic*]' for referring to the Almighty as 'He'. Crusader even rewrote the Lord's Prayer, changing the introductory invocation to Our Father-Mother God'.

Bibliography

1. *Selected List of Works of Charles Kingsley*

1848 *The Saint's Tragedy*

1849 *Alton Locke*

1849 *Yeast*

1849 *Twenty-five Village Sermons*

1852 *Phaeton*

1853 *Hypatia*

1855 *Glaucus*

1855 *Westward Ho!*

1856 *The Heroes*

1857 *Two Years Ago*

1858 *Andromeda and other Poems*

1859 *Miscellanies*

1860 *The Limits of Exact Science applied to History* (*Inaugural Lecture*).

1863 *The Water-Babies*

1866 *Hereward the Wake*

1869 *The Hermits*

1869 *Madam How and Lady Why*

1871 *At Last*

1873 *Prose Idylls*

2. *Selected List of Printed Authorities*

Baldwin, Stanley E.: *Charles Kingsley* (Cornell University Press, Ithaca, 1934)

Brown, W. Henry: *Charles Kingsley: The Work and Influence of Parson Lot* (The Co-operative Union Ltd, Manchester, 1924)

Cottingham, C. Elizabeth: *A Little History of Eversley Collected from Various Sources* (Henry T. Morley, Reading)

Davenport, Reginald C.: *A Brief Account of the Kingsley Family*, by An Outside Member (privately printed, 1911)

Egner, G. *Apologia pro Charles Kingsley* (Sheed and Ward, 1969)

Ellis, S. M.: *Henry Kingsley, 1830-1876: Towards a Vindication* (Grant Richards, 1931)

Faber, Geoffrey: *Oxford Apostles: A Character Study of the Oxford Movement* (Faber and Faber, 1933)

Gosse, Edmund: *Father and Son* (William Heinemann, 1907)

Graves, Charles L.: *Life and Letters of Alexander Macmillan* (Macmillan and Co., 1910)

Jagow, Kurt, ed: *Letters of the Prince Consort, 1831–1861* (John Murray, 1938)

Kendall, Guy: *Charles Kingsley and His Ideas* (Hutchinson and Co., 1947)

Kingsley, Charles: *Alton Locke, Tailor and Poet. An Autobiography* with a prefatory memoir by Thomas Hughes (Macmillan and Co., 1876)

—— *The Tutor's Story* with an introduction by Lucas Malet (Smith Elder and Co., 1916)

—— *The Water-Babies* with an introduction by Rose Kingsley (Everyman, 1908)

Kingsley, Frances E., ed.: *Charles Kingsley: His Letters and Memories of His Life* edited by His Wife, 2 vols. (Henry S. King and Co., 1877)

Kingsley, George Henry: *Notes on Sport and Travel*, with a Memoir by His Daughter Mary H. Kingsley (Macmillan and Co., 1900)

Kingsley, Rose: *Eversley Gardens.* (George Allen, 1907)

—— *South by West, or Winter in the Rocky Mountains and Spring in Mexico* with a preface by Charles Kingsley (Isbister, 1874)

Lee, Sidney: *King Edward VII: A Biography* (Macmillan and Co, 1925–7)

Ludlow, John Malcolm: 'Some of the Christian Socialists of 1848 and the Following Years. I', *Economic Review* (October 1893) pp. 486–500.

—— 'Some of the Christian Socialists of 1848 and the Following Years. II', *Economic Review* (January 1894) pp. 24–42.

Mack, Edward C. and Armytage, W. H. G.: *Thomas Hughes: The Life of the Author of Tom Brown's Schooldays* (Ernest Benn, 1952)

Martin, Robert Bernard, ed.: *Charles Kingsley's American Notes: Letters from a Lecture Tour, 1874* (Princeton University Library, Princeton, 1958)

—— *The Dust of Combat: A Life of Charles Kingsley* (Faber and Faber Ltd, 1959)

Martineau, Violet: *John Martineau: Pupil of Kingsley* (Edward Arnold, 1921)

Maurice, Frederick, ed: *Life of Frederick Denison Maurice, Chiefly Told in His Own Letters*, 2 vols. (Macmillan and Co., 3rd ed., 1884)

Paul, Herbert: *The Life of Froude* (Sir Isaac Pitman and Sons, 1905)

Pope-Hennessy, Una: *Canon Charles Kingsley* (Chatto and Windus, 1948)

Raven, Charles E.: *Christian Socialism, 1848–1854* (Macmillan and Co., 1920)

Stanley, Dean A. P.: *Funeral Sermon for Charles Kingsley* (Privately printed, 1875)

Tennyson, Hallam: *Alfred Lord Tennyson: A Memoir by His Son*, 4 vols. (Macmillan and Co, 1898)

Thorp, Margaret Farraud: *Charles Kingsley, 1819–1875* (Princeton University Press, Princeton, 1937)

Ward, Wilfred: *The Life of John Henry Cardinal Newman*, 2 vols. (Longman, Green and Co., 1912)

—— ed.: *Newman's Apologia pro Vita Sua: The Two Versions of 1864 and 1865*, preceded by Newman's and Kingsley's Pamphlets (Oxford University Press, 1931)

Index

Abbey Square, Chester, 273
Abbott, George, 23, 105
Abergeldie Castle, 251
Aberystwyth, 301
Ackland, Dr W. H., 50n, 173, 238
Adam, 167
Afterthoughts, 195n, 271
Agde, 233
Ainsworth, Harrison, 134
Airly Beacon, 102
Albert, Prince Consort, 104, 108, 154, 169, 197, 201, 203, 203n, 205, 214, 240, 299
Alcibiades, 187
Aldershot, 67, 67n, 196, 269
Alexandra, Princess, 214
Alexandria, 151, 152
Algeria, 233
Alleyne, Agnes Rebecca Augusta, 223n
Alma, 169
Almack's, 69
Alps, 194
Alresford, 218
Alton Locke, 15, 107n, 129, 130–46, 166, 185, 204, 273
American Civil War, 215n, 242, 255
Ancient Mariner, The, 100
Andromeda, 156, 179, 220
Anglo Saxon Chronicle, 244
Anne, Queen, 224
Antigua, 260
Apennines, 183
Apologia Pro Charles Kingsley, 236
Apologia Pro Vita Sua, 235–7
Appledore, 169
Arcadia, 170
Argentina, 268
Argyll, Duke of, 210
Arnold, Matthew, 294
Arnold, Dr Thomas, 41
Arthur's Club, 92
Ashburton, Lady, 210
Ask if I Love Thee, 148
Atlantic, 127, 168, 173
At Last, 36n, 225, 259, 263–4
Australia, 121, 182, 188, 242, 276, 289
Avery, Gillian, 219n
Avignon, 74

Babylon, 71, 184
Baby Sings not on its Mother's Breast, The, 148

Baden, 61
Bagshot, 194, 215
Bain, 243
Baitsbite Lock, 212
Balaklava, 169, 299
Banks, Sir Joseph, 24
Bannister, Mr, 208, 208n
Barbados, 24, 35, 242, 265
Barcelona, 234
Bardon Hall, 170n
Barnack, 23, 26, 28–9, 32, 34, 260
Barnstaple, 168, 173
Barnwell, 57
Barry, F. R., 284n
Barton Hall, 215
Bateson, Dr W. H., 62
Bath, 87, 232
Battersea, 49
B. B. C., 15, 135n
Beacon Street, 287
Bear Wood, 251
Beddgelert, 184
Beethoven, 272, 279
Belgrave Square, 174
Belgravia, 159
Bell, Dr, 291
Bemerton, 97
Benson, E. W., 192
Benson, Mrs E. W., 241
Beowulf, 115
Bergun's Park, 291
Bermondsey, 130, 134
Bermondsey Abbey, 130n
Bernard Street, Bloomsbury, 277
Bethnal Green, 175
Béziers, 233
Biarritz, 232
Bideford, 18, 34, 38, 39, 168, 173, 238
Birds of America, 216n
Birmingham, 229, 237
Bitburg, 150
Black Beauty, 16, 162
Blackmore, Susannah, 39
Blackwater, 67
Blackwater, Vale of, 229
Blackwell, Dr Elizabeth, 254
Blomfield, Dr C. J., 144
Blunt, Rev and Mrs, 276
Bocas Islands, 261
Bodley Head, publisher, 141n

Bolderwood, Ralph, 188
Bolitho, family of, 41
Boltwood, Charles D., 259n, 302
Bonn, 151
Bonney, T. G., 225
Borlase, family of, 41
Borneo, 170
Boston, 287-8
Bournemouth, 116, 256n, 279
Bovisand, 36
Bowdler, Mrs M. A., 223n
Bramshill, 67, 105, 106, 162, 163, 269, 278
Brasenose College, 24
Braunton Hills, 173
Brave Words for Brave Soldiers, 169, 300
Braziers Park, 54
Brazil, 176
Bremer, Frederika, 59, 143
Brick Hill House, 158
Bridal Veil Fall, 291
Bridge Hall, 38
Bridgeland Street, 173
Bridgewater Treatise, 73
Bristol, 40, 174
British Museum, 61n, 76n, 110, 259n, 283
Brompton, 182, 207
Brontë, Rev Patrick, 30
Brooke, Rajah Sir James, 170
Brooks, Shirley, 284
Brown, John, 134
Brownhill, Father, 122
Browning, Robert, 159, 183
Bryanston School, 81
Buckingham Palace, 201, 204
Buckland, William, 73
Buckle, Henry Thomas, 211
Bude, 232
Bullar, John, 50n, 204n, 239n
Bulteel, Miss, 258
Bunbury, Sir Charles, 215, 227, 248, 259, 266, 275, 280
Bunsen, Baron de, 104, 123, 154, 257
Buried Life, The, 294
Bursden, 37
Burton, Democritus, 110
Burton, Mrs Hyford, 175
Burton-on-Trent, 26
Button Cap, 27
Buxton, 222
Byrom, Thomas, 133n
Byron, Lord, 24, 35, 159n
Byzant, 233

Cadogan, Lord and Lady, 48
Cadogan estates, 47
Caird, Sir James, 294
California, 161, 163, 165, 291
Callista, 153
Cam, 53, 56

Cambridge, 15, 25, 26, 32, 51-62, 70, 77, 79, 82, 89, 95, 100, 101, 114, 119, 128, 134, 138, 144, 153, 173, 174, 176, 196, 204-6, 208, 210-15, 225, 226, 228, 239, 242, 243, 244, 249, 250, 257, 259, 261, 268, 273, 280, 285
Cambridge, Mass, 287
Campbell, Pitcairn, 56
Campbell, 188, 276
Canada, 289
Canning, George, 69
Carleill, Christopher, 36
Carlisle, Lord, 131
Carlsbad, 61
Carlton House Terrace, 154
Carlyle, Thomas, 49, 61, 94, 109n, 123, 133, 186, 211, 242, 257
Carmichael, Mr, 256
Carnbrae, 266
Carroll, Lewis, 153, 277
Carthage, 233
Cary, family of, 36
Cary, Will, 36
Castle End, 57
Castle Street, 133n
Cater's Beam, 128
Cavendish, Thomas, 36
Cawsand, 36
Cazamian, Louis, 133n
Cette, 233
Ceylon, 216
Chalk Stream Studies, 53n, 195
Chagford, 128
Chambers, Dr, 50
Chanter, Rev J. M., 189
Chanter, Mrs J. M., 27, 39, 39n, 49, 87, 188
Chapel Royal, St James, 201
Chaplin, George, 295
Chapman, Annie, 191n
Chapman, George, 173n
Charge of the Light Brigade, The, 158
Charles I, 23
Charles Kingsley: His Letters and Memories of his Life. Edited by his wife, 16
Charles River, 287
Chartism, 107-9, 111, 121, 123, 129
Cheap Clothes and Nasty, 132, 172
Checkenden, 54
Cheddar, 83, 87, 88
Chelsea, 48-9, 58-60, 79, 88, 93, 102, 145, 148, 151, 174, 188, 206, 207
Chequers, the, 189n
Chester, 258, 259, 268-82
Chester Natural Science Society, 274
Chiffinch, 288
Child's History of England, 205n, 244
Chimney Sweepers Regulation Act, 222
Christchurch Cathedral, 110
Christian Socialist, The, 142
Chronological Historical Rhymes 42n
Cirencester, 268

Clacy, George, 105, 139
Clacy, Mrs George, 106
Clapham, 102
Clapham, West Indies, 266
Clare, John, 32
Clarke, Sir James, 231, 250
Clifden, Nellie, 214
Clifton, 41
Clough, Arthur, 104
Clovelly, 34–9, 41n, 45, 48, 49, 50, 125, 127, 128, 168, 180, 260, 272
Codrington, Sir Edward, 36
Colebrook, 128
Coleridge, The Rev Derwent, 41, 42, 42n, 44, 46, 70, 83n, 104
Coleridge, Mrs Derwent, 42
Coleridge, Lord Chief Justice, 41
Coleridge, Samuel Taylor, 100
Collier, 44n
Collins, publisher, 133n
Cologne, 149
Colorado, 280, 291
Colorado Springs, 280, 291, 292, 294
Columbus, Christopher, 36
Comte, Auguste, 211, 257
Connan, Dr D. M., 132n
Conrad of Morpurg, 103
Cook, Capt James, 35
Cooper, Mr, of Sligo, 210
Cooper, Thomas, 111, 133, 133n
Cooper, Walter, 133n
Co-operative Movement, 134n
Cooper's Magazine, 142
Cope, Sir John, 67, 93, 95, 105, 106, 139, 145
Cope, Sir William, 95n, 145 161, 163, 165, 177, 280
Cork, County, 54
Cornish Magazine, The, 44n
Cornwall, 54, 55, 83
Cottesmore, 32
Council Bluffs, 290
Covey-Crump, A., 17
Cowper, William, 178, 178n
Cox, Mark, 34
Craigenputtock, 49
Cranbourne Chase, 82, 90
Crediton, 128
Cricketer's Magazine, The, 191n
Crimea, 155
Crimean War, 169, 176, 180, 227, 298–301
Cromwell, Oliver, 300
Crowland Abbey, 252, 252n
Crystal Palace, 143
Cuba, 263
Cumberland, 36
Cunnack, E. M., 41n
Cyrene, 233

Dade, Miss, 30
Daily Telegraph, 18, 222

Daily Thoughts, 18
D'Alembert, 75
Dalesman Publishing Co, 193n
Dampier, William, 35
Dante, 40, 95, 219
Dart, 25, 129
Dartmoor, 65, 128, 129
Darwin, Charles, 15, 211, 214, 215, 259
David, 52, 173, 272
David and Charles, publisher, 127n
David and Other Sermons, 255n
Dawkings, Mrs Nancy, 156n
Dee, 220, 275
Delamere Forest, 23
Demerara, 242
Demonstrable Heights, 301
Dent, publisher, 246
Denver, 280, 291
Devon, 65, 168, 171, 173
Dial House, 68n
Dickens, Charles, 18, 130, 131, 134, 174, 287
Dickens, Mrs Charles, 174
Dickenson, Lowes, 161
Dietrich of Thuringia, 77
Disraeli, Benjamin, 134, 191, 257
Dodd, Edgar, 128n
Dodgson, see Carroll, Lewis
Dolby, Miss, 192
Doneraile, Lord, 54
Dorset, 81, 89, 90, 91
Douglas, Camp, 290
Drake, Sir Francis, 36
Dresden, 150
Dressors, 188, 256n
Drew, Rev D. S., 144
Drifting Away, 238
Drosier, Rev Thomas, 128
Druitt, M. J., 191n
Duffy, Maureen, 220
Dust of Combat, 287n, 288n
Durham, 257
Durweston, 81–2, 84, 90, 91
Duxford, 56

East End, London, 132
East India College, Haileybury, 177
Easton-on-the-Hill, 34
Eastward Ho!, 173n
Economic Review, 108n
Edinburgh, 163, 211, 232
Edinburgh Daily Review, 276
Edward, Prince of Wales, 213, 214, 214n, 251, 269, 281, 295, 296
Edwards, Mary Stella, 50n
Egner, G., 236
Egypt, 233
Eifel mountain, 148, 232
Elegy, 129
Eliot, George, 173
Eliot Place, Blackheath, 191, 192

Elizabeth, Queen, 49
Ellis, S. M., 278n
Ely, 26, 52, 213, 239
Embury Beacon, 37n
Emerson, R. W., 152, 254
Emma, Queen, 239–41, 255
Ems, 147, 149
England, 109, 110, 216, 234, 300
Erasmus, Desiderius, 247
Erotic World of Faery, The, 220
Erskine, Henry, 238
Erskine, Rt Hon Thomas, 161, 238
Esquemeling, 35
Essay on Shelley and Byron, 159n
Eton, 41
Euphues, 170, 256
Eversley, 15, 18, 45, 66–71, 87–97, 100, 105–7, 116, 120, 121, 123, 129, 130, 137–45, 158, 160, 163, 164, 165n, 176, 177, 183, 185, 188–92, 194, 196, 206, 208, 215n, 226, 229n, 231, 234, 238, 240, 250, 251, 253, 253n, 254, 258, 260, 268, 269, 270, 279, 280, 281, 284, 285, 289, 292, 293, 294, 296, 297, 298
Eversley, Lord, 240, 251
Eversley Gardens, 253n
Everyman, publisher, 133n
Exeter College, Oxford, 104, 121
Eyre, Governor Edward John, 241–2

Farley Court, 177, 179
Farley Hall, 35
Farnham, 159, 195
Farnham Castle, 66
Farrington, 158
Farson, Daniel, 191n
Father and Son, 191n
Fens, 34
Fez Club, 187
Fields, Annie, 287
Fir Grove, 161
Firs, The, 159n
Fisher, Herbert, 213
Fitzmaurice, Col the Hon A., 296
Fitzwilliam Museum, 226
Fleetwood, George, 23
Flintshire, 180
Florida State University, 216
Flowers of the Field, 42
Folly Ditch, 130, 132, 132n, 135
Forum, 134
Foster, Dr, 160
Fox, Caroline, 172
Fox, George, 239
France, 59, 187, 232, 235, 247
Franco–Prussian War, 275
Fraser's Magazine, 34, 42, 104, 106, 107, 111, 158, 172, 194, 195, 205, 215n, 248
French Revolution, The, 257
Frimley, 139
Friswell, J. H., 240n

Frith, W. P., 285
Frobisher, Martin, 36
Froissart, 35
From Ocean to Sea, 233n
Froude, J. A., 72, 104, 121, 122, 160, 183, 186, 209, 212, 212n, 229, 231, 232, 234, 248
Froude, Mrs J. A., 54, 72, 85, 121, 122, 160, 208, 209
Froude, Richard Hurrell, 121
Fry, Mrs Elizabeth, 48n

Gainsborough, Lady, 61
Gardiner, Miss, 121
Garth, the, 105n, 141
Geological Society, 49, 215, 247n
Germany, 61, 74, 106, 146, 147–50, 156, 160, 187, 232, 275, 299
Gibbons, Grindling, 284n
Gibraltar, 231
Gilbert, Geoffrey, 170n
Gilbert, Sir Humphrey, 270
Giorgione, 123
Gladstone, W. E., 257, 281, 282, 284, 299
Glaucus, or the Wonders of the Shore, 167, 177, 182
Glover, Mrs, 170n
Glyder, 159, 181
Glyn's bank, 106
God in History, 257
Goderich, Lord, 174, 178, 299
Good Time Coming, The, 142
Good Words, 246, 247, 247n, 259
Goode, William, 65
Goodrington, 166
Gordon, 241
Gordon, Sir Arthur, 259–63
Gosse, Edmund, 166
Gosse, Philip, 138n, 166, 167, 174
Grange, The, 210
Granta, 56
Grant Richards, publisher, 278n
Gray, Asa, 287
Great Exhibition, 143
Great Marlow, 54
Greece, 233, 301
Greg, W. R., 171
Grenfell, Charles Pascoe, 155, 178
Grenfell, Charlotte, niece of Mrs Charles Kingsley Jr., 182
Grenfell, Charlotte, sister of Mrs Charles Kingsley Jr., see Froude, Mrs J. A.
Grenfell, Frances Eliza, see Kingsley, Mrs Charles Jr
Grenfell, Geogina, see Müller, Mrs Max
Grenfell, Georgiana, 54, 72–3, 87
Grenfell, Henrietta, 54, 72
Grenfell, Mary, 276
Grenfell, Riversdale Pascoe, 54, 79, 83, 155
Grenville, Sir Richard, 36, 189
Guadeloupe, 260

Guardian, The, 144
Guildford, 189n
Gull, Sir William, 295, 296n
Gurney, A. W., 41n
Gurney, Archer Thompson, 41, 41n, 157, 158n, 159n
Gurney, Rev R. H. 41n, 157n, 158n

Habershon, Mr, 177
Hakluyt, Richard, 173, 270
Hallam, A. H., 52
Hamlyn-Williams, Sir James, 34, 36, 49
Hampshire, 66, 78, 107, 139, 175
Hampton Court, 195
Hardinge, Lord, 299
Hare, Archdeacon, 109
Harmony Hall, 266
Harold, 246
Harrison, Frederick, 134
Harrison, William, 270
Harrow, 279, 280, 287, 289
Hartford Bridge Flat, 232
Hartland Point, 37, 152
Hawk, Edward, 45
Hawker, Rev R. S., 141
Hawkins, William, 36
Hawthorne, Nathaniel, 17, 77, 179
Hawtrey, Dr E. C., 41
Haynes, Mr, 271
Hazelwood, Sarah Kingsley, see Kingsley, Mrs Henry
Health and Education, 297
Heaven on Earth, 96n
Heckfield Place, 25
Hedges, Mrs, 240
Helpston, 32
Helston, 41, 41n, 43, 45, 46, 46n, 47, 48, 49, 83n, 266
Hennessy, Una Pope, 153
Henry, Bishop of Exeter, 166
Henry VII, 83
Henry Kingsley, 1830-1876. Towards a Vindication, 278n
Herbert, George, 97
Herbert, Sidney, 299
Hereward the Wake, 15, 161, 170, 218, 233n, 255, 255n, 281n
Hermits, The, 252, 255n
Heroes, The, 15, 179, 216n
Hertha, 90
Heynes, Dr, 294, 296
Highgate, 278
Hill, Mrs Frederick, 83
Hill Street, 122
Hillyars and the Burtons, The, 49
Himalayas, 194
Hinson, R. and L., 193n
History of the Public Health Department of Bermondsey, 132n

Hodder and Stoughton, publisher, 219n, 220n, 284n
Hoe, 36
Holland, 246
Holme, 32
Holne, 25, 34, 65, 105, 128
Holyoake, 155, 155n
Home, Emma, 175
Homer, 270
Hood, Robin, 245
Hopkins, Gerard Manley, 159
Horse Guards, 299
Houghton, Lord, 277
Housman, A. E., 227
House of Commons, 108, 251, 300
Howson, Dr J. S. 258, 273
Hughes, Thomas, 107n, 110, 111, 143, 145, 145n, 155, 159, 159n, 161, 162, 169, 176, 178, 182, 183, 184, 187, 190, 195, 238, 241, 242, 285, 298
Hullah, John P., 158, 192
Humboldt, 261
Hungary, 301
Hunt, Dr James, 193
Hunt, John, 24
Huntingdon, 32
Hurlbert, W. H. 288, 288n
Hurst Castle, 267,
Hutton, R. H., 230, 235, 235n
Huxley, T. H., 241, 248, 274
Hypatia, 15, 149, 151-6, 166, 167, 172, 175, 203, 228, 252
Hypotheses Hypochondriacae, 46n

Ilfracombe, 34, 118, 120, 188
Illustrated News, 93
Indian Civil Service, 244
Indian Mutiny, 192
Inferno, 218
Inkerman, 169
In Memoriam, 158
Intimations of Immortality, 204
Inverary Castle, 210
Ipsden, 54, 75
Ireland, 108, 171, 209-10
Isaiah, 186
Isle of Ely, 245
Isle of Wight, 98, 158
Italy, 146, 233
Itchen, 218

Jack the Ripper, 191
Jackson of Paul's, 187
Jacob's Island, 130-5, 181
Jacob Street, 132n
Jamaica, 241
Jamieson, Mrs, 119, 120
Jason, 179
Jelf, Dr R. W., 111, 155

John Martineau: Pupil of Charles Kingsley, 124n, 138n

John O'London's Weekly, 191

Johns, Charles Alexander, 42, 42n, 44, 45n, 83, 83n, 229n, 238, 251, 278, 278n, 280, 281, 293

Johns, Mrs Charles, 85, 251, 293, 293n

Johnson, Capt Charles, 35

Jonathan, 52

Jonson, Ben, 173n

Joshua, 172

Journal of Association, 242

Kennington Common, 108, 145

Kensington, 47, 284

Kentish Town, 278

Keys, 253n

Kingdom of Christ, The, 70, 100, 257

Kings College, Cambridge, 104

King's College, London, 49, 54, 101, 111, 155, 159n

Kings College School, 116

King's Parade, 225

Kings Road, 48n

Kingsley, Mrs, of Dulwich, 161

Kingsley, Mrs Charles Jr., 16, 17, 30, then throughout

Kingsley, Rev Charles, Sr., 23–6, 30, 31, 32, 34, 35, 36, 39, 41, 41n, 47, 48, 49, 54, 55, 60, 77, 87, 104, 105, 120, 150, 161, 188, 206, 207

Kingsley, Mrs Charles, Sr , 24–7, 28, 39, 47, 48, 100, 103, 105, 147, 150, 151, 188, 207, 208, 256n, 277n, 280

Kingsley, Charlotte, see Chanter, Mrs J. M.

Kingsley, Frank, 18

Kingsley, George, 27, 30, 35n, 39, 54, 107, 123, 151, 161, 174, 180, 182, 278, 291

Kingsley, Gerald, 2, 26, 30, 49, 54, 100

Kingsley, Grenville Arthur, 189, 190, 216, 232, 239n, 247, 251, 252, 256, 271, 278, 279, 289

Kingsley, Henry, 27, 39, 39n, 49, 53, 54, 62, 68, 75, 94, 116, 128, 146, 147–50, 161, 187, 188, 188n, 242, 269, 276–9, 296

Kingsley, Mrs Henry, 276, 277

Kingsley, Herbert, 26, 30, 39, 44, 45, 46

Kingsley, Louisa Mary, 28

Kingsley, Mary, daughter of Charles Jr., 36, 133, 133n, 144, 160, 161, 163, 165, 179, 187n, 190, 216, 232, 253, 269

Kingsley, Mary, daughter of George, 35n, 278

Kingsley, Maurice, 17, 98, 118, 122, 128, 143, 158, 166, 179, 189, 190, 191, 192, 203, 205, 216, 243, 244, 250, 268, 280, 281, 291, 292, 294

Kingsley, Mrs Maurice, 292

Kingsley, Ralph, 18

Kingsley, Ranulph de, 23

Kingsley, Rose, 93, 93n, 98, 99, 100, 118, 122, 128, 139, 143, 161, 162, 165, 166, 179, 188n, 190, 195, 216, 253, 253n, 254, 259–67, 276, 280, 288, 290, 290n, 291, 295

Kingsley, William, 23

Kingsley et Thomas Cooper Etude sur une Source d'Alton Locke, 133n

Kirkdale Ragged School, 216

Knight, John, 39n

Knight, Rev William, 39, 40

Knowles, Betsy, 27, 28, 30, 208

Labuan, 170

Lamb's Tales from Shakespeare, 179

Lancashire Cotton Famine, 215

Lancelot, 57, 144

Landes, 232

Land's End, 266

Lane, John, 141n

Langa - Willi, 188

Langham, A. and M., 127n

Leader, 155

Leamington High School for Girls, 253

Leamington Spa, 253

Lear, Edward, 216, 216n

Leben Jesu, 142

Lees, Mr, 139, 146

Leigh, family of, 170n

Leonardo da Vinci, 272

Lewis, Naomi, 135n

Liddell, Col, 203

Life of St Elizabeth, The, 77, 79, 87, 126

Limerick, Bishop of, 257

Lincoln, 242, 245

Lincoln's Inn, 101, 174

Lind, Jenny, 253

Linneaus, 143, 196

Little Cloister, 283

Liverpool, 274

Lloyds, 38

Lodge, David, 133n

Logan River, 239n

London, 68n, 71, 107, 110, 123, 125, 129, 130, 132, 134, 143, 145, 159, 165, 174, 176, 193, 206, 218, 224, 225, 283, 284, 293, 295, 297

London Bridge, 147

Longfellow, H. W., 287, 288

Looe, 45, 266

Lorelei, 148

Lotos Club, 286

Lowndes Square, 83

Lucas, Nathan, 24

Ludlow, John Malcom, 52n, 101, 107, 108, 108n, 109, 110, 111, 116, 120, 121, 122, 123, 126, 132, 142, 155, 156, 157, 159n, 160, 172, 176, 187, 221, 241, 242, 285, 298, 299

Lundy, 127, 127n, 171

Luther, 70

Lyell, Sir Charles, 15, 215, 274

Lyly, John, 170

Lymington, 23

Lynmouth, 121, 122

Lynn, 114

Lytton, Bulmer, 174, 246, 281

McCarthy, Justin, 53, 211, 212, 212n
McCarthy, Mary, 216, 216n
McCleod, Norman, 280
Macedon, 301
Mackaye, Sandy, 133, 134
Macmillan, publisher, 15, 158, 172, 182, 187, 188, 197, 231, 247, 277, 300
Macmillan, Alexander, 125, 168n, 172, 188, 235, 249, 255, 258, 289n, 296
Macmillan, Daniel, 172
Macmillan's Magazine, 229, 231, 246
Madam How and Lady Why, 247, 255n
Madingley Hall, 213, 214
Madrid, 231
Magdalene College, Cambridge, 51, 56, 138
Malet, Lucas, see Kingsley, Mary, daughter of Charles Jr
Malham Cove, 193
Malham Tarn House, 193
Manchester, 112, 134, 134n, 160, 215
Manfred, 62
Mansfield, Charles Blanchford, 52, 53, 54, 57, 101, 107, 109, 110, 111, 116, 118, 119, 120, 121, 130, 132, 159, 172, 176, 176n, 177, 285, 298n
Man's Working Day, 95n
Marguerite of Navarre, 247
Marienbad, 61
Marius the Epicurean, 153
Markree Castle, 210
Marlborough House, 281
Marlow, Mr, 192
Marsh, Herbert, 26, 28
Marston, John, 173n
Martin, R. B., 287n, 288n
Martineau, Harriet, 53, 137, 160
Martineau, John, 16, 124n, 139, 145, 296
Martineau, Violet, 124n, 138n
Mary Barton, 134
Marx, Mrs, 175, 218
Masson, David, 123
Matthews, Jessie, 216
Maud, 158, 158n
Maurice, Frederick Denison, 70, 100, 101, 101n, 102, 104, 108, 109, 110, 111, 116, 119, 123, 137, 155, 157, 159n, 163, 186, 207, 215, 235, 238, 243, 249, 257, 280, 285
Mechanics Institute, Bristol, 192
Mediterranean, 233, 234
Mee, Arthur, 34
Melvill, Henry, 178
Merced, 291
Meredith, George, 121
Meredith, Mrs George, 121
Meta, River, 171
Mexico, 280, 292
Middleham, 95n
Middlesex Hospital, 176
Middle West, 289
Milford, 102

Mill, John Stuart, 211, 241, 253, 254
Mill Lane, Bermondsey, 130, 131
Mill Pond, Bermondsey, 130
Milnes, Monkton, 174, 237
Milton, John, 294
Miscellanies, 41n
Mississippi, 289, 290n, 292
Mitford, Mary Russell, 143, 144
Mlle. Lili, 232
Moberley, Dr George, 258
Mono, 261
Montagu, James, 206
Montalambert, Count, 76
Montserrat, 263, 263n
Mordaunt, Lady, 214
Moreau, General, 290
Morning Chronicle, The, 130, 131
Morrison, Walter, 193
Morte Sands, 119
Moses, 144
Moulins, Camille des, 158
Mount Batten, 36
Mount Edgecumb, 36
Mountains of the Moon, 174
Mountfield Court, 250
Moxon, publisher, 104
Mozley, 156
Mr Kingsley and Dr Newman, 230n
Mudie, librarian, 182
Müller, Prof Max, 15, 204, 228, 296
Müller, Mrs Max, 204
Murray, publisher, 104
My Winter Garden, 47n, 55n, 57n, 67n, 194

Naples, 287
National Gallery, 106, 110
National Library of Scotland, 29
Nauvoo, 290n
Navarino, 36
Neckinger, River 130
Needles, 266
Nelson, Horatio, 243
Nemesis of Faith, 121
New England, 165, 287
New Forest, 102, 105
New Lanark Mills, 111
Newman, Francis, 123
Newman, Cardinal, John Henry, 15, 53, 59, 106, 121, 123n, 153, 229–37, 238, 239
Newton, Isaac, 257
New Rochelle, 18
New York, 158, 286, 287, 288, 292, 294
New York Daily Tribune, 286
New York World, The, 288
Niagara Falls, 289
Nice, 74–5, 82, 99, 174, 219n
Nicholas I, Tzar, 169
Nicolai, Christoph, 49
Nîmes, 74, 233, 234
Nineteenth Century Children, 219n

Noah, 184
North British Review, 167
North Clifton, 26, 32
North Devon, 34n, 35n, 37n, 38n, 120, 127n, 128n
Norfolk, 134
Northdown House, 168, 169, 173
Norwich, 24, 222
Notes on Sports and Travel, 35n
Notre Dame, 231
Nun's Pool, The, 143, 143n

Oakshot Castle, 269
O'Connor, Feargus, 108
Oddicombe, 166
Ode to the North-East Wind, 225n
Odin, 245
Oenone, 156
Oh! that we two were Maying, 62
Oh! Thou hadst been a Wife for Shakespeare's Self, 148
Old Church Street, 48n
Oliver Twist, 130
Omaha, 290
Omphalos, 167
On the Death of a Certain Periodical, 110n
On Time, 294
Origin of Species, 135–6, 167, 215
Orinoco, 265
Orkney, Earl of, 155
Osborne, Georgie, 90
Osborne, Lord Sydney Godolphin, 81, 83, 87, 89, 90, 91, 92, 110, 132, 281
Osborne, Lady, 78, 90, 92
Our American Cousin, 183n
Our Village, 143
Owen, Robert, 110
Owen, Mrs, 181, 184
Oxford, 15, 24, 53, 62, 110, 124, 128, 131, 140, 147, 149, 172, 187, 188, 204, 213, 228, 229, 237, 253
Oxford Movement, 76
Oxfordshire, 54

Paine, John, 159
Paine, Tom, 155
Palestine, 233
Palinodia, 53
Pall Mall Gazette, 216
Palmer, 65
Palmerston, Lord, 176, 178, 178n, 253, 298
Paraguay, 176
Paraguay, Brazil and the Plate, 176n
Parfitt, Mr, 145, 145n
Paris, 74, 85, 107, 176, 180, 231, 235
Parker, John, 104, 106, 107, 109, 110, 111, 123, 144, 172, 186, 204, 215n, 248
Park Lane, 159
Park Place, 55
Parnassus, 157

Parracombe, 39
Pater, Walter, 153
Pau, 232, 247
Paul, Charles Kegan, 140
Peakirk, 32
Peck, chemist, 226
Pelham, Alice, 27
Pennington, 102
Penrose, Frank, 77, 172, 176
Penrose, John, 32
Period of my Life, 284n
Perrot, Mr, 128
Perseus, 179
Peterborough, 26, 32, 245, 246
Petit Tor, 166
Phaethon, 152
Phelps, wine merchant, 125
Philadelphia, 288
Philip of Macedon, 95
Piccadilly, 221
Pic du Mìdi, 233
Pickering, publisher, 104
Pike's Peak, 291
Pilgrimage of Grace, 187, 193
Pimperne, 83, 89, 91
Plas Gwynant, 160
Plate, 176
Plato, 49, 101
Plautus, 45
Plough Inn, 218
Plymouth, 36, 44
Poland, 301
Politics for the People, 109–10, 115, 142, 143, 172
Pont de Gard, 74, 234
Port of Spain, 260, 263
Portland, Lord, 225
Portman, Lord, 83, 83n, 281
Porphyry and Iamblichus, 43, 152
Potter, Rev Horatio, 286
Powles, Cowley, 42, 45–7, 48, 52, 62, 65, 83, 87, 104, 121, 191, 281
Prestoe, Mr, 263
Preston, 36
Prose Idylls, 34n, 35n, 47n, 53n, 55n, 57n, 67n, 77n, 127n, 128n, 233n
Prussia, Crown Prince and Princess of, 201
Psyche, 46
Punch, 132, 183, 284
Purgatory of Suicides, The, 111
Pusey, Dr E. B., 53, 54, 55, 56, 65–6
Pyranees, 232

Queen's College, London, 111, 115, 119
Queensland, 243
Queen Square, 40, 87

Rab and his Friends, 134
Rabelais, Francois, 143n, 247
Raglan, Lord, 169, 299
Raleigh, Sir Walter, 36, 51–2

Ranke, Leopold Von, 204
Ravenshoe, 277
Ray Lodge, 155, 168, 272
Reading, 67, 68n, 189n, 192
Recollections of Geoffrey Hamlyn, The, 187, 188
Redpath, James, 286n
Reminiscences, Justin McCarthy's 212n
Reubens, P. P., 77
Reynolds, Sir Joshua, 23
Rhine, 147
Richard of Ely, 246
Richmond Terrace, 39
Rights of Man, The, 155
Ripon, 87
Robbery Under Arms, 188
Robinson, Henry Crabb, 173
Rochester, 257
Rocky Mountains, 290
Rodney, Lord and Lady, 272
Rogers, 35
Rogers, Dr, 227
Roman and the Teuton, The, 211n, 248
Rome, 59, 106, 112, 115, 122, 150, 230, 247
Rose, The, 253n
Roses and Rose Growing, 253n
Rotherhithe Society, 132n
Rough Rhyme on a Rough Matter, A, 113
Rousseau, J. J., 75
Royal Academy, 174
Royal Cornwall Gazette, 42
Royal Literary Fund, 277
Royalty Theatre, 216
Rugby, 41
Runnamede Villa, 118
Ruskin, John, 49, 159, 159n, 183, 242
Russell, Sir Charles, 296
Russell, G. W. E., 89, 195, 195n, 271, 271n
Russell, Lord John, 131

Sackville College, 125
Sacred and Legendary Art, 119
St Andrews, 212n
St Anthony, 252
St Augustine, 149, 270
St Bernard of Clairvaux, 76
St Elizabeth of Hungary, 76–7, 102–4, 203
St Guthlac, 252
St John's Church, Charlotte Street, 144
St John's Wood, 176
St Leger, Miss, 54
St Louis, 289, 290
St Lucia, 260
St Luke's, Chelsea, 47, 49, 66, 100, 101, 104, 172, 207, 276, 285
St Mary's, Oxford, 228, 230
St Paul, 186, 252
St Paul's, 77, 178
St Peter's, Belgrave Square, 122
St Peter's Terrace, 213, 226
St Pierre, Bernardin de, 75

St Saviour's Dock, 130, 132n
St Sexburga, 245
Saint's Tragedy, The, 62, 77n, 97n, 102–3, 104, 116, 140
St Thomas, Virgin Islands, 259
St Vincent, 24
Salisbury, 258
Salisbury, Bishop of, 257
Salt Lake City, 290, 291
Sand, George, 53
Sandhurst, 70, 81
Sandringham, 214, 256
Sands of Dee, The, 220n, 275
Sandwich Islands, 239
San Francisco, 291
Santa Maura, 156, 157
Sarawak, 170
Sargasso Sea, 36
Saturday Review, 196, 248, 249
Sydney, 170
Scarborough, 232
Schuyler, Capt Howard, 255
Scotland, 252
Scott, Sir Walter, 213
Scutari, 169
Seaward, James, 222
Sebastopol, 169
Sedan, 276
Sedgwick, Prof, 56
Seeley, J. R., 258
Selwyn, George Augustus, 170
Senior, Mrs, 175
Sewell, Anna, 221
Sewell, William, 121
Shakespeare, William, 104, 294
Sharp, Cecil, 113
Shaw-Lefevre, Emma, 251, 259
Shelford, 61
Shelley, Percy B., 159
Shelrocke, 35
Ship Aground, The, 132n
Ship Tavern, 168
Shropshire Lad, A. 102
Sicily, 234
Sidney Sussex College, 25
Silcote of Silcotes, 277
Simpson, Annie, 34, 156n
Sims, Mr, 271
Singapore, 170
Skipton, 193
Slyfield, George, 141
Smith, Charles, 106
Smith, Col Hamilton, 263
Smith, Joseph, 290n
Smith, Percy, 124, 140
Smithfield, 121
Snowdon, 181, 183, 184, 185
Song upon Life, 29
South America, 171
South Berkshire, the, 105n

Southwark and Vauxhall Water Company, 132
South Wind, The, 67n
Spain, 231, 232, 247
Spectator, 230, 235n
Spencer, Herbert, 272
Stamford, 26
Stamford Mercury, 28n
Stanley, Arthur Penryn, 18, 189, 283, 293, 296–7
Stanley, Harold, 52n
Stapleton, Augustus Granville, 69, 81, 163, 213, 229, 272
Stapleton, Frederick, 235
Stephen, Sir James, 204
Stewart, Mr, 52
Stowe, Harriet Beecher, 156, 162–3
Strand, 104, 109
Strange, Col, 289
Stratfield Saye, 251
Strauss, 142
Stretton, 187
Stubbs, William, 52, 212
Subjugation of Women, The, 253
Suffolk, 100
Sumner, Charles, 288
Sunday Companion, 97n
Supposititious works, 301
Surrey, 139
Sussex, 139
Swallowfield, 143, 177
Swanage, 193
Swinburne, Algernon, 277
Sybil, 134
Sydney Street, Kensington, 47

Tanglewood Tales, 179
Taplow Court, 155, 168
Taw, 168
Taylor, Leonard, 97n
Taylor, Tom, 132, 183, 183n, 184
Teign, 128
Temple Bar, 101
Tennyson, Lord Alfred, 19, 52, 75, 101, 154, 158, 169, 240, 242
Thackeray, Anne, 147
Thackeray, William M., 19, 147
Thames, 49, 107, 130, 132
Thekla, 205
Theological Essays, 155
Theseus, 179
Thompson, Dr W. H., 257, 258
Thorpe-le-Soken, 301
Three Fishers, The, 144
Three Lectures on the Ancient Régime, 249, 255n
Ticknor and Fields, publisher, 287
Times, The, 90, 132, 164, 215, 220, 249, 250, 251, 296, 299, 300
Tintoretto, 77
Titian, 90

Toad Lane, 134n
Tom Brown's Schooldays, 110, 159, 187, 238, 240
Toovey-Hawley, Rev John, 68, 94
Tor Abbey, 166
Torbay, 167, 168
Torquay, 164, 165, 166, 208
Torres Straights, 100
Torridge, 52, 168, 173
Totnes, Archdeacon of, 121
Trafalgar Square, 107
Transcendentalists, The, 41
Tregarva, 112–14
Trehill Well, 46n, 220
Trent, 26
Tresavean, 83
Trier, 149, 150, 152
Trinidad, 259, 260, 261, 263, 263n, 265, 266, 295
Trinity Church, Bath, 87
Trinity College, Cambridge, 206, 243, 257
Trinity Hall, 25
Trumpington, 56
Truro, 54
Turton, Doctor William, 39
Tutor's Story, The, 133n, 187n
Twain, Mark, 285
Two Dispensations, The, 70
Twopenny, Rev R., 54
Two Years Ago, 38n, 145, 150, 158, 159, 179–84, 197, 246, 254, 288n
Tyrateus, 169
Uncle Tom's Cabin, 44, 156, 163
United States of America, 83n, 93, 158, 161, 254, 261, 283–97, 301

Vallings, Gabrielle, 17, 44
Van Dyck, 23
Vanity Fair, 147
Venezuela, 265
Venice, 183
Victoria, Australia, 188
Victoria, Princess, 256
Victoria, Queen, 15, 23, 107, 108, 138, 154, 197, 201, 203, 214, 239, 240, 250, 257, 257n, 258, 282, 294
Vieuxbois, Lord, 114
25 Village Sermons, 95n, 96n
Virgil, 42, 140
Virgin Islands, 259
Von Weser, Baroness, 175

Wales, 160, 183, 208
Wales, Sir Charles, 61
Walsh, Charles, 131
Walter, John, 251
Wandsworth, 172
Warbrook, 69, 272
Wargrave, 276, 277
Warre, Mrs Caroline, 78, 83, 87, 88, 120, 122, 132

Washington, 288

Water-Babies, The, 15, 18, 27, 31, 102, 133, 136, 167, 168, 179, 187, 189, 193, 209, 211–23, 224, 225, 227n, 240

Waterloo, 110

Waterloo Bridge, 108, 181

Water of Life and Other Sermons, The, 255n

Waud, Dr Sammuel, 51, 62

Weidenfeld and Nicolson, publisher, 216n

Wellesley, Emily, 43

Wellesley, Gerald, 71, 201n, 281, 282

Wellington, Duke of, 48n, 107, 108, 187, 229, 241, 251

Wellington, College, 189n, 192, 233, 239, 241, 243

Welsford, 37

West, Mr and Mrs, 208

West End, London, 49, 132

West Indies, 23, 35, 87, 191, 242, 259–67, 270

West London Observer, 207

Westminster Abbey, 15, 18, 109, 145, 178, 282, 284, 285, 288, 293

Westminster Hospital, 295

Westminster Review, 173

Westward Ho!, 15, 34n, 127, 164–78, 182, 229, 232, 246, 275

Weybridge, 176

Wharfedale, 193n

What is the Real Error of the Tracts for the Times? 70

What Then Does Dr Newman Mean? 231

When all the World was Young Lad, 227

Whewell, Dr William, 206, 206n, 257

Whitchurch, 224–5

White, George, 99, 190

White, Gilbert, 228

White Hart, Whitchurch, 224

Whitehouse, Mrs, 126

Whitfield, Mr and Mrs, 127

Whittier, J. G., 287

Whittlesea, 32

Wilberforce, Bishop Samuel, 131, 133n, 228

Willesden, 284

William I, 245–6

William III, 213

Wimble, Mr, 126

Wimbledon, 159n

Winchester, 67, 218, 251, 281, 293

Winchester, Bishop of, 66, 95, 284, 296

Winchester Training College, 96

Windrush, Professor, 152

Windsor Castle, 201, 204, 294, 297

Windsor Forest, 67

Winn, W. J., 45n

Winton House, 251, 279

Wisdom and Innocence, 230, 231

Wokingham, 110, 222, 241, 294

Wolsely Street, 132n

Women's Sanitary League, 283

Wood, Peter, 69, 102

Woodford Bridge, 71

Woodham, Mr, 250

Woodside, Harrow-on-the-Hill, 280

Woolner, Thomas, 18

Worcester, 257

Worcester College, Oxford, 147

Wordsworth, William, 98, 294

Working Men's College, 141, 159n

Wright, John, 222

Wyndham, Dr T., 83, 90, 90n

Yeast, 90, 95, 111–15, 116, 118, 122, 133, 134, 143n, 144, 166, 180, 182, 195n, 204, 220

Yosemite, 163, 218, 291

York, 187

Yorke, Marie, see Kingsley, Mrs Maurice

Yorkshire, 102, 162, 187, 193

Young, Brigham, 290